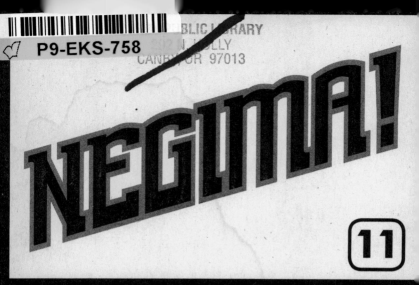

NEGIMA!

11

Ken Akamatsu

TRANSLATED BY
Toshifumi Yoshida

ADAPTED BY
T. Ledoux

LETTERING AND RETOUCH BY
Steve Palmer

DEL REY

BALLANTINE BOOKS · NEW YORK

A Del Rey Trade Paperback Original

Negima! volume 11 copyright © 2005 by Ken Akamatsu

English translation copyright © 2006 by Ken Akamatsu

Published in the United States by Del Rey, an imprint of The Random House Publishing Group, a division of Random House, Inc., New York.

Del Rey is a registered trademark and the Del Rey colophon is a trademark of Random House, Inc.

Publication rights arranged through Kodansha Ltd., Tokyo

First published in Japan in 2005 by Kodansha Ltd., Tokyo

ISBN-10 0-345-49231-5

Printed in the United States of America

www.delreymanga.com

9 8 7 6 5 4 3 2 1

Translator —Toshifumi Yoshida
Adaptor—T. Ledoux
Lettering and retouch—Steve Palmer
Cover Design—David Stevenson

Honorifics

Throughout the Del Rey Manga books, you will find Japanese honorifics left intact in the translations. For those not familiar with how the Japanese use honorifics and, more important, how they differ from American honorifics, we present this brief overview.

Politeness has always been a critical facet of Japanese culture. Ever since the feudal era, when Japan was a highly stratified society, use of honorifics—which can be defined as polite speech that indicates relationship or status—has played an essential role in the Japanese language. When addressing someone in Japanese, an honorific usually takes the form of a suffix attached to one's name (example: "Asuna-san"), or as a title at the end of one's name or in place of the name itself (example: "Negi-sensei," or simply "Sensei!").

Honorifics can be expressions of respect or endearment. In the context of manga and anime, honorifics give insight into the nature of the relationship between characters. Many translations into English leave out these important honorifics, and therefore distort the "feel" of the original Japanese. Because Japanese honorifics contain nuances that English honorifics lack, it is our policy at Del Rey not to translate them. Here, instead, is a guide to some of the honorifics you may encounter in Del Rey Manga.

-*san*: This is the most common honorific, and is equivalent to Mr., Miss, Ms., or Mrs. It is the all-purpose honorific and can be used in any situation where politeness is required.

-*sama*: This is one level higher than "-san." It is used to confer great respect.

-*dono*: This comes from the word "tono," which means "lord." It is an even higher level than "-sama," and confers utmost respect.

-kun: This suffix is used at the end of boys' names to express familiarity or endearment. It is also sometimes used by men among friends, or when addressing someone younger or of a lower station.

-chan: This is used to express endearment, mostly toward girls. It is also used for little boys, pets, and even among lovers. It gives a sense of childish cuteness.

Bozu: This is an informal way to refer to a boy, similar to the English term "kid" or "squirt."

Senpai/sempai: This title suggests that the addressee is one's senior in a group or organization. It is most often used in a school setting, where underclassmen refer to their upperclassmen as "senpai." It can also be used in the workplace, such as when a newer employee addresses an employee who has seniority in the company.

Kohai: This is the opposite of "sempai," and is used toward underclassmen in school or newcomers in the workplace. It connotes that the addressee is of lower station.

Sensei: Literally meaning "one who has come before," this title is used for teachers, doctors, or masters of any profession or art.

Anesan (or *nesan*): A generic term for a girl, usually older, that means sister.

Ojôsama: A way of referring to the daughter or sister of someone with high political or social status.

-[blank]: Usually forgotten in these lists, but perhaps the most significant difference between Japanese and English. The lack of honorific means that the speaker has permission to address the person in a very intimate way. Usually, only family, spouses, or very close friends have this kind of permission. Known as *yobisute,* it can be gratifying when someone who has earned the intimacy starts to call one by one's name without an honorific. But when that intimacy hasn't been earned, it can also be very insulting.

A Word from the Author

It's Day Two of MahoraFest and the start of the Mahora "Budokai" Martial Arts Tournament! Right from the start, it's been pretty much one match after another. Who will prove victorious...? Some of the story's most popular chapters yet, in collected form at last...! As of this volume, there'll be many battles depicted—although, on the grand *Negima!* scale of things, it won't be so much. (^^;) Readers craving the *rabu-kome* "love comedy" angle of things have nothing to worry about—there's still all of Day Three remaining.

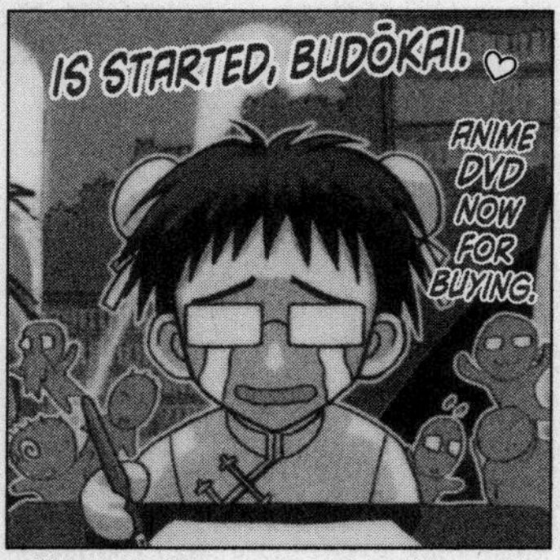
IS STARTED, BUDŌKAI. ♡
ANIME DVD NOW FOR BUYING.

Finally, although the anime version of *Negima!* (in Japan) has come to an end, the CDs and DVDs will still be released regularly. Those of you who may have missed them, please give them a look!

Ken Akamatsu
www.ailove.net

魔法先生
ネギま!
MAGISTER NEGI MAGI

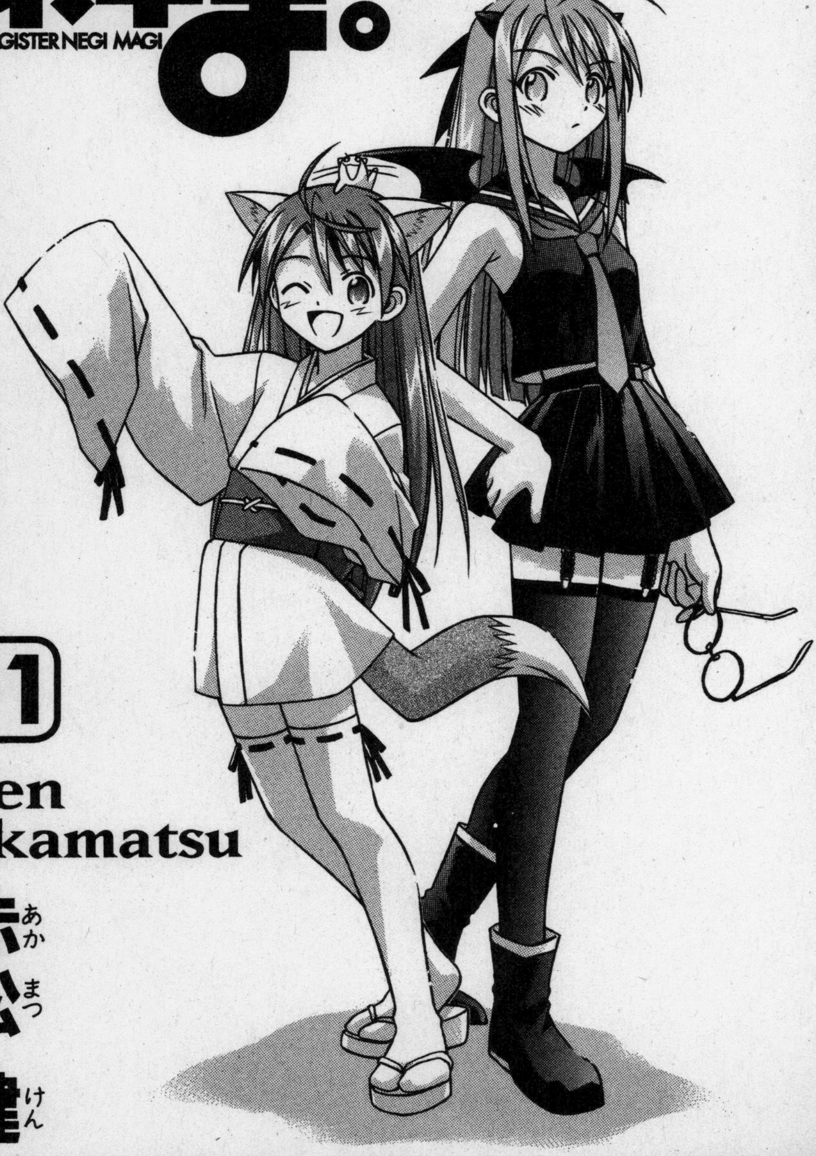

11

Ken Akamatsu

赤松健

Contents

Ninetieth Period: In Which All (?) Is Set A'Right: Evening Events........3

Ninety-first Period: Wise in the Ways of Cosplay ♡........21

Ninety-second Period: Promise to a Rival........37

Ninety-third Period: Enter Kotarō! The Budōkai Begins........55

Ninety-fourth Period: Extreme Combat! Tatsumiya vs. Ku Fei........73

Ninety-fifth Period: The Latest Weapon...and a Tradition of Fighting Spirit........91

Ninety-sixth Period: Courage—the Key to Victory!........109

Ninety-seventh Period: Takamichi Gets Really Real........127

Ninety-eighth Period: Negi! Get Up!!........145

Niney-ninth Period: The Hidden Technique Bursts Through........163

Festival Timetable........182

Fan Art Corner........184

3-D Background Explanations........186

Character Concept Sketches........189

Lexicon Magicum Negimarium........191

About the Creator........194

Translation Notes........195

Preview of *Negima!* Vol. 12 197

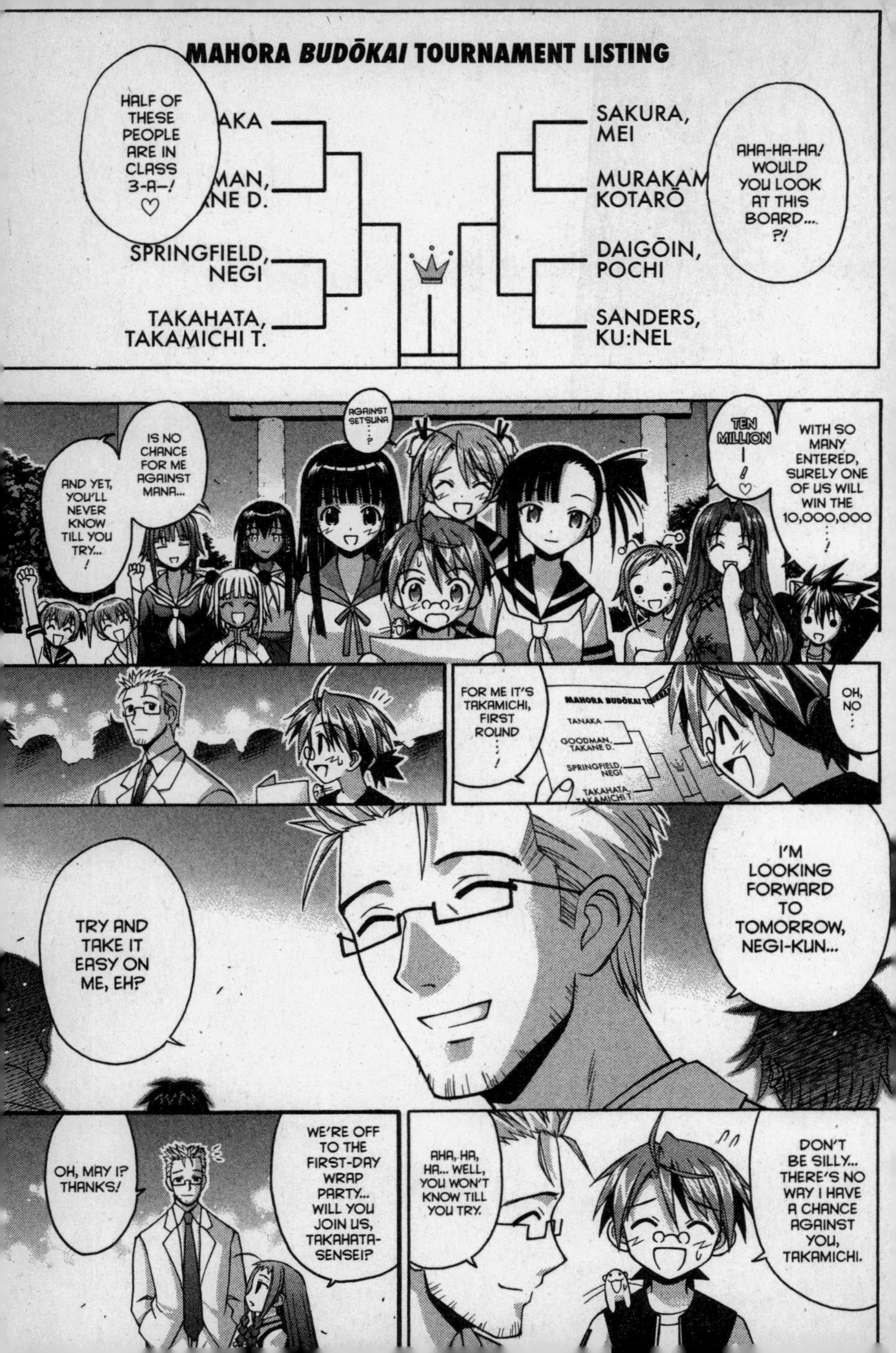
MAHORA BUDŌKAI TOURNAMENT LISTING
AKA
MAN,
ANE D.
SPRINGFIELD, NEGI
TAKAHATA, TAKAMICHI T.
SAKURA, MEI
MURAKAM KOTARŌ
DAIGŌIN, POCHI
SANDERS, KU:NEL
AHA-HA-HA! WOULD YOU LOOK AT THIS BOARD...?!
HALF OF THESE PEOPLE ARE IN CLASS 3-A–! ♡
WITH SO MANY ENTERED, SURELY ONE OF US WILL WIN THE 10,000,000...!
TEN MILLION—!♡
AGAINST SETSUNA...?
IS NO CHANCE FOR ME AGAINST MANA...
AND YET, YOU'LL NEVER KNOW TILL YOU TRY...!
OH, NO...
FOR ME IT'S TAKAMICHI, FIRST ROUND...!
MAHORA BUDŌKAI TOURNA
TANAKA
GOODMAN, TAKANE D.
SPRINGFIELD, NEGI
TAKAHATA, TAKAMICHI T.
I'M LOOKING FORWARD TO TOMORROW, NEGI-KUN...
TRY AND TAKE IT EASY ON ME, EH?
DON'T BE SILLY... THERE'S NO WAY I HAVE A CHANCE AGAINST YOU, TAKAMICHI.
AHA, HA, HA... WELL, YOU WON'T KNOW TILL YOU TRY.
WE'RE OFF TO THE FIRST-DAY WRAP PARTY... WILL YOU JOIN US, TAKAHATA-SENSEI?
OH, MAY I? THANKS!

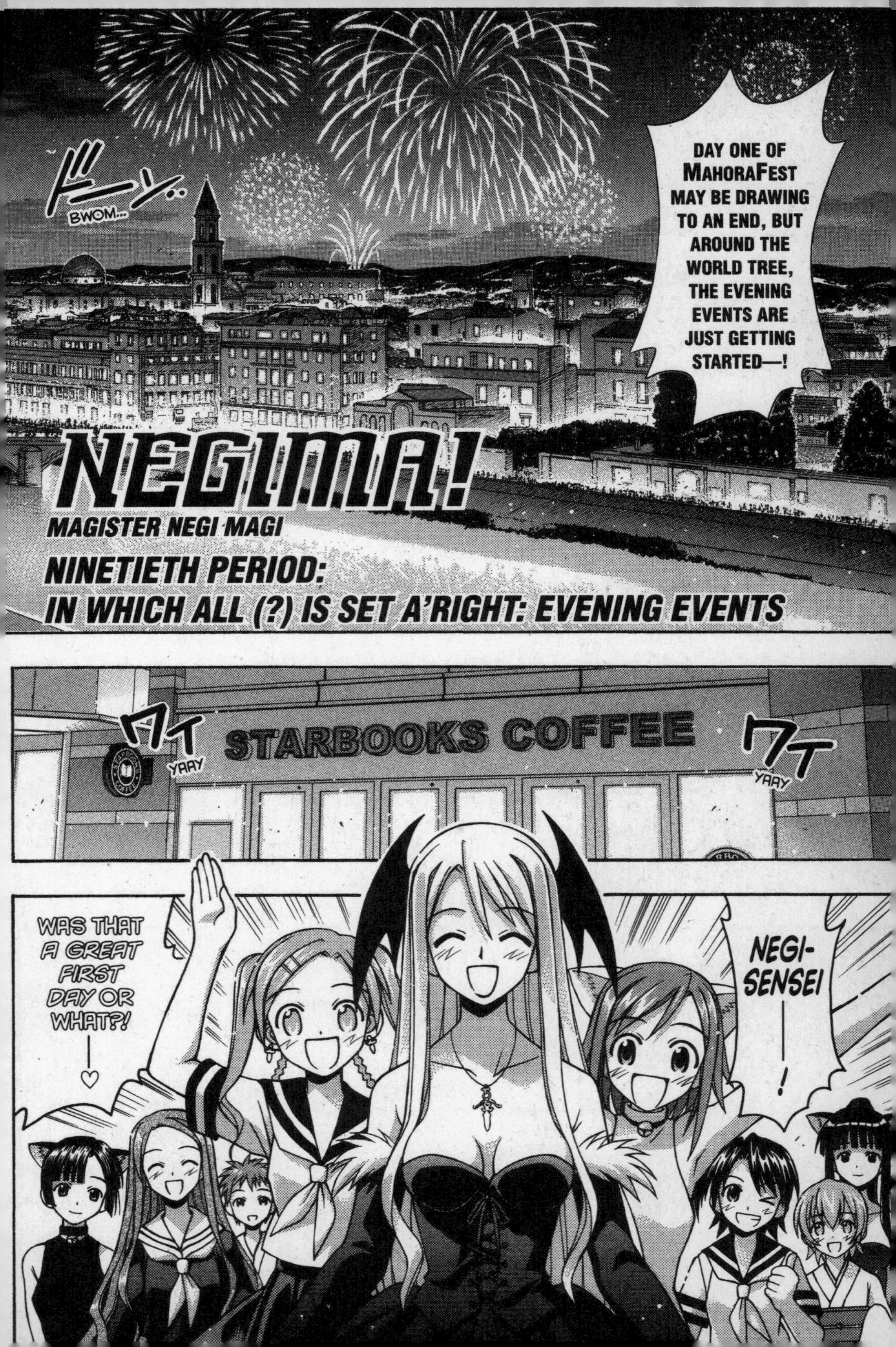
DAY ONE OF MAHORAFEST MAY BE DRAWING TO AN END, BUT AROUND THE WORLD TREE, THE EVENING EVENTS ARE JUST GETTING STARTED—!
ドーン..
BWOM...
NEGIMA!
MAGISTER NEGI MAGI
NINETIETH PERIOD:
IN WHICH ALL (?) IS SET A'RIGHT: EVENING EVENTS
ワイ
YAAY
STARBOOKS COFFEE
ワイ
YAAY
NEGI-SENSEI!
WAS THAT A GREAT FIRST DAY OR WHAT?! ♡

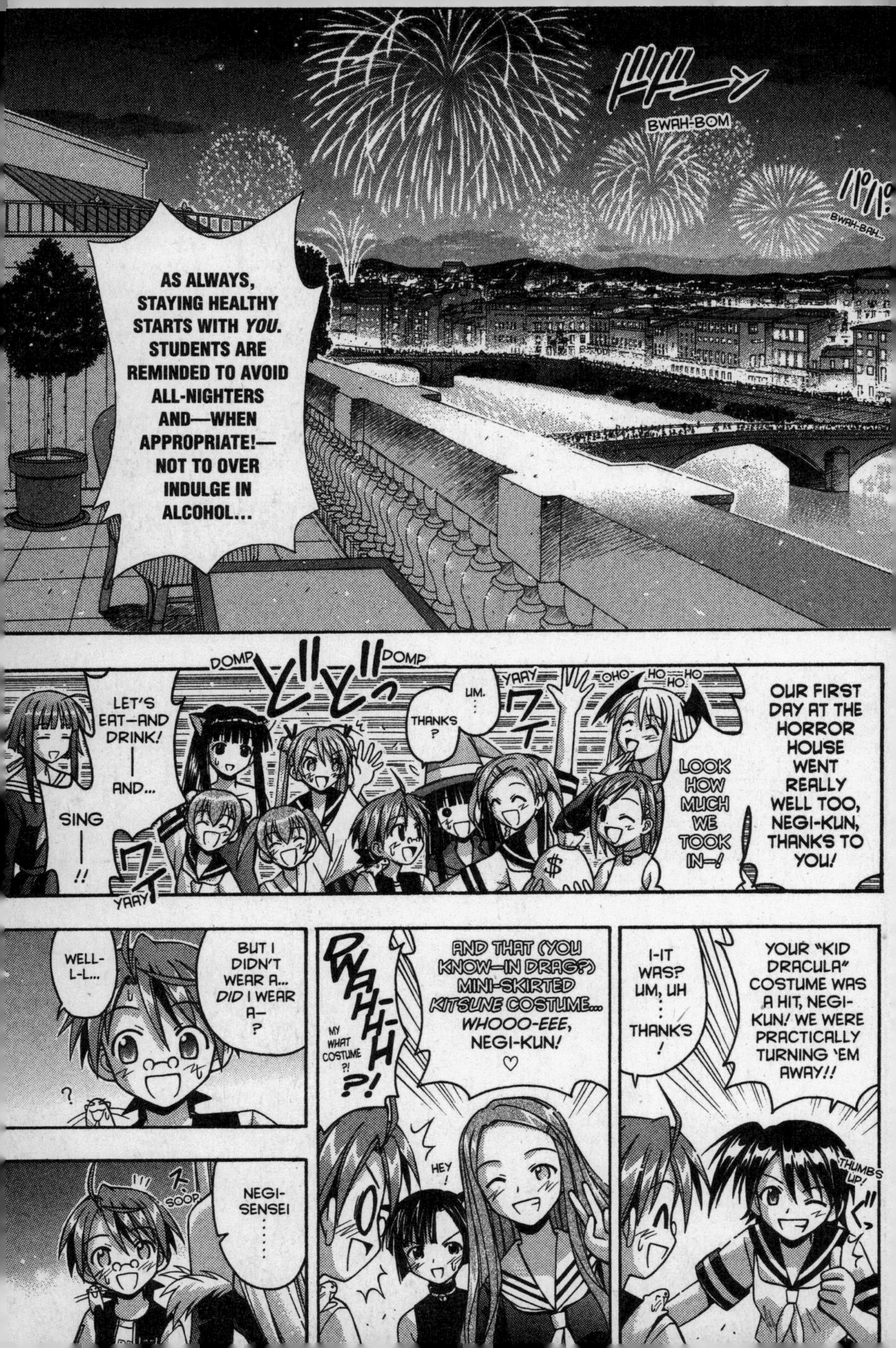
BWAH-BOM
BWAH-BAH...
AS ALWAYS, STAYING HEALTHY STARTS WITH *YOU*. STUDENTS ARE REMINDED TO AVOID ALL-NIGHTERS AND—WHEN APPROPRIATE!—NOT TO OVER INDULGE IN ALCOHOL...
OUR FIRST DAY AT THE HORROR HOUSE WENT REALLY WELL TOO, NEGI-KUN, THANKS TO YOU!
LOOK HOW MUCH WE TOOK IN—!
OHO HO HO HO
YAAY
UM. ... THANKS?
DOMP DOMP
LET'S EAT—AND DRINK! | AND... SING | !!
YAAY
YOUR "KID DRACULA" COSTUME WAS A HIT, NEGI-KUN! WE WERE PRACTICALLY TURNING 'EM AWAY!!
I-IT WAS? UM, UH ... THANKS!
THUMBS UP!
AND THAT (YOU KNOW—IN DRAG?) MINI-SKIRTED *KITSUNE* COSTUME... *WHOOO-EEE*, NEGI-KUN! ♡
BWAHHH-H?!
MY WHAT COSTUME?!
HEY!
WELL-L-L...
BUT I DIDN'T WEAR A... *DID* I WEAR A—?
SOOP
NEGI-SENSEI ......

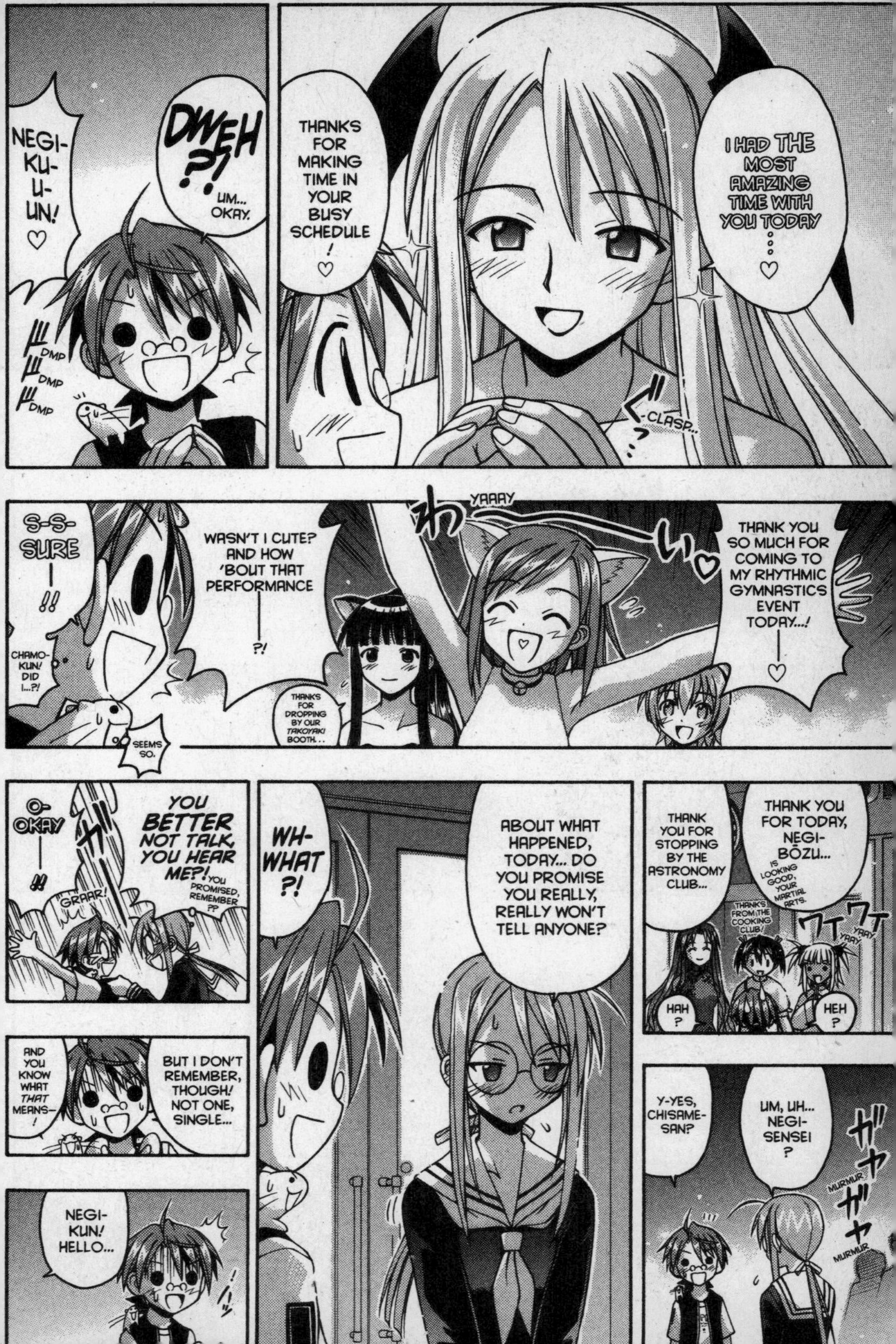
I HAD THE MOST AMAZING TIME WITH YOU TODAY... ♡
THANKS FOR MAKING TIME IN YOUR BUSY SCHEDULE! ♡
CLASP...
DWEH?!
UM... OKAY.
NEGI-KU-U-UN! ♡
DMP
DMP
DMP
THANK YOU SO MUCH FOR COMING TO MY RHYTHMIC GYMNASTICS EVENT TODAY...! ♡
YAAAY
WASN'T I CUTE? AND HOW 'BOUT THAT PERFORMANCE—?!
THANKS FOR DROPPING BY OUR TAKOYAKI BOOTH...
S-S-SURE—!!
CHAMO-KUN! DID I...?!
SEEMS SO.
THANK YOU FOR TODAY, NEGI-BŌZU...
IS LOOKING GOOD, YOUR MARTIAL ARTS.
THANK YOU FOR STOPPING BY THE ASTRONOMY CLUB...
THANKS FROM THE COOKING CLUB!
YAAY
YAAY
HEH?
HAH?
UM, UH... NEGI-SENSEI?
Y-YES, CHISAME-SAN?
MURMUR
MURMUR
ABOUT WHAT HAPPENED, TODAY... DO YOU PROMISE YOU REALLY, REALLY WON'T TELL ANYONE?
WH-WHAT?!
YOU BETTER NOT TALK, YOU HEAR ME?!
YOU PROMISED, REMEMBER??
GRAAR!
O-OKAY—!!
BUT I DON'T REMEMBER, THOUGH! NOT ONE, SINGLE...
AND YOU KNOW WHAT THAT MEANS—!
NEGI-KUN! HELLO...

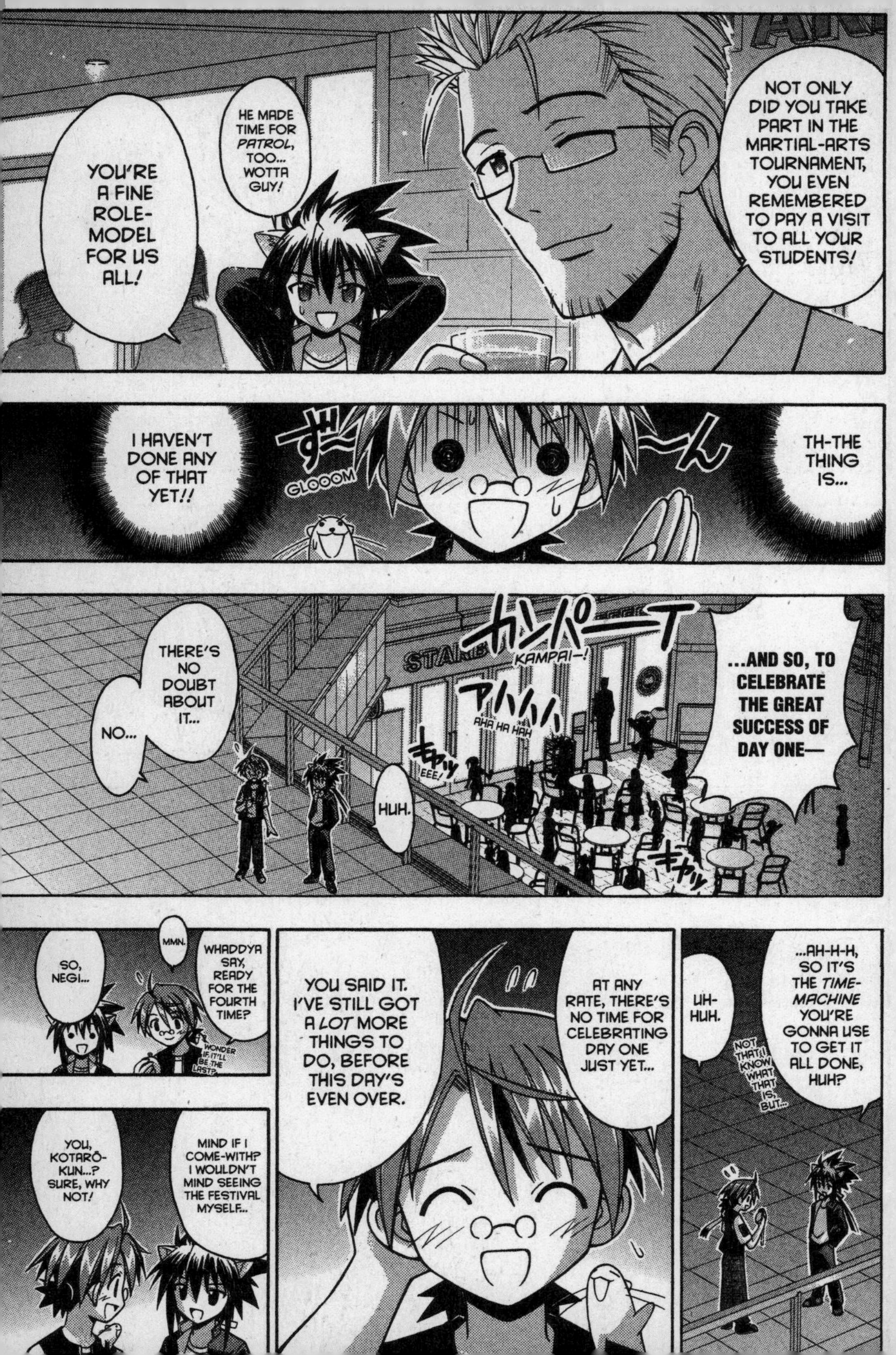
NOT ONLY DID YOU TAKE PART IN THE MARTIAL-ARTS TOURNAMENT, YOU EVEN REMEMBERED TO PAY A VISIT TO ALL YOUR STUDENTS!
HE MADE TIME FOR *PATROL*, TOO... WOTTA GUY!
YOU'RE A FINE ROLE-MODEL FOR US ALL!
TH-THE THING IS...
ずーん
GLOOOM
I HAVEN'T DONE ANY OF THAT YET!!
...AND SO, TO CELEBRATE THE GREAT SUCCESS OF DAY ONE—
カンパーイ
KAMPAI—!
アハハハ
AHA HA HAH
キャッ
EEE!
キャッ
HUH.
THERE'S NO DOUBT ABOUT IT...
NO...
...AH-H-H, SO IT'S THE *TIME-MACHINE* YOU'RE GONNA USE TO GET IT ALL DONE, HUH?
NOT THAT I KNOW WHAT THAT IS, BUT...
UH-HUH.
AT ANY RATE, THERE'S NO TIME FOR CELEBRATING DAY ONE JUST YET...
YOU SAID IT. I'VE STILL GOT A *LOT* MORE THINGS TO DO, BEFORE THIS DAY'S EVEN OVER.
WHADDYA SAY, READY FOR THE FOURTH TIME?
MMN.
SO, NEGI...
WONDER IF IT'LL BE THE LAST?
MIND IF I COME WITH? I WOULDN'T MIND SEEING THE FESTIVAL MYSELF...
YOU, KOTARŌ-KUN...? SURE, WHY NOT!

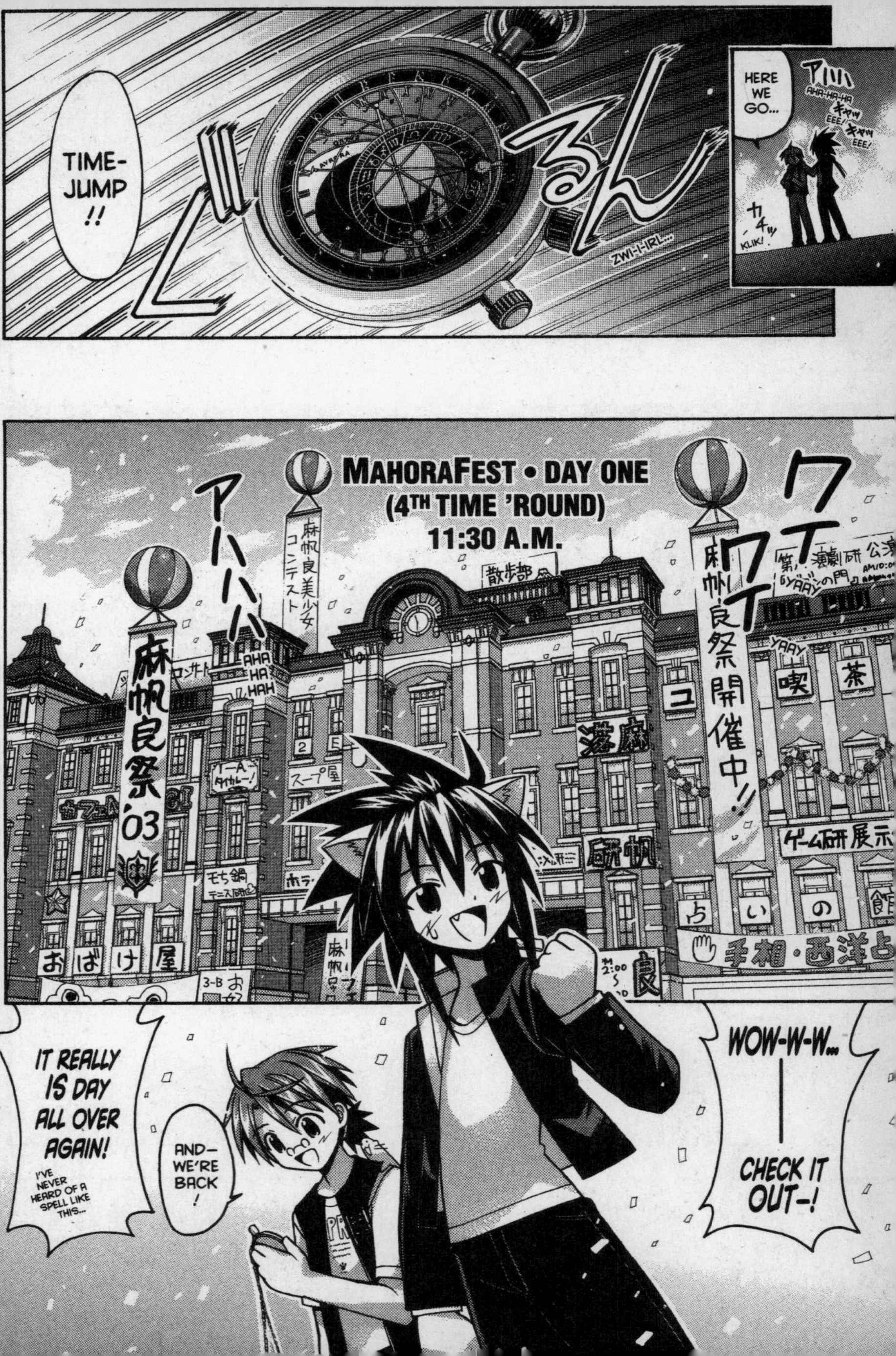

HERE WE GO...
アハハ
AHA-HA-HA
キャッ
EEE!
キャッ
EEE!
カチッ
KLIK!
TIME-JUMP!!
ZWI-I-IRL...
MAHORAFEST • DAY ONE
(4TH TIME 'ROUND)
11:30 A.M.
アハハハ
AHA HA HAH
ワイワイ
YAAY
YAAY
麻帆良祭'03
麻帆良美少女コンテスト
麻帆良祭開催中!!
WOW-W-W...
CHECK IT OUT-!
AND—WE'RE BACK!
IT REALLY IS DAY ALL OVER AGAIN!
I'VE NEVER HEARD OF A SPELL LIKE THIS...

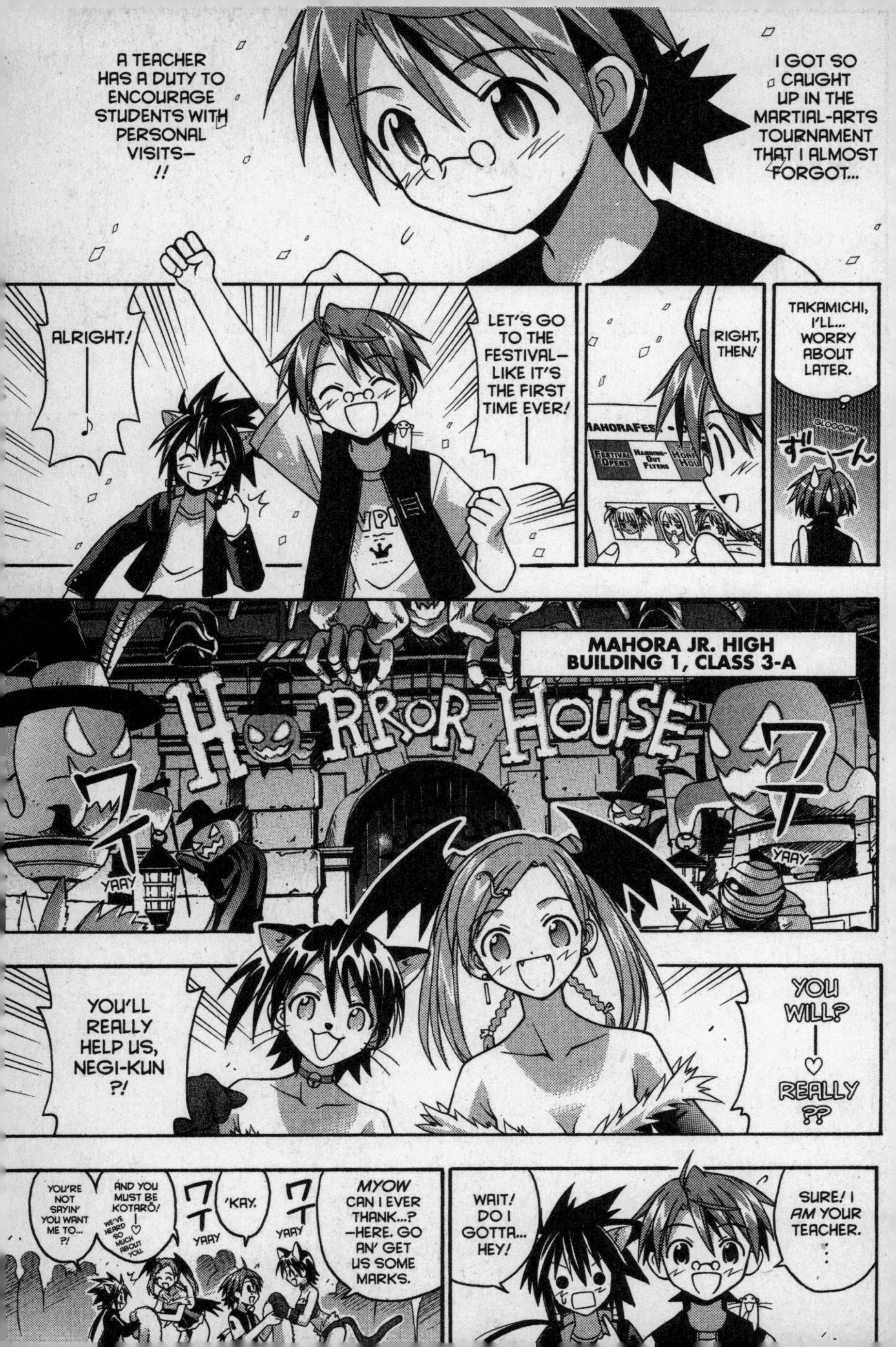
I GOT SO CAUGHT UP IN THE MARTIAL-ARTS TOURNAMENT THAT I ALMOST FORGOT...
A TEACHER HAS A DUTY TO ENCOURAGE STUDENTS WITH PERSONAL VISITS— !!
TAKAMICHI, I'LL... WORRY ABOUT LATER.
GLOOOOM
ずーーん
RIGHT, THEN!
MAHORAFES
FESTIVAL OPENS
HANDING-OUT FLYERS
LET'S GO TO THE FESTIVAL—LIKE IT'S THE FIRST TIME EVER!
ALRIGHT! ♪
MAHORA JR. HIGH BUILDING 1, CLASS 3-A
H RROR HOUSE
ワ
ア
YAAY
ワ
イ
YAAY
YOU WILL? ♡ REALLY ??
YOU'LL REALLY HELP US, NEGI-KUN ?!
SURE! I *AM* YOUR TEACHER. ...
WAIT! DO I GOTTA... HEY!
MYOW CAN I EVER THANK...? —HERE. GO AN' GET US SOME MARKS.
ワイ
YAAY
'KAY.
ワイ
YAAY
AND YOU MUST BE KOTARŌ! ♡
WE'VE HEARD SO MUCH ABOUT YOU.
YOU'RE NOT SAYIN' YOU WANT ME TO...?!

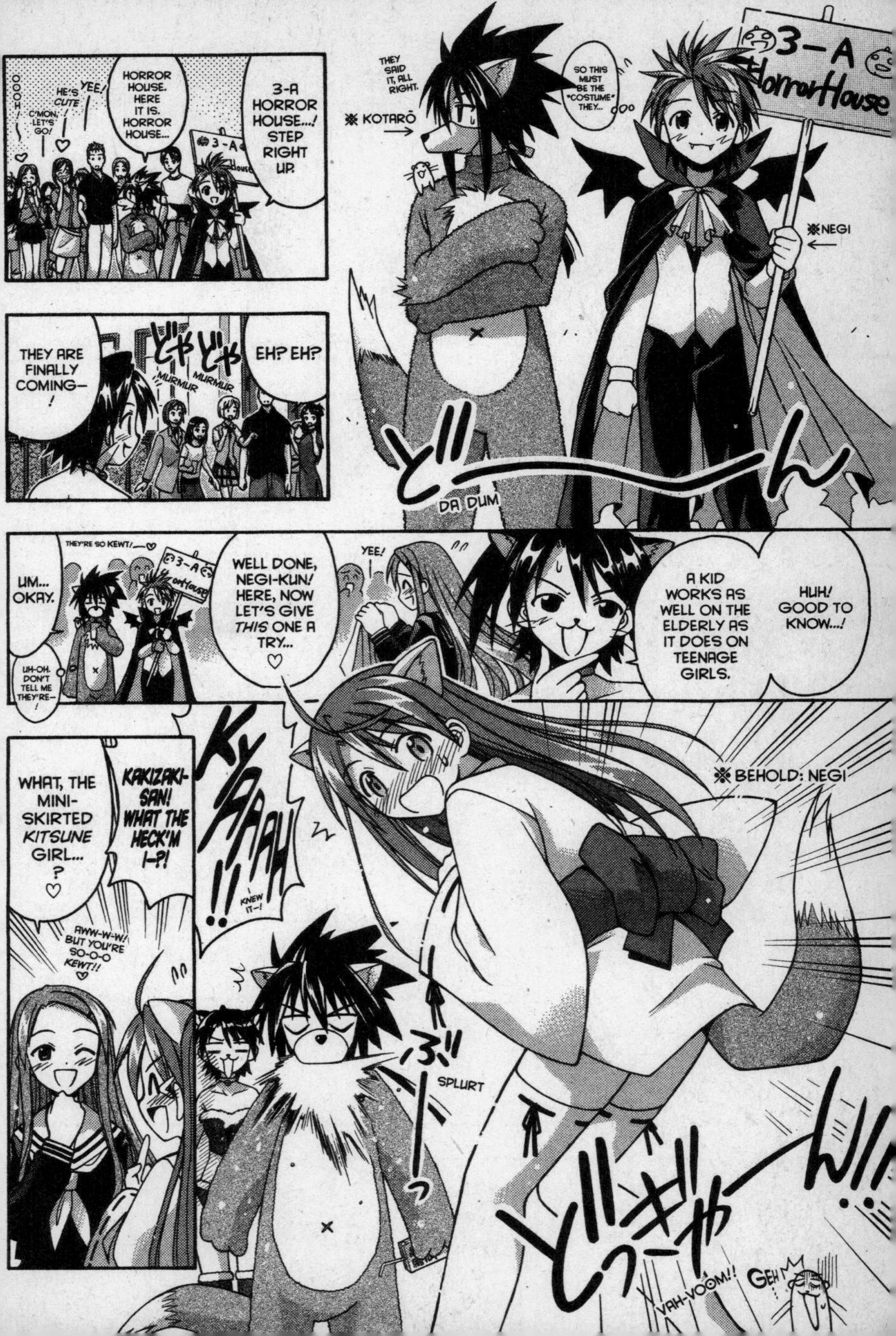
3-A Horror House
SO THIS MUST BE THE "COSTUME" THEY...
THEY SAID IT, ALL RIGHT.
※KOTARŌ
※NEGI
DA DUM
3-A HORROR HOUSE...! STEP RIGHT UP.
HORROR HOUSE. HERE IT IS. HORROR HOUSE...
YEE!
HE'S CUTE!
C'MON, LET'S GO!
OOOH!
3-A
EH? EH?
MURMUR
MURMUR
THEY ARE FINALLY COMING—!
HUH! GOOD TO KNOW...!
A KID WORKS AS WELL ON THE ELDERLY AS IT DOES ON TEENAGE GIRLS.
YEE!
WELL DONE, NEGI-KUN! HERE, NOW LET'S GIVE THIS ONE A TRY... ♡
THEY'RE SO KEWT! ♡
3-A
UM... OKAY.
UH-OH. DON'T TELL ME THEY'RE—!
※BEHOLD: NEGI
KYAAAH!!
KNEW IT—!
KAKIZAKI-SAN! WHAT THE HECK'M I—?!
WHAT, THE MINI-SKIRTED KITSUNE GIRL...? ♡
AWW-W-W! BUT YOU'RE SO-O-O KEWT!! ♡
SPLURT
VAH-VOOM!!
GEH

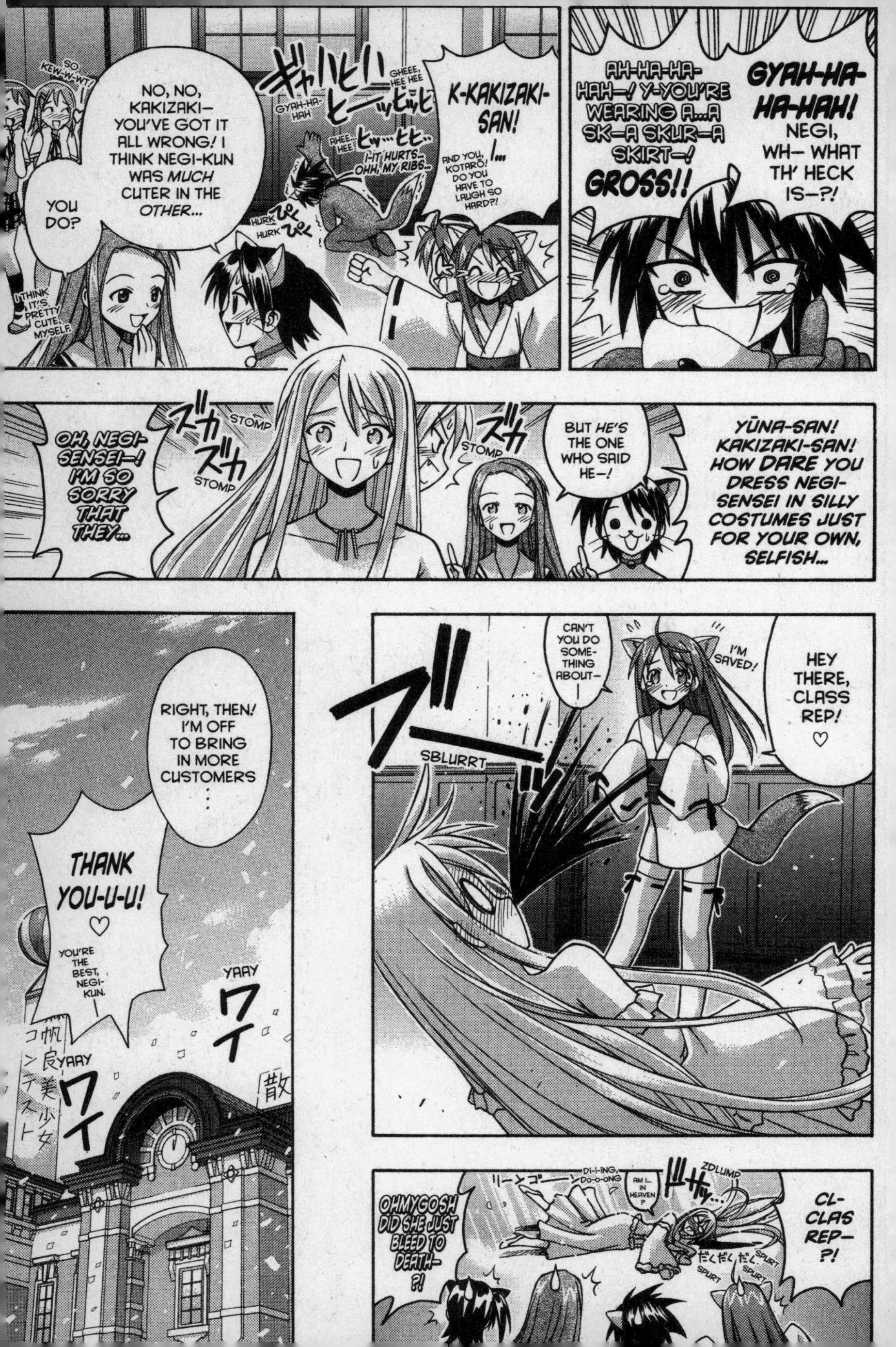
GYAH-HA-HA-HAH! NEGI, WH— WHAT TH' HECK IS—?!
AH-HA-HA-HAH—! Y-YOU'RE WEARING A...A SK—A SKUR—A SKIRT—! GROSS!!
K-KAKIZAKI-SAN! I...
AND YOU, KOTARŌ! DO YOU HAVE TO LAUGH SO HARD?!
GHEEE, HEE HEE
ヒーッヒッヒ
GYAH-HA-HAH
AHEE HEE
ヒッ…ヒヒ…
I-IT HURTS... OHH, MY RIBS...
HURK
HURK
NO, NO, KAKIZAKI— YOU'VE GOT IT ALL WRONG! I THINK NEGI-KUN WAS MUCH CUTER IN THE OTHER...
YOU DO?
SO KEW-W-WT!
I THINK IT'S PRETTY CUTE, MYSELF.
YŪNA-SAN! KAKIZAKI-SAN! HOW DARE YOU DRESS NEGI-SENSEI IN SILLY COSTUMES JUST FOR YOUR OWN, SELFISH...
BUT HE'S THE ONE WHO SAID HE—!
ズカ
STOMP
ズカ
STOMP
ズカ
STOMP
OH, NEGI-SENSEI—! I'M SO SORRY THAT THEY...
HEY THERE, CLASS REP! ♡
I'M SAVED!
CAN'T YOU DO SOMETHING ABOUT—
SBLURRT
CL-CLAS REP—?!
ZDLUMP
AM I... IN HEAVEN?
DI-I-ING, DO-O-ONG
リーンゴーン
だくだく だく
SPURT
SPURT
SPURT
OHMYGOSH DID SHE JUST BLEED TO DEATH—?!
RIGHT, THEN! I'M OFF TO BRING IN MORE CUSTOMERS...
THANK YOU-U-U! ♡
YOU'RE THE BEST, NEGI-KUN.
YAAY
ワイ
YAAY
ワイ
帆良美少女コンテスト
散

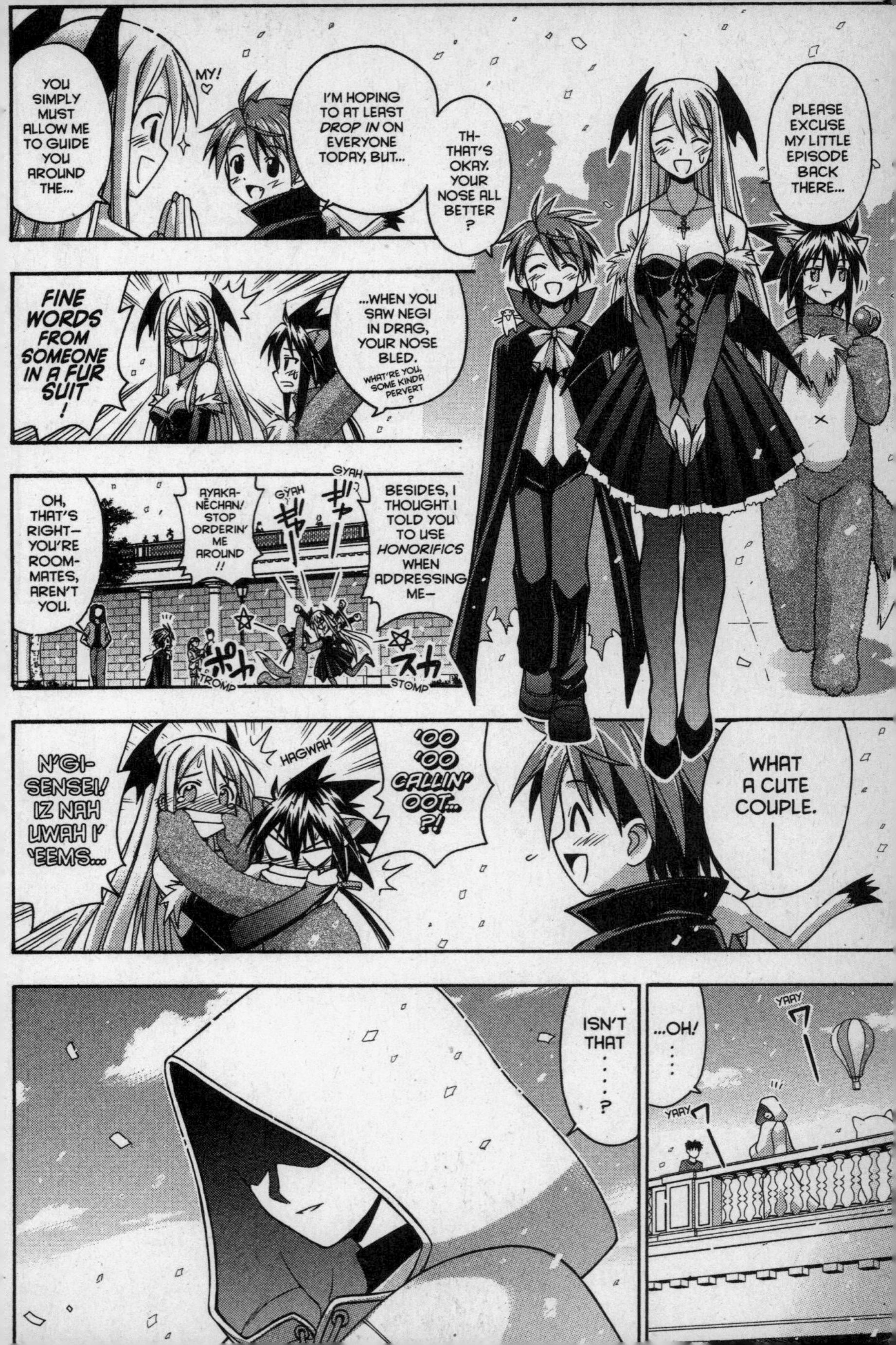
PLEASE EXCUSE MY LITTLE EPISODE BACK THERE...
TH-THAT'S OKAY. YOUR NOSE ALL BETTER?
I'M HOPING TO AT LEAST *DROP IN* ON EVERYONE TODAY, BUT...
MY! ♡
YOU SIMPLY MUST ALLOW ME TO GUIDE YOU AROUND THE...
...WHEN YOU SAW NEGI IN DRAG, YOUR NOSE BLED.
WHAT'RE YOU, SOME KINDA PERVERT?
FINE WORDS FROM SOMEONE IN A FUR SUIT!
BESIDES, I THOUGHT I TOLD YOU TO USE *HONORIFICS* WHEN ADDRESSING ME—
STOMP
GYAH
AYAKA-NÈCHAN! STOP ORDERIN' ME AROUND!!
GYAH
TROMP
OH, THAT'S RIGHT— YOU'RE ROOM-MATES, AREN'T YOU.
WHAT A CUTE COUPLE.
'OO 'OO CALLIN' OOT...?!
HAGWAH
N'GI-SENSEI! IZ NAH UWAH I' 'EEMS...
...OH! ....
YAAY
YAAY
ISN'T THAT ....?

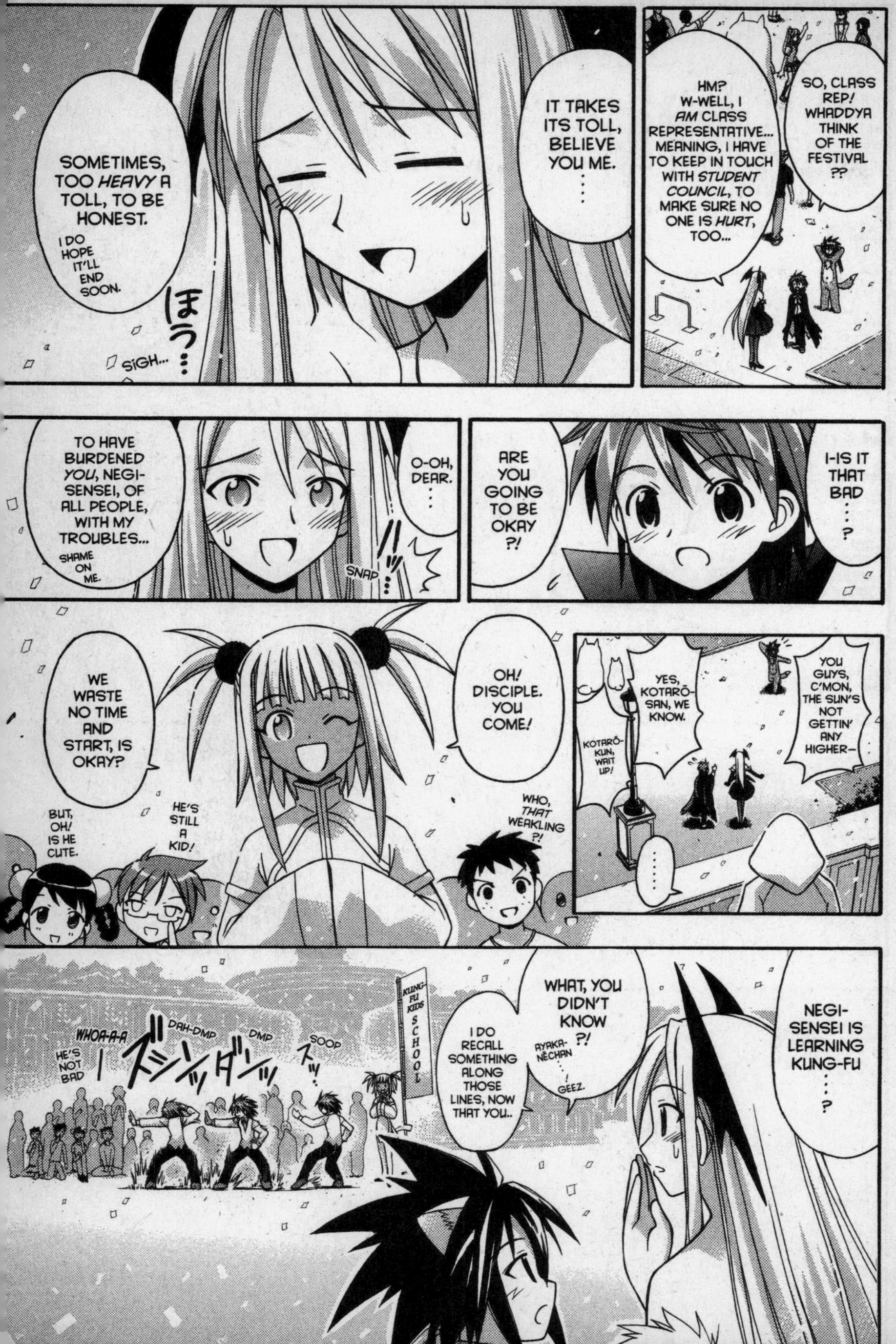
SO, CLASS REP! WHADDYA THINK OF THE FESTIVAL ??
HM? W-WELL, I AM CLASS REPRESENTATIVE... MEANING, I HAVE TO KEEP IN TOUCH WITH STUDENT COUNCIL, TO MAKE SURE NO ONE IS HURT, TOO...
IT TAKES ITS TOLL, BELIEVE YOU ME. ...
SOMETIMES, TOO HEAVY A TOLL, TO BE HONEST.
I DO HOPE IT'LL END SOON.
ほう
SIGH...
I-IS IT THAT BAD ...?
ARE YOU GOING TO BE OKAY ?!
O-OH, DEAR. ...
SNAP
TO HAVE BURDENED YOU, NEGI-SENSEI, OF ALL PEOPLE, WITH MY TROUBLES...
SHAME ON ME.
YOU GUYS, C'MON, THE SUN'S NOT GETTIN' ANY HIGHER–
YES, KOTARŌ-SAN, WE KNOW.
KOTARŌ-KUN, WAIT UP!
......
OH! DISCIPLE. YOU COME!
WE WASTE NO TIME AND START, IS OKAY?
WHO, THAT WEAKLING ?!
HE'S STILL A KID!
BUT, OH! IS HE CUTE.
NEGI-SENSEI IS LEARNING KUNG-FU ...?
WHAT, YOU DIDN'T KNOW ?!
AYAKA-NĒCHAN ...! GEEZ.
I DO RECALL SOMETHING ALONG THOSE LINES, NOW THAT YOU..
KUNG-FU KIDS SCHOOL
SOOP
DMP
DAH-DMP
WHOA-A-A
HE'S NOT BAD

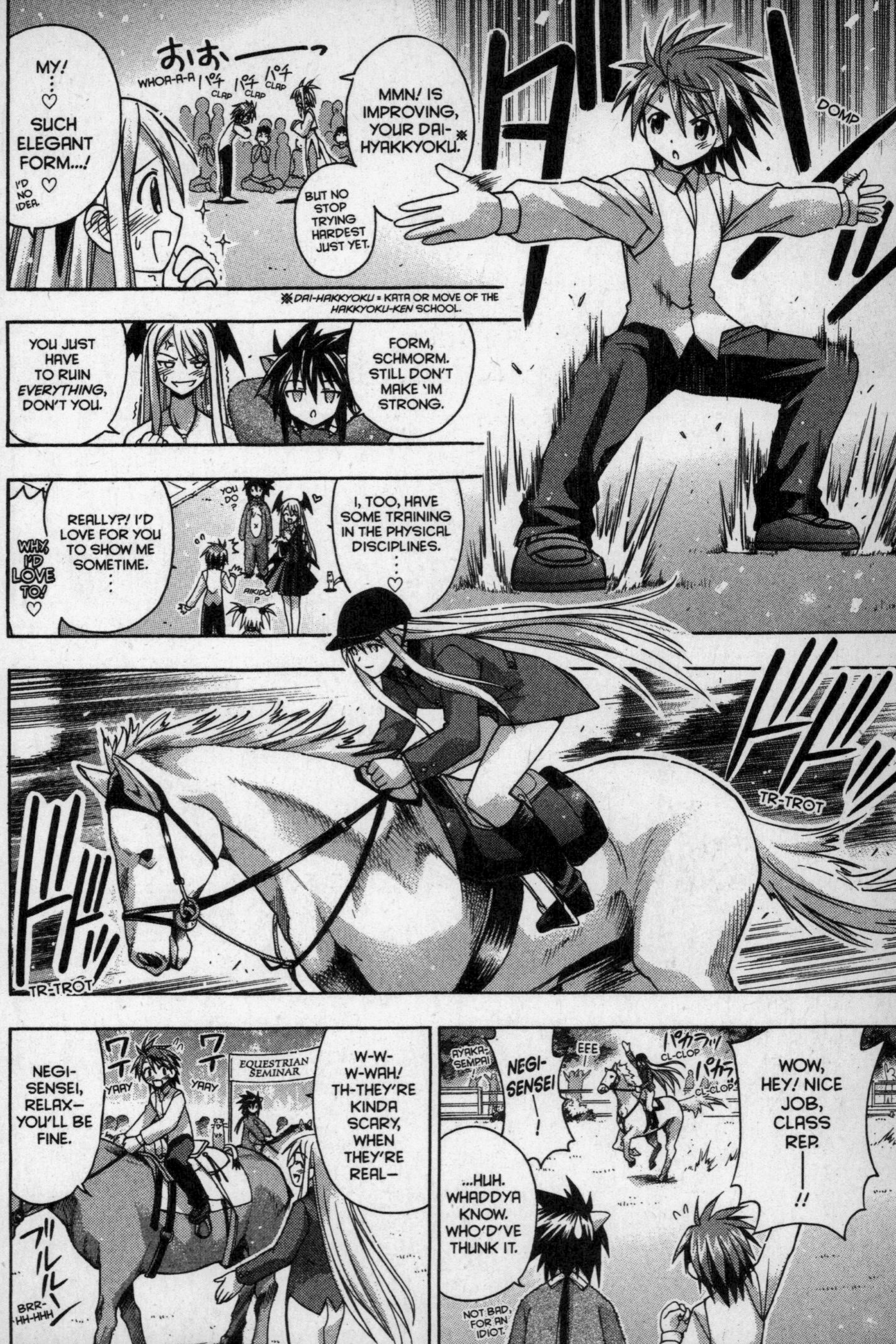
DOMP
MMN! IS IMPROVING, YOUR DAI-HYAKKYOKU.※
BUT NO STOP TRYING HARDEST JUST YET.
おお一一っ WHOA-A-A
パチ CLAP パチ CLAP パチ CLAP
MY! ... ♡ SUCH ELEGANT FORM...!
I'D NO IDEA. ♡
※DAI-HAKKYOKU = KATA OR MOVE OF THE HAKKYOKU-KEN SCHOOL.
FORM, SCHMORM. STILL DON'T MAKE 'IM STRONG.
YOU JUST HAVE TO RUIN EVERYTHING, DON'T YOU.
I, TOO, HAVE SOME TRAINING IN THE PHYSICAL DISCIPLINES. ... ♡
YOU DO?
AIKIDO?
REALLY?!? I'D LOVE FOR YOU TO SHOW ME SOMETIME. ...
WHY, I'D LOVE TO! ♡
TR-TROT
TR-TROT
WOW, HEY! NICE JOB, CLASS REP. !!
パカラッ CL-CLOP
パカラ CL-CLOP
EEE
AYAKA-SENPAI
NEGI-SENSEI!
...HUH. WHADDYA KNOW. WHO'D'VE THUNK IT.
NOT BAD, FOR AN IDIOT.
W-W-W-WAH! TH-THEY'RE KINDA SCARY, WHEN THEY'RE REAL—
ワイ YAAY
ワイ YAAY
EQUESTRIAN SEMINAR
NEGI-SENSEI, RELAX—YOU'LL BE FINE.
ブルルル BRR-HH-HHH

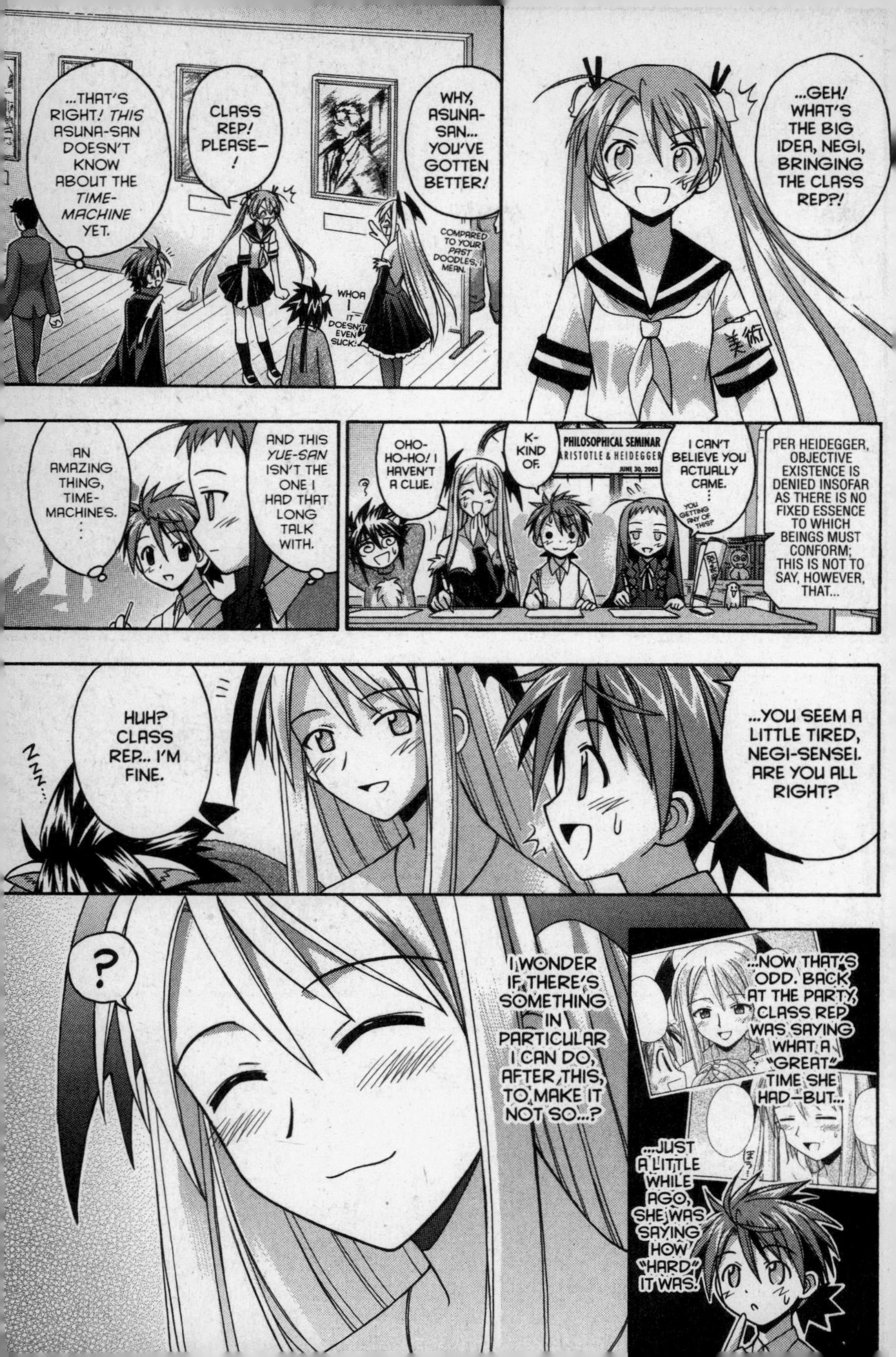

...GEH! WHAT'S THE BIG IDEA, NEGI, BRINGING THE CLASS REP?!
WHY, ASUNA-SAN... YOU'VE GOTTEN BETTER!
COMPARED TO YOUR *PAST* DOODLES, I MEAN.
CLASS REP! PLEASE—!
WHOA! IT DOESN'T EVEN SUCK!
...THAT'S RIGHT! *THIS* ASUNA-SAN DOESN'T KNOW ABOUT THE *TIME-MACHINE* YET.
PER HEIDEGGER, OBJECTIVE EXISTENCE IS DENIED INSOFAR AS THERE IS NO FIXED ESSENCE TO WHICH BEINGS MUST CONFORM; THIS IS NOT TO SAY, HOWEVER, THAT...
PHILOSOPHICAL SEMINAR
ARISTOTLE & HEIDEGGER
JUNE 30, 2003
I CAN'T BELIEVE YOU ACTUALLY CAME. ...
YOU GETTING ANY OF THIS?
K-KIND OF.
OHO-HO-HO! I HAVEN'T A CLUE.
AND THIS *YUE-SAN* ISN'T THE ONE I HAD THAT LONG TALK WITH.
AN AMAZING THING, TIME-MACHINES. ...
...YOU SEEM A LITTLE TIRED, NEGI-SENSEI. ARE YOU ALL RIGHT?
HUH? CLASS REP... I'M FINE.
ZZZ...
...NOW THAT'S ODD. BACK AT THE PARTY, CLASS REP WAS SAYING WHAT A "GREAT" TIME SHE HAD—BUT...
...JUST A LITTLE WHILE AGO, SHE WAS SAYING HOW "HARD" IT WAS.
I WONDER IF THERE'S SOMETHING IN PARTICULAR I CAN DO, AFTER THIS, TO MAKE IT NOT SO...?
?

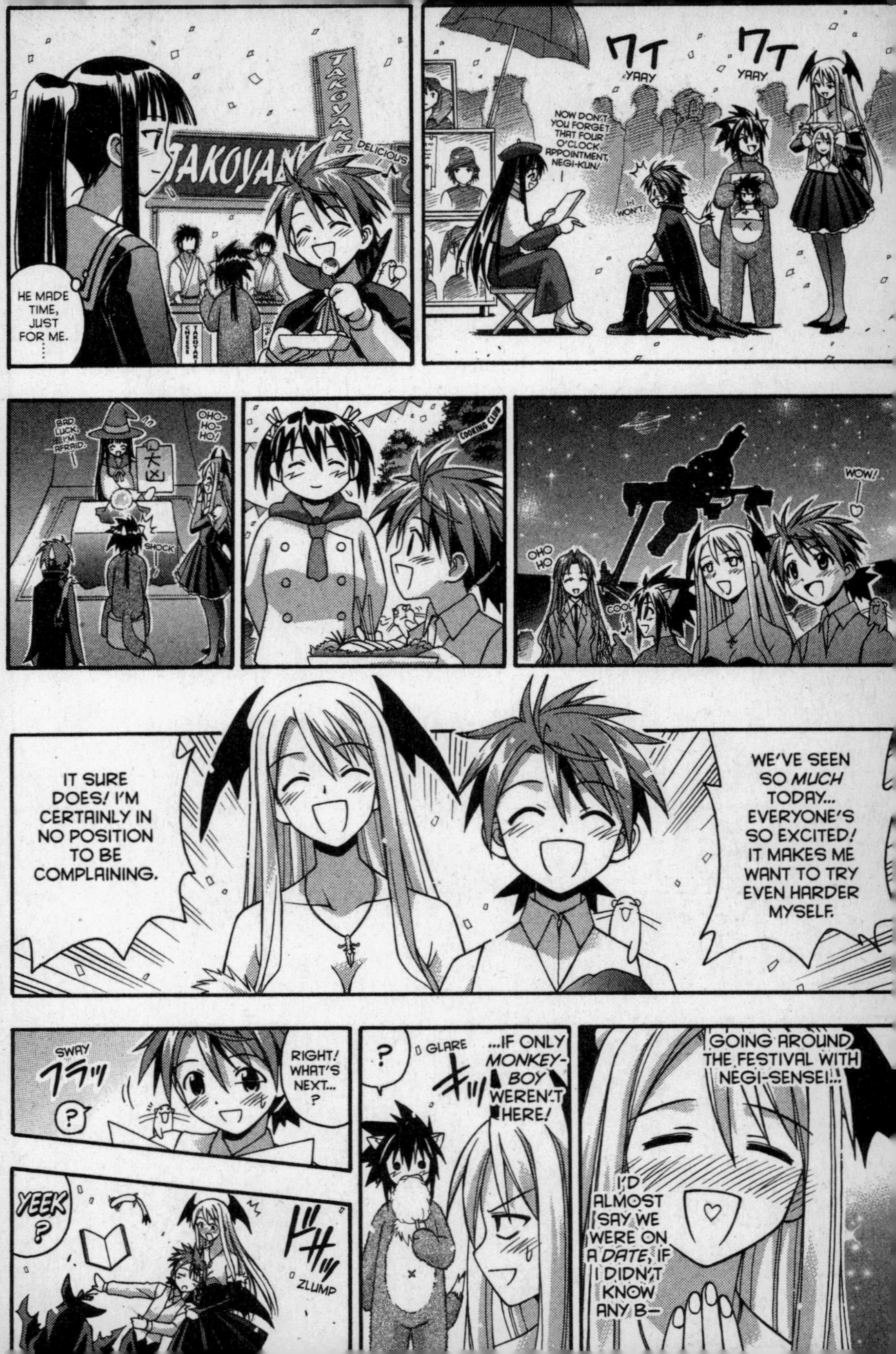
ワイ
YAAY
ワイ
YAAY
NOW DON'T YOU FORGET THAT FOUR O'CLOCK APPOINTMENT, NEGI-KUN!
I-I WON'T!
TAKOYAKI
TAKOYAKI
DELICIOUS ♪
HE MADE TIME, JUST FOR ME. ...
WOW!
OHO HO
COOL
COOKING CLUB
OHO-HO-HO!
BAD LUCK, I'M AFRAID.
大凶
SHOCK
WE'VE SEEN SO *MUCH* TODAY... EVERYONE'S SO EXCITED! IT MAKES ME WANT TO TRY EVEN HARDER MYSELF.
IT SURE DOES! I'M CERTAINLY IN NO POSITION TO BE COMPLAINING.
GOING AROUND THE FESTIVAL WITH NEGI-SENSEI...
I'D ALMOST SAY WE WERE ON A *DATE*, IF I DIDN'T KNOW ANY B—
...IF ONLY *MONKEY-BOY* WEREN'T HERE!
GLARE
?
RIGHT! WHAT'S NEXT... ?
SWAY
?
ZLUMP
YEEK ?

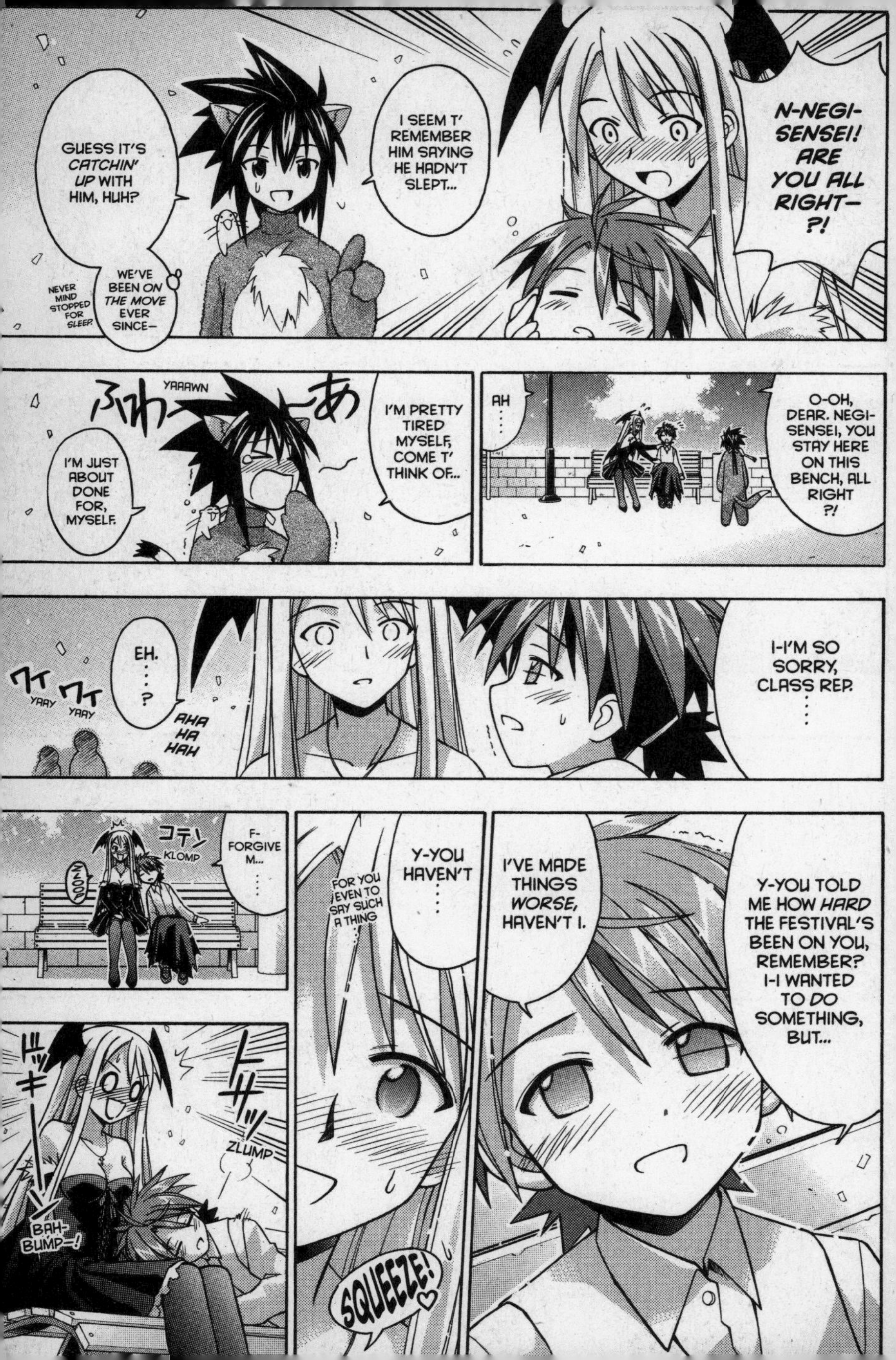
N-NEGI-SENSEI! ARE YOU ALL RIGHT—?!
I SEEM T' REMEMBER HIM SAYING HE HADN'T SLEPT...
GUESS IT'S CATCHIN' UP WITH HIM, HUH?
WE'VE BEEN ON THE MOVE EVER SINCE—
NEVER MIND STOPPED FOR SLEEP.
O-OH, DEAR. NEGI-SENSEI, YOU STAY HERE ON THIS BENCH, ALL RIGHT?!
AH ...
ふわ〜〜あ
YAAAWN
I'M PRETTY TIRED MYSELF, COME T' THINK OF...
I'M JUST ABOUT DONE FOR, MYSELF.
I-I'M SO SORRY, CLASS REP. ...
EH. ...?
AHA HA HAH
ワイ ワイ
YAAY YAAY
Y-YOU TOLD ME HOW HARD THE FESTIVAL'S BEEN ON YOU, REMEMBER? I-I WANTED TO DO SOMETHING, BUT...
I'VE MADE THINGS WORSE, HAVEN'T I.
Y-YOU HAVEN'T ...
FOR YOU EVEN TO SAY SUCH A THING ...
SQUEEZE!
F-FORGIVE M... ...
コテン
KLOMP
ZLOOP
ドサッ
ZLUMP
ドッキー
BAH-BUMP—!

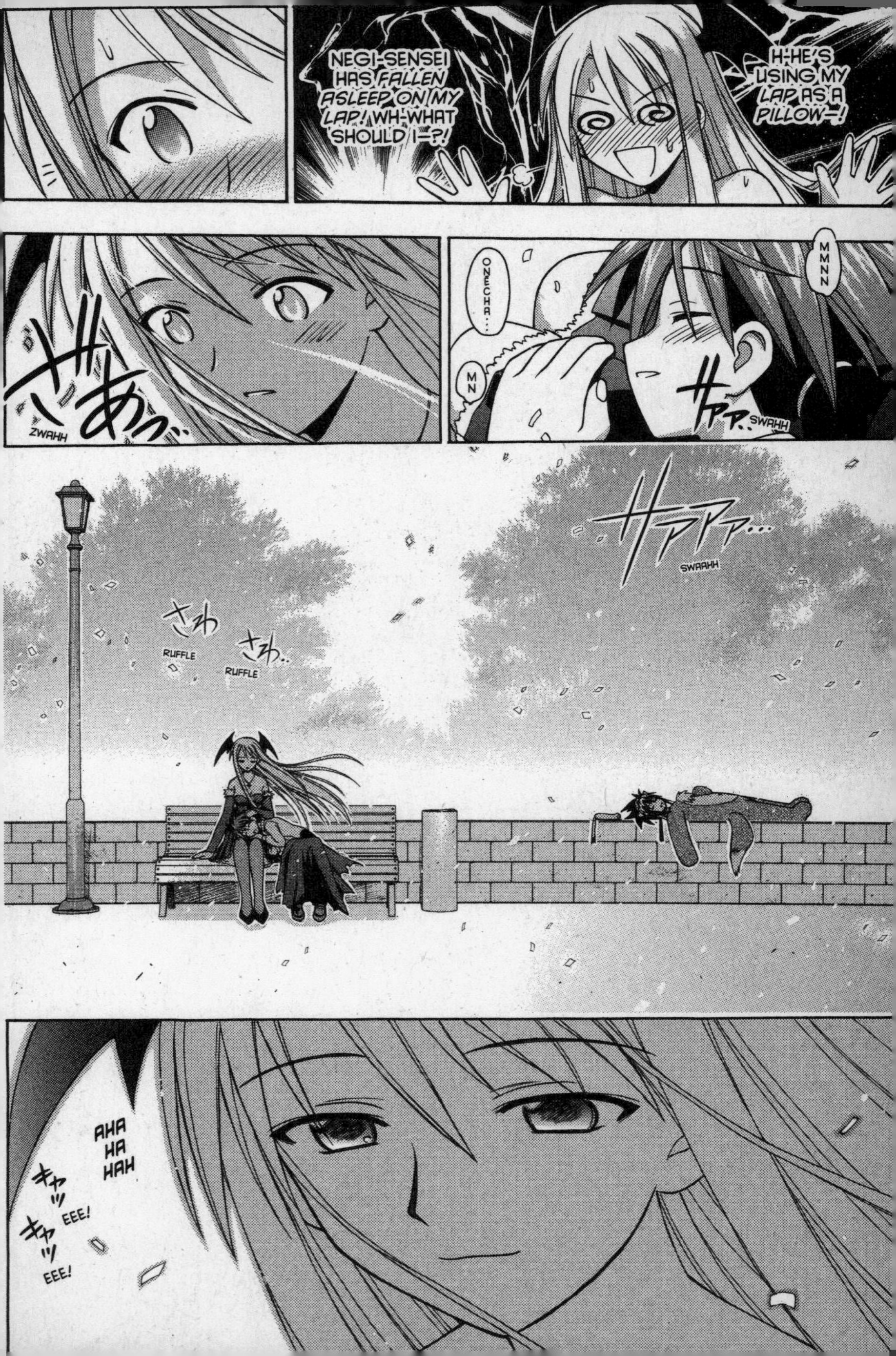
H-HE'S USING MY LAP AS A PILLOW--!
NEGI-SENSEI HAS FALLEN ASLEEP ON MY LAP! WH-WHAT SHOULD I--?!
MMNN
ONECHA...
MN
ザァァ..
SWAHH
ざあっ
ZWAHH
ザァァァ..
SWAAHH
さわ
RUFFLE
さわ..
RUFFLE
AHA HA HAH
キャッ
EEE!
キャッ
EEE!

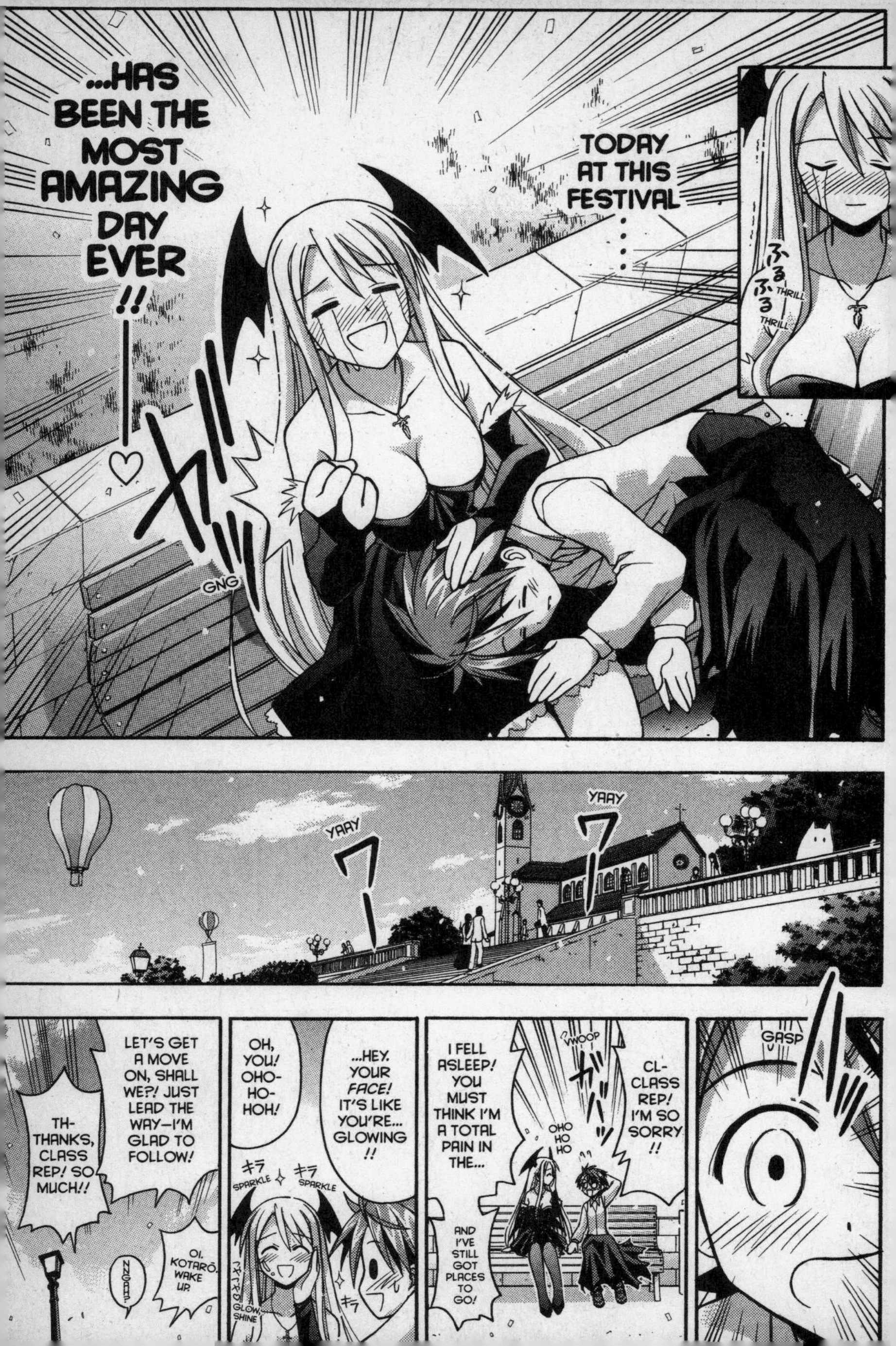
ふる ふる
THRILL THRILL
TODAY AT THIS FESTIVAL...
...HAS BEEN THE MOST AMAZING DAY EVER!!—♡
GNG
YAAY
YAAY
GASP
CL-CLASS REP! I'M SO SORRY!!
I FELL ASLEEP! YOU MUST THINK I'M A TOTAL PAIN IN THE...
VWOOP
OHO HO HO
AND I'VE STILL GOT PLACES TO GO!
...HEY. YOUR FACE! IT'S LIKE YOU'RE... GLOWING!!
OH, YOU! OHO-HO-HOH!
キラ SPARKLE キラ SPARKLE
GLOW, SHINE
LET'S GET A MOVE ON, SHALL WE?! JUST LEAD THE WAY—I'M GLAD TO FOLLOW!
TH-THANKS, CLASS REP! SO MUCH!!
OI. KOTARŌ. WAKE UP.
NNGAH?

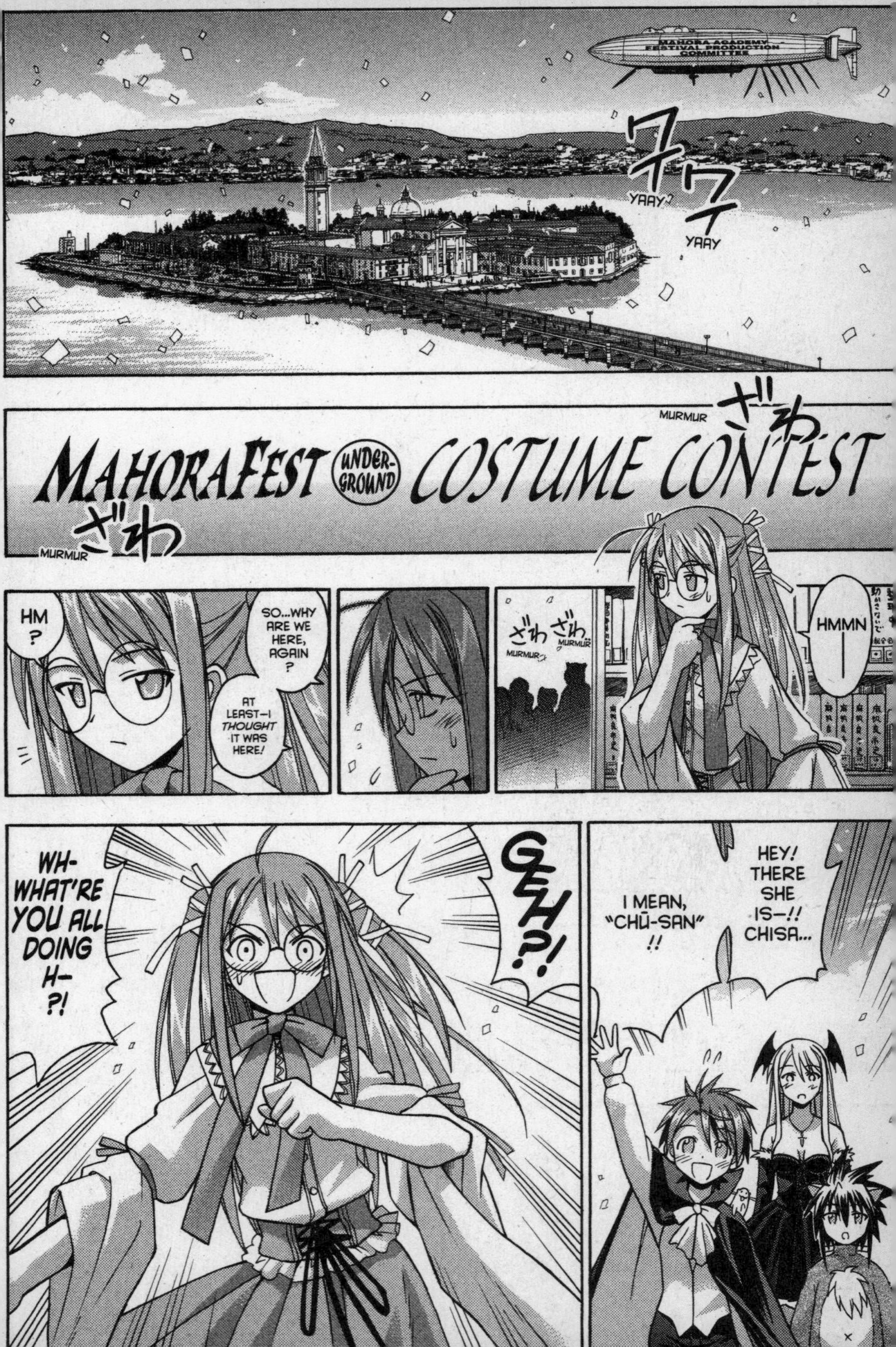
MAHORA ACADEMY FESTIVAL PRODUCTION COMMITTEE
ワイワイ
YAAY
YAAY
ざわ
MURMUR
MAHORAFEST UNDERGROUND COSTUME CONTEST
ざわ
MURMUR
HMMN—
ざわ ざわ
MURMUR MURMUR
SO...WHY ARE WE HERE, AGAIN?
AT LEAST—I THOUGHT IT WAS HERE!
HM?
HEY! THERE SHE IS—!! CHISA...
I MEAN, "CHŪ-SAN"!!
GEH?!
WH-WHAT'RE YOU ALL DOING H-?!

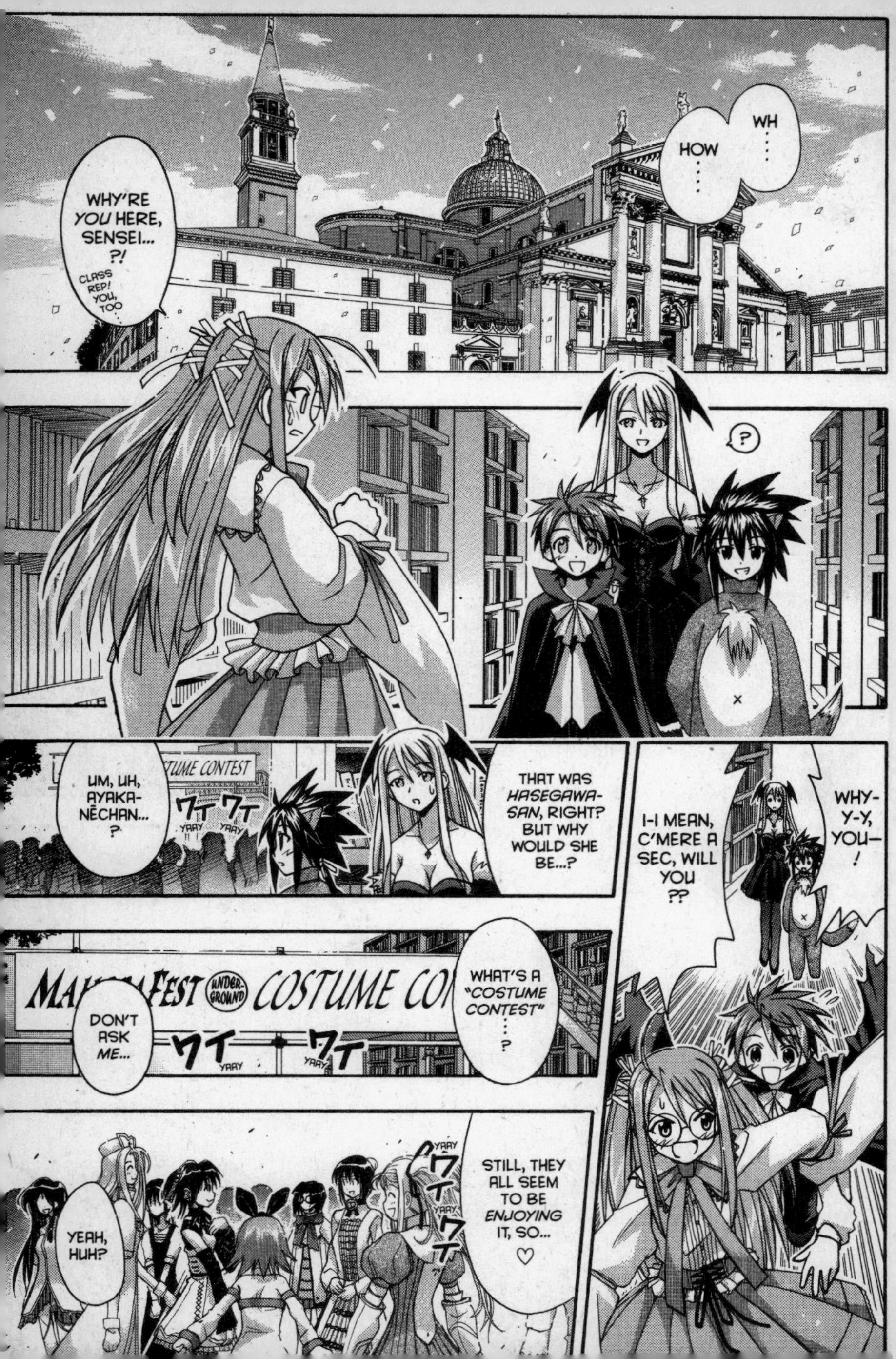

WH......
HOW......
WHY'RE YOU HERE, SENSEI...?!
CLASS REP! YOU, TOO...
?
WHY-Y-Y, YOU—!
I-I MEAN, C'MERE A SEC, WILL YOU??
THAT WAS HASEGAWA-SAN, RIGHT? BUT WHY WOULD SHE BE...?
UM, UH, AYAKA-NĒCHAN...?
STUME CONTEST
YAAY YAAY
WHAT'S A "COSTUME CONTEST"...?
DON'T ASK ME...
UNDER-GROUND COSTUME CON
YAAY YAAY
STILL, THEY ALL SEEM TO BE ENJOYING IT, SO... ♡
YEAH, HUH?
YAAY YAAY

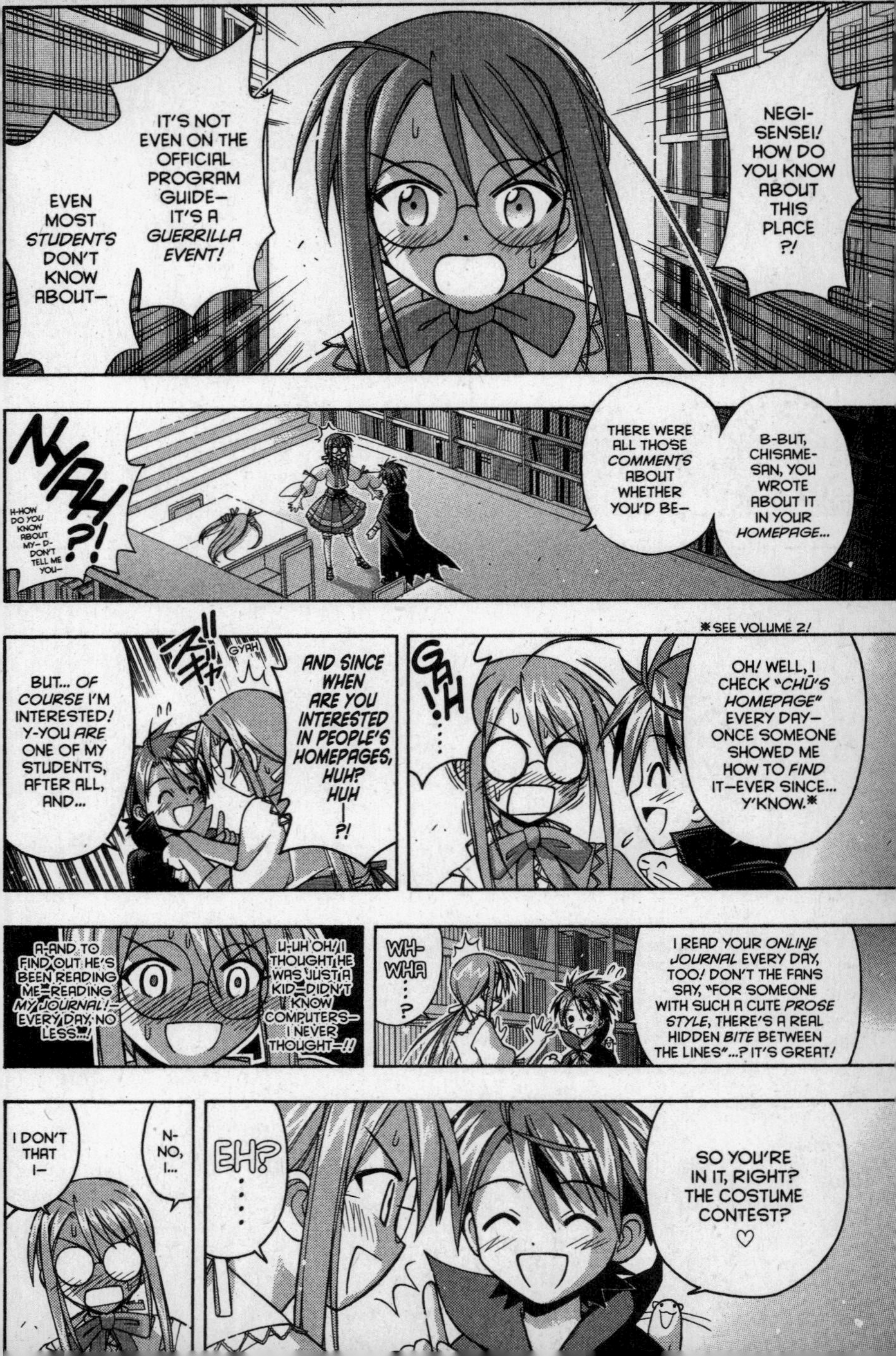
NEGI-SENSEI! HOW DO YOU KNOW ABOUT THIS PLACE?!
IT'S NOT EVEN ON THE OFFICIAL PROGRAM GUIDE— IT'S A *GUERRILLA EVENT!*
EVEN MOST *STUDENTS* DON'T KNOW ABOUT—
B-BUT, CHISAME-SAN, YOU WROTE ABOUT IT IN YOUR *HOMEPAGE...*
THERE WERE ALL THOSE *COMMENTS* ABOUT WHETHER YOU'D BE—
NYAH?!
H-HOW DO YOU KNOW ABOUT MY— D-DON'T TELL ME YOU—
*SEE VOLUME 2!
OH! WELL, I CHECK "CHŪ'S HOMEPAGE" EVERY DAY— ONCE SOMEONE SHOWED ME HOW TO *FIND* IT—EVER SINCE... Y'KNOW.*
GAH!...
AND SINCE WHEN ARE YOU INTERESTED IN PEOPLE'S HOMEPAGES, HUH? HUH—?!
GYAH
BUT... *OF COURSE* I'M INTERESTED! Y-YOU *ARE* ONE OF MY STUDENTS, AFTER ALL, AND...
I READ YOUR *ONLINE JOURNAL* EVERY DAY, TOO! DON'T THE FANS SAY, "FOR SOMEONE WITH SUCH A CUTE *PROSE STYLE*, THERE'S A REAL HIDDEN *BITE* BETWEEN THE LINES"...? IT'S GREAT!
WH-WHA...?
U-UH OH! I THOUGHT HE WAS JUST A KID—DIDN'T KNOW COMPUTERS— I NEVER THOUGHT—!!
A-AND TO FIND OUT HE'S BEEN READING ME—READING *MY JOURNAL!*—EVERY DAY, NO LESS...!
SO YOU'RE IN IT, RIGHT? THE COSTUME CONTEST? ♡
EH?....
N-NO, I...
I DON'T THAT I—

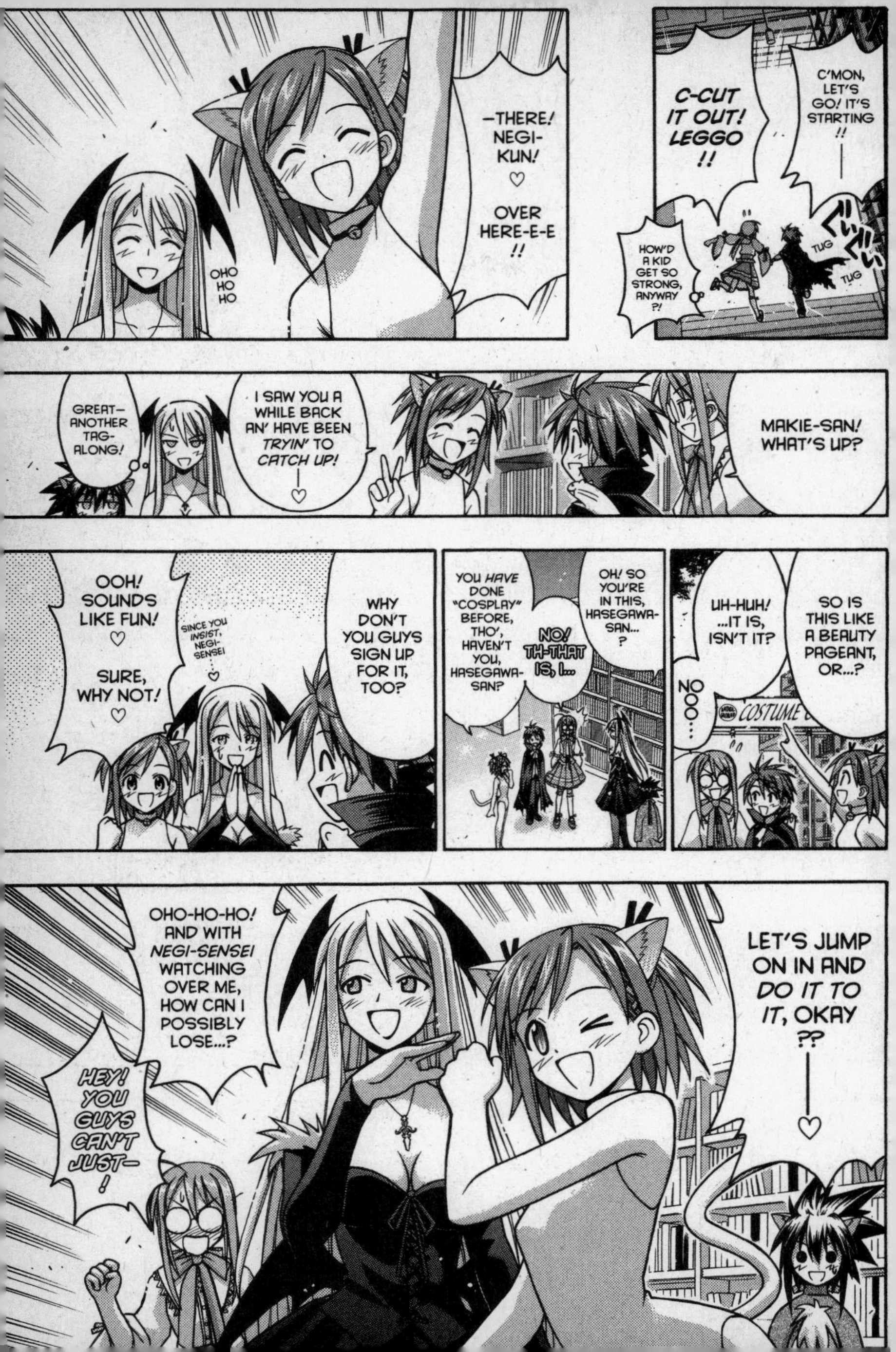
C'MON, LET'S GO! IT'S STARTING !!
C-CUT IT OUT! LEGGO !!
HOW'D A KID GET SO STRONG, ANYWAY ?!
TUG
TUG
—THERE! NEGI-KUN! ♡ OVER HERE-E-E !!
OHO HO HO
MAKIE-SAN! WHAT'S UP?
I SAW YOU A WHILE BACK AN' HAVE BEEN TRYIN' TO CATCH UP! ♡
GREAT—ANOTHER TAG-ALONG!
SO IS THIS LIKE A BEAUTY PAGEANT, OR...?
UH-HUH! ...IT IS, ISN'T IT?
NOOO...
COSTUME
OH! SO YOU'RE IN THIS, HASEGAWA-SAN...?
YOU HAVE DONE "COSPLAY" BEFORE, THO', HAVEN'T YOU, HASEGAWA-SAN?
NO! TH-THAT IS, I...
WHY DON'T YOU GUYS SIGN UP FOR IT, TOO?
OOH! SOUNDS LIKE FUN! ♡ SURE, WHY NOT! ♡
SINCE YOU INSIST, NEGI-SENSEI... ♡
LET'S JUMP ON IN AND DO IT TO IT, OKAY ?? ♡
OHO-HO-HO! AND WITH NEGI-SENSEI WATCHING OVER ME, HOW CAN I POSSIBLY LOSE...?
HEY! YOU GUYS CAN'T JUST— !

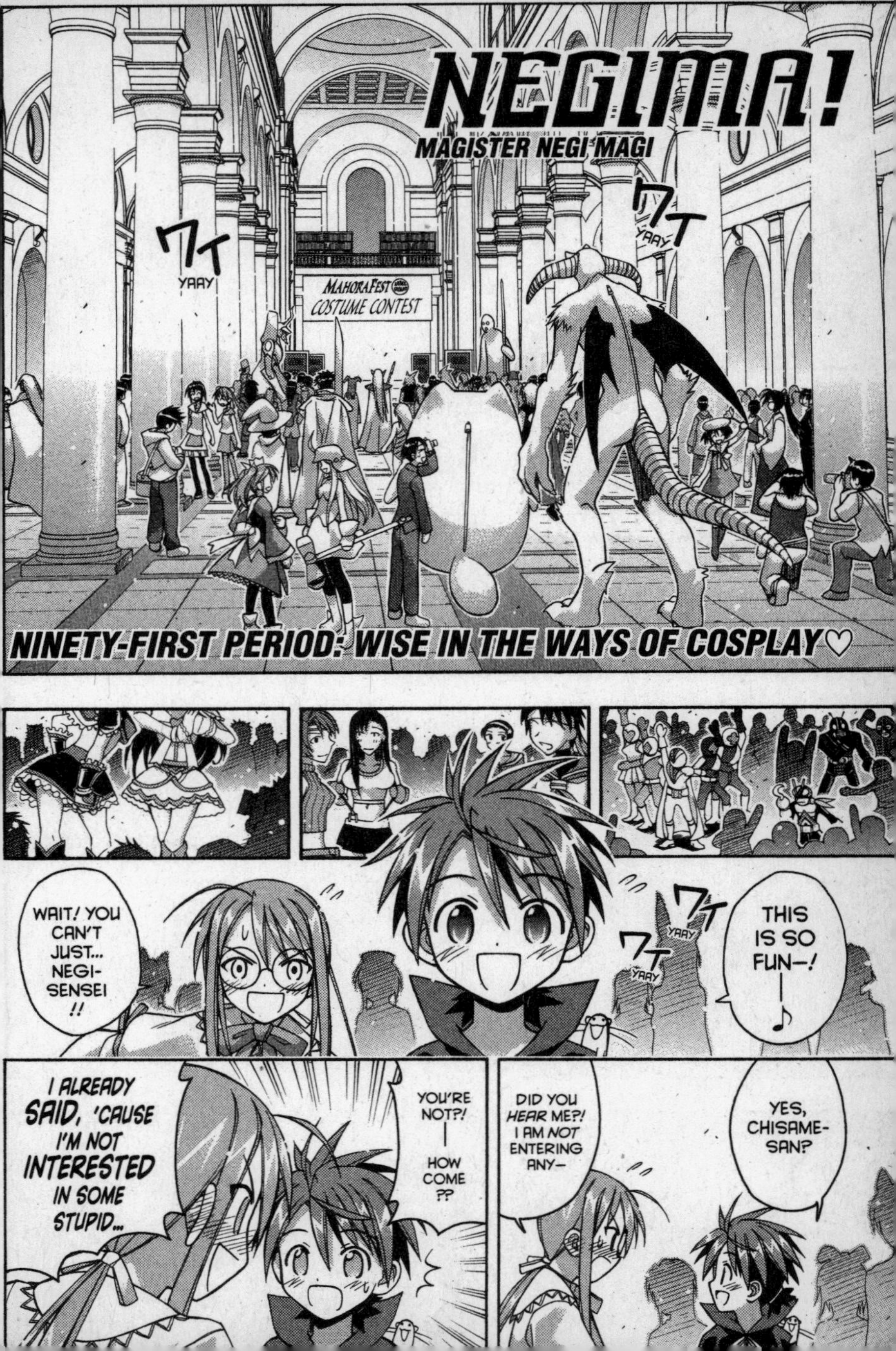
NEGIMA!
MAGISTER NEGI MAGI
ワイ
YAAY
ワイ
YAAY
MAHORAFEST
COSTUME CONTEST
NINETY-FIRST PERIOD: WISE IN THE WAYS OF COSPLAY♡
THIS IS SO FUN—! ♪
ワイ
YAAY
ワイ
YAAY
WAIT! YOU CAN'T JUST... NEGI-SENSEI!!
YES, CHISAME-SAN?
DID YOU HEAR ME?! I AM NOT ENTERING ANY—
YOU'RE NOT?! HOW COME??
I ALREADY SAID, 'CAUSE I'M NOT INTERESTED IN SOME STUPID...

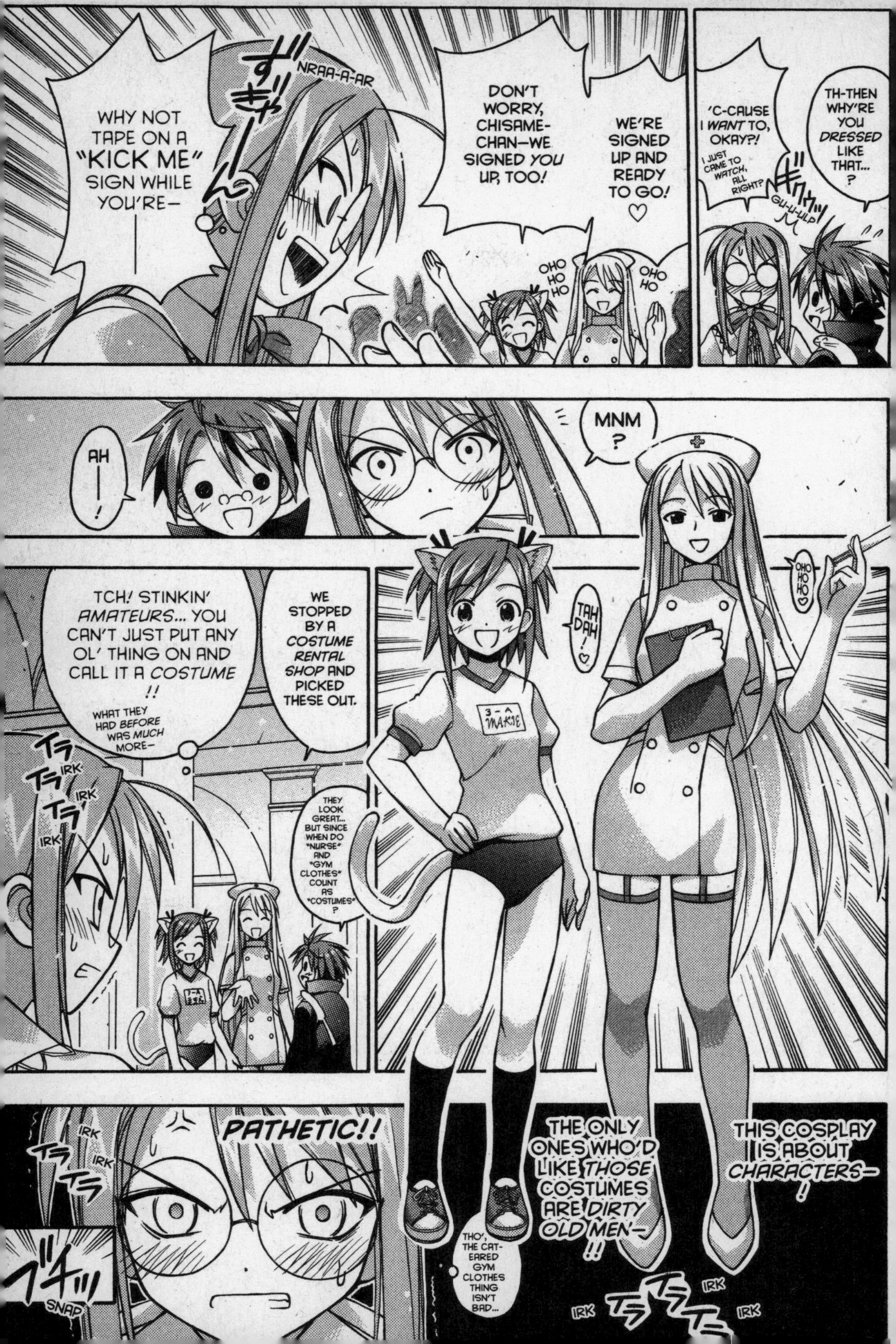
TH-THEN WHY'RE YOU DRESSED LIKE THAT...?
'C-CAUSE I WANT TO, OKAY?!
I JUST CAME TO WATCH, ALL RIGHT?
GU-U-ULP
WE'RE SIGNED UP AND READY TO GO! ♡
DON'T WORRY, CHISAME-CHAN—WE SIGNED YOU UP, TOO!
OHO HO
OHO HO HO
NRAA-A-AR
WHY NOT TAPE ON A "KICK ME" SIGN WHILE YOU'RE— —
MNM?
AH—!
OHO HO HO ♡
TAH DAH! ♡
3-A MAKIE
WE STOPPED BY A COSTUME RENTAL SHOP AND PICKED THESE OUT.
TCH! STINKIN' AMATEURS... YOU CAN'T JUST PUT ANY OL' THING ON AND CALL IT A COSTUME!!
WHAT THEY HAD BEFORE WAS MUCH MORE—
THEY LOOK GREAT... BUT SINCE WHEN DO "NURSE" AND "GYM CLOTHES" COUNT AS "COSTUMES"?
IRK
IRK
IRK
THIS COSPLAY IS ABOUT CHARACTERS—!
THE ONLY ONES WHO'D LIKE THOSE COSTUMES ARE DIRTY OLD MEN—!!
THO', THE CAT-EARED GYM CLOTHES THING ISN'T BAD...
IRK
IRK
IRK
PATHETIC!!
IRK
IRK
SNAP

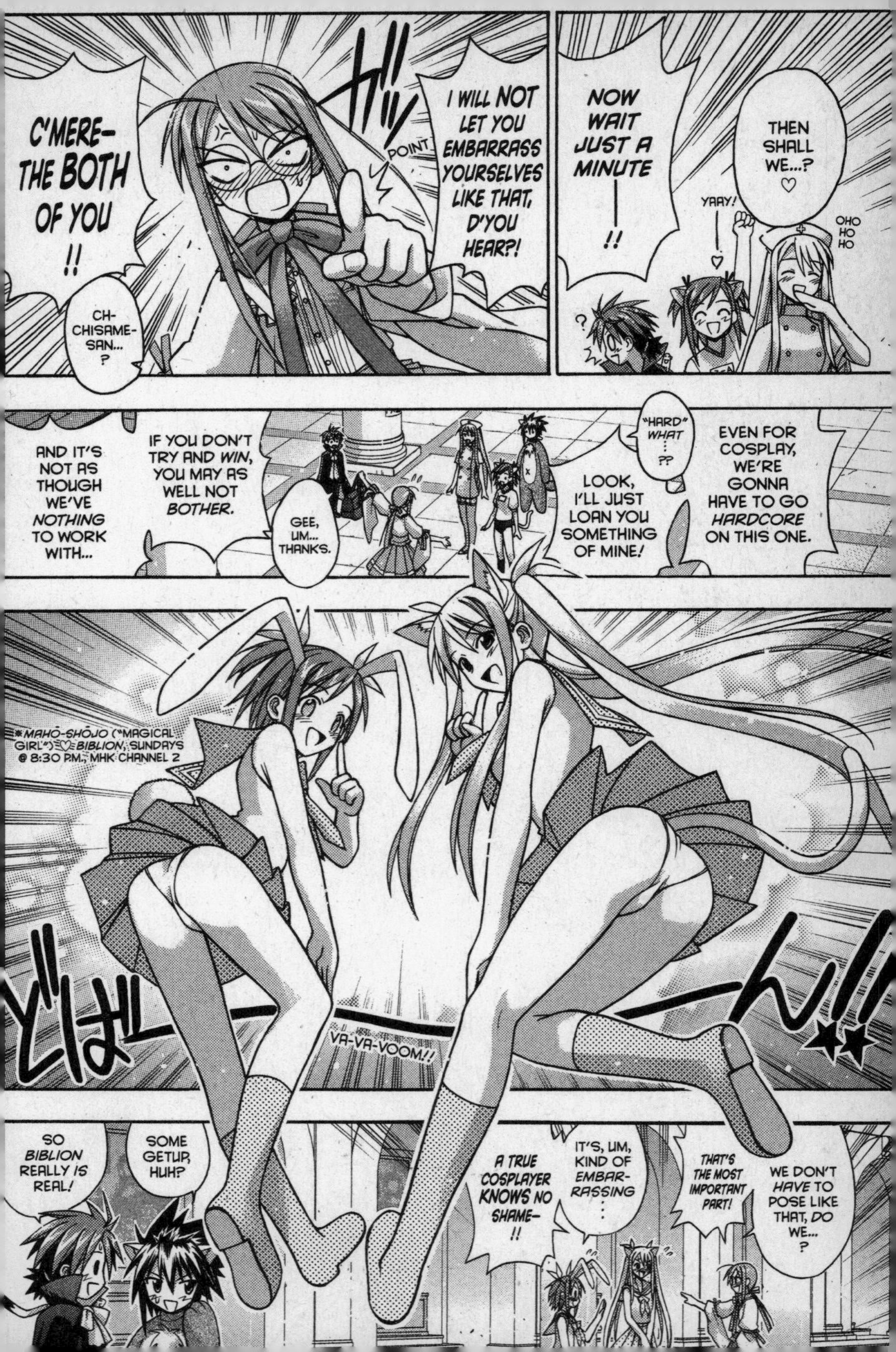

NOW WAIT JUST A MINUTE—!!
THEN SHALL WE...? ♡
YAAY! —♡
OHO HO HO
I WILL NOT LET YOU EMBARRASS YOURSELVES LIKE THAT, D'YOU HEAR?!
POINT
C'MERE—THE BOTH OF YOU!!
CH-CHISAME-SAN...?
EVEN FOR COSPLAY, WE'RE GONNA HAVE TO GO HARDCORE ON THIS ONE.
"HARD" WHAT...??
LOOK, I'LL JUST LOAN YOU SOMETHING OF MINE!
GEE, UM... THANKS.
IF YOU DON'T TRY AND WIN, YOU MAY AS WELL NOT BOTHER.
AND IT'S NOT AS THOUGH WE'VE NOTHING TO WORK WITH...
*MAHO-SHOJO ("MAGICAL GIRL")♡BIBLION, SUNDAYS @ 8:30 P.M., MHK CHANNEL 2
VA-VA-VOOM!!
WE DON'T HAVE TO POSE LIKE THAT, DO WE...?
THAT'S THE MOST IMPORTANT PART!
IT'S, UM, KIND OF EMBARRASSING...
A TRUE COSPLAYER KNOWS NO SHAME—!!
SOME GETUP, HUH?
SO BIBLION REALLY IS REAL!

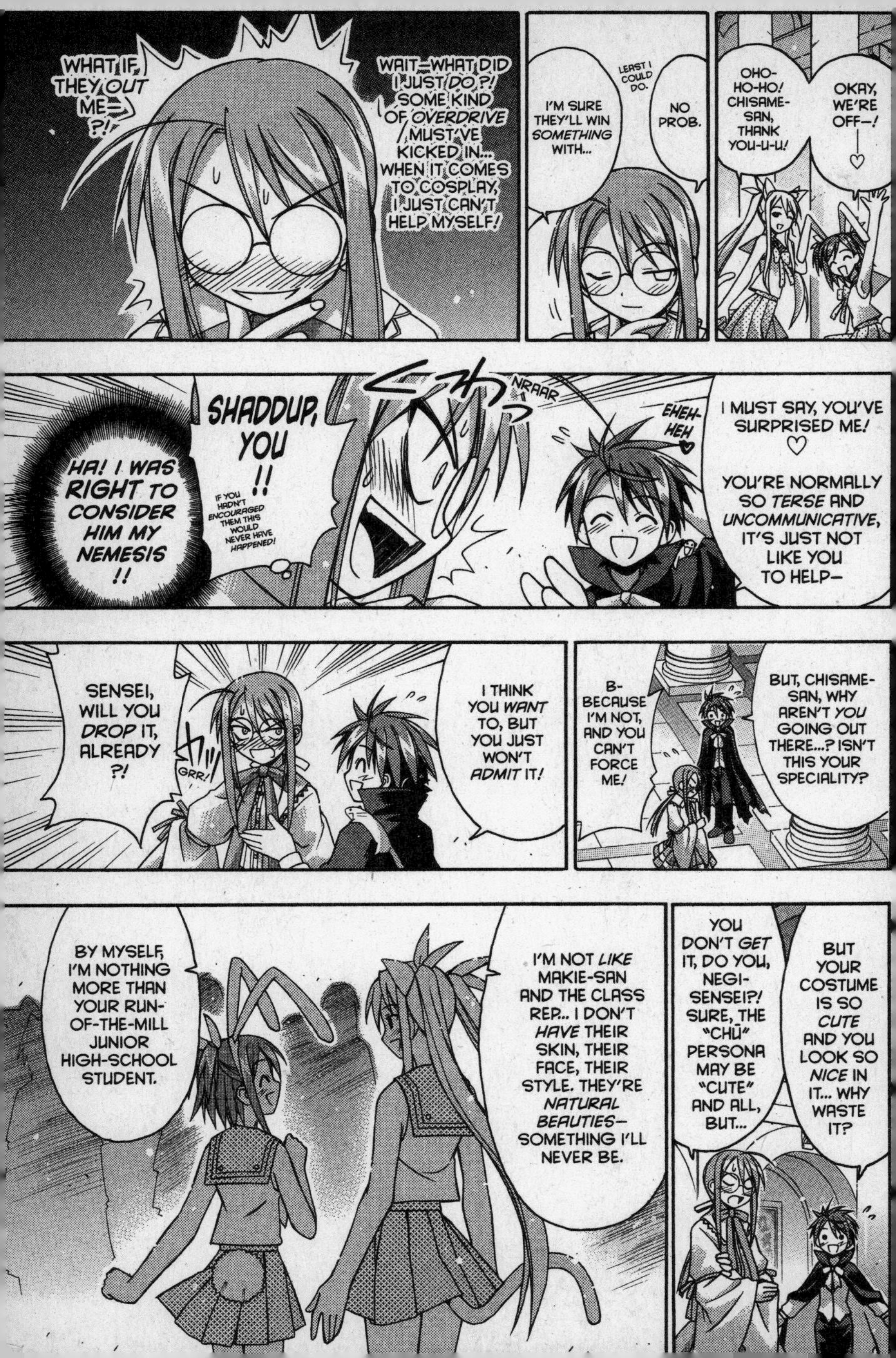

OKAY, WE'RE OFF—! ♡
OHO-HO-HO! CHISAME-SAN, THANK YOU-U-U!
NO PROB.
LEAST I COULD DO.
I'M SURE THEY'LL WIN SOMETHING WITH...
WAIT—WHAT DID I JUST DO?! SOME KIND OF OVERDRIVE MUST'VE KICKED IN... WHEN IT COMES TO COSPLAY, I JUST CAN'T HELP MYSELF!
WHAT IF THEY OUT ME—?!
I MUST SAY, YOU'VE SURPRISED ME! ♡
YOU'RE NORMALLY SO TERSE AND UNCOMMUNICATIVE, IT'S JUST NOT LIKE YOU TO HELP—
EHEH-HEH ♡
NRAAR
SHADDUP, YOU!!
IF YOU HADN'T ENCOURAGED THEM THIS WOULD NEVER HAVE HAPPENED!
HA! I WAS RIGHT TO CONSIDER HIM MY NEMESIS!!
BUT, CHISAME-SAN, WHY AREN'T YOU GOING OUT THERE...? ISN'T THIS YOUR SPECIALITY?
B-BECAUSE I'M NOT, AND YOU CAN'T FORCE ME!
I THINK YOU WANT TO, BUT YOU JUST WON'T ADMIT IT!
SENSEI, WILL YOU DROP IT, ALREADY?!
GRR!
BUT YOUR COSTUME IS SO CUTE AND YOU LOOK SO NICE IN IT... WHY WASTE IT?
YOU DON'T GET IT, DO YOU, NEGI-SENSEI?! SURE, THE "CHŪ" PERSONA MAY BE "CUTE" AND ALL, BUT...
I'M NOT LIKE MAKIE-SAN AND THE CLASS REP... I DON'T HAVE THEIR SKIN, THEIR FACE, THEIR STYLE. THEY'RE NATURAL BEAUTIES—SOMETHING I'LL NEVER BE.
BY MYSELF, I'M NOTHING MORE THAN YOUR RUN-OF-THE-MILL JUNIOR HIGH-SCHOOL STUDENT.

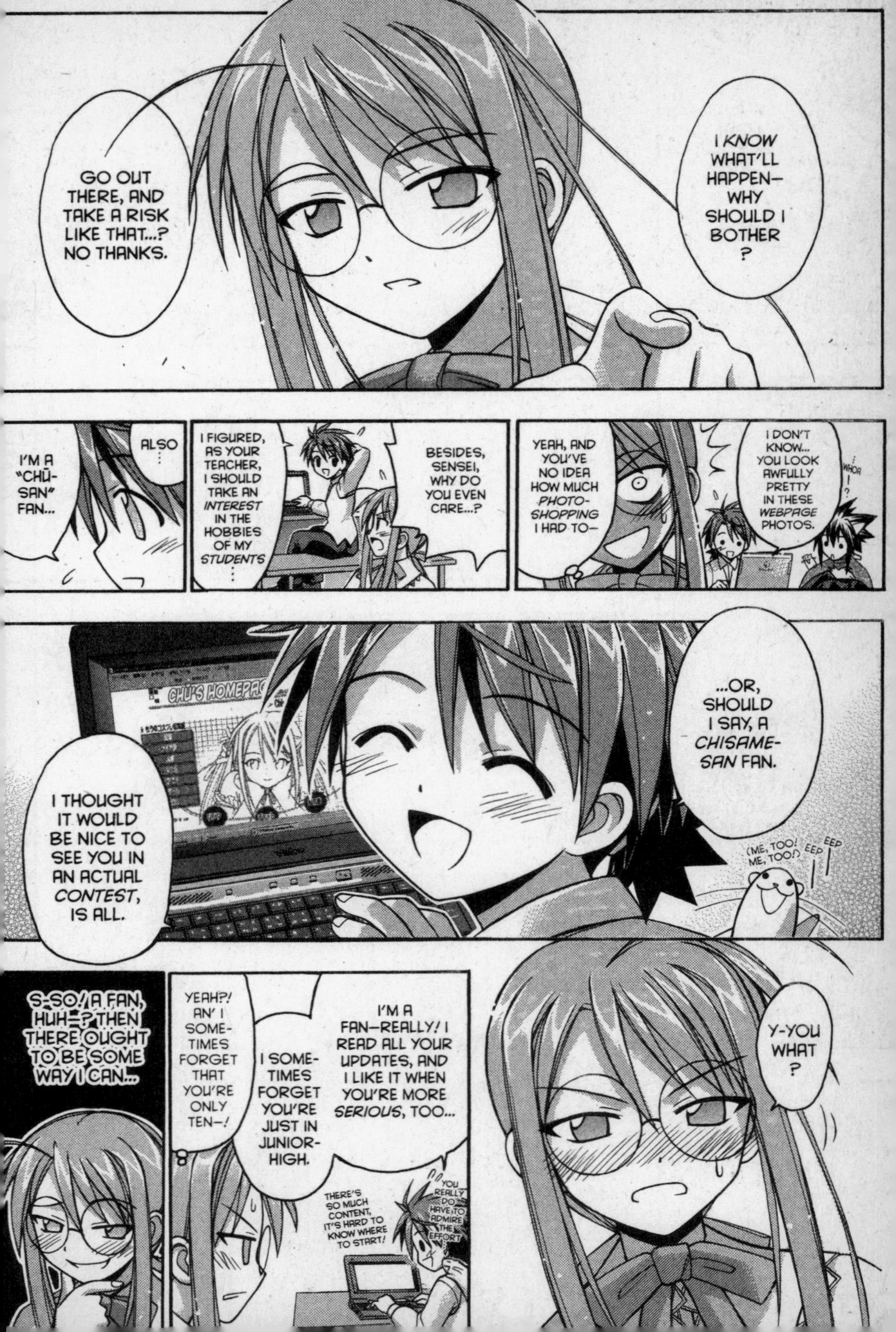
I KNOW WHAT'LL HAPPEN— WHY SHOULD I BOTHER ?
GO OUT THERE, AND TAKE A RISK LIKE THAT...? NO THANKS.
I DON'T KNOW... YOU LOOK AWFULLY PRETTY IN THESE WEBPAGE PHOTOS.
WHOA !?
YEAH, AND YOU'VE NO IDEA HOW MUCH PHOTO-SHOPPING I HAD TO—
BESIDES, SENSEI, WHY DO YOU EVEN CARE...?
I FIGURED, AS YOUR TEACHER, I SHOULD TAKE AN INTEREST IN THE HOBBIES OF MY STUDENTS...
ALSO...
I'M A "CHŪ-SAN" FAN...
...OR, SHOULD I SAY, A CHISAME-SAN FAN.
(ME, TOO! ME, TOO!)
EEP EEP
I THOUGHT IT WOULD BE NICE TO SEE YOU IN AN ACTUAL CONTEST, IS ALL.
Y-YOU WHAT ?
I'M A FAN—REALLY! I READ ALL YOUR UPDATES, AND I LIKE IT WHEN YOU'RE MORE SERIOUS, TOO...
I SOME-TIMES FORGET YOU'RE JUST IN JUNIOR-HIGH.
YEAH?! AN' I SOME-TIMES FORGET THAT YOU'RE ONLY TEN—!
YOU REALLY DO HAVE TO ADMIRE THE EFFORT
THERE'S SO MUCH CONTENT, IT'S HARD TO KNOW WHERE TO START!
S-SO! A FAN, HUH—? THEN THERE OUGHT TO BE SOME WAY I CAN...

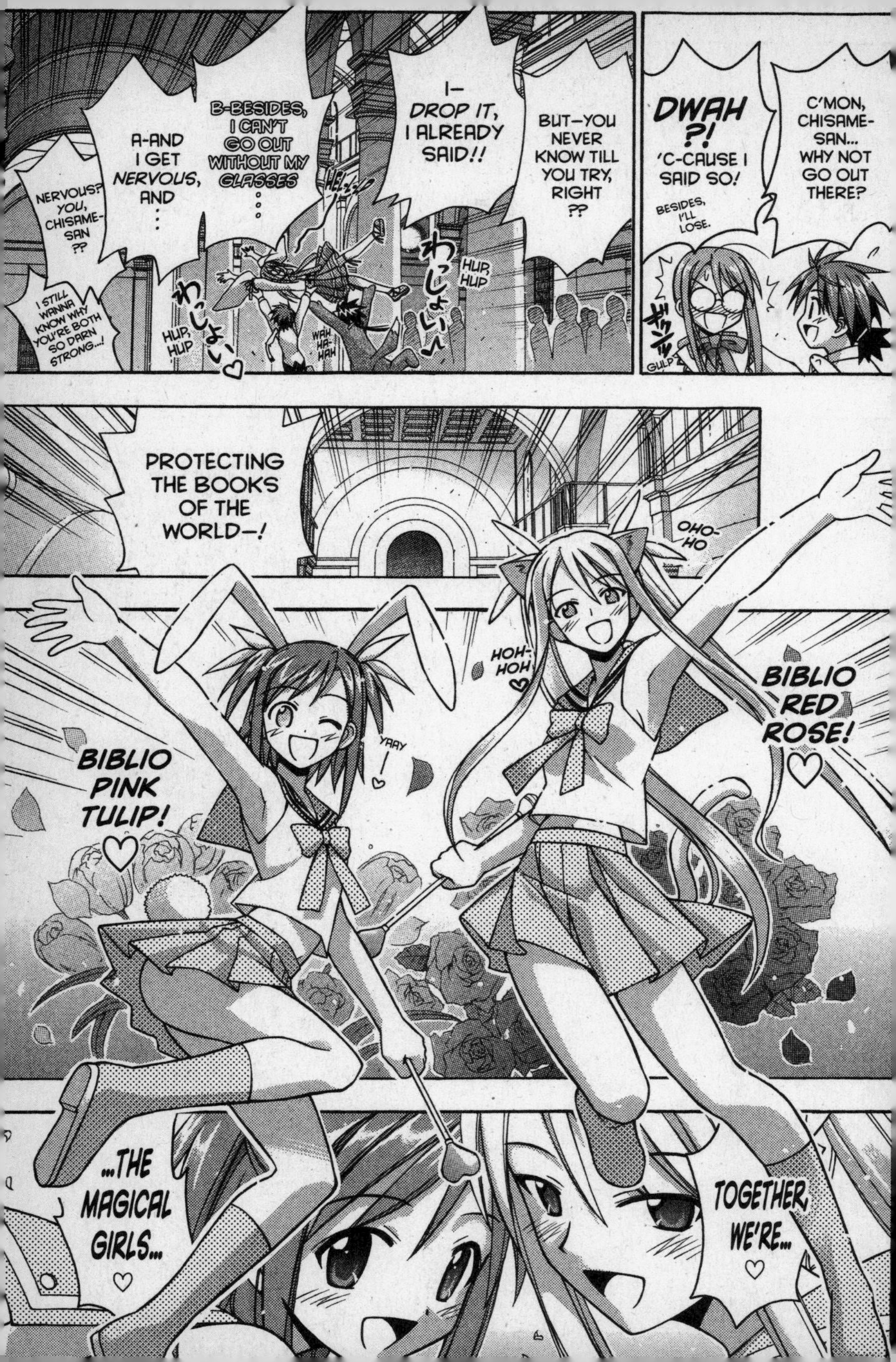
C'MON, CHISAME-SAN... WHY NOT GO OUT THERE?
DWAH?! 'C-CAUSE I SAID SO!
BESIDES, I'LL LOSE.
GULP
BUT—YOU NEVER KNOW TILL YOU TRY, RIGHT??
I— DROP IT, I ALREADY SAID!!
HUP, HUP
わっしょい♪
B-BESIDES, I CAN'T GO OUT WITHOUT MY GLASSES...
A-AND I GET NERVOUS, AND...
NERVOUS? YOU, CHISAME-SAN??
WAH HA HAH
わっしょい♡
HUP, HUP
I STILL WANNA KNOW WHY YOU'RE BOTH SO DARN STRONG...!
PROTECTING THE BOOKS OF THE WORLD—!
OHO-HO
BIBLIO RED ROSE! ♡
HOH-HOH ♡
YAAY ♡
BIBLIO PINK TULIP! ♡
TOGETHER, WE'RE... ♡
...THE MAGICAL GIRLS... ♡

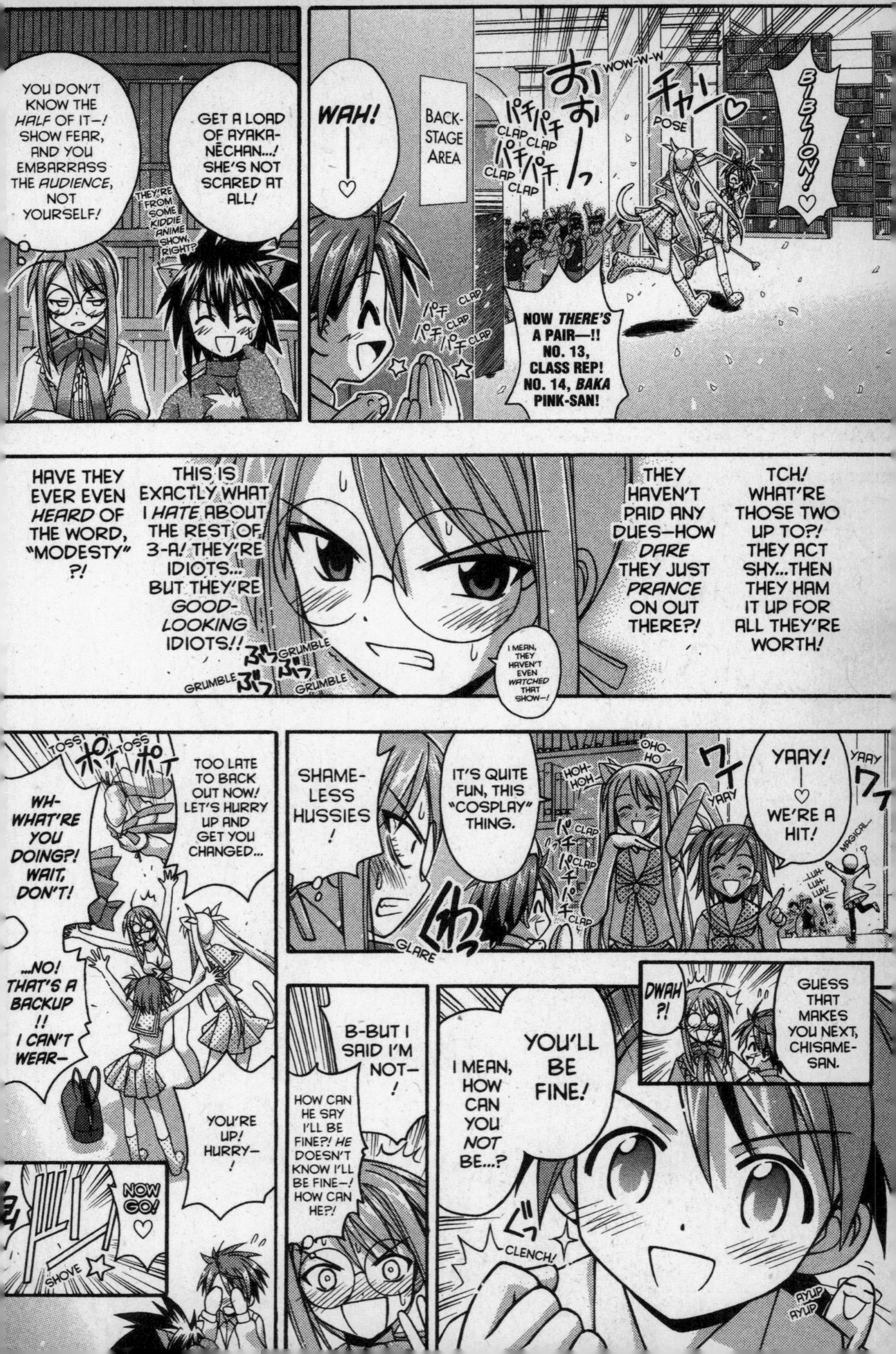
BIBLION! ♡
POSE
WOW-W-W
CLAP CLAP CLAP CLAP
NOW THERE'S A PAIR—!! NO. 13, CLASS REP! NO. 14, BAKA PINK-SAN!
WAH! ♡
BACK-STAGE AREA
CLAP CLAP CLAP
GET A LOAD OF AYAKA-NĒCHAN...! SHE'S NOT SCARED AT ALL!
THEY'RE FROM SOME KIDDIE ANIME SHOW, RIGHT?
YOU DON'T KNOW THE HALF OF IT—! SHOW FEAR, AND YOU EMBARRASS THE AUDIENCE, NOT YOURSELF!
TCH! WHAT'RE THOSE TWO UP TO?! THEY ACT SHY...THEN THEY HAM IT UP FOR ALL THEY'RE WORTH!
THEY HAVEN'T PAID ANY DUES—HOW DARE THEY JUST PRANCE ON OUT THERE?!
I MEAN, THEY HAVEN'T EVEN WATCHED THAT SHOW—!
THIS IS EXACTLY WHAT I HATE ABOUT THE REST OF 3-A! THEY'RE IDIOTS... BUT THEY'RE GOOD-LOOKING IDIOTS!!
HAVE THEY EVER EVEN HEARD OF THE WORD, "MODESTY"?!
GRUMBLE GRUMBLE GRUMBLE GRUMBLE
YAAY! ♡ WE'RE A HIT!
YAAY
YAAY
MAGICAL...
...LUH-LUH-LUH!
OHO-HO
HOH-HOH
CLAP CLAP CLAP
IT'S QUITE FUN, THIS "COSPLAY" THING.
SHAME-LESS HUSSIES!
GLARE
TOO LATE TO BACK OUT NOW! LET'S HURRY UP AND GET YOU CHANGED...
TOSS TOSS
WH-WHAT'RE YOU DOING?! WAIT, DON'T!
...NO! THAT'S A BACKUP!! I CAN'T WEAR—
YOU'RE UP! HURRY—!
GUESS THAT MAKES YOU NEXT, CHISAME-SAN.
DWAH?!
YOU'LL BE FINE!
I MEAN, HOW CAN YOU NOT BE...?
CLENCH!
AYUP AYUP
B-BUT I SAID I'M NOT—!
HOW CAN HE SAY I'LL BE FINE?! HE DOESN'T KNOW I'LL BE FINE—! HOW CAN HE?!
NOW GO! ♡
SHOVE

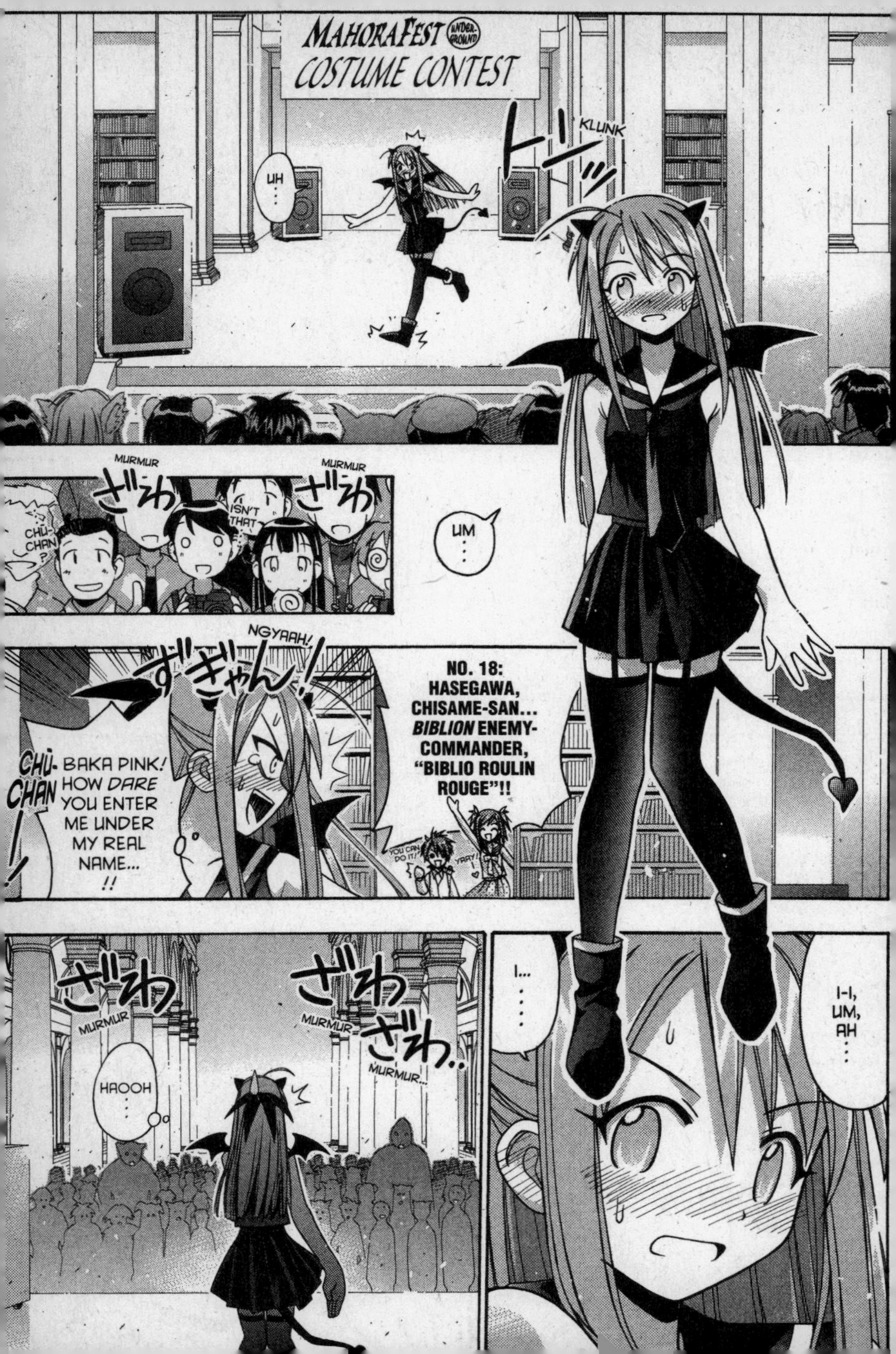
MAHORAFEST UNDERGROUND
COSTUME CONTEST
KLUNK
UH...
UM...
MURMUR
ざわ
MURMUR
ざわ
ISN'T THAT
CHU-CHAN?
NO. 18: HASEGAWA, CHISAME-SAN... *BIBLION* ENEMY-COMMANDER, "BIBLIO ROULIN ROUGE"!!
YAAY!
YOU CAN DO IT!
NGYAAH!
ずぎゃん!
BAKA PINK! HOW *DARE* YOU ENTER ME UNDER MY REAL NAME...!!
CHU-CHAN!
I-I, UM, AH...
I...
ざわ
MURMUR
ざわ
ざわ..
MURMUR...
ざわ
MURMUR
HAOOH...

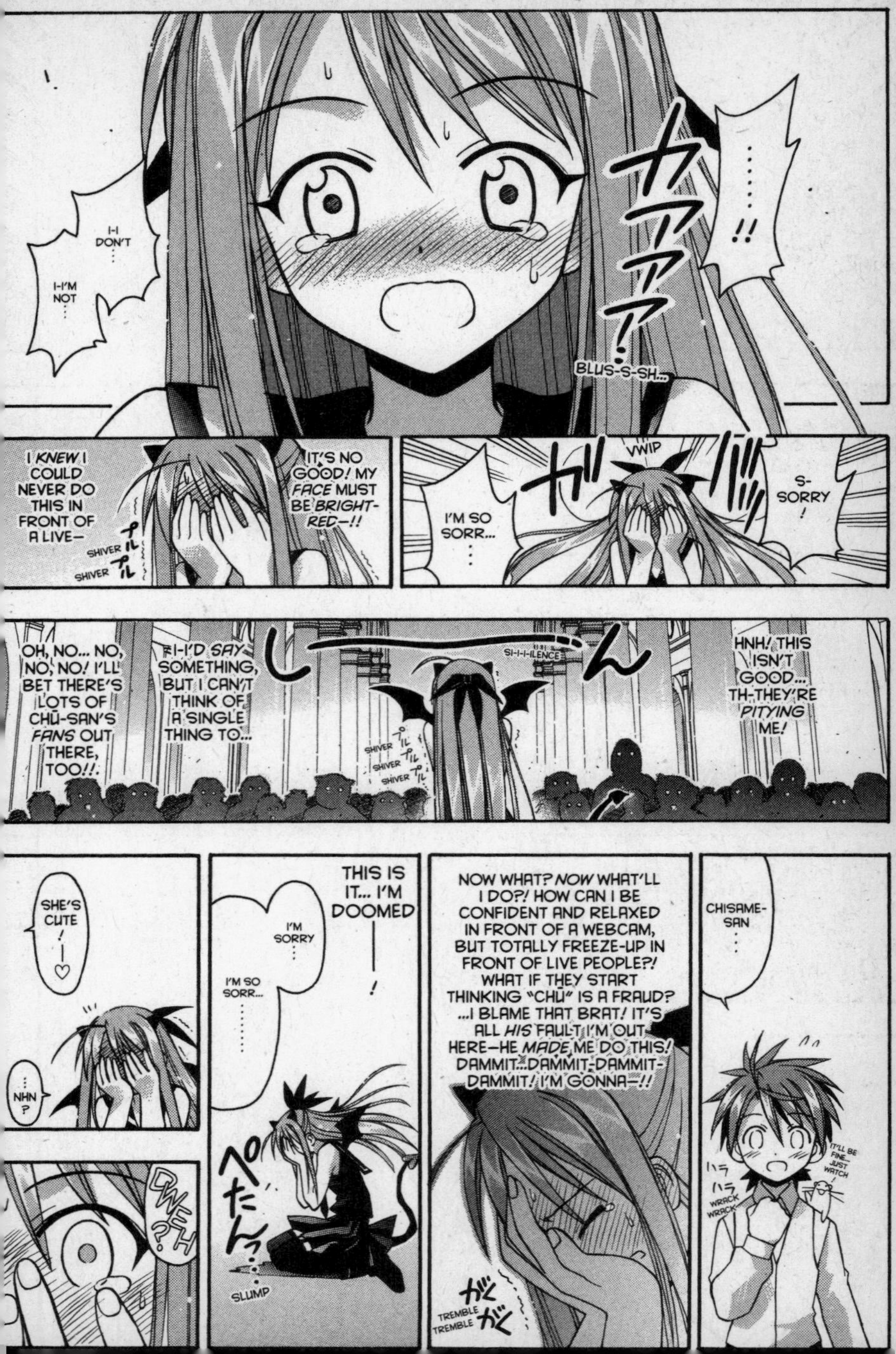
......!!
BLUS-S-SH...
I-I DON'T... I-I'M NOT...
!.
S-SORRY!
VWIP
I'M SO SORR......
IT'S NO GOOD! MY FACE MUST BE BRIGHT-RED—!!
I KNEW I COULD NEVER DO THIS IN FRONT OF A LIVE—
SHIVER SHIVER
HNH! THIS ISN'T GOOD... TH-THEY'RE PITYING ME!
SI-I-I-ILENCE
SHIVER SHIVER SHIVER
I-I'D SAY SOMETHING, BUT I CAN'T THINK OF A SINGLE THING TO...
OH, NO... NO, NO, NO! I'LL BET THERE'S LOTS OF CHŪ-SAN'S FANS OUT THERE, TOO!!
CHISAME-SAN...
IT'LL BE FINE. JUST WATCH!
WRACK WRACK
NOW WHAT? NOW WHAT'LL I DO?! HOW CAN I BE CONFIDENT AND RELAXED IN FRONT OF A WEBCAM, BUT TOTALLY FREEZE-UP IN FRONT OF LIVE PEOPLE?! WHAT IF THEY START THINKING "CHŪ" IS A FRAUD? ...I BLAME THAT BRAT! IT'S ALL HIS FAULT I'M OUT HERE—HE MADE ME DO THIS! DAMMIT...DAMMIT-DAMMIT-DAMMIT! I'M GONNA—!!
TREMBLE TREMBLE
THIS IS IT... I'M DOOMED—!
I'M SORRY...
I'M SO SORR......
SLUMP
SHE'S CUTE!—♡
...NHN?
DWEH?!

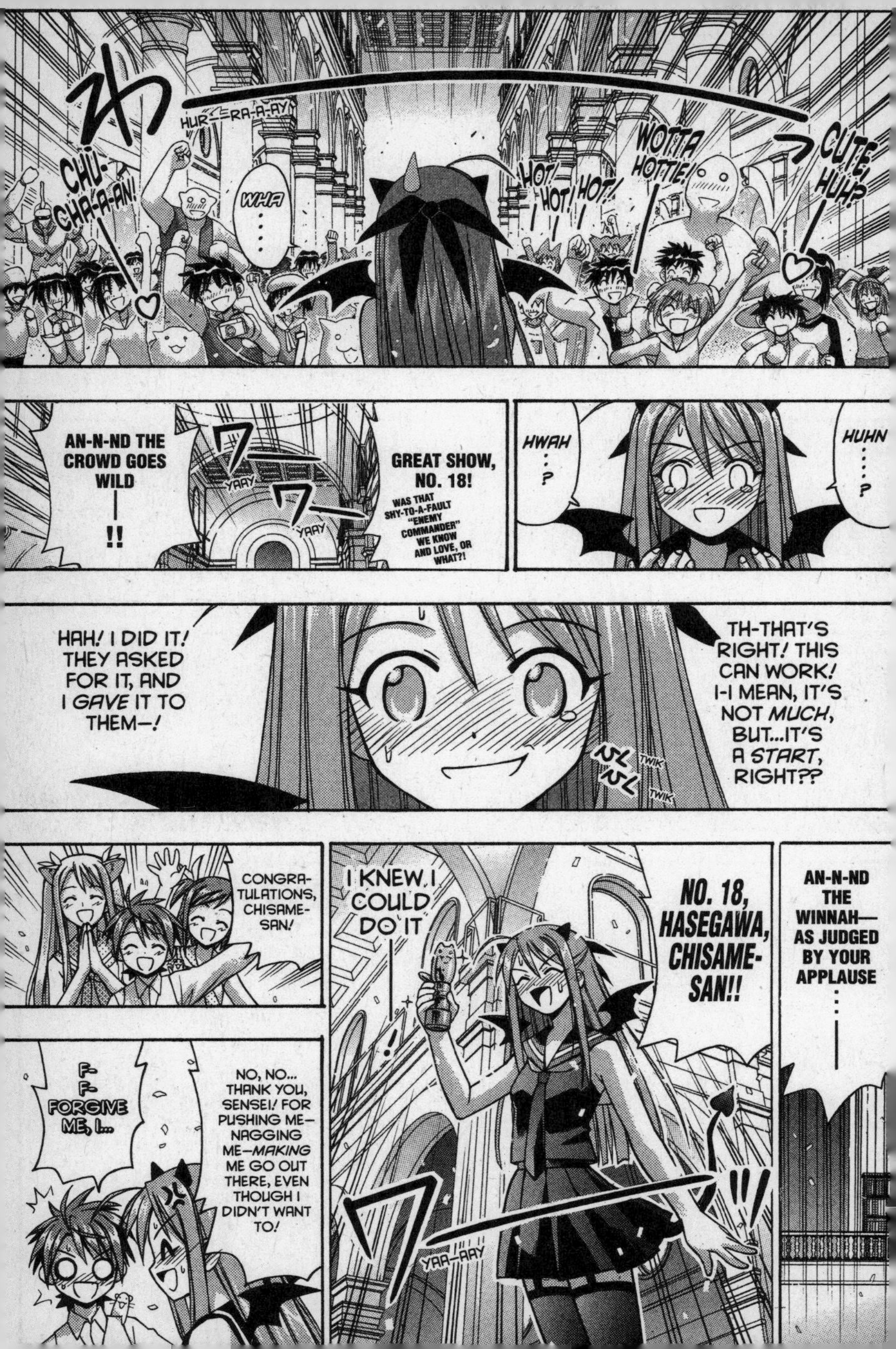
CUTE, HUH?
WOTTA HOTTIE!
HOT! HOT! HOT!
HUR—RA-A-AY
WHA...
CHU-CHA-A-AN!
HUHN.....?
HWAH..?
GREAT SHOW, NO. 18!
WAS THAT SHY-TO-A-FAULT "ENEMY COMMANDER" WE KNOW AND LOVE, OR WHAT?!
YAAY
YAAY
AN-N-ND THE CROWD GOES WILD—!!
TH-THAT'S RIGHT! THIS CAN WORK! I-I MEAN, IT'S NOT MUCH, BUT...IT'S A START, RIGHT??
TWIK
TWIK
HAH! I DID IT! THEY ASKED FOR IT, AND I GAVE IT TO THEM—!
AN-N-ND THE WINNAH—AS JUDGED BY YOUR APPLAUSE...—
NO. 18, HASEGAWA, CHISAME-SAN!!
I KNEW I COULD DO IT—!
YAR—AAY
CONGRATULATIONS, CHISAME-SAN!
NO, NO... THANK YOU, SENSEI! FOR PUSHING ME—NAGGING ME—MAKING ME GO OUT THERE, EVEN THOUGH I DIDN'T WANT TO!
F-F-FORGIVE ME, I...

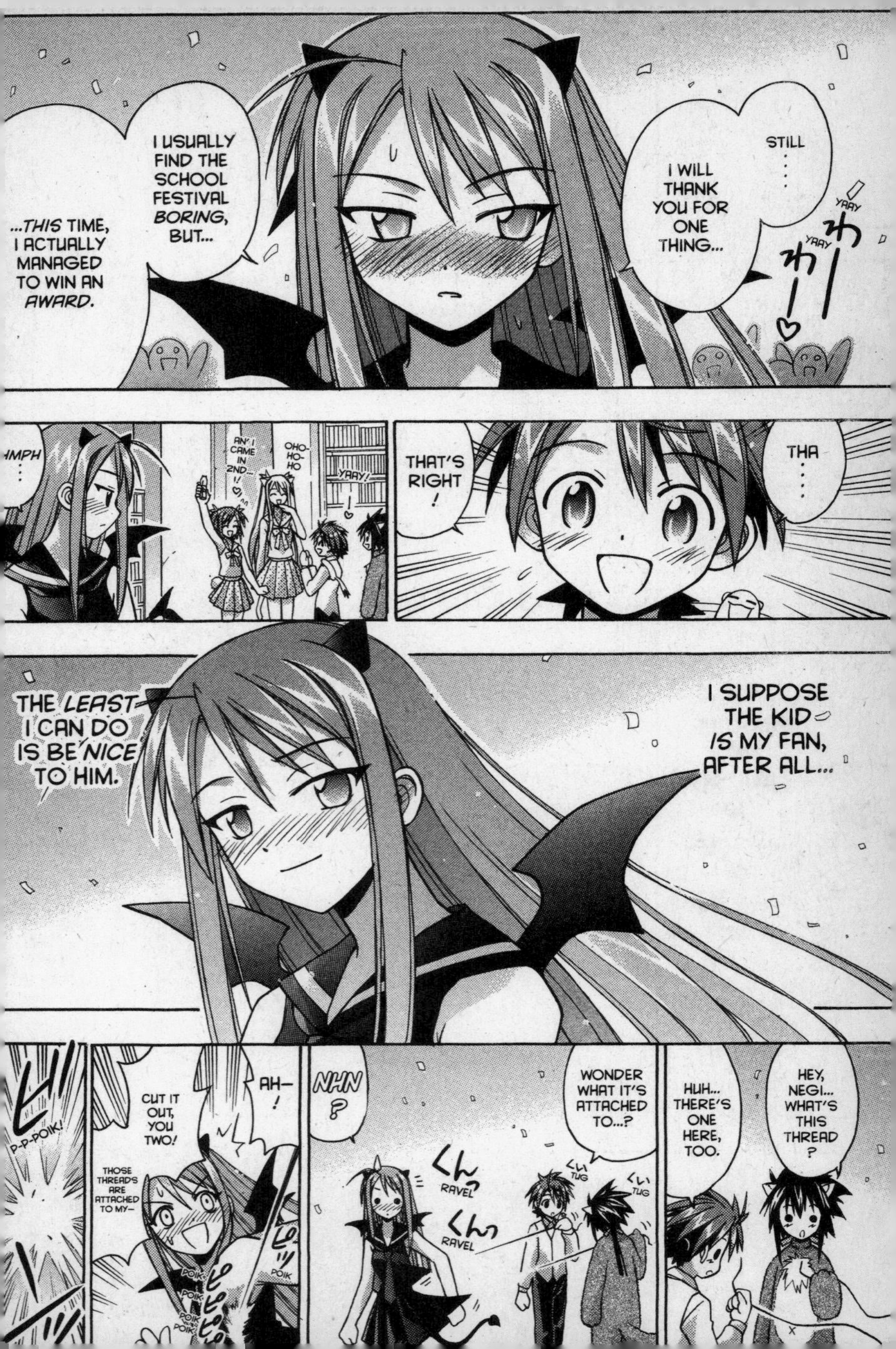

STILL...
I WILL THANK YOU FOR ONE THING...
わーわー♡
YAAY YAAY
I USUALLY FIND THE SCHOOL FESTIVAL BORING, BUT...
...THIS TIME, I ACTUALLY MANAGED TO WIN AN AWARD.
THA...
THAT'S RIGHT!
OHO-HO-HO
YAAY!
AN' I CAME IN 2ND...!!
HMPH...
I SUPPOSE THE KID IS MY FAN, AFTER ALL...
THE LEAST I CAN DO IS BE NICE TO HIM.
HEY, NEGI... WHAT'S THIS THREAD?
HUH... THERE'S ONE HERE, TOO.
WONDER WHAT IT'S ATTACHED TO...?
くい TUG
くい TUG
NHN?
くんっ RAVEL
くんっ RAVEL
AH—!
CUT IT OUT, YOU TWO!
THOSE THREADS ARE ATTACHED TO MY—
POIK POIK POIK POIK
P-P-POIK!

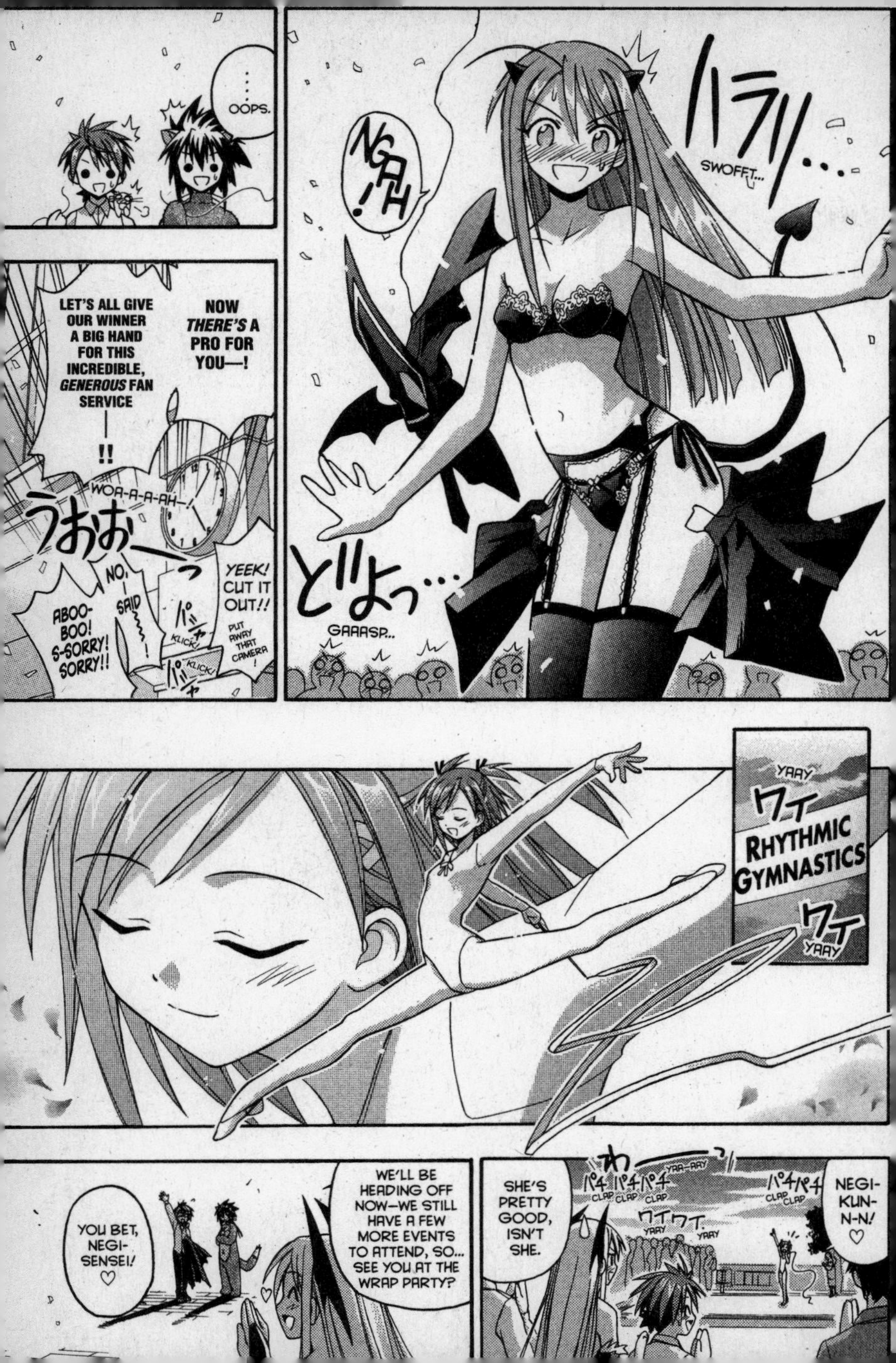
ハラリ…
SWOFFT…
NGAH!
どよっ…
GAAASP...
…OOPS.
NOW THERE'S A PRO FOR YOU—!
LET'S ALL GIVE OUR WINNER A BIG HAND FOR THIS INCREDIBLE, GENEROUS FAN SERVICE—!!
うおおーっ
WOA-A-A-AH—!
YEEK! CUT IT OUT!!
PUT AWAY THAT CAMERA!
パシャ
KLICK!
パシャ
KLICK!
NO I SAID ~!
ABOO-BOO! S-SORRY! SORRY!!
ワイ
YAAY
RHYTHMIC GYMNASTICS
ワイ
YAAY
NEGI-KUN-N-N! ♡
わーっ
YAA-AAY
パチパチパチ
CLAP CLAP CLAP
パチパチ
CLAP CLAP
ワイワイ
YAAY YAAY
SHE'S PRETTY GOOD, ISN'T SHE.
WE'LL BE HEADING OFF NOW—WE STILL HAVE A FEW MORE EVENTS TO ATTEND, SO... SEE YOU AT THE WRAP PARTY?
YOU BET, NEGI-SENSEI! ♡

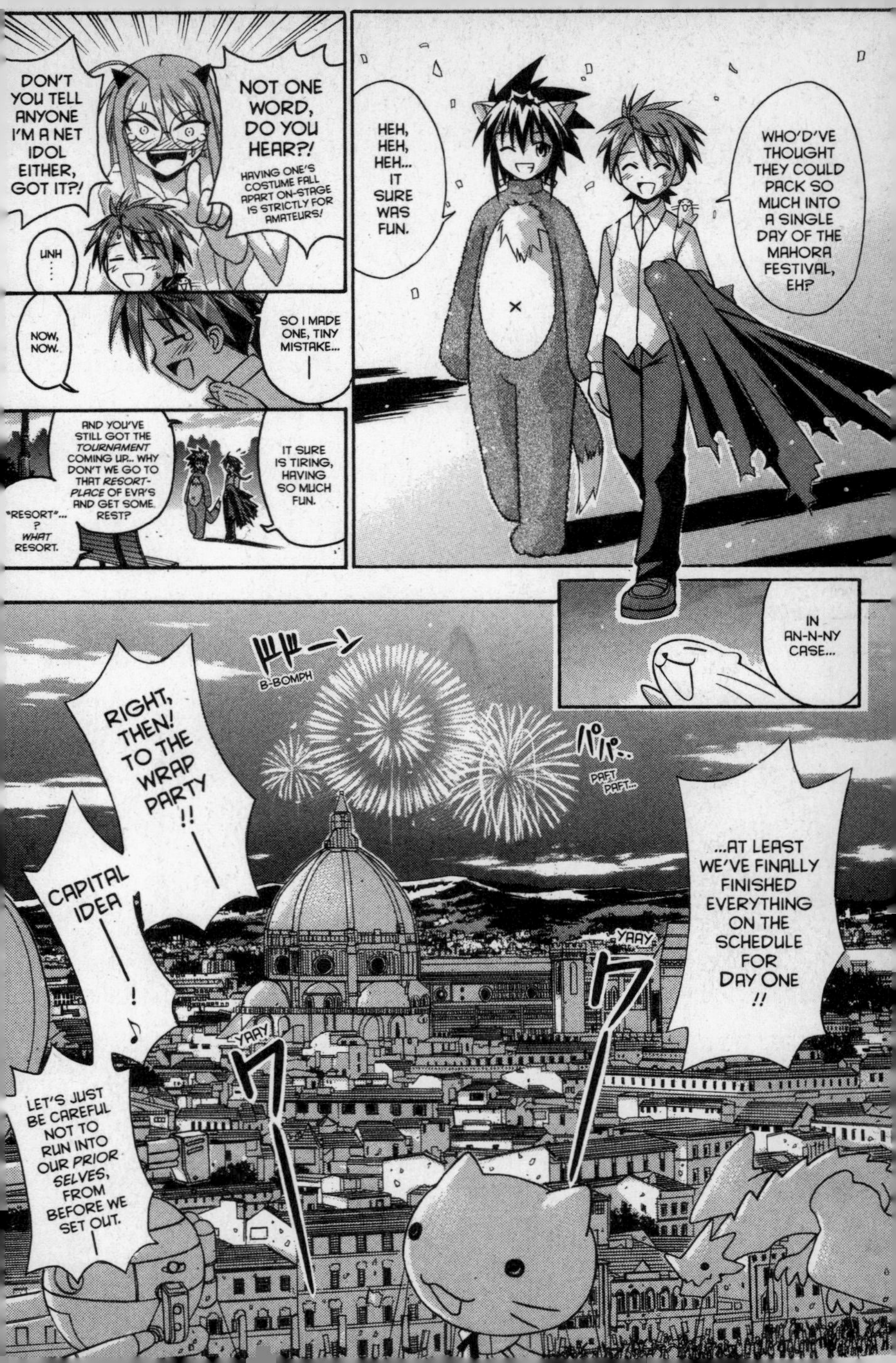

WHO'D'VE THOUGHT THEY COULD PACK SO MUCH INTO A SINGLE DAY OF THE MAHORA FESTIVAL, EH?
HEH, HEH, HEH... IT SURE WAS FUN.
NOT ONE WORD, DO YOU HEAR?!
HAVING ONE'S COSTUME FALL APART ON-STAGE IS STRICTLY FOR AMATEURS!
DON'T YOU TELL ANYONE I'M A NET IDOL EITHER, GOT IT?!
UNH ...
SO I MADE ONE, TINY MISTAKE...
NOW, NOW.
IT SURE IS TIRING, HAVING SO MUCH FUN.
AND YOU'VE STILL GOT THE *TOURNAMENT* COMING UP.. WHY DON'T WE GO TO THAT *RESORT-PLACE* OF EVA'S AND GET SOME REST?
"RESORT"... ? *WHAT* RESORT.
IN AN-N-NY CASE...
...AT LEAST WE'VE FINALLY FINISHED EVERYTHING ON THE SCHEDULE FOR DAY ONE !!
PAFT PAFT...
B-BOMPH
RIGHT, THEN! TO THE WRAP PARTY !!
YAAY
CAPITAL IDEA—!
YAAY
LET'S JUST BE CAREFUL NOT TO RUN INTO OUR *PRIOR SELVES*, FROM BEFORE WE SET OUT.

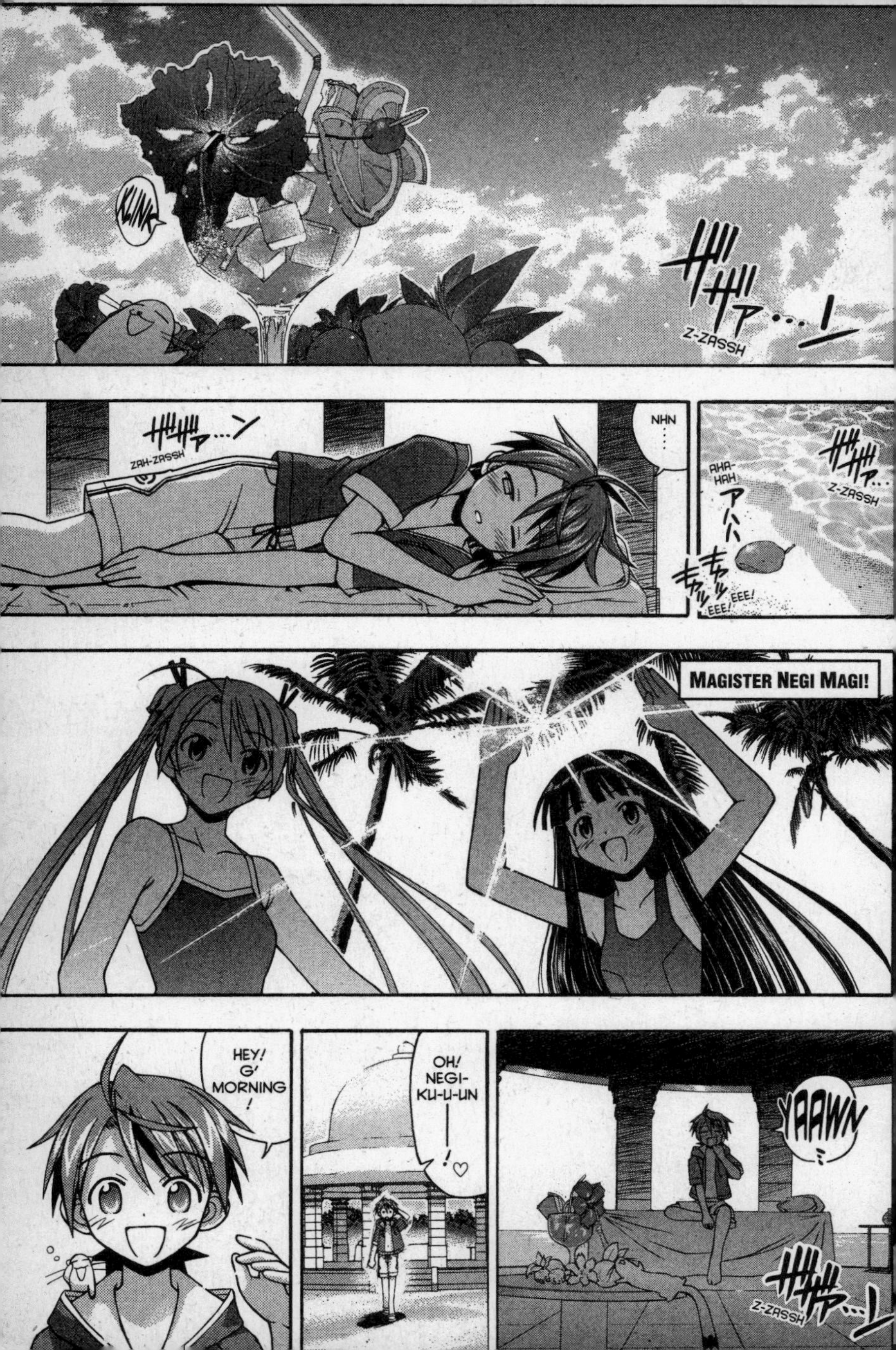
Z-ZASSH
KLINK
Z-ZASSH
AHA-HAH
EEE!
EEE!
NHN...
ZAH-ZASSH
MAGISTER NEGI MAGI!
YAAWN
Z-ZASSH
OH! NEGI-KU-U-UN—!♡
HEY! G' MORNING!

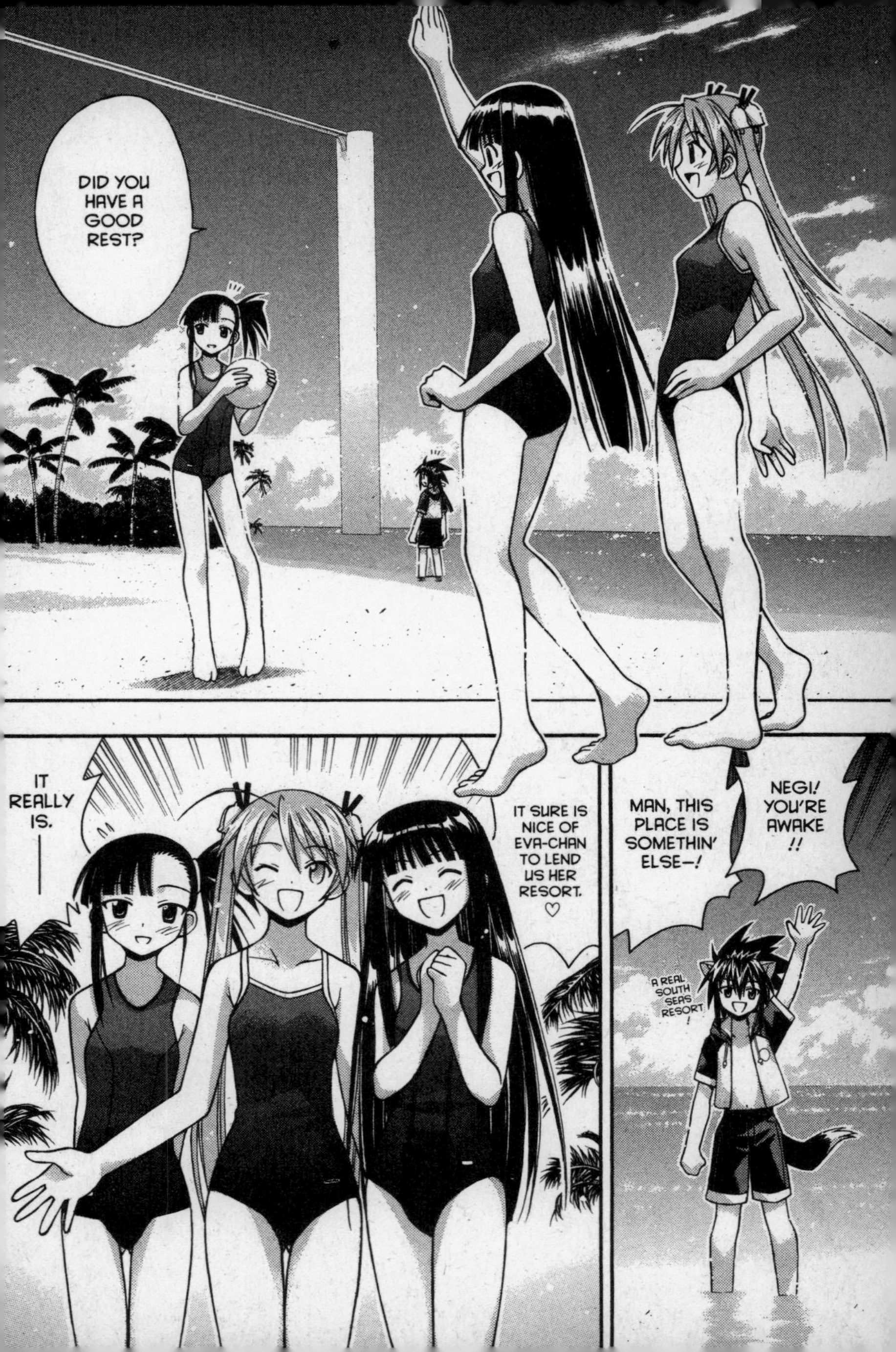
DID YOU HAVE A GOOD REST?
NEGI! YOU'RE AWAKE!!
MAN, THIS PLACE IS SOMETHIN' ELSE—!
A REAL SOUTH SEAS RESORT!
IT SURE IS NICE OF EVA-CHAN TO LEND US HER RESORT. ♡
IT REALLY IS.

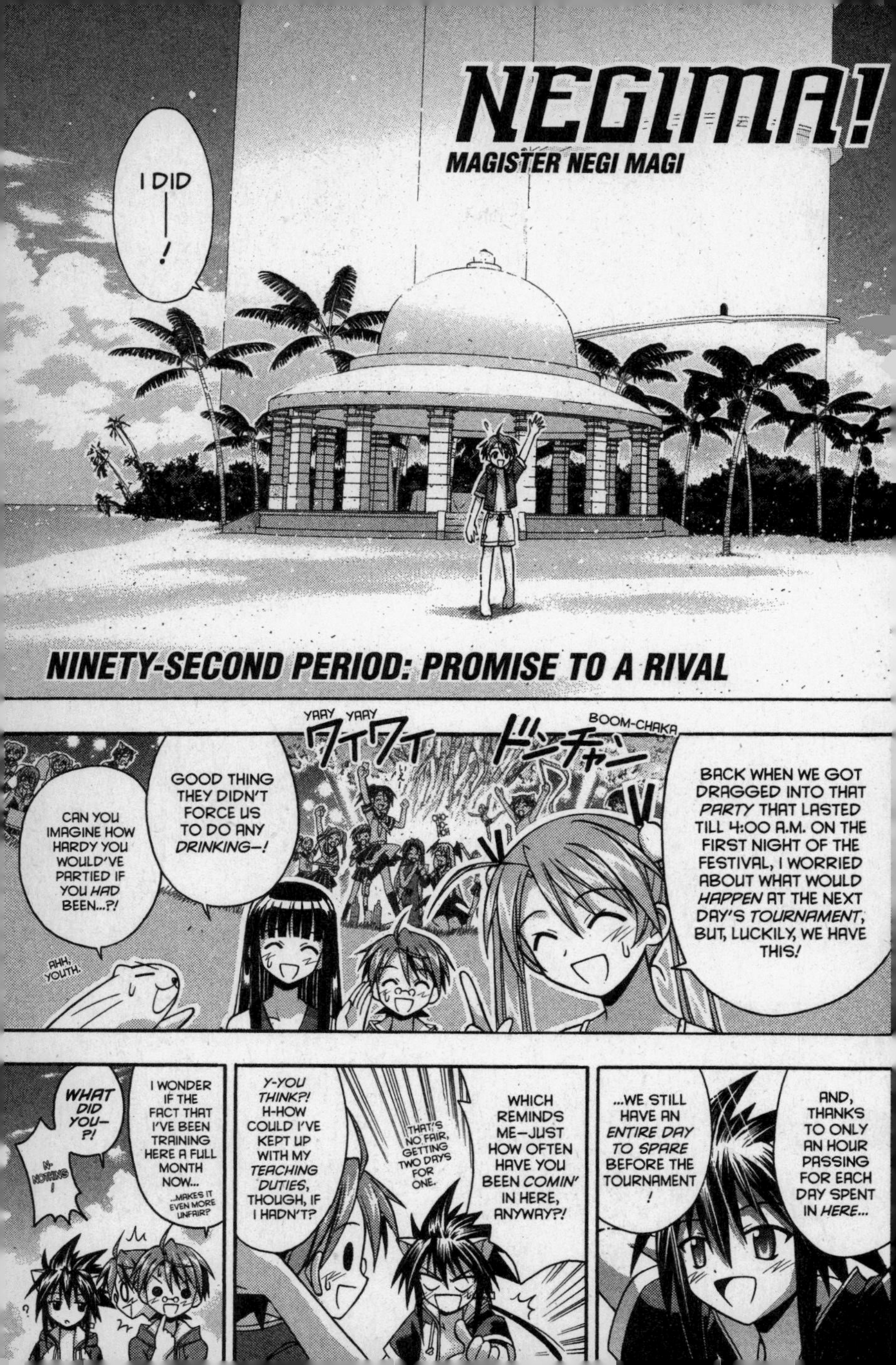
NEGIMA!
MAGISTER NEGI MAGI
I DID —!
NINETY-SECOND PERIOD: PROMISE TO A RIVAL
BACK WHEN WE GOT DRAGGED INTO THAT PARTY THAT LASTED TILL 4:00 A.M. ON THE FIRST NIGHT OF THE FESTIVAL, I WORRIED ABOUT WHAT WOULD HAPPEN AT THE NEXT DAY'S TOURNAMENT, BUT, LUCKILY, WE HAVE THIS!
BOOM-CHAKA
YAAY YAAY
GOOD THING THEY DIDN'T FORCE US TO DO ANY DRINKING—!
CAN YOU IMAGINE HOW HARDY YOU WOULD'VE PARTIED IF YOU HAD BEEN...?!
AHH, YOUTH.
AND, THANKS TO ONLY AN HOUR PASSING FOR EACH DAY SPENT IN HERE...
...WE STILL HAVE AN ENTIRE DAY TO SPARE BEFORE THE TOURNAMENT!
WHICH REMINDS ME—JUST HOW OFTEN HAVE YOU BEEN COMIN' IN HERE, ANYWAY?!
THAT'S NO FAIR, GETTING TWO DAYS FOR ONE.
Y-YOU THINK?! H-HOW COULD I'VE KEPT UP WITH MY TEACHING DUTIES, THOUGH, IF I HADN'T?
I WONDER IF THE FACT THAT I'VE BEEN TRAINING HERE A FULL MONTH NOW...
...MAKES IT EVEN MORE UNFAIR?
WHAT DID YOU—?!
N-NOTHING!

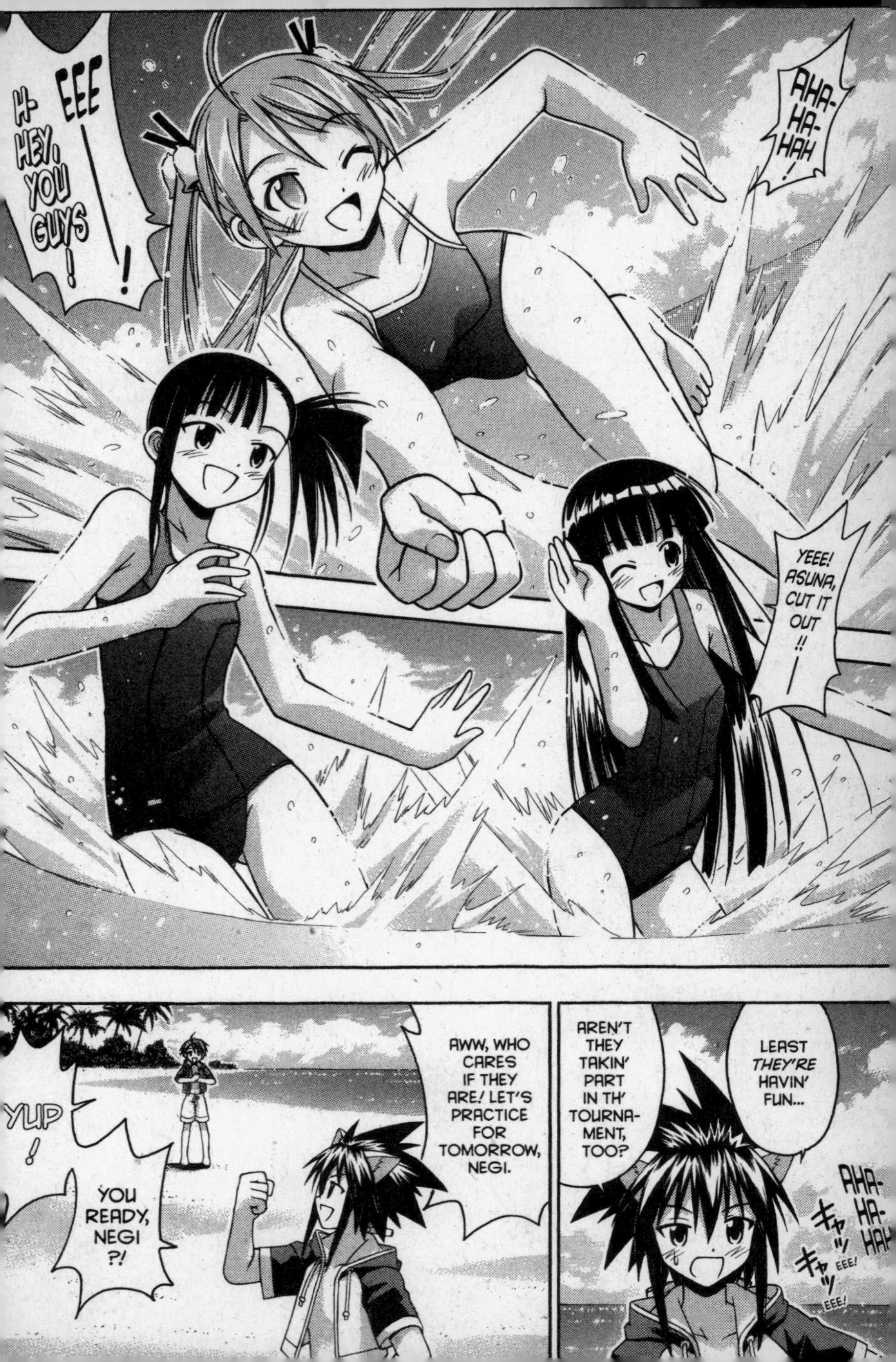
AHA-HA-HAH!
EEE—!
H-HEY, YOU GUYS!
YEEE! ASUNA, CUT IT OUT!!—
LEAST THEY'RE HAVIN' FUN...
AREN'T THEY TAKIN' PART IN TH' TOURNAMENT, TOO?
AHA-HA-HAH
キャッ キャッ
EEE!
EEE!
AWW, WHO CARES IF THEY ARE! LET'S PRACTICE FOR TOMORROW, NEGI.
YUP!
YOU READY, NEGI?!

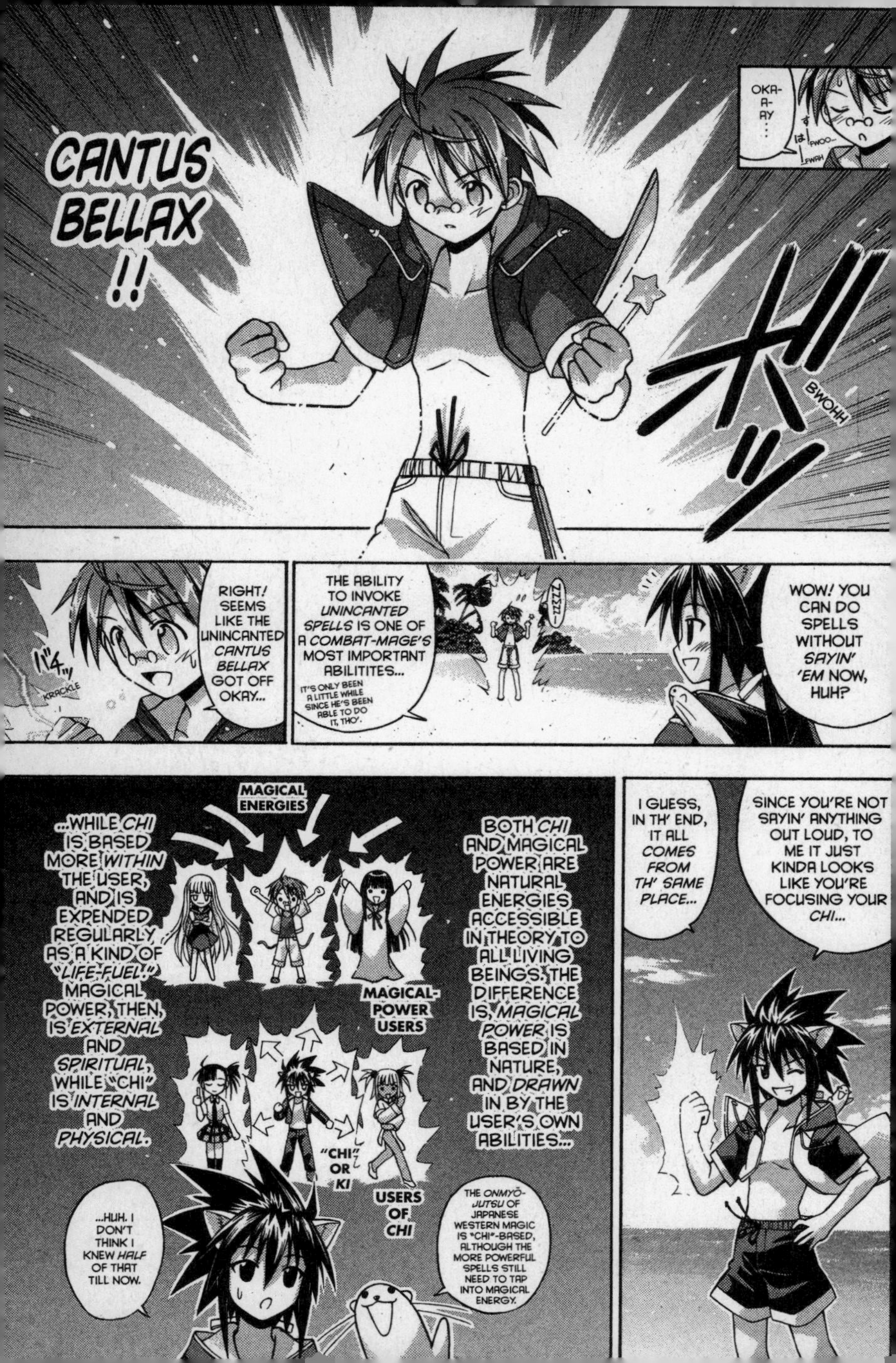
OKA-A-AY...
PWOO-
FWAH
CANTUS BELLAX!!
BWOHH
WOW! YOU CAN DO SPELLS WITHOUT SAYIN' 'EM NOW, HUH?
ZZZZZ
THE ABILITY TO INVOKE UNINCANTED SPELLS IS ONE OF A COMBAT-MAGE'S MOST IMPORTANT ABILITITES...
IT'S ONLY BEEN A LITTLE WHILE SINCE HE'S BEEN ABLE TO DO IT, THO'.
RIGHT! SEEMS LIKE THE UNINCANTED CANTUS BELLAX GOT OFF OKAY...
KRACKLE
SINCE YOU'RE NOT SAYIN' ANYTHING OUT LOUD, TO ME IT JUST KINDA LOOKS LIKE YOU'RE FOCUSING YOUR CHI...
I GUESS, IN TH' END, IT ALL COMES FROM TH' SAME PLACE...
BOTH CHI AND MAGICAL POWER ARE NATURAL ENERGIES ACCESSIBLE IN THEORY TO ALL LIVING BEINGS. THE DIFFERENCE IS, MAGICAL POWER IS BASED IN NATURE, AND DRAWN IN BY THE USER'S OWN ABILITIES...
MAGICAL ENERGIES
...WHILE CHI IS BASED MORE WITHIN THE USER, AND IS EXPENDED REGULARLY AS A KIND OF "LIFE-FUEL." MAGICAL POWER, THEN, IS EXTERNAL AND SPIRITUAL, WHILE "CHI" IS INTERNAL AND PHYSICAL.
MAGICAL-POWER USERS
"CHI" OR KI
USERS OF CHI
THE ONMYŌ-JUTSU OF JAPANESE WESTERN MAGIC IS "CHI"-BASED, ALTHOUGH THE MORE POWERFUL SPELLS STILL NEED TO TAP INTO MAGICAL ENERGY.
...HUH. I DON'T THINK I KNEW HALF OF THAT TILL NOW.

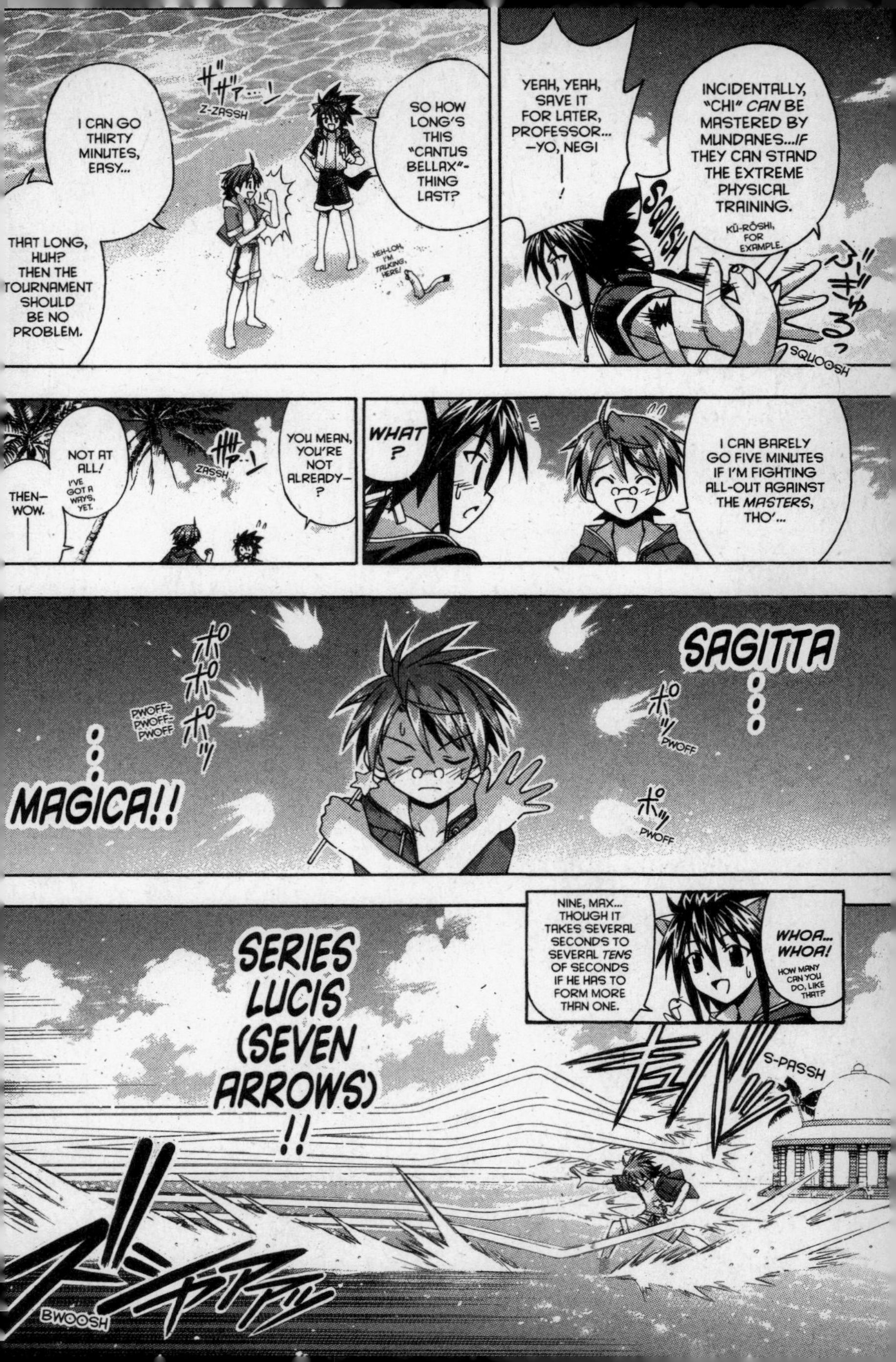
INCIDENTALLY, "CHI" *CAN* BE MASTERED BY MUNDANES...*IF* THEY CAN STAND THE EXTREME PHYSICAL TRAINING.
KŪ-RŌSHI, FOR EXAMPLE.
SQUISH
YEAH, YEAH, SAVE IT FOR LATER, PROFESSOR... —YO, NEGI ! !
SQUOOSH
SO HOW LONG'S THIS "CANTUS BELLAX"-THING LAST?
Z-ZASSH
I CAN GO THIRTY MINUTES, EASY...
HEH-LOH, I'M TALKING, HERE!
THAT LONG, HUH? THEN THE TOURNAMENT SHOULD BE NO PROBLEM.
I CAN BARELY GO FIVE MINUTES IF I'M FIGHTING ALL-OUT AGAINST THE *MASTERS*, THO'...
WHAT?
YOU MEAN, YOU'RE NOT ALREADY—?
ZASSH
NOT AT ALL!
I'VE GOT A WAYS, YET.
THEN— WOW.
SAGITTA...
PWOFF
PWOFF
PWOFF-PWOFF-PWOFF
...MAGICA!!
WHOA... WHOA!
HOW MANY CAN YOU DO, LIKE THAT?
NINE, MAX... THOUGH IT TAKES SEVERAL SECONDS TO SEVERAL *TENS* OF SECONDS IF HE HAS TO FORM MORE THAN ONE.
S-PASSH
SERIES LUCIS (SEVEN ARROWS)!!
BWOOSH

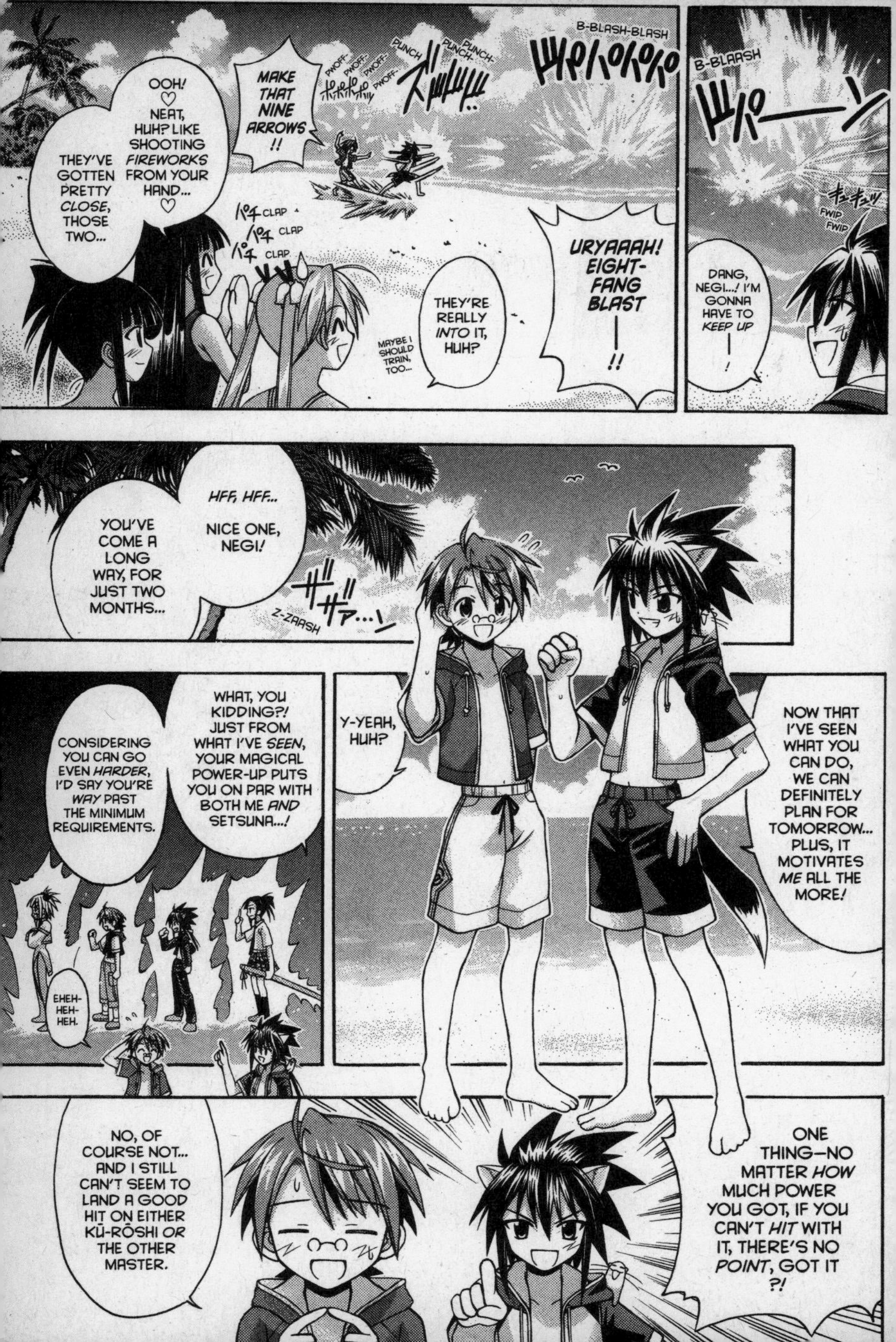
B-BLAASH
FWIP
FWIP
DANG, NEGI...! I'M GONNA HAVE TO KEEP UP—!
B-BLASH-BLASH
PUNCH-PUNCH-PUNCH
PWOFF-PWOFF-PWOFF-PWOFF-
MAKE THAT NINE ARROWS!!
URYAAAH! EIGHT-FANG BLAST—!!
THEY'RE REALLY INTO IT, HUH?
MAYBE I SHOULD TRAIN, TOO...
OOH! ♡ NEAT, HUH? LIKE SHOOTING FIREWORKS FROM YOUR HAND... ♡
CLAP
CLAP
CLAP
THEY'VE GOTTEN PRETTY CLOSE, THOSE TWO...
HFF, HFF... NICE ONE, NEGI!
YOU'VE COME A LONG WAY, FOR JUST TWO MONTHS...
Z-ZAASH
NOW THAT I'VE SEEN WHAT YOU CAN DO, WE CAN DEFINITELY PLAN FOR TOMORROW... PLUS, IT MOTIVATES ME ALL THE MORE!
Y-YEAH, HUH?
WHAT, YOU KIDDING?! JUST FROM WHAT I'VE SEEN, YOUR MAGICAL POWER-UP PUTS YOU ON PAR WITH BOTH ME AND SETSUNA...!
CONSIDERING YOU CAN GO EVEN HARDER, I'D SAY YOU'RE WAY PAST THE MINIMUM REQUIREMENTS.
EHEH-HEH-HEH.
ONE THING—NO MATTER HOW MUCH POWER YOU GOT, IF YOU CAN'T HIT WITH IT, THERE'S NO POINT, GOT IT?!
NO, OF COURSE NOT... AND I STILL CAN'T SEEM TO LAND A GOOD HIT ON EITHER KŪ-RŌSHI OR THE OTHER MASTER.

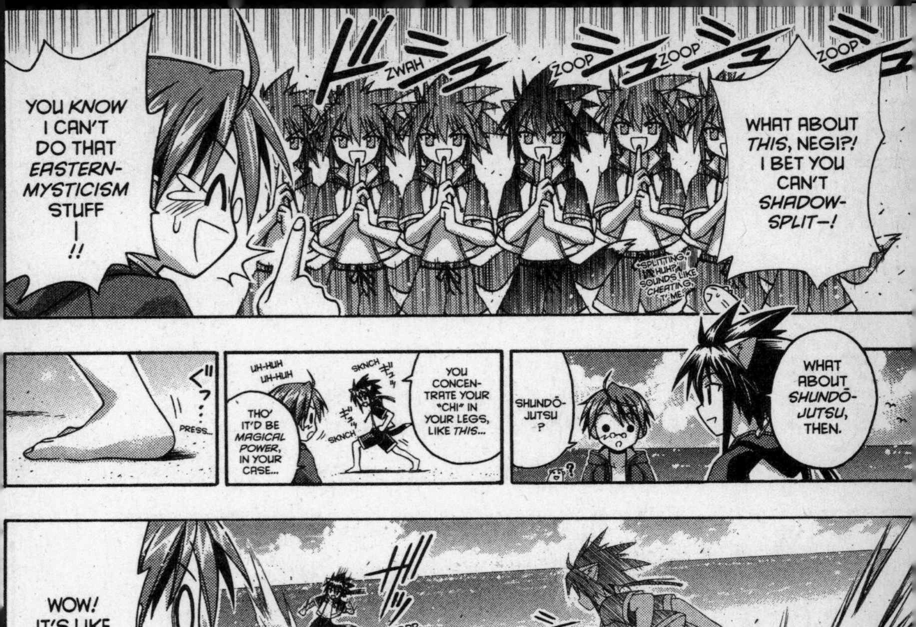
ZWAH
ZOOP
ZOOP
ZOOP
WHAT ABOUT THIS, NEGI?! I BET YOU CAN'T SHADOW-SPLIT—!
YOU KNOW I CAN'T DO THAT EASTERN-MYSTICISM STUFF—!!
"SPLITTING," HUH? SOUNDS LIKE CHEATING T' ME.
WHAT ABOUT SHUNDŌ-JUTSU, THEN.
SHUNDŌ-JUTSU?
SKNCH
YOU CONCENTRATE YOUR "CHI" IN YOUR LEGS, LIKE THIS...
UH-HUH UH-HUH
THO' IT'D BE MAGICAL POWER, IN YOUR CASE...
SKNCH
PRESS...
SPROING
SHWOO
ZOPP
SEE?
WOW! IT'S LIKE YOU JUST TELEPORTED!!
WOAH!
BWOP-
BWOP-
BWOP-
Z-BWOP-
THAT'S "SHUNDŌ-JUTSU," ALL RIGHT! IT RANGES THREE TO SEVEN METERS...
I GOT A WAYS T' GO, MYSELF.
AN' LEAVE AFTER-IMAGES, LIKE THIS.
IT'S PRETTY HANDY T' KNOW, WHEN FIGHTIN' A MASTER...
YOU TRY IT!!
ME?!

※ **SHADOW-SPLITTING** (*KAGE-BUNSHIN*): IMAGES HAVE ACTUAL PHYSICAL SUBSTANCE.
TELEPORTATION (*BUNSHIN*): AFTER-IMAGES CREATED BY EXTREME HIGH SPEED, GIVING APPEARANCE OF GREATER PRESENCE.

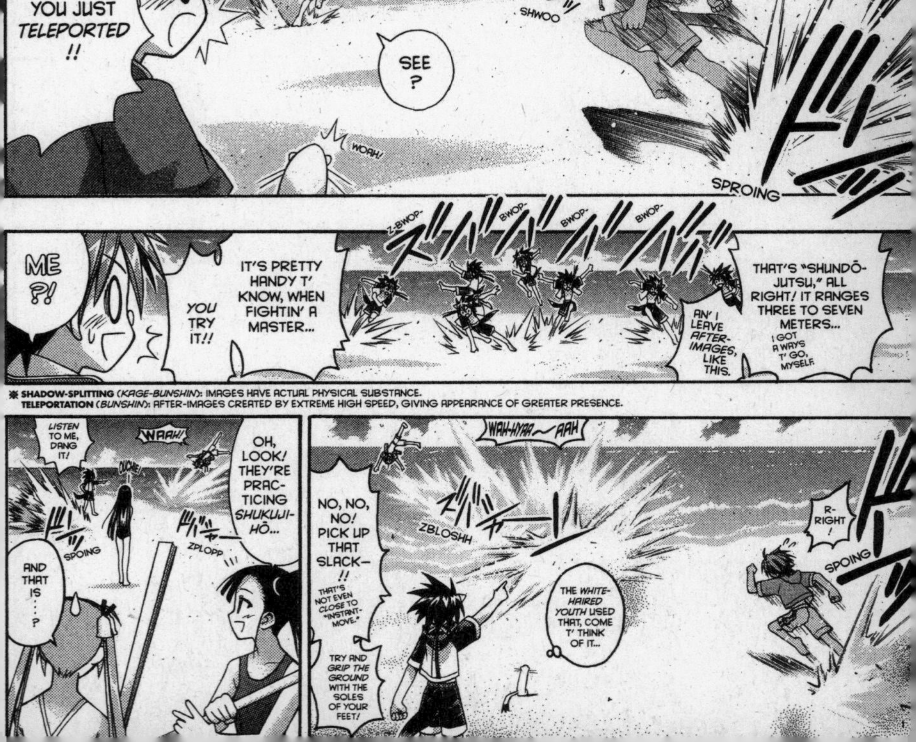
R-RIGHT!
SPOING
WAH-HYAA~AAH
ZBLOSHH
NO, NO, NO! PICK UP THAT SLACK—!!
THAT'S NOT EVEN CLOSE TO "INSTANT-MOVE."
THE WHITE-HAIRED YOUTH USED THAT, COME T' THINK OF IT...
TRY AND GRIP THE GROUND WITH THE SOLES OF YOUR FEET!
OH, LOOK! THEY'RE PRACTICING SHUKUJI-HŌ...
WAAH!
OUCH!
LISTEN TO ME, DANG IT!
ZPLOPP
SPOING
AND THAT IS...?

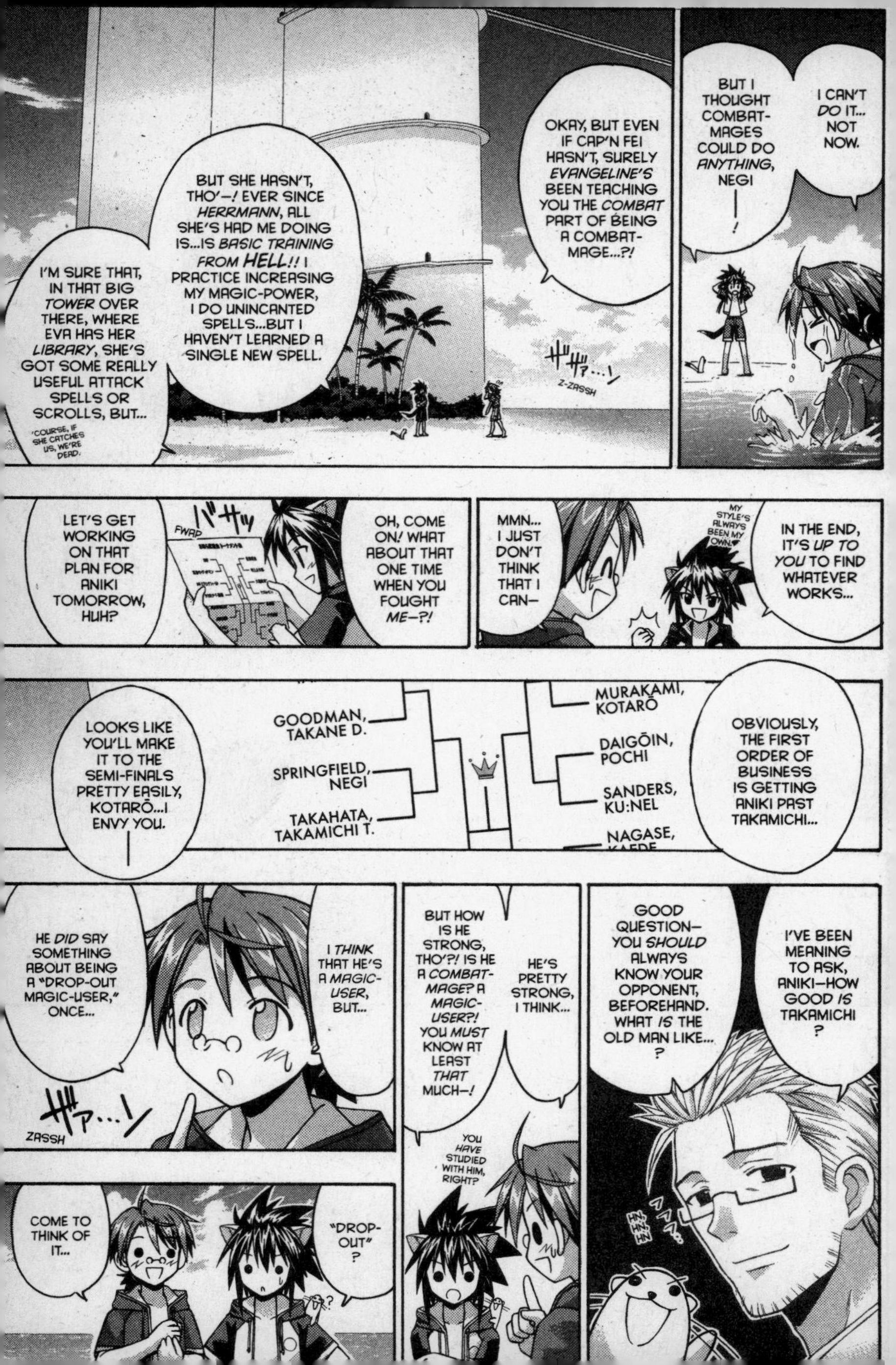
I CAN'T DO IT... NOT NOW.
BUT I THOUGHT COMBAT-MAGES COULD DO ANYTHING, NEGI—!
OKAY, BUT EVEN IF CAP'N FEI HASN'T, SURELY EVANGELINE'S BEEN TEACHING YOU THE COMBAT PART OF BEING A COMBAT-MAGE...?!
Z-ZASSH
BUT SHE HASN'T, THO'—! EVER SINCE HERRMANN, ALL SHE'S HAD ME DOING IS...IS BASIC TRAINING FROM HELL!! I PRACTICE INCREASING MY MAGIC-POWER, I DO UNINCANTED SPELLS...BUT I HAVEN'T LEARNED A SINGLE NEW SPELL.
I'M SURE THAT, IN THAT BIG TOWER OVER THERE, WHERE EVA HAS HER LIBRARY, SHE'S GOT SOME REALLY USEFUL ATTACK SPELLS OR SCROLLS, BUT...
'COURSE, IF SHE CATCHES US, WE'RE DEAD.
IN THE END, IT'S UP TO YOU TO FIND WHATEVER WORKS...
MY STYLE'S ALWAYS BEEN MY OWN.
MMN... I JUST DON'T THINK THAT I CAN—
OH, COME ON! WHAT ABOUT THAT ONE TIME WHEN YOU FOUGHT ME—?!
FWAP
LET'S GET WORKING ON THAT PLAN FOR ANIKI TOMORROW, HUH?
OBVIOUSLY, THE FIRST ORDER OF BUSINESS IS GETTING ANIKI PAST TAKAMICHI...
MURAKAMI, KOTARŌ
DAIGŌIN, POCHI
SANDERS, KU:NEL
NAGASE,
GOODMAN, TAKANE D.
SPRINGFIELD, NEGI
TAKAHATA, TAKAMICHI T.
LOOKS LIKE YOU'LL MAKE IT TO THE SEMI-FINALS PRETTY EASILY, KOTARŌ...I ENVY YOU.
I'VE BEEN MEANING TO ASK, ANIKI—HOW GOOD IS TAKAMICHI?
GOOD QUESTION—YOU SHOULD ALWAYS KNOW YOUR OPPONENT, BEFOREHAND. WHAT IS THE OLD MAN LIKE...?
HN, HN, HN
HE'S PRETTY STRONG, I THINK...
BUT HOW IS HE STRONG, THO'?! IS HE A COMBAT-MAGE? A MAGIC-USER?! YOU MUST KNOW AT LEAST THAT MUCH—!
YOU HAVE STUDIED WITH HIM, RIGHT?
I THINK THAT HE'S A MAGIC-USER, BUT...
HE DID SAY SOMETHING ABOUT BEING A "DROP-OUT MAGIC-USER," ONCE...
ZASSH
"DROP-OUT"?
COME TO THINK OF IT...

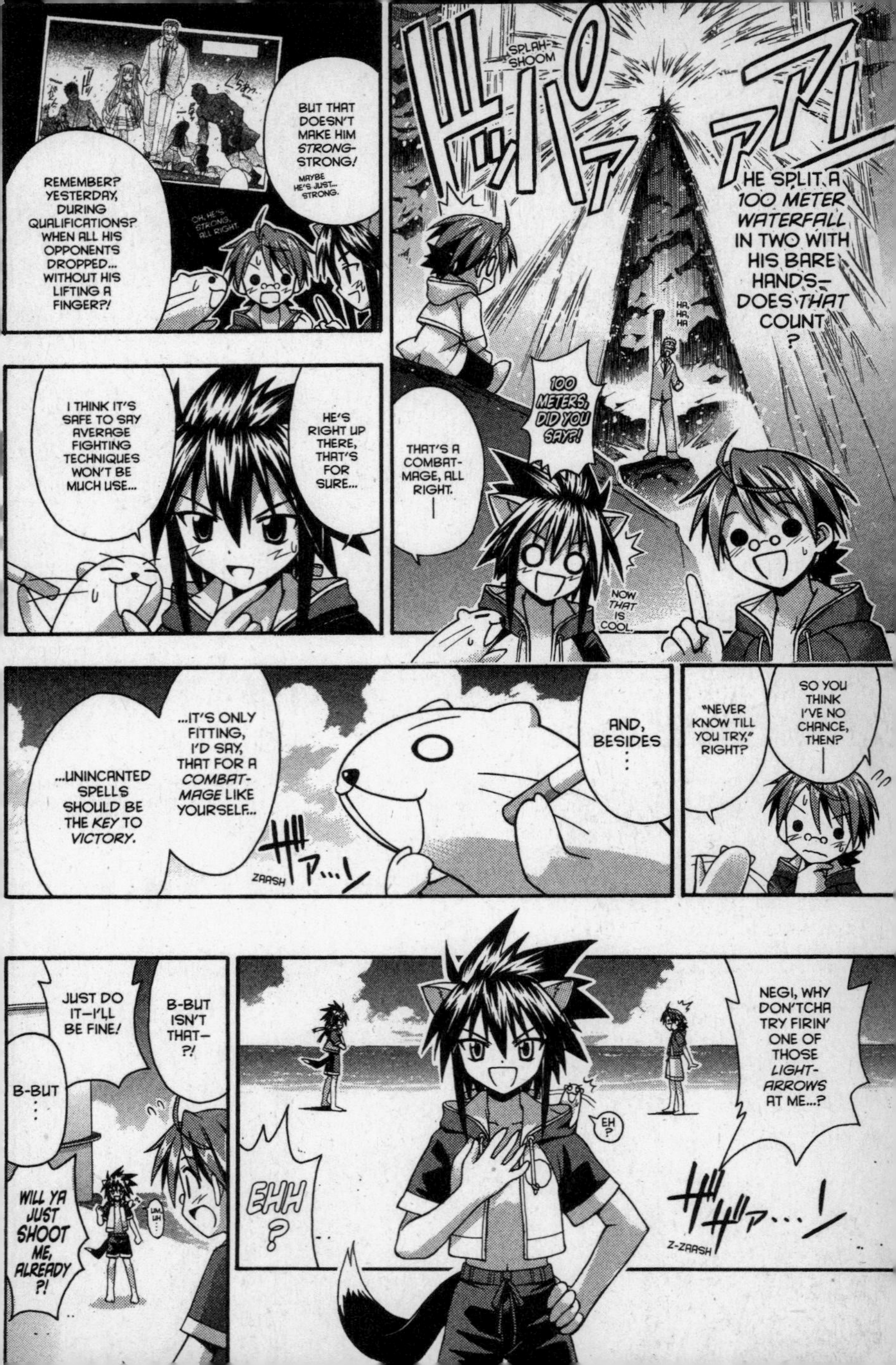
SPLAH-SHOOM
HE SPLIT A 100 METER WATERFALL IN TWO WITH HIS BARE HANDS—DOES THAT COUNT?
HA, HA, HA
100 METERS, DID YOU SAY?!
THAT'S A COMBAT-MAGE, ALL RIGHT.
NOW THAT IS COOL.
BUT THAT DOESN'T MAKE HIM STRONG-STRONG!
MAYBE HE'S JUST... STRONG.
REMEMBER? YESTERDAY, DURING QUALIFICATIONS? WHEN ALL HIS OPPONENTS DROPPED... WITHOUT HIS LIFTING A FINGER?!
OH, HE'S STRONG, ALL RIGHT.
HE'S RIGHT UP THERE, THAT'S FOR SURE...
I THINK IT'S SAFE TO SAY AVERAGE FIGHTING TECHNIQUES WON'T BE MUCH USE...
SO YOU THINK I'VE NO CHANCE, THEN?
"NEVER KNOW TILL YOU TRY," RIGHT?
AND, BESIDES...
...IT'S ONLY FITTING, I'D SAY, THAT FOR A COMBAT-MAGE LIKE YOURSELF...
...UNINCANTED SPELLS SHOULD BE THE KEY TO VICTORY.
ZAASH
NEGI, WHY DON'TCHA TRY FIRIN' ONE OF THOSE LIGHT-ARROWS AT ME...?
Z-ZAASH
EH?
EHH?
B-BUT ISN'T THAT—?!
JUST DO IT—I'LL BE FINE!
B-BUT...
UM, UH...
WILL YA JUST SHOOT ME, ALREADY?!

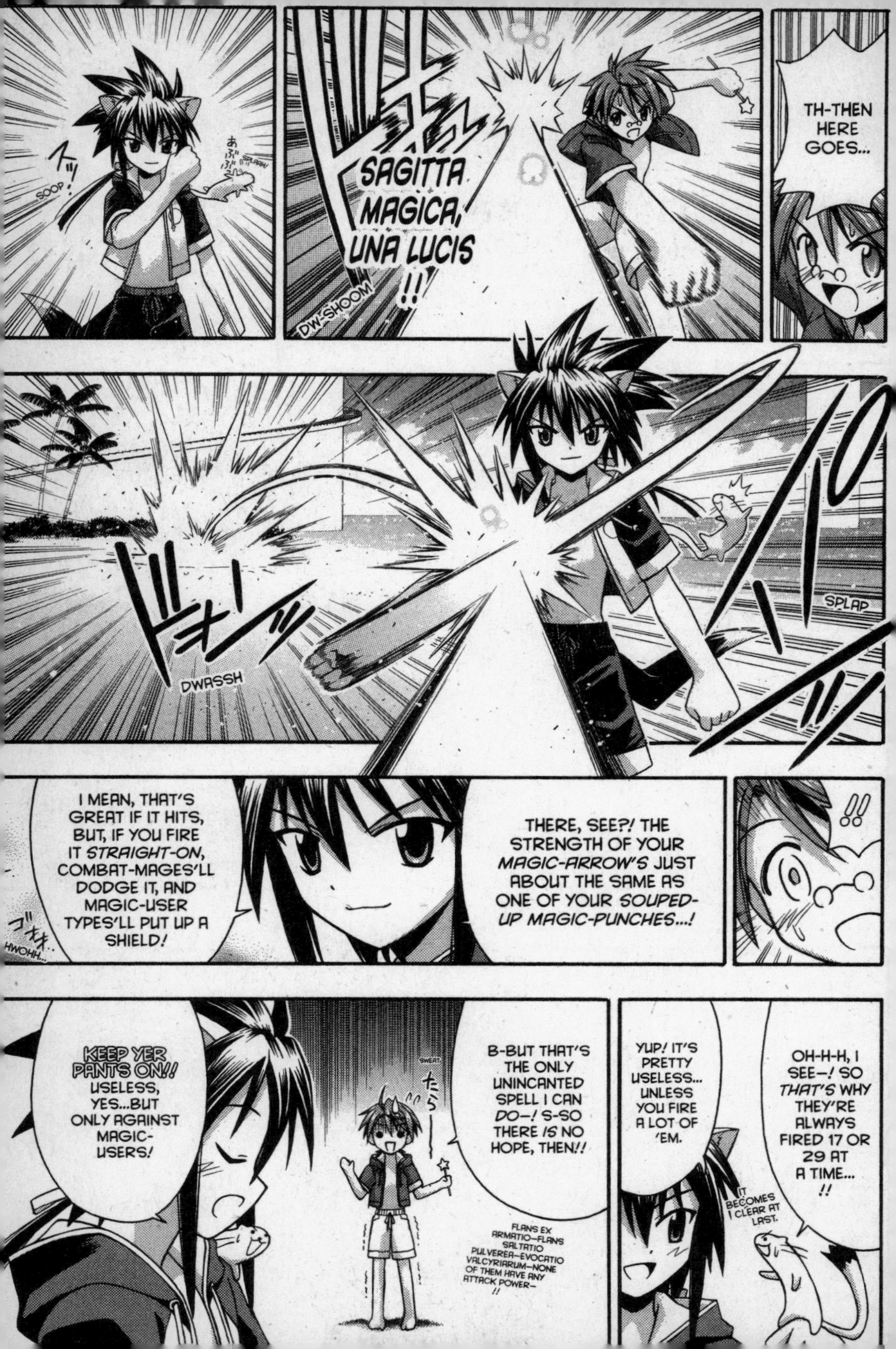
TH-THEN HERE GOES...
SAGITTA MAGICA, UNA LUCIS !!
DW-SHOOM
SPLASH
SOOP
SPLAP
DWASSH
!!
THERE, SEE?! THE STRENGTH OF YOUR MAGIC-ARROW'S JUST ABOUT THE SAME AS ONE OF YOUR SOUPED-UP MAGIC-PUNCHES...!
I MEAN, THAT'S GREAT IF IT HITS, BUT, IF YOU FIRE IT STRAIGHT-ON, COMBAT-MAGES'LL DODGE IT, AND MAGIC-USER TYPES'LL PUT UP A SHIELD!
HWOHH...
OH-H-H, I SEE—! SO THAT'S WHY THEY'RE ALWAYS FIRED 17 OR 29 AT A TIME... !!
YUP! IT'S PRETTY USELESS... UNLESS YOU FIRE A LOT OF 'EM.
IT BECOMES CLEAR AT LAST.
B-BUT THAT'S THE ONLY UNINCANTED SPELL I CAN DO—! S-SO THERE IS NO HOPE, THEN!!
SWEAT
FLANS EX ARMATIO—FLANS SALTATIO PULVEREA—EVOCATIO VALCYRIARUM—NONE OF THEM HAVE ANY ATTACK POWER— !!
KEEP YER PANTS ON!! USELESS, YES...BUT ONLY AGAINST MAGIC-USERS!

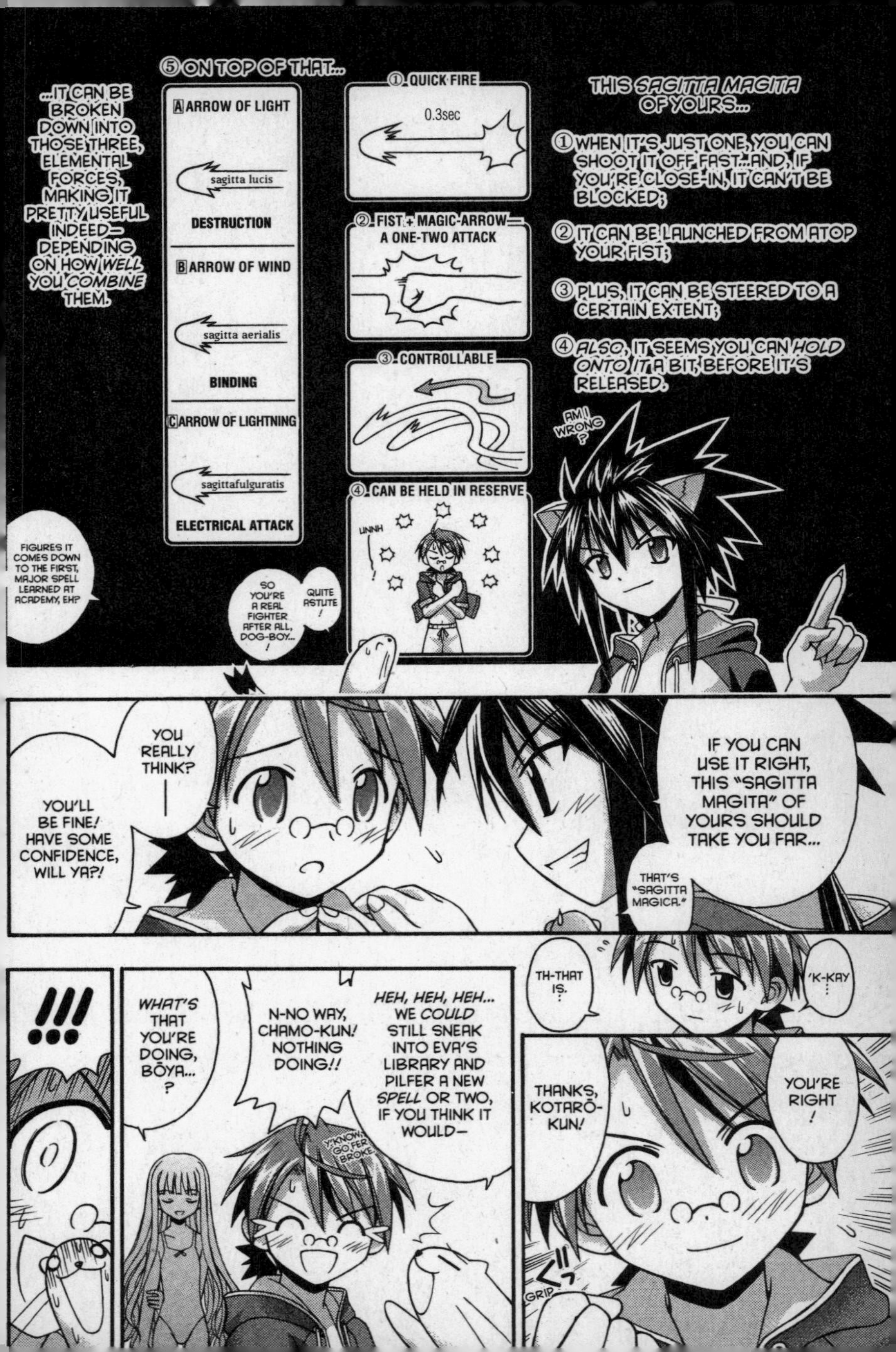

THIS SAGITTA MAGITA OF YOURS...
① WHEN IT'S JUST ONE, YOU CAN SHOOT IT OFF FAST...AND, IF YOU'RE CLOSE-IN, IT CAN'T BE BLOCKED;
② IT CAN BE LAUNCHED FROM ATOP YOUR FIST;
③ PLUS, IT CAN BE STEERED TO A CERTAIN EXTENT;
④ ALSO, IT SEEMS YOU CAN HOLD ONTO IT A BIT, BEFORE IT'S RELEASED.
AM I WRONG?
① QUICK FIRE
0.3sec
② FIST + MAGIC-ARROW— A ONE-TWO ATTACK
③ CONTROLLABLE
④ CAN BE HELD IN RESERVE
UNNH
⑤ ON TOP OF THAT...
A ARROW OF LIGHT
sagitta lucis
DESTRUCTION
B ARROW OF WIND
sagitta aerialis
BINDING
C ARROW OF LIGHTNING
sagittafulguratis
ELECTRICAL ATTACK
...IT CAN BE BROKEN DOWN INTO THOSE THREE, ELEMENTAL FORCES, MAKING IT PRETTY USEFUL INDEED—DEPENDING ON HOW WELL YOU COMBINE THEM.
QUITE ASTUTE!
SO YOU'RE A REAL FIGHTER AFTER ALL, DOG-BOY...!
FIGURES IT COMES DOWN TO THE FIRST, MAJOR SPELL LEARNED AT ACADEMY, EH?
IF YOU CAN USE IT RIGHT, THIS "SAGITTA MAGITA" OF YOURS SHOULD TAKE YOU FAR...
THAT'S "SAGITTA MAGICA."
YOU REALLY THINK?
YOU'LL BE FINE! HAVE SOME CONFIDENCE, WILL YA?!
'K-KAY...
TH-THAT IS.
YOU'RE RIGHT!
THANKS, KOTARŌ-KUN!
GRIP
HEH, HEH, HEH... WE COULD STILL SNEAK INTO EVA'S LIBRARY AND PILFER A NEW SPELL OR TWO, IF YOU THINK IT WOULD—
Y'KNOW, GO FER BROKE
N-NO WAY, CHAMO-KUN! NOTHING DOING!!
WHAT'S THAT YOU'RE DOING, BŌYA...?
!!!

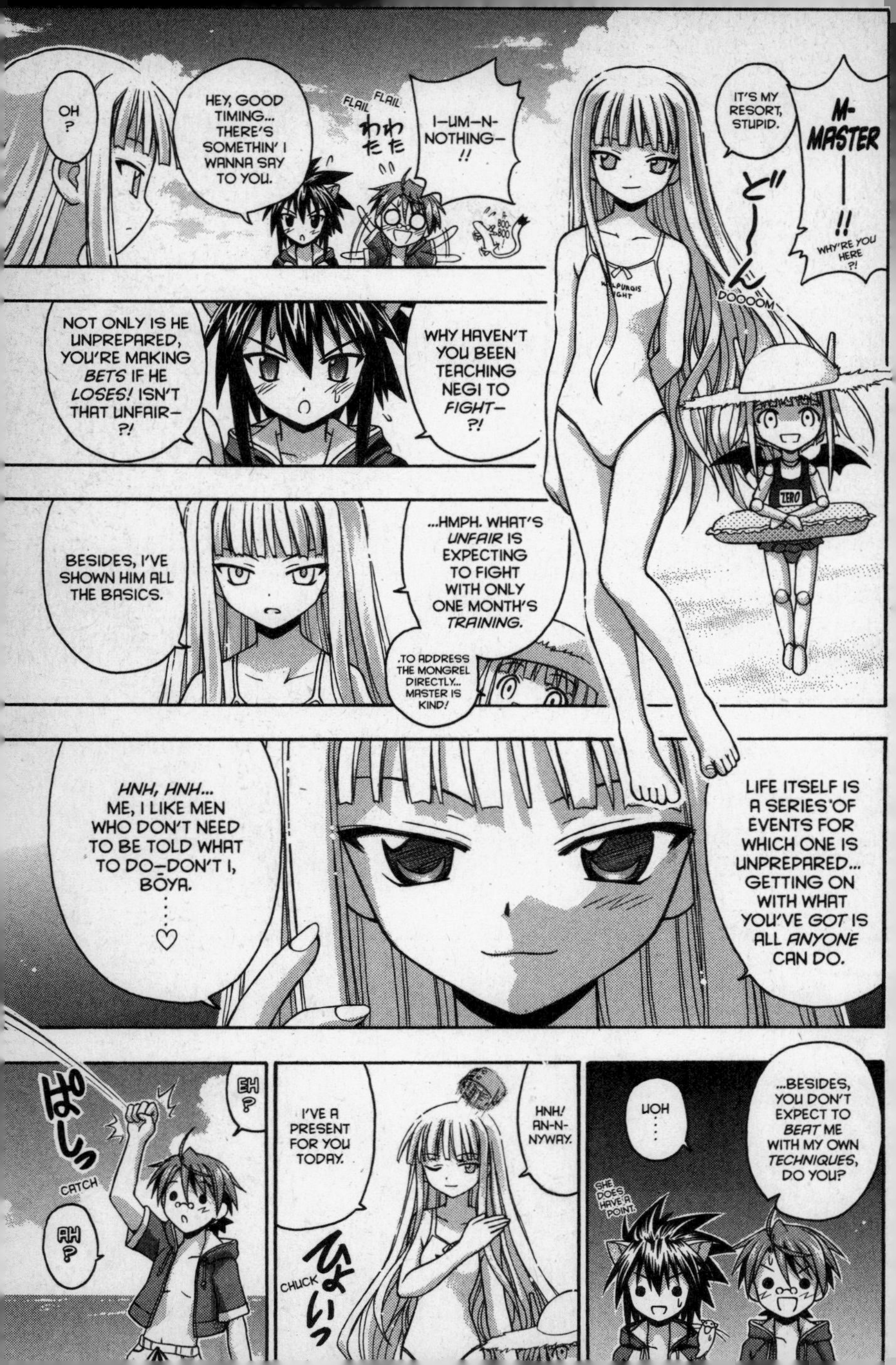
M-MASTER—!!
WHY'RE YOU HERE?!
IT'S MY RESORT, STUPID.
ど~ん
DOOOOM
I-UM-N-NOTHING—!!
FLAIL FLAIL
わわたた
HEY, GOOD TIMING... THERE'S SOMETHIN' I WANNA SAY TO YOU.
OH?
WHY HAVEN'T YOU BEEN TEACHING NEGI TO *FIGHT*—?!
NOT ONLY IS HE UNPREPARED, YOU'RE MAKING *BETS* IF HE *LOSES!* ISN'T THAT UNFAIR—?!
...HMPH. WHAT'S *UNFAIR* IS EXPECTING TO FIGHT WITH ONLY ONE MONTH'S *TRAINING*.
BESIDES, I'VE SHOWN HIM ALL THE BASICS.
.TO ADDRESS THE MONGREL DIRECTLY... MASTER IS KIND!
LIFE ITSELF IS A SERIES OF EVENTS FOR WHICH ONE IS UNPREPARED... GETTING ON WITH WHAT YOU'VE *GOT* IS ALL *ANYONE* CAN DO.
HNH, HNH... ME, I LIKE MEN WHO DON'T NEED TO BE TOLD WHAT TO DO—DON'T I, BOYA. ...♡
...BESIDES, YOU DON'T EXPECT TO *BEAT* ME WITH MY OWN *TECHNIQUES*, DO YOU?
UOH ....
SHE DOES HAVE A POINT.
HNH! AN-N-NYWAY.
I'VE A PRESENT FOR YOU TODAY.
ひょいっ
CHUCK
EH?
ぱしっ
CATCH
AH?

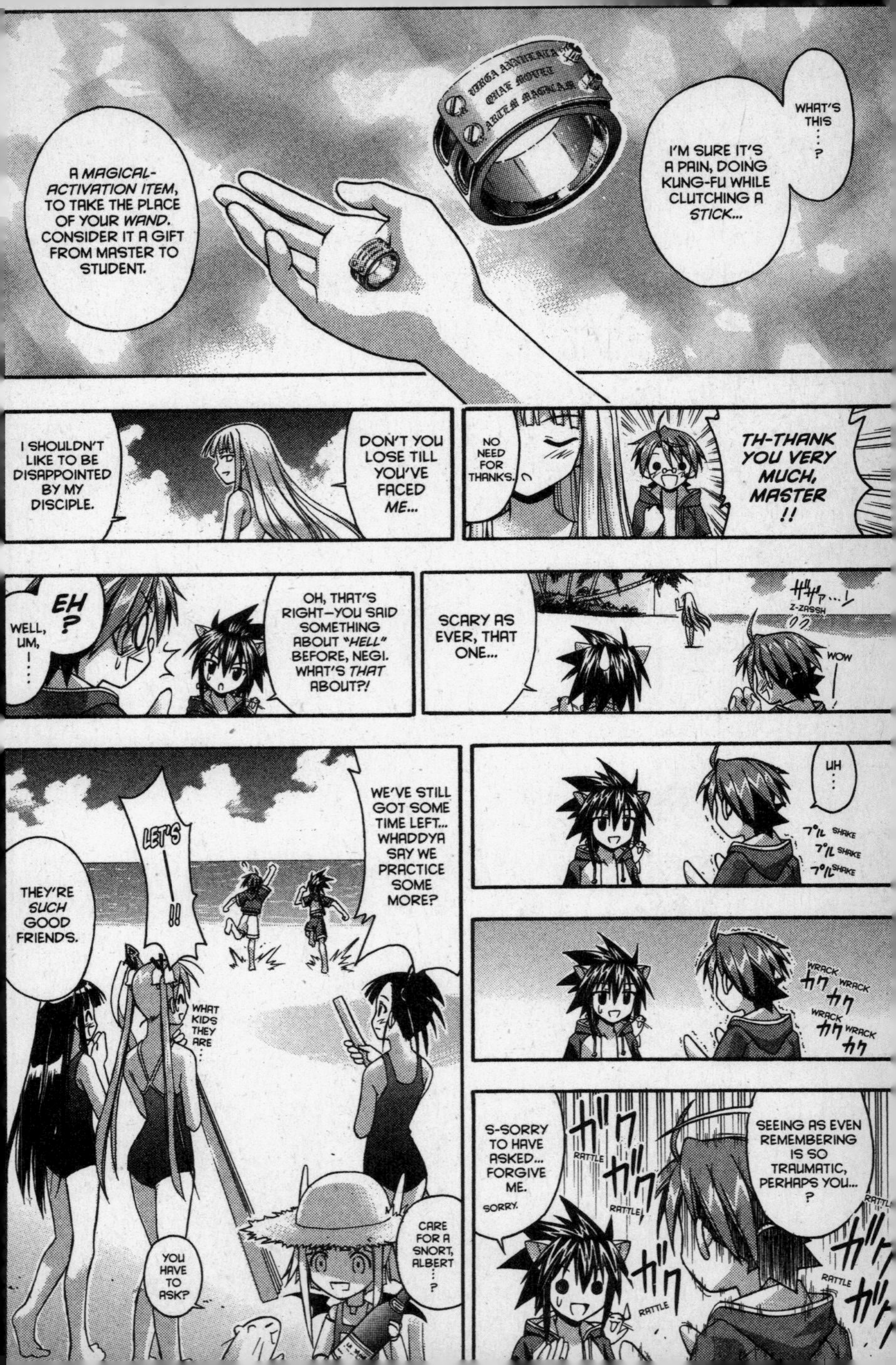
WHAT'S THIS...?
I'M SURE IT'S A PAIN, DOING KUNG-FU WHILE CLUTCHING A *STICK*...
A *MAGICAL-ACTIVATION ITEM*, TO TAKE THE PLACE OF YOUR *WAND*. CONSIDER IT A GIFT FROM MASTER TO STUDENT.
TH-THANK YOU VERY MUCH, MASTER!!
NO NEED FOR THANKS.
DON'T YOU LOSE TILL YOU'VE FACED *ME*...
I SHOULDN'T LIKE TO BE DISAPPOINTED BY MY DISCIPLE.
Z-ZASSH
WOW!
SCARY AS EVER, THAT ONE...
OH, THAT'S RIGHT—YOU SAID SOMETHING ABOUT *"HELL"* BEFORE, NEGI. WHAT'S *THAT* ABOUT?!
EH?
WELL, UM, !...
UH...
SHAKE SHAKE SHAKE
WRACK WRACK WRACK WRACK
SEEING AS EVEN REMEMBERING IS SO TRAUMATIC, PERHAPS YOU...?
RATTLE RATTLE RATTLE RATTLE RATTLE
S-SORRY TO HAVE ASKED... FORGIVE ME.
SORRY.
WE'VE STILL GOT SOME TIME LEFT... WHADDYA SAY WE PRACTICE SOME MORE?
LET'S—!!
THEY'RE *SUCH* GOOD FRIENDS.
WHAT KIDS THEY ARE...
CARE FOR A SNORT, ALBERT...?
YOU HAVE TO ASK?

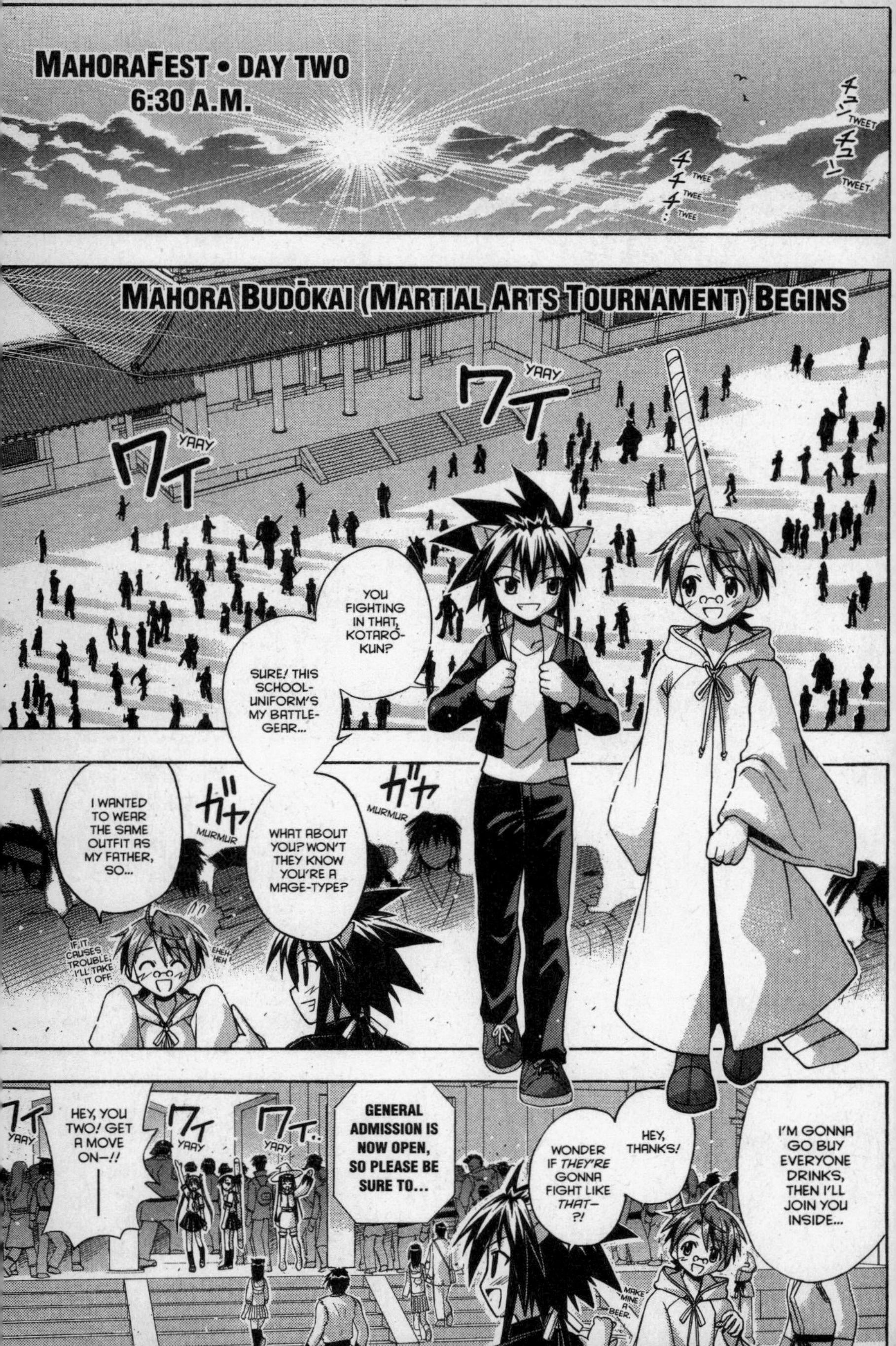

MahoraFest • Day Two
6:30 A.M.
チュン TWEET
チュン TWEET
チチチ TWEE TWEE TWEE
Mahora Budōkai (Martial Arts Tournament) Begins
ワイ YAAY
ワイ YAAY
YOU FIGHTING IN THAT, KOTARŌ-KUN?
SURE! THIS SCHOOL-UNIFORM'S MY BATTLE-GEAR...
ガヤ MURMUR
WHAT ABOUT YOU? WON'T THEY KNOW YOU'RE A MAGE-TYPE?
ガヤ MURMUR
I WANTED TO WEAR THE SAME OUTFIT AS MY FATHER, SO...
EHEH HEH
IF IT CAUSES TROUBLE, I'LL TAKE IT OFF.
I'M GONNA GO BUY EVERYONE DRINKS, THEN I'LL JOIN YOU INSIDE...
HEY, THANKS!
MAKE MINE A BEER.
WONDER IF THEY'RE GONNA FIGHT LIKE THAT—?!
GENERAL ADMISSION IS NOW OPEN, SO PLEASE BE SURE TO...
ワイ YAAY
ワイ YAAY
HEY, YOU TWO! GET A MOVE ON—!!
ワイ YAAY

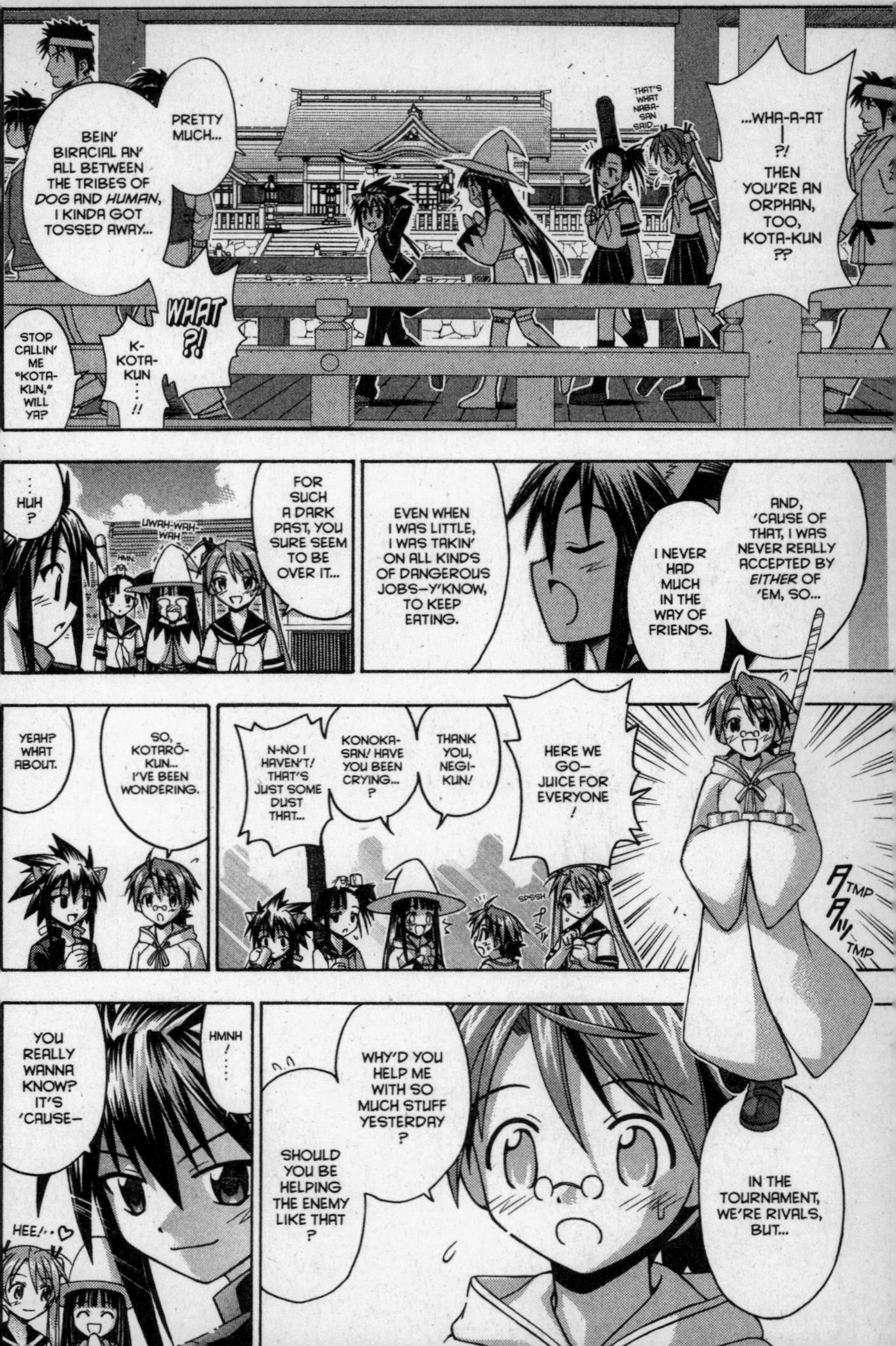

...WHA-A-AT! ?! THEN YOU'RE AN ORPHAN, TOO, KOTA-KUN??
THAT'S WHAT NABA-SAN SAID...
PRETTY MUCH...
BEIN' BIRACIAL AN' ALL BETWEEN THE TRIBES OF *DOG AND HUMAN*, I KINDA GOT TOSSED AWAY...
WHAT ?!
K-KOTA-KUN...!!
STOP CALLIN' ME "KOTA-KUN," WILL YA?
AND, 'CAUSE OF THAT, I WAS NEVER REALLY ACCEPTED BY *EITHER* OF 'EM, SO...
I NEVER HAD MUCH IN THE WAY OF FRIENDS.
EVEN WHEN I WAS LITTLE, I WAS TAKIN' ON ALL KINDS OF DANGEROUS JOBS—Y'KNOW, TO KEEP EATING.
FOR SUCH A DARK PAST, YOU SURE SEEM TO BE OVER IT...
UWAH-WAH-WAH
HMN.
...HUH?
TMP
TMP
HERE WE GO—JUICE FOR EVERYONE!
THANK YOU, NEGI-KUN!
KONOKA-SAN! HAVE YOU BEEN CRYING...?
N-NO I HAVEN'T! THAT'S JUST SOME DUST THAT...
SPSSH
SO, KOTARŌ-KUN... I'VE BEEN WONDERING.
YEAH? WHAT ABOUT.
IN THE TOURNAMENT, WE'RE RIVALS, BUT...
WHY'D YOU HELP ME WITH SO MUCH STUFF YESTERDAY?
SHOULD YOU BE HELPING THE ENEMY LIKE THAT?
HMNH!....
YOU REALLY WANNA KNOW? IT'S 'CAUSE—
HEE!..♡

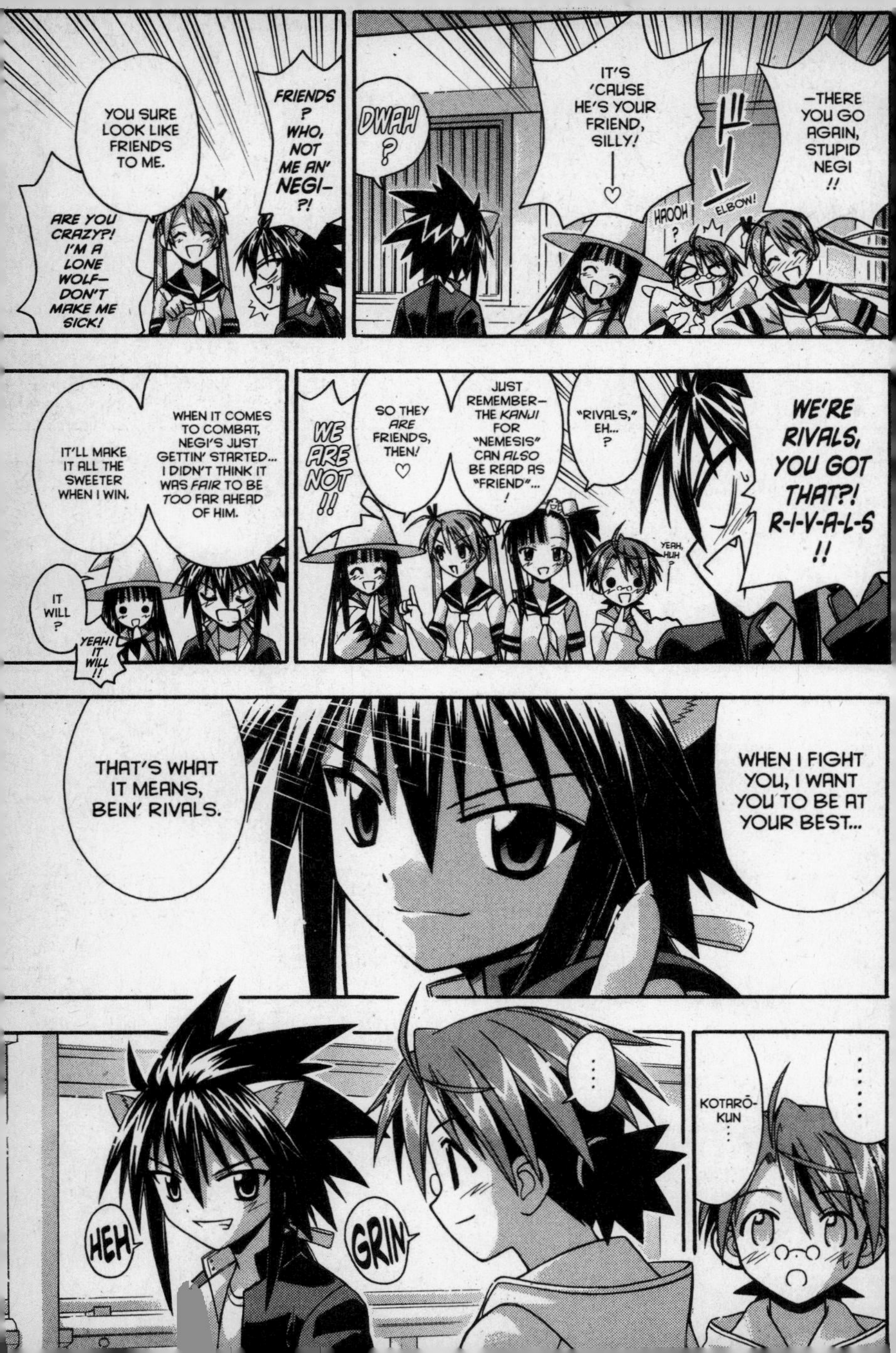
—THERE YOU GO AGAIN, STUPID NEGI!!
ELBOW!
HAOOH?
IT'S 'CAUSE HE'S YOUR FRIEND, SILLY! ♡
DWAH?
FRIENDS? WHO, NOT ME AN' NEGI—?!
YOU SURE LOOK LIKE FRIENDS TO ME.
ARE YOU CRAZY?! I'M A LONE WOLF—DON'T MAKE ME SICK!
WE'RE RIVALS, YOU GOT THAT?! R-I-V-A-L-S!!
"RIVALS," EH...?
YEAH, HUH?
JUST REMEMBER—THE KANJI FOR "NEMESIS" CAN ALSO BE READ AS "FRIEND"...!
SO THEY ARE FRIENDS, THEN! ♡
WE ARE NOT!!
WHEN IT COMES TO COMBAT, NEGI'S JUST GETTIN' STARTED... I DIDN'T THINK IT WAS FAIR TO BE TOO FAR AHEAD OF HIM.
IT'LL MAKE IT ALL THE SWEETER WHEN I WIN.
IT WILL?
YEAH! IT WILL!!
WHEN I FIGHT YOU, I WANT YOU TO BE AT YOUR BEST...
THAT'S WHAT IT MEANS, BEIN' RIVALS.
......
KOTARŌ-KUN...
....
GRIN
HEH

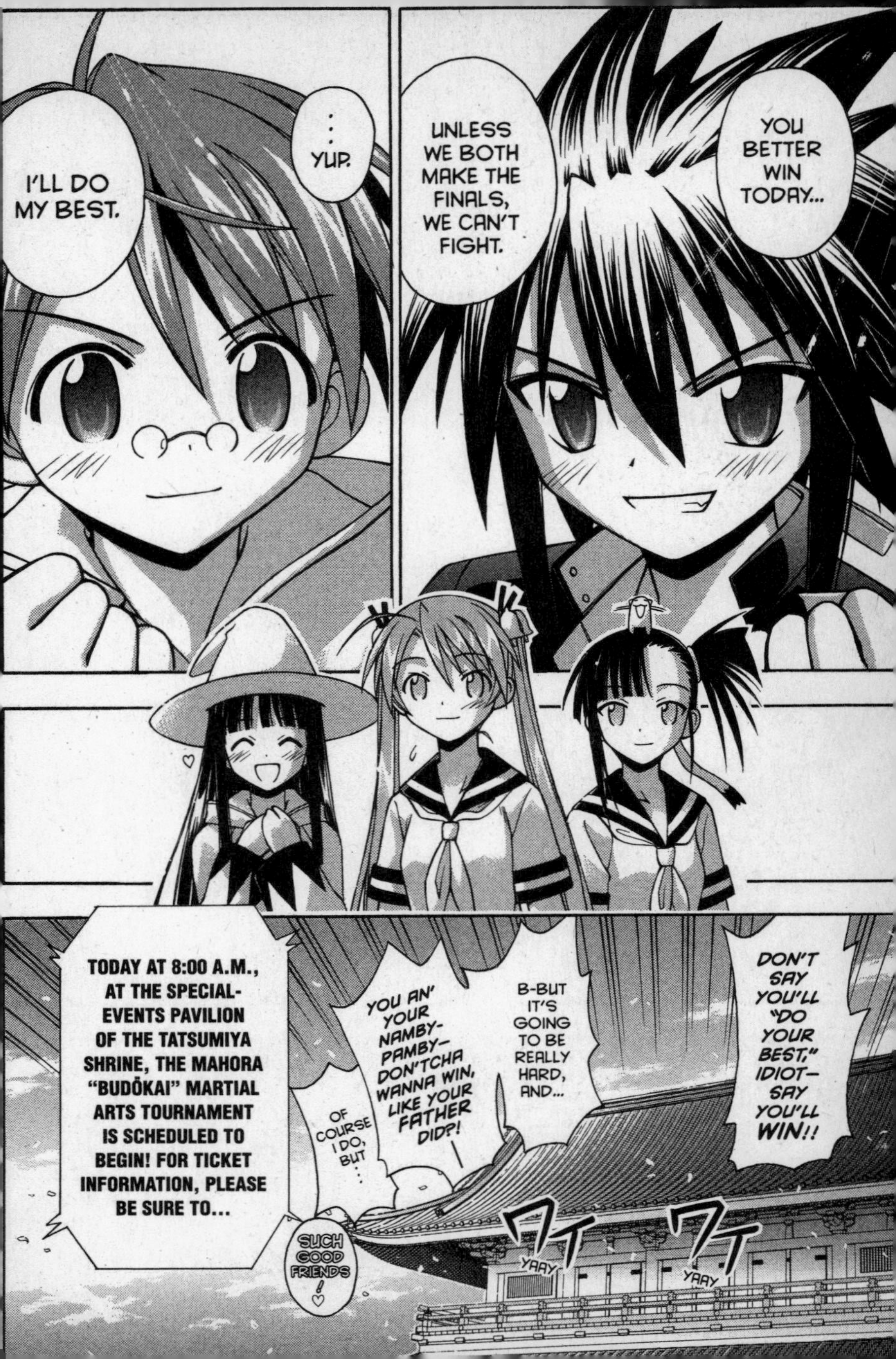
YOU BETTER WIN TODAY...
UNLESS WE BOTH MAKE THE FINALS, WE CAN'T FIGHT.
. . . YUP.
I'LL DO MY BEST.
DON'T SAY YOU'LL "DO YOUR BEST," IDIOT— SAY YOU'LL WIN!!
B-BUT IT'S GOING TO BE REALLY HARD, AND...
YOU AN' YOUR NAMBY-PAMBY— DON'TCHA WANNA WIN, LIKE YOUR FATHER DID?!
OF COURSE I DO, BUT . . .
YAAY
YAAY
SUCH GOOD FRIENDS ! ♡
TODAY AT 8:00 A.M., AT THE SPECIAL-EVENTS PAVILION OF THE TATSUMIYA SHRINE, THE MAHORA "BUDŌKAI" MARTIAL ARTS TOURNAMENT IS SCHEDULED TO BEGIN! FOR TICKET INFORMATION, PLEASE BE SURE TO...

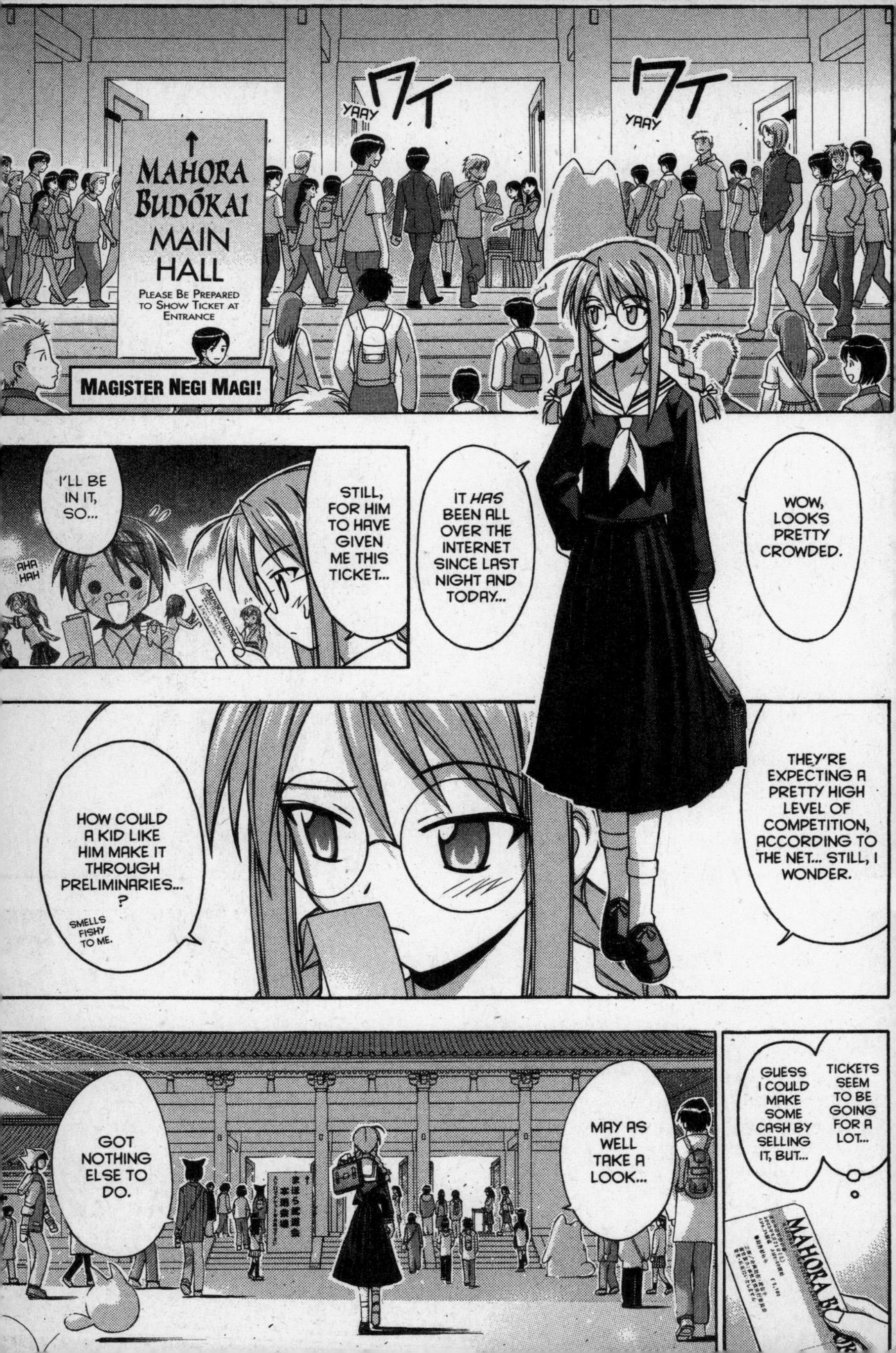

ワイ
YAAY
ワイ
YAAY
MAHORA BUDÓKAI MAIN HALL
Please Be Prepared to Show Ticket at Entrance
MAGISTER NEGI MAGI!
WOW, LOOKS PRETTY CROWDED.
IT *HAS* BEEN ALL OVER THE INTERNET SINCE LAST NIGHT AND TODAY...
STILL, FOR HIM TO HAVE GIVEN ME THIS TICKET...
I'LL BE IN IT, SO...
AHA HAH
THEY'RE EXPECTING A PRETTY HIGH LEVEL OF COMPETITION, ACCORDING TO THE NET... STILL, I WONDER.
HOW COULD A KID LIKE HIM MAKE IT THROUGH PRELIMINARIES... ?
SMELLS FISHY TO ME.
TICKETS SEEM TO BE GOING FOR A LOT...
GUESS I COULD MAKE SOME CASH BY SELLING IT, BUT...
MAY AS WELL TAKE A LOOK...
GOT NOTHING ELSE TO DO.

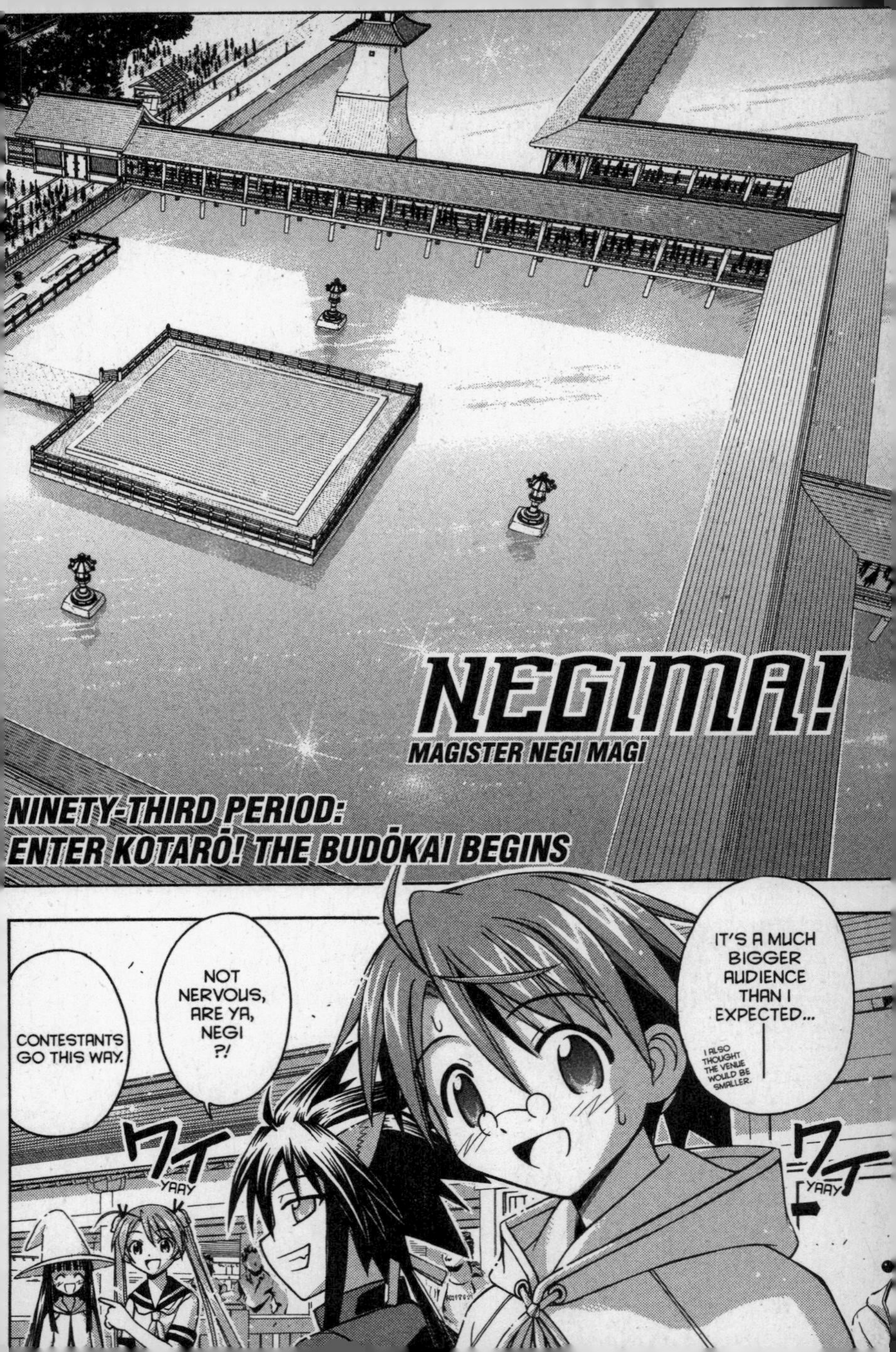
NEGIMA!
MAGISTER NEGI MAGI
NINETY-THIRD PERIOD:
ENTER KOTARŌ! THE BUDŌKAI BEGINS
IT'S A MUCH BIGGER AUDIENCE THAN I EXPECTED...
I ALSO THOUGHT THE VENUE WOULD BE SMALLER.
ワイ
YAAY
NOT NERVOUS, ARE YA, NEGI ?!
ワイ
YAAY
CONTESTANTS GO THIS WAY.

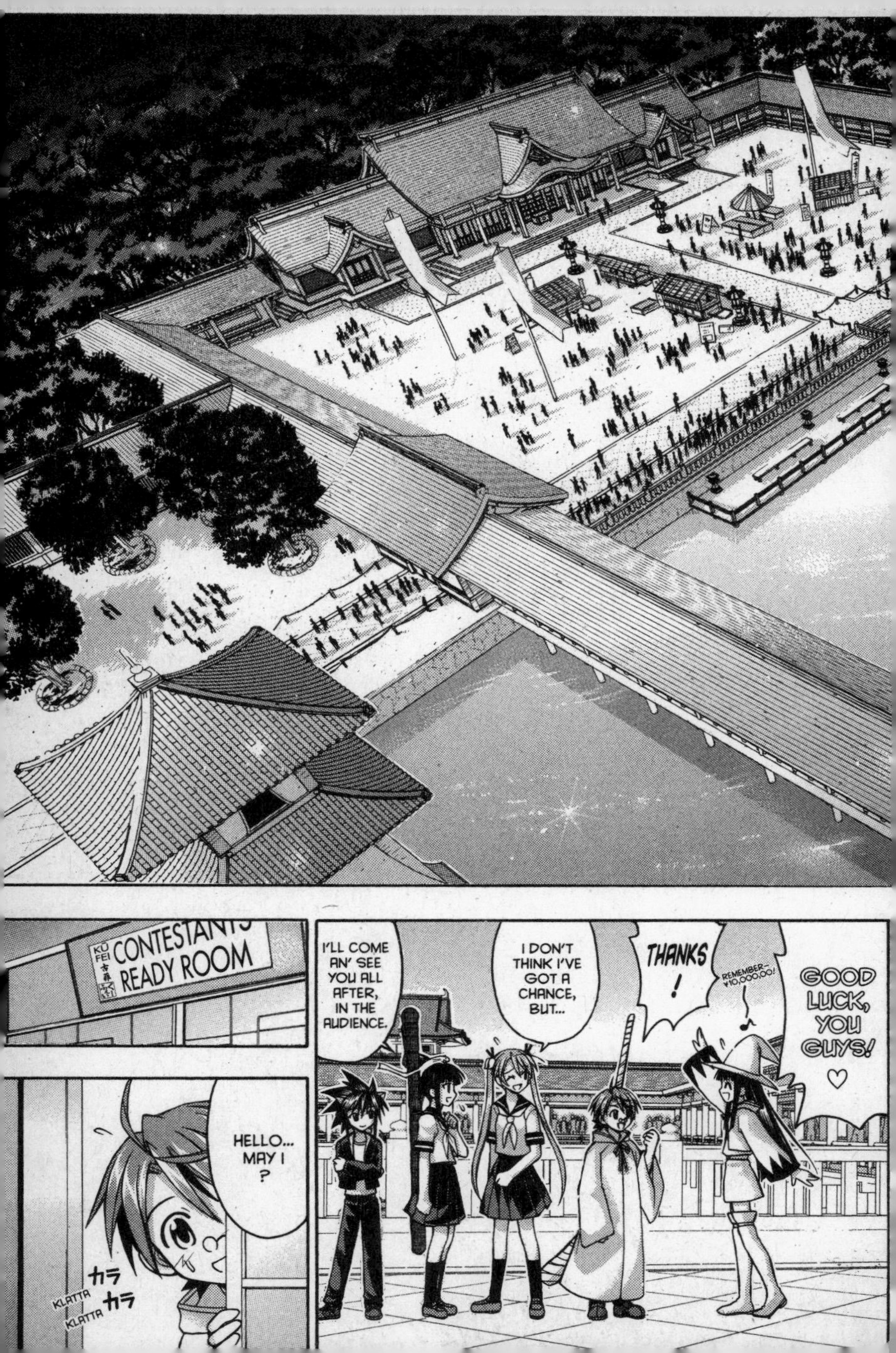
GOOD LUCK, YOU GUYS! ♥
REMEMBER— ¥10,000,00!
THANKS!
I DON'T THINK I'VE GOT A CHANCE, BUT...
I'LL COME AN' SEE YOU ALL AFTER, IN THE AUDIENCE.
KŪ FEI
CONTESTANTS READY ROOM
HELLO... MAY I ?
カラ カラ
KLATTA KLATTA

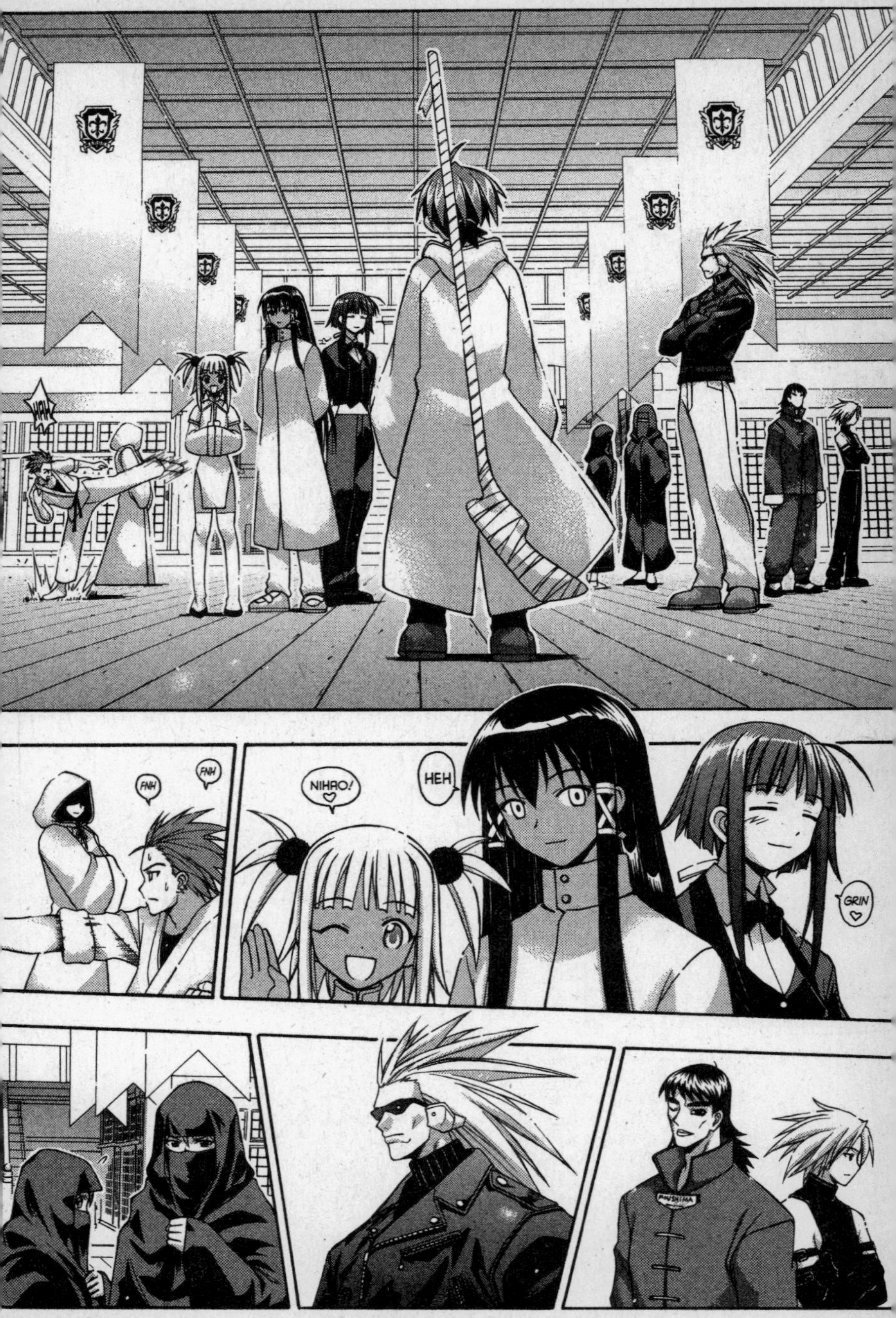
HAH
HEH
NIHAO! ♡
GRIN ♡
FNH
FNH

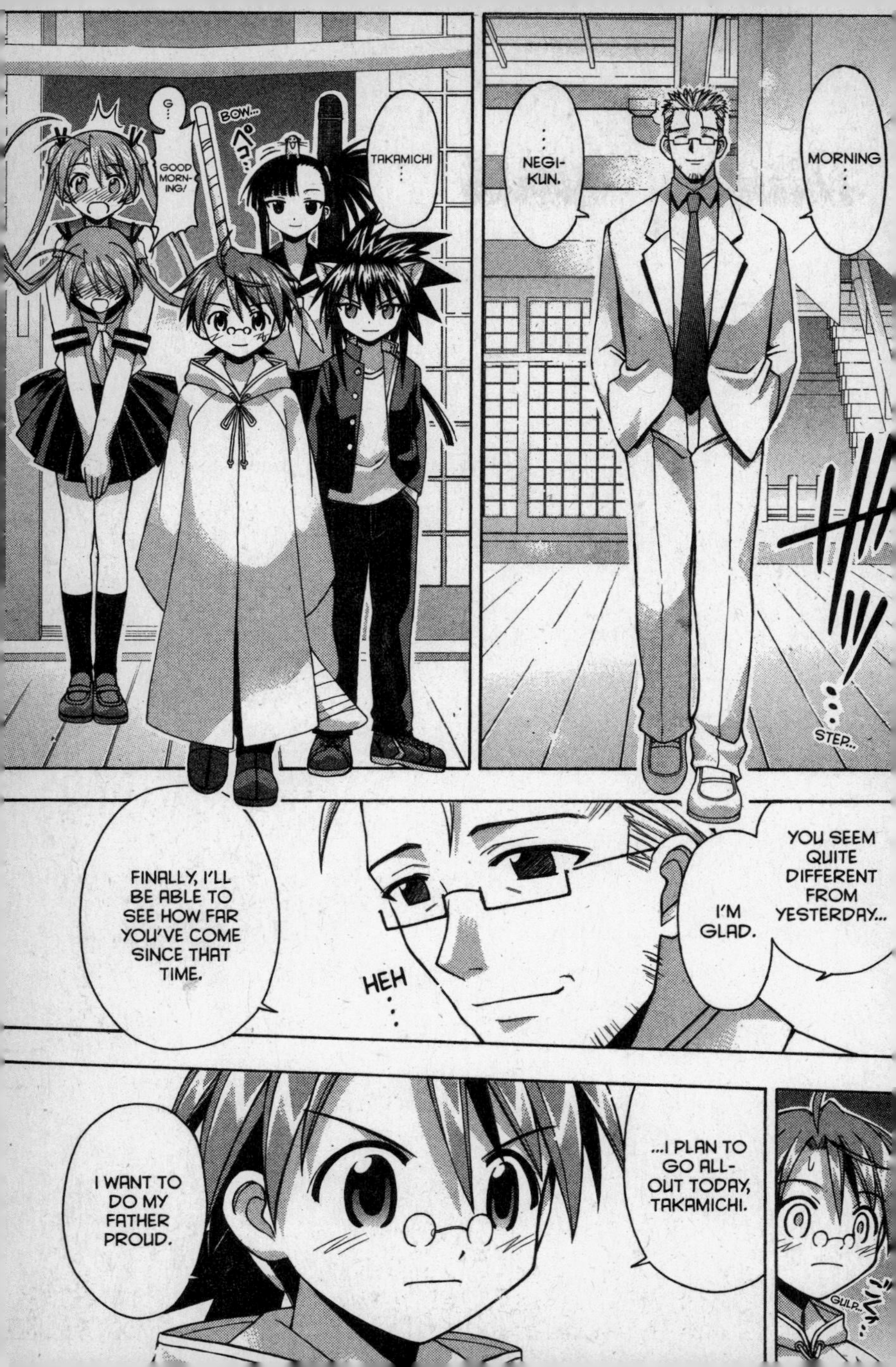

MORNING...
...NEGI-KUN.
STEP...
TAKAMICHI...
BOW...
G...
GOOD MORNING!
YOU SEEM QUITE DIFFERENT FROM YESTERDAY...
I'M GLAD.
HEH...
FINALLY, I'LL BE ABLE TO SEE HOW FAR YOU'VE COME SINCE THAT TIME.
GULP...
...I PLAN TO GO ALL-OUT TODAY, TAKAMICHI.
I WANT TO DO MY FATHER PROUD.

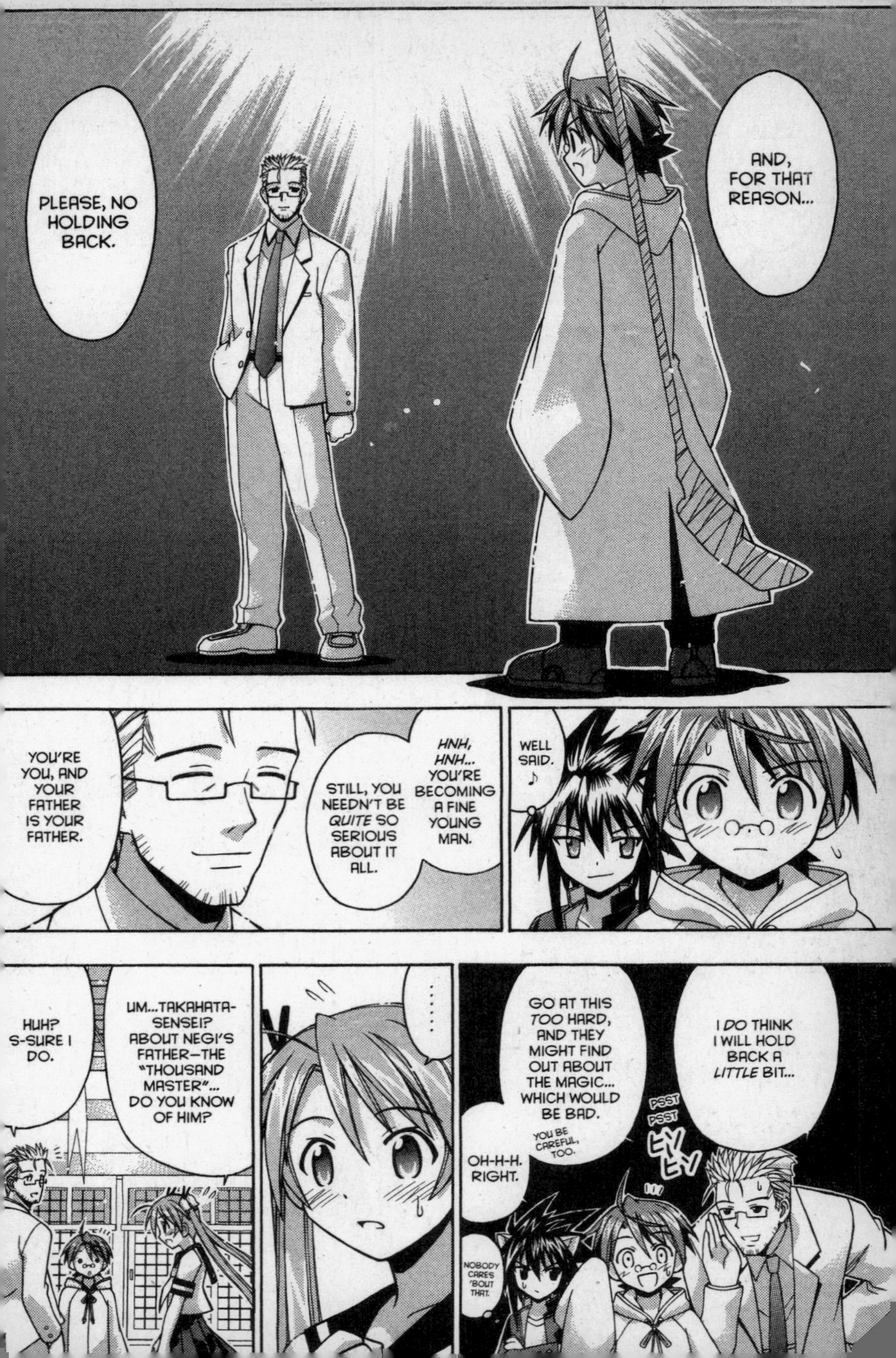
AND, FOR THAT REASON...
PLEASE, NO HOLDING BACK.
WELL SAID. ♪
HNH, HNH... YOU'RE BECOMING A FINE YOUNG MAN.
STILL, YOU NEEDN'T BE *QUITE* SO SERIOUS ABOUT IT ALL.
YOU'RE YOU, AND YOUR FATHER IS YOUR FATHER.
I *DO* THINK I WILL HOLD BACK A *LITTLE* BIT...
GO AT THIS *TOO* HARD, AND THEY MIGHT FIND OUT ABOUT THE MAGIC... WHICH WOULD BE BAD.
PSST PSST
ヒソ ヒソ
YOU BE CAREFUL, TOO.
OH-H-H. RIGHT.
NOBODY CARES 'BOUT THAT.
......
UM...TAKAHATA-SENSEI? ABOUT NEGI'S FATHER—THE "THOUSAND MASTER"... DO YOU KNOW OF HIM?
HUH? S-SURE I DO.

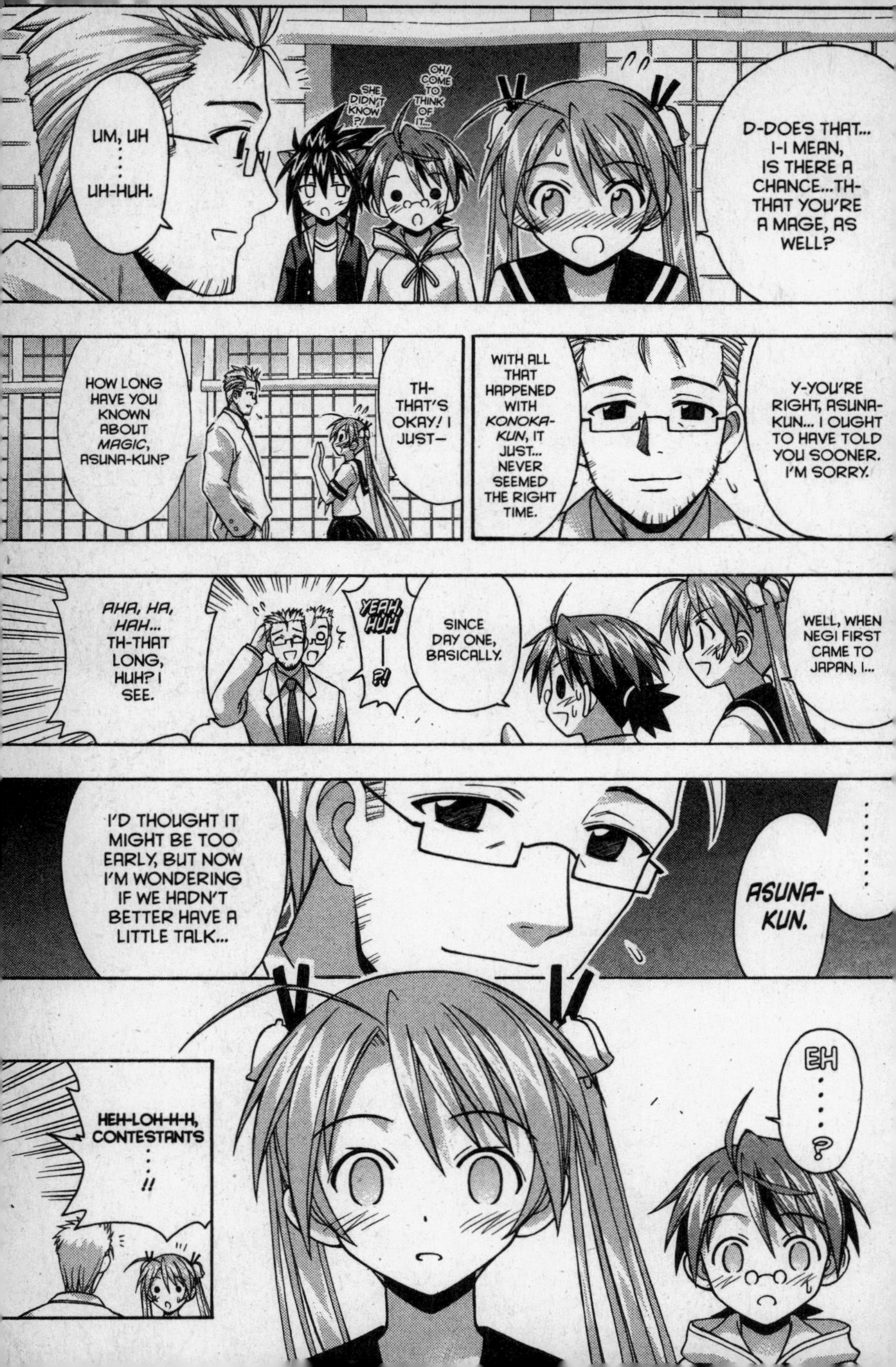
D-DOES THAT... I-I MEAN, IS THERE A CHANCE...TH-THAT YOU'RE A MAGE, AS WELL?
OH! COME TO THINK OF IT...
SHE DIDN'T KNOW ?!
UM, UH ...... UH-HUH.
Y-YOU'RE RIGHT, ASUNA-KUN... I OUGHT TO HAVE TOLD YOU SOONER. I'M SORRY.
WITH ALL THAT HAPPENED WITH *KONOKA-KUN*, IT JUST... NEVER SEEMED THE RIGHT TIME.
TH-THAT'S OKAY! I JUST—
HOW LONG HAVE YOU KNOWN ABOUT *MAGIC*, ASUNA-KUN?
WELL, WHEN NEGI FIRST CAME TO JAPAN, I...
SINCE DAY ONE, BASICALLY.
YEAH, HUH—?!
AHA, HA, HAH... TH-THAT LONG, HUH? I SEE.
......
ASUNA-KUN.
I'D THOUGHT IT MIGHT BE TOO EARLY, BUT NOW I'M WONDERING IF WE HADN'T BETTER HAVE A LITTLE TALK...
EH.....?
HEH-LOH-H-H, CONTESTANTS ...!!

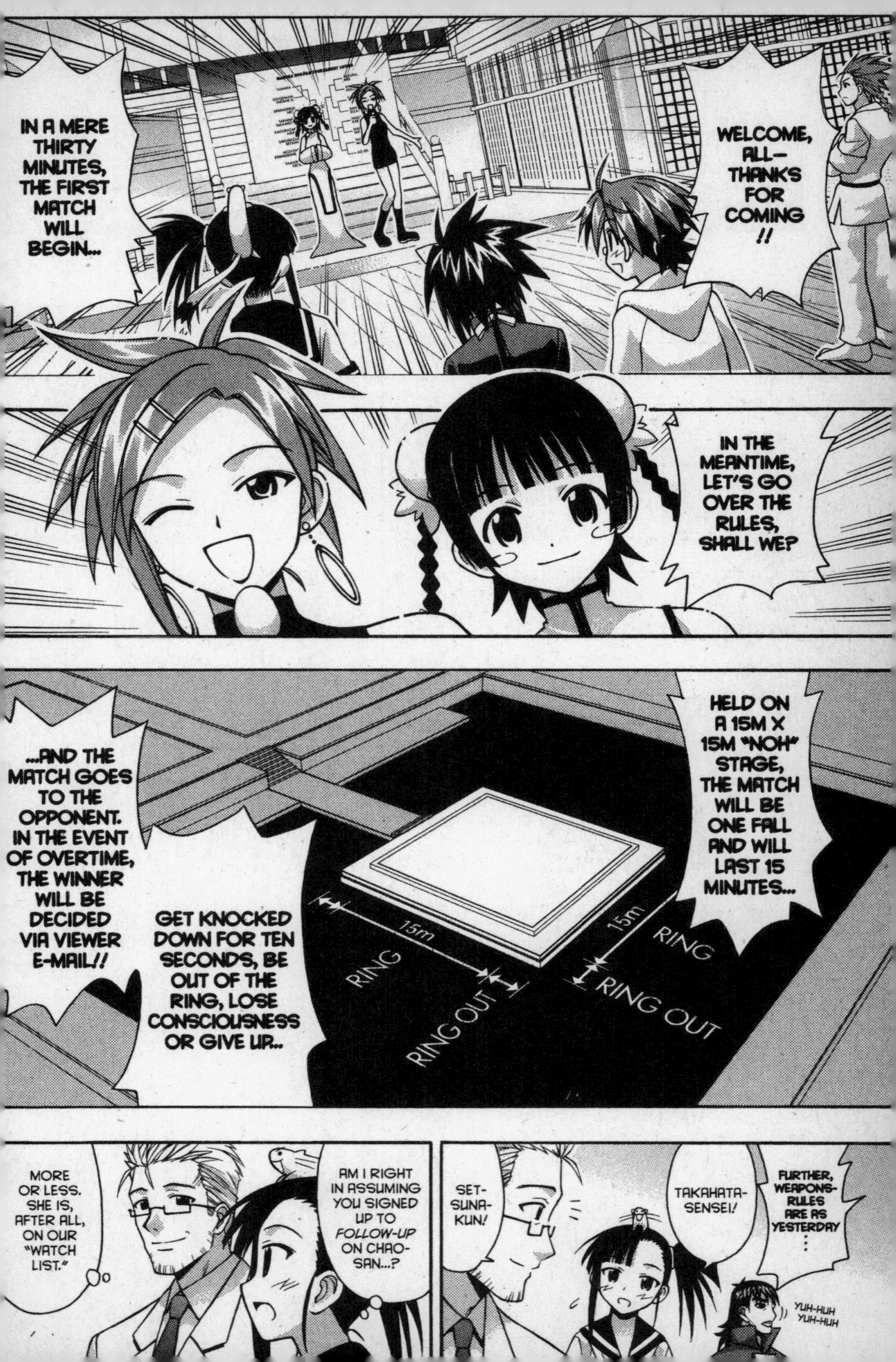
WELCOME, ALL— THANKS FOR COMING!!
IN A MERE THIRTY MINUTES, THE FIRST MATCH WILL BEGIN...
IN THE MEANTIME, LET'S GO OVER THE RULES, SHALL WE?
HELD ON A 15M X 15M "NOH" STAGE, THE MATCH WILL BE ONE FALL AND WILL LAST 15 MINUTES...
15m
15m
RING
RING
RING OUT
RING OUT
GET KNOCKED DOWN FOR TEN SECONDS, BE OUT OF THE RING, LOSE CONSCIOUSNESS OR GIVE UP...
...AND THE MATCH GOES TO THE OPPONENT. IN THE EVENT OF OVERTIME, THE WINNER WILL BE DECIDED VIA VIEWER E-MAIL!!
FURTHER, WEAPONS-RULES ARE AS YESTERDAY...
YUH-HUH YUH-HUH
TAKAHATA-SENSEI!
SET-SUNA-KUN!
AM I RIGHT IN ASSUMING YOU SIGNED UP TO *FOLLOW-UP* ON CHAO-SAN...?
MORE OR LESS. SHE IS, AFTER ALL, ON OUR "WATCH LIST."

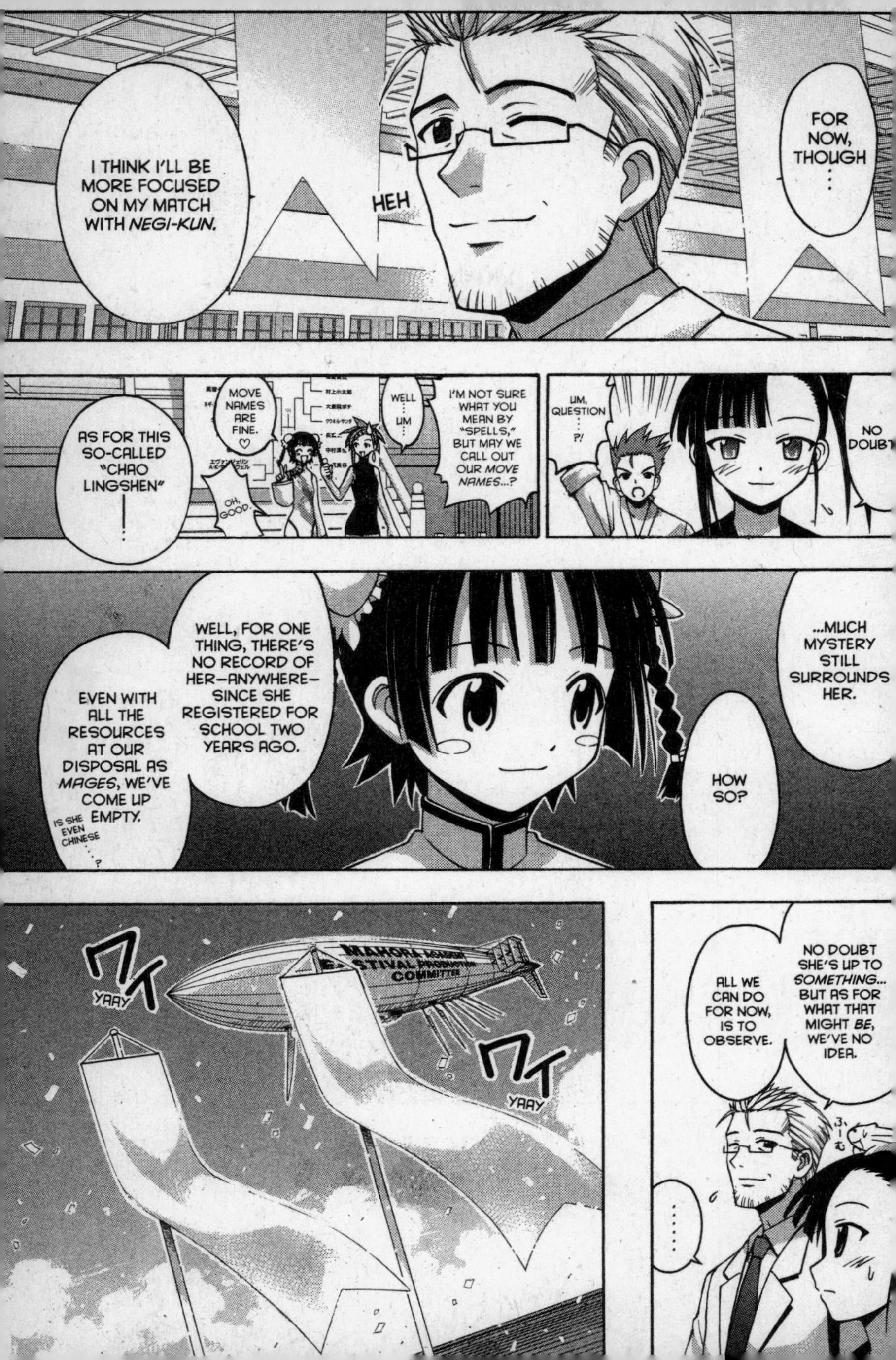
FOR NOW, THOUGH...
HEH
I THINK I'LL BE MORE FOCUSED ON MY MATCH WITH *NEGI-KUN.*
NO DOUBT
UM, QUESTION...?!
I'M NOT SURE WHAT YOU MEAN BY "SPELLS," BUT MAY WE CALL OUT OUR *MOVE NAMES*...?
WELL... UM
MOVE NAMES ARE FINE. ♡
OH, GOOD.
AS FOR THIS SO-CALLED "CHAO LINGSHEN" ...!
...MUCH MYSTERY STILL SURROUNDS HER.
HOW SO?
WELL, FOR ONE THING, THERE'S NO RECORD OF HER—ANYWHERE—SINCE SHE REGISTERED FOR SCHOOL TWO YEARS AGO.
EVEN WITH ALL THE RESOURCES AT OUR DISPOSAL AS *MAGES*, WE'VE COME UP EMPTY.
IS SHE EVEN CHINESE...?
NO DOUBT SHE'S UP TO *SOMETHING*... BUT AS FOR WHAT THAT MIGHT *BE*, WE'VE NO IDEA.
ALL WE CAN DO FOR NOW, IS TO OBSERVE.
ふーむ
......
YAAY
COMMITTEE
YAAY

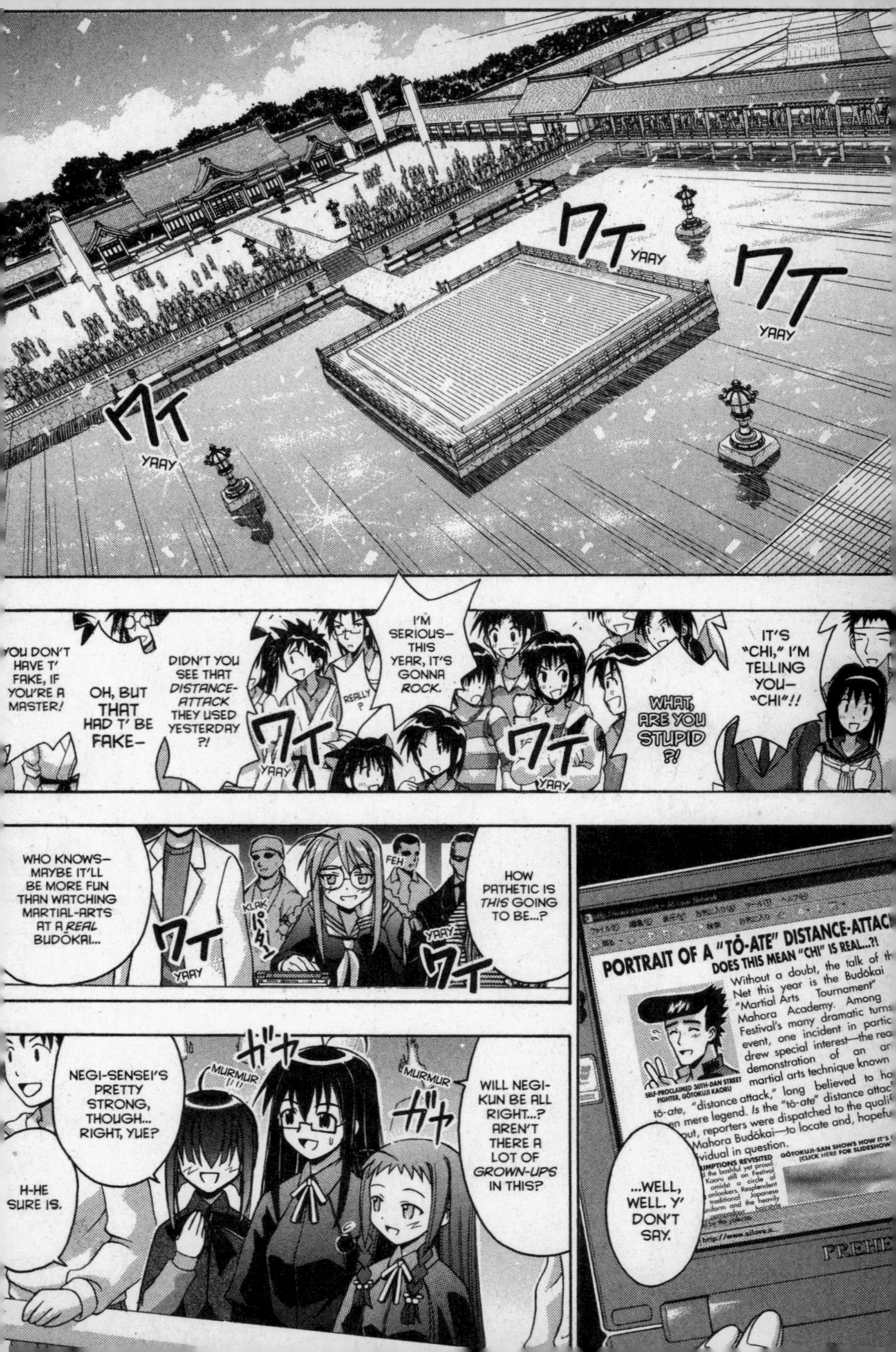

YAAY
YAAY
YAAY
IT'S "CHI," I'M TELLING YOU— "CHI"!!
WHAT, ARE YOU STUPID ?!
YAAY
I'M SERIOUS— THIS YEAR, IT'S GONNA ROCK.
REALLY ?
YAAY
DIDN'T YOU SEE THAT DISTANCE-ATTACK THEY USED YESTERDAY ?!
OH, BUT THAT HAD T' BE FAKE—
YOU DON'T HAVE T' FAKE, IF YOU'RE A MASTER!
PORTRAIT OF A "TŌ-ATE" DISTANCE-ATTAC
DOES THIS MEAN "CHI" IS REAL...?!
SELF-PROCLAIMED 30TH-DAN STREET FIGHTER, GŌTOKUJI KAORU
GŌTOKUJI-SAN SHOWS HOW IT'S
...WELL, WELL. Y' DON'T SAY.
HOW PATHETIC IS THIS GOING TO BE...?
YAAY
FEH
KLAK
WHO KNOWS— MAYBE IT'LL BE MORE FUN THAN WATCHING MARTIAL-ARTS AT A REAL BUDŌKAI...
YAAY
WILL NEGI-KUN BE ALL RIGHT...? AREN'T THERE A LOT OF GROWN-UPS IN THIS?
MURMUR
MURMUR
NEGI-SENSEI'S PRETTY STRONG, THOUGH... RIGHT, YUE?
H-HE SURE IS.

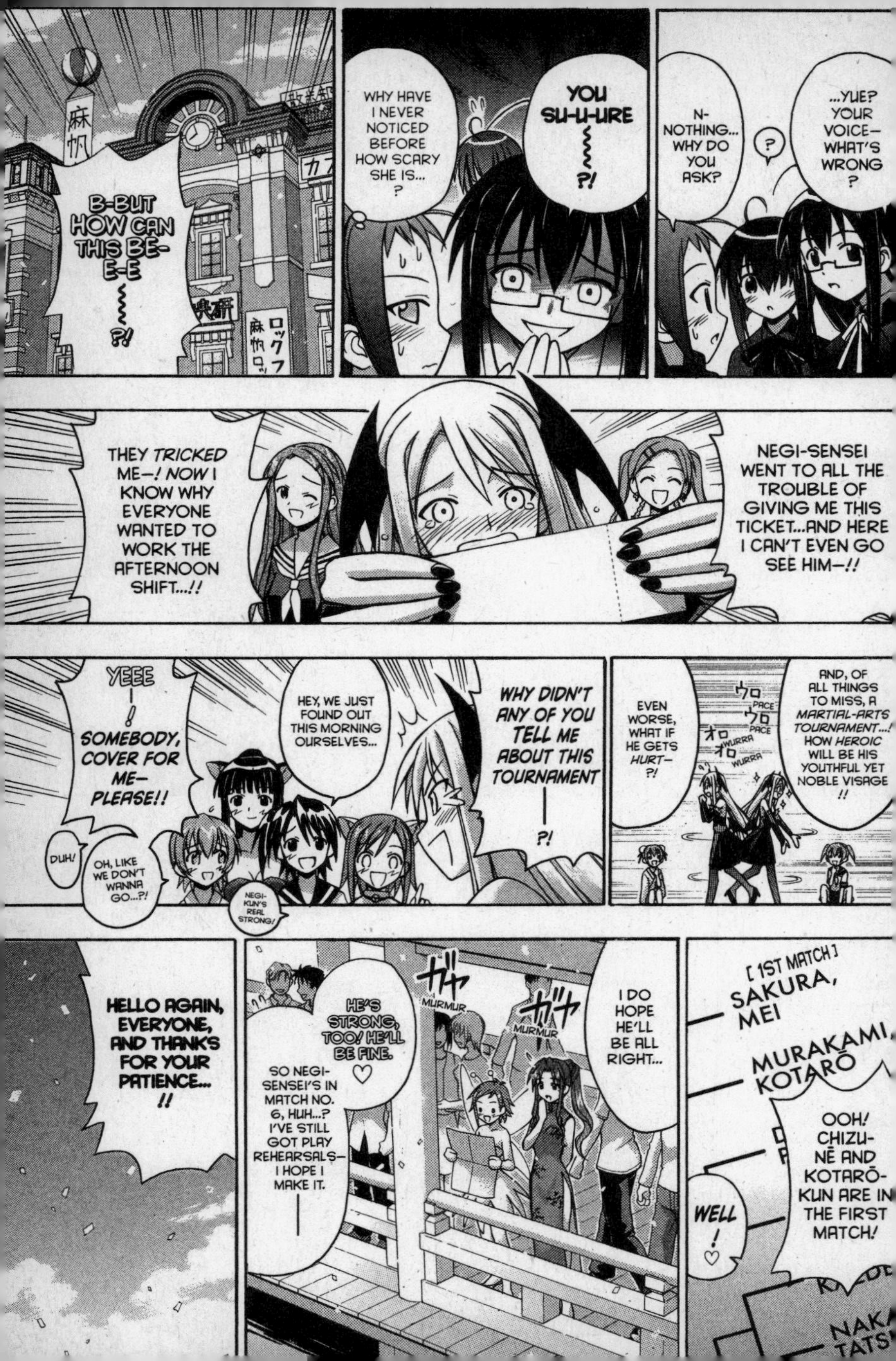
...YUE? YOUR VOICE—WHAT'S WRONG ?
?
N-NOTHING... WHY DO YOU ASK?
YOU SU-U-URE ~~~ ?!
WHY HAVE I NEVER NOTICED BEFORE HOW SCARY SHE IS... ?
B-BUT HOW CAN THIS BE-E-E ~~~ ?!
NEGI-SENSEI WENT TO ALL THE TROUBLE OF GIVING ME THIS TICKET...AND HERE I CAN'T EVEN GO SEE HIM—!!
THEY *TRICKED* ME—! *NOW* I KNOW WHY EVERYONE WANTED TO WORK THE AFTERNOON SHIFT...!!
AND, OF ALL THINGS TO MISS, A *MARTIAL-ARTS TOURNAMENT*...! HOW *HEROIC* WILL BE HIS YOUTHFUL YET NOBLE VISAGE !!
ウロ PACE ウロ PACE
オロ WURRA オロ WURRA
EVEN WORSE, WHAT IF HE GETS *HURT*— ?!
WHY DIDN'T ANY OF YOU TELL ME ABOUT THIS TOURNAMENT — ?!
HEY, WE JUST FOUND OUT THIS MORNING OURSELVES...
YEEE — ! SOMEBODY, COVER FOR ME— PLEASE!!
DUH!
OH, LIKE WE DON'T WANNA GO...?!
NEGI-KUN'S REAL STRONG!
[1ST MATCH] SAKURA, MEI
MURAKAMI, KOTARŌ
OOH! CHIZU-NĒ AND KOTARŌ-KUN ARE IN THE FIRST MATCH!
WELL! ♡
I DO HOPE HE'LL BE ALL RIGHT...
ガヤ MURMUR
ガヤ MURMUR
HE'S STRONG, TOO! HE'LL BE FINE. ♡
SO NEGI-SENSEI'S IN MATCH NO. 6, HUH...? I'VE STILL GOT PLAY REHEARSALS—I HOPE I MAKE IT. —
HELLO AGAIN, EVERYONE, AND THANKS FOR YOUR PATIENCE... !!

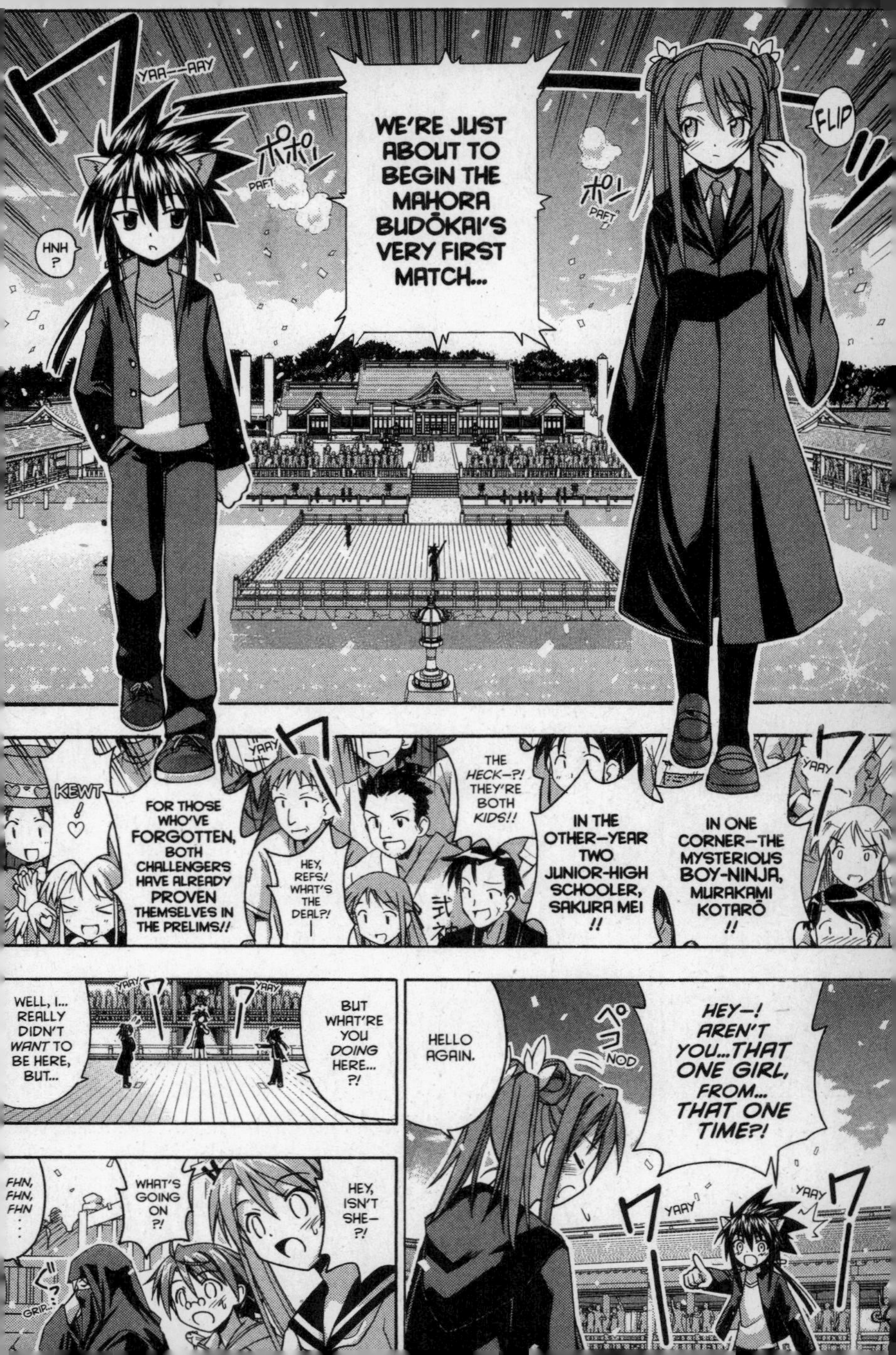
FLIP
PAFT
WE'RE JUST ABOUT TO BEGIN THE MAHORA BUDŌKAI'S VERY FIRST MATCH...
PAFT
YAAA—AAY
HNH ?
YAAY
IN ONE CORNER—THE MYSTERIOUS BOY-NINJA, MURAKAMI KOTARŌ !!
IN THE OTHER—YEAR TWO JUNIOR-HIGH SCHOOLER, SAKURA MEI !!
THE *HECK*—?! THEY'RE BOTH *KIDS*!!
YAAY
HEY, REFS! WHAT'S THE DEAL?!
FOR THOSE WHO'VE FORGOTTEN, BOTH CHALLENGERS HAVE ALREADY PROVEN THEMSELVES IN THE PRELIMS!!
KEWT ! ♡
HEY—! AREN'T YOU...THAT ONE GIRL, FROM... THAT ONE TIME?!
NOD
HELLO AGAIN.
YAAY
YAAY
BUT WHAT'RE YOU *DOING* HERE... ?!
YAAY
YAAY
WELL, I... REALLY DIDN'T *WANT* TO BE HERE, BUT...
HEY, ISN'T SHE— ?!
WHAT'S GOING ON ?!
FHN, FHN, FHN . . .
GRIP...

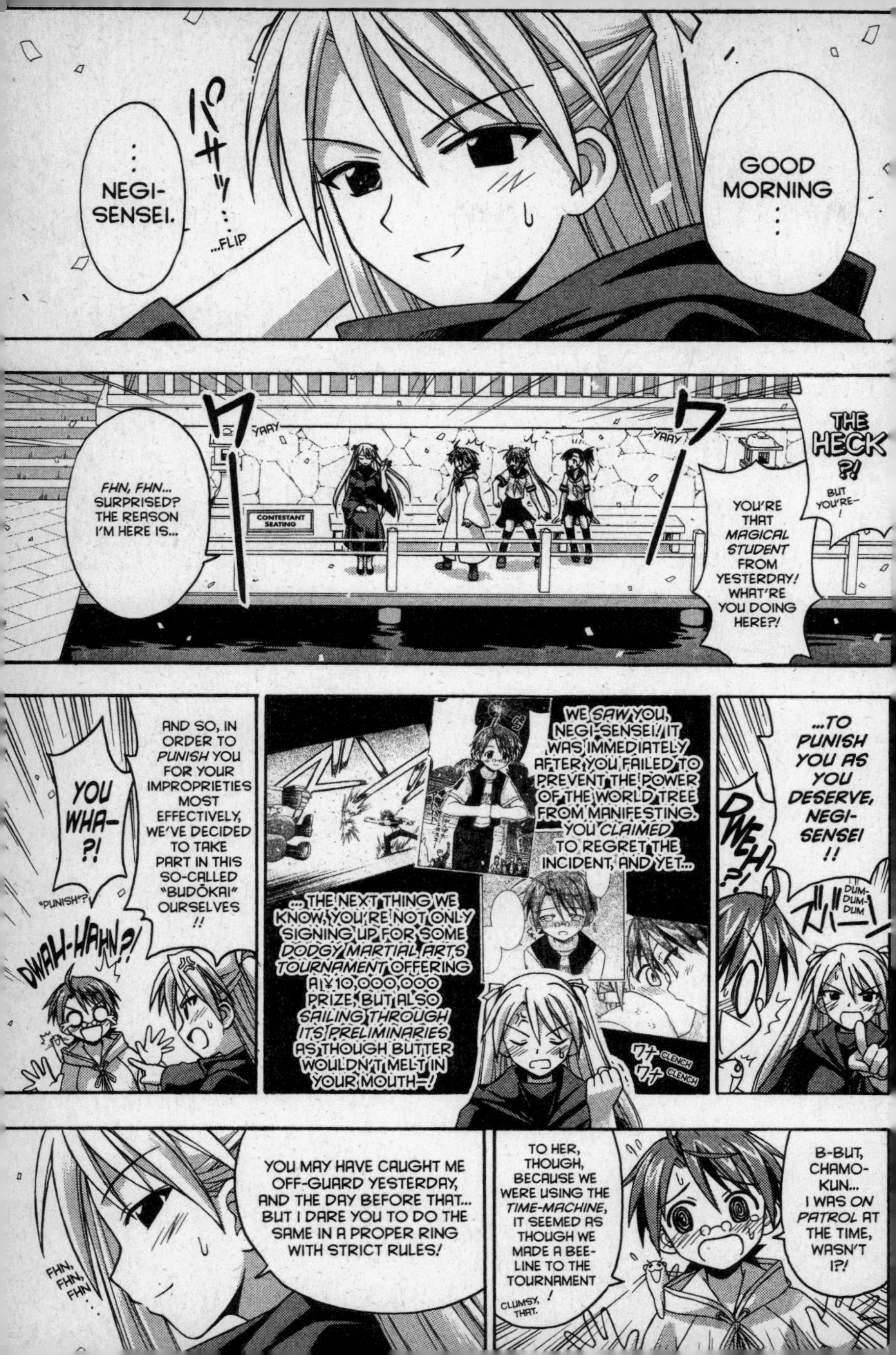
GOOD MORNING...
パサッ... ...FLIP
...NEGI-SENSEI.
THE HECK?!
BUT YOU'RE-!
YOU'RE THAT MAGICAL STUDENT FROM YESTERDAY! WHAT'RE YOU DOING HERE?!
ワー YAAY
ワー YAAY
CONTESTANT SEATING
FHN, FHN... SURPRISED? THE REASON I'M HERE IS...
...TO PUNISH YOU AS YOU DESERVE, NEGI-SENSEI!!
DWEH?!
DUM-DUM-DUM
WE SAW YOU, NEGI-SENSEI! IT WAS IMMEDIATELY AFTER YOU FAILED TO PREVENT THE POWER OF THE WORLD TREE FROM MANIFESTING. YOU CLAIMED TO REGRET THE INCIDENT, AND YET...
...THE NEXT THING WE KNOW, YOU'RE NOT ONLY SIGNING UP FOR SOME DODGY MARTIAL ARTS TOURNAMENT OFFERING A ¥10,000,000 PRIZE, BUT ALSO SAILING THROUGH ITS PRELIMINARIES AS THOUGH BUTTER WOULDN'T MELT IN YOUR MOUTH-!
ワナ CLENCH ワナ CLENCH
AND SO, IN ORDER TO PUNISH YOU FOR YOUR IMPROPRIETIES MOST EFFECTIVELY, WE'VE DECIDED TO TAKE PART IN THIS SO-CALLED "BUDŌKAI" OURSELVES!!
YOU WHA-?!
PUNISH?
DWAH-HAHN?!
B-BUT, CHAMO-KUN... I WAS ON PATROL AT THE TIME, WASN'T I?!
TO HER, THOUGH, BECAUSE WE WERE USING THE TIME-MACHINE, IT SEEMED AS THOUGH WE MADE A BEE-LINE TO THE TOURNAMENT
CLUMSY, THAT!
YOU MAY HAVE CAUGHT ME OFF-GUARD YESTERDAY, AND THE DAY BEFORE THAT... BUT I DARE YOU TO DO THE SAME IN A PROPER RING WITH STRICT RULES!
FHN, FHN, FHN...

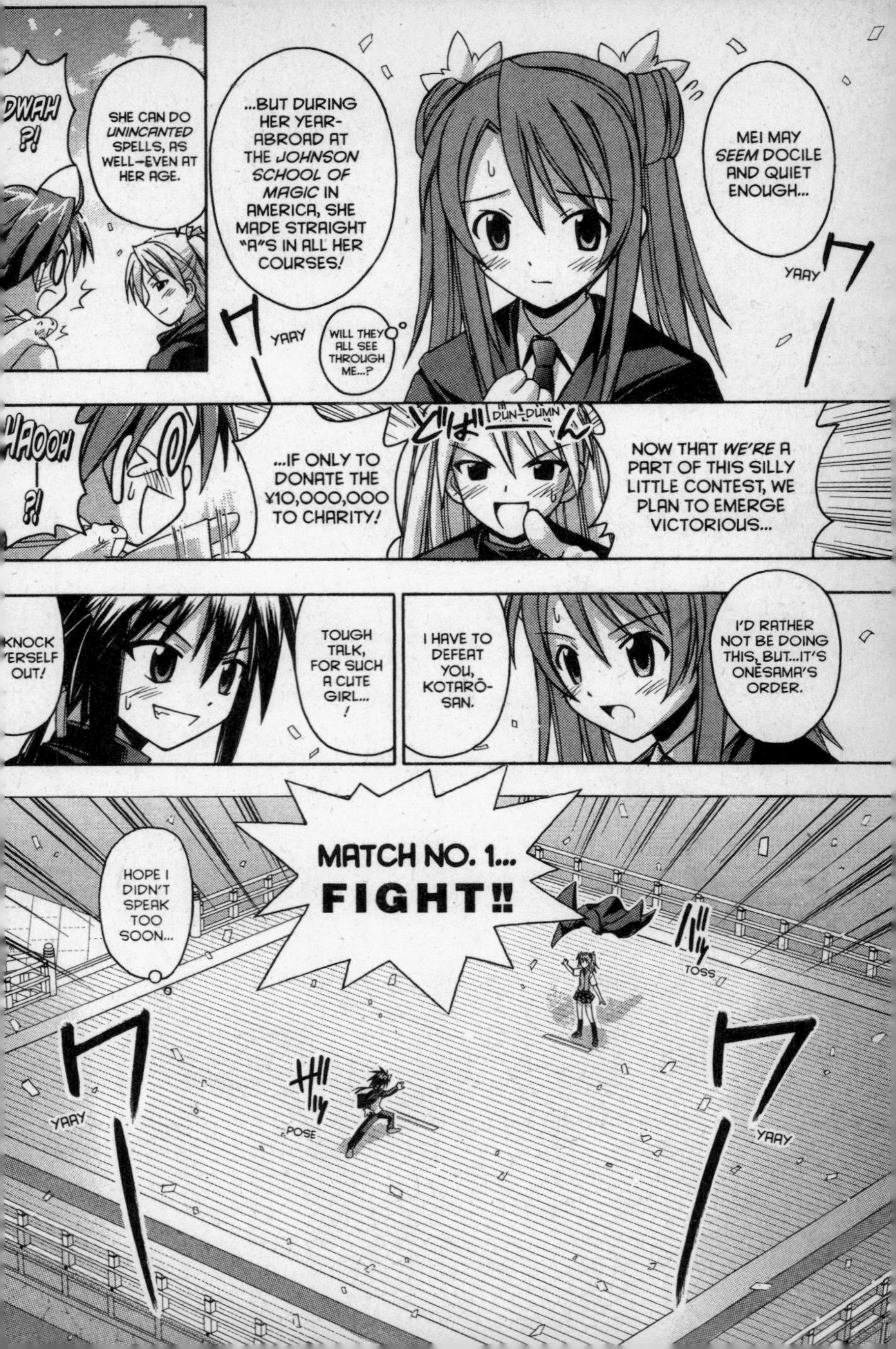
MEI MAY *SEEM* DOCILE AND QUIET ENOUGH...
YAAY
...BUT DURING HER YEAR-ABROAD AT THE *JOHNSON SCHOOL OF MAGIC* IN AMERICA, SHE MADE STRAIGHT "A"S IN ALL HER COURSES!
WILL THEY ALL SEE THROUGH ME...?
YAAY
SHE CAN DO *UNINCANTED* SPELLS, AS WELL—EVEN AT HER AGE.
DWAH ?!
NOW THAT *WE'RE* A PART OF THIS SILLY LITTLE CONTEST, WE PLAN TO EMERGE VICTORIOUS...
DUN-DUMN
...IF ONLY TO DONATE THE ¥10,000,000 TO CHARITY!
HAOOH ?!
I'D RATHER NOT BE DOING THIS, BUT...IT'S ONĒSAMA'S ORDER.
I HAVE TO DEFEAT YOU, KOTARŌ-SAN.
TOUGH TALK, FOR SUCH A CUTE GIRL...!
KNOCK YERSELF OUT!
MATCH NO. 1... FIGHT!!
TOSS
YAAY
HOPE I DIDN'T SPEAK TOO SOON...
POSE
YAAY

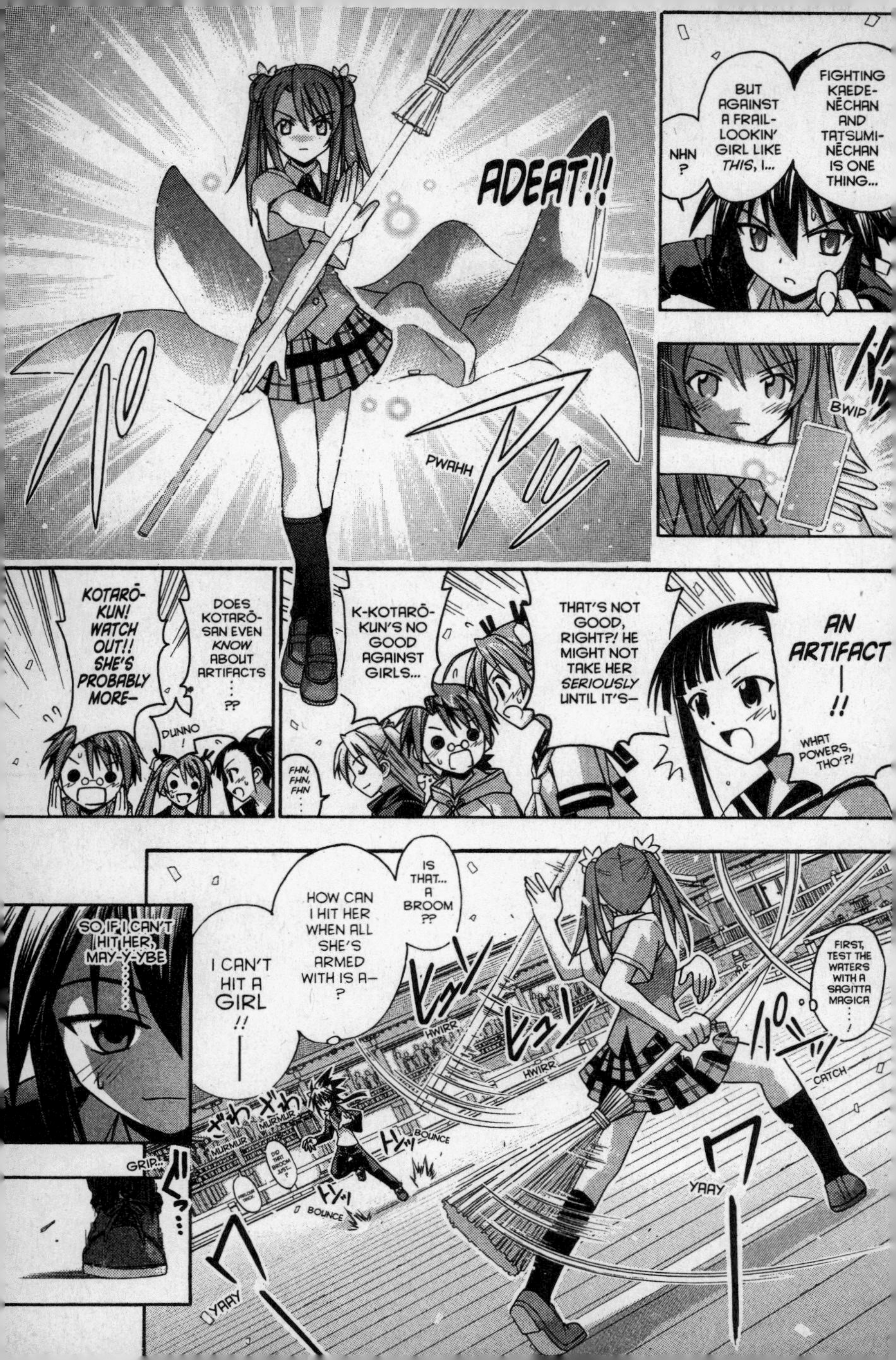
FIGHTING KAEDE-NĒCHAN AND TATSUMI-NĒCHAN IS ONE THING...
BUT AGAINST A FRAIL-LOOKIN' GIRL LIKE *THIS*, I...
NHN?
BWIP
ADEAT!!
PWAHH
AN ARTIFACT—!!
THAT'S NOT GOOD, RIGHT?! HE MIGHT NOT TAKE HER *SERIOUSLY* UNTIL IT'S—
WHAT POWERS, THO'?!
K-KOTARŌ-KUN'S NO GOOD AGAINST GIRLS...
FHN, FHN, FHN...
DOES KOTARŌ-SAN EVEN *KNOW* ABOUT ARTIFACTS...??
KOTARŌ-KUN! WATCH OUT!! SHE'S PROBABLY MORE—
DUNNO!
??
FIRST, TEST THE WATERS WITH A SAGITTA MAGICA...!
CATCH
IS THAT... A BROOM??
HOW CAN I HIT HER WHEN ALL SHE'S ARMED WITH IS A—?
HWIRR
HWIRR
YAAY
BOUNCE
MURMUR
MURMUR
DID THAT BROOM JUST...?
BOUNCE
YAAY
I CAN'T HIT A GIRL!!—
SO IF I CAN'T HIT HER, MAY-Y-YBE......
GRIP...

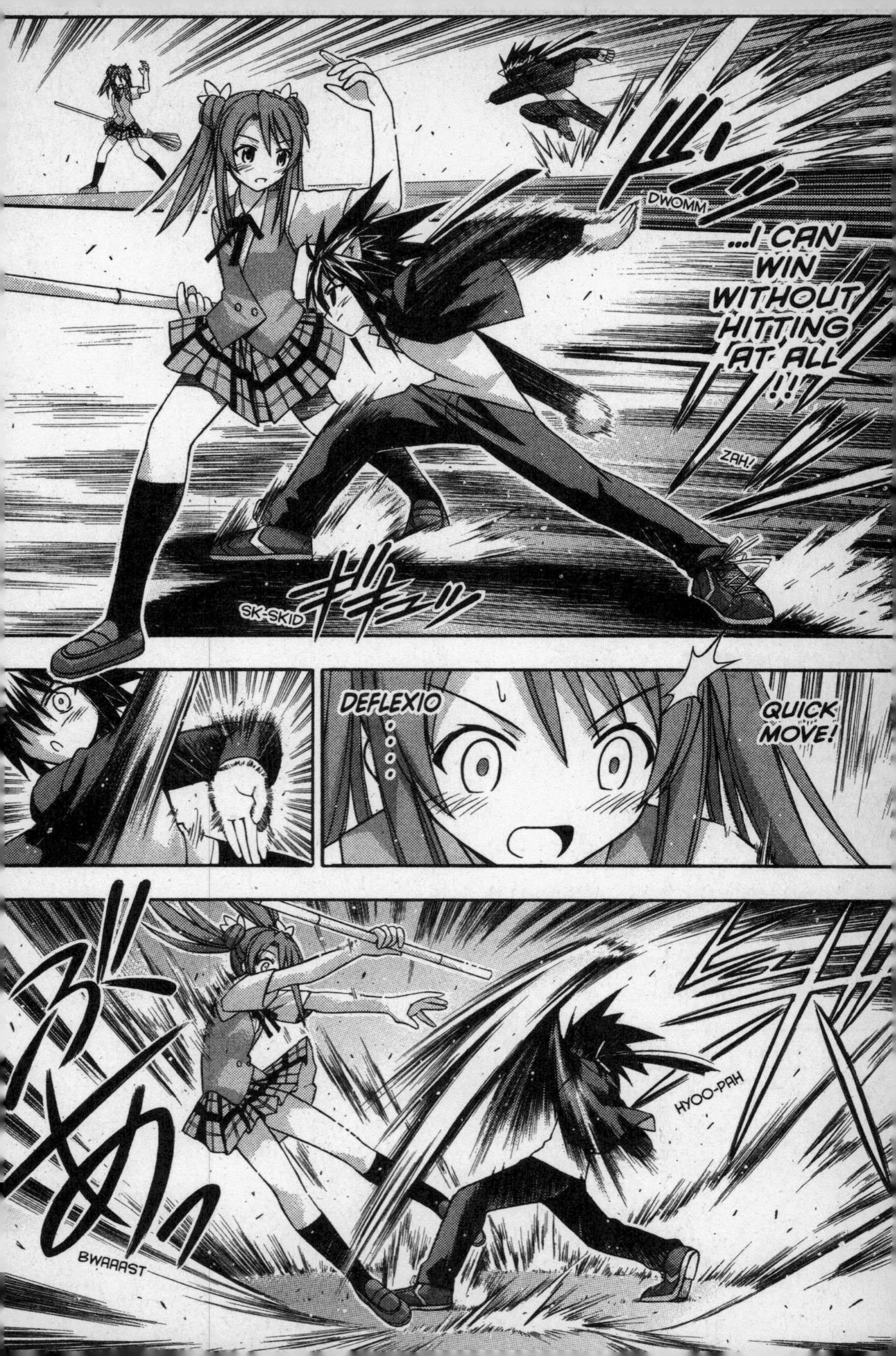
DWOMM
...I CAN WIN WITHOUT HITTING AT ALL!!
ZAH!
SK-SKID
QUICK MOVE!
DEFLEXIO
HYOO-PAH
BWAAAST

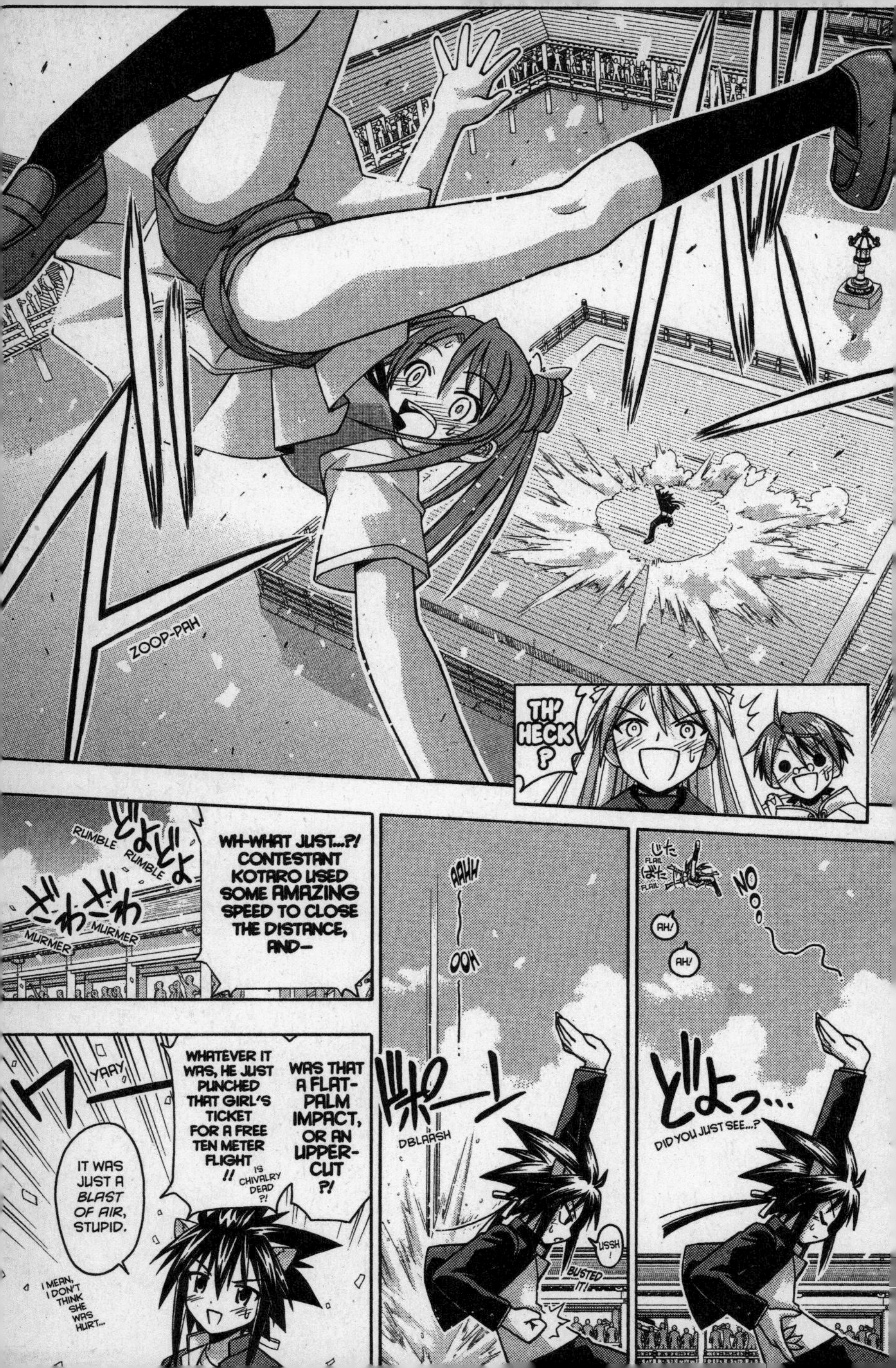

ZOOP-PAH
TH' HECK ?
じたばた
FLAIL FLAIL
NOOO
AH!
AH!
どよっ…
DID YOU JUST SEE...?
AAHH—OOH
ドポーー!
DBLAASH
USSH
BUSTED IT!
どよどよ
RUMBLE RUMBLE
ざわざわ
MURMER MURMER
WH-WHAT JUST...?! CONTESTANT KOTARO USED SOME AMAZING SPEED TO CLOSE THE DISTANCE, AND—
WAS THAT A FLAT-PALM IMPACT, OR AN UPPER-CUT ?!
WHATEVER IT WAS, HE JUST PUNCHED THAT GIRL'S TICKET FOR A FREE TEN METER FLIGHT !!
IS CHIVALRY DEAD ?!
ワー
YAAY
IT WAS JUST A BLAST OF AIR, STUPID.
I MEAN, I DON'T THINK SHE WAS HURT...

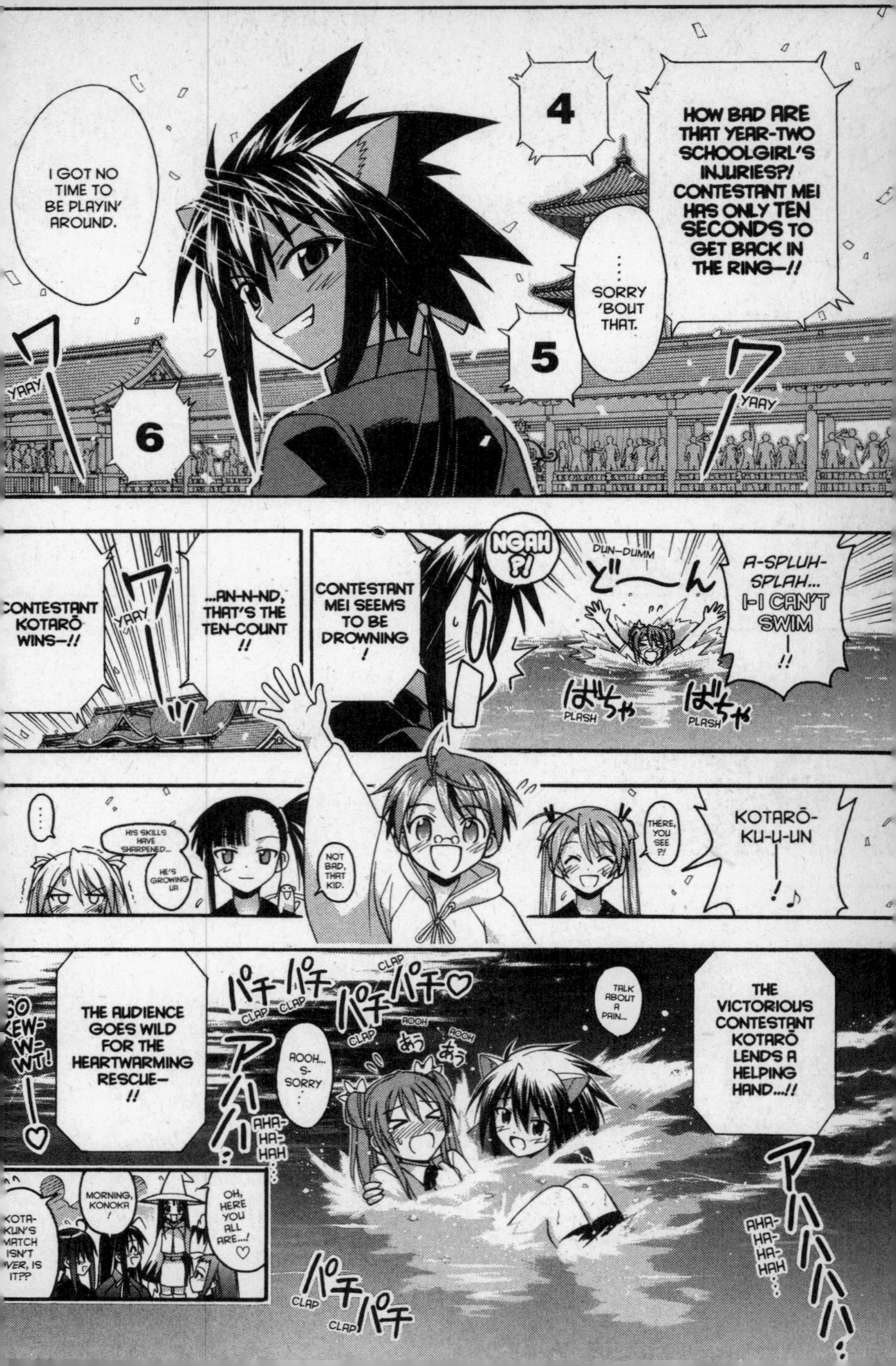
HOW BAD ARE THAT YEAR-TWO SCHOOLGIRL'S INJURIES?! CONTESTANT MEI HAS ONLY TEN SECONDS TO GET BACK IN THE RING—!!
4
... SORRY 'BOUT THAT.
5
YAAY
I GOT NO TIME TO BE PLAYIN' AROUND.
6
YAAY
A-SPLUH-SPLAH... I-I CAN'T SWIM—!!
DUN-DUMM
どーん
ばちゃ PLASH
ばちゃ PLASH
NGAH ?!
CONTESTANT MEI SEEMS TO BE DROWNING!
...AN-N-ND, THAT'S THE TEN-COUNT!!
YAAY
CONTESTANT KOTARŌ WINS—!!
KOTARŌ-KU-U-UN—!♪
THERE, YOU SEE?!
NOT BAD, THAT KID.
HIS SKILLS HAVE SHARPENED... HE'S GROWING UP.
......
THE VICTORIOUS CONTESTANT KOTARŌ LENDS A HELPING HAND...!!
TALK ABOUT A PAIN...
AHA-HA-HA-HAH
あう AOOH
あう AOOH
AOOH... S-SORRY...
パチパチ CLAP CLAP
パチパチ♡ CLAP CLAP
AHA-HA-HAH
THE AUDIENCE GOES WILD FOR THE HEARTWARMING RESCUE—!!
SO KEW-W-WT!♥
パチパチ CLAP CLAP
OH, HERE YOU ALL ARE...!♡
MORNING, KONOKA!
KOTA-KUN'S MATCH ISN'T VER, IS IT??

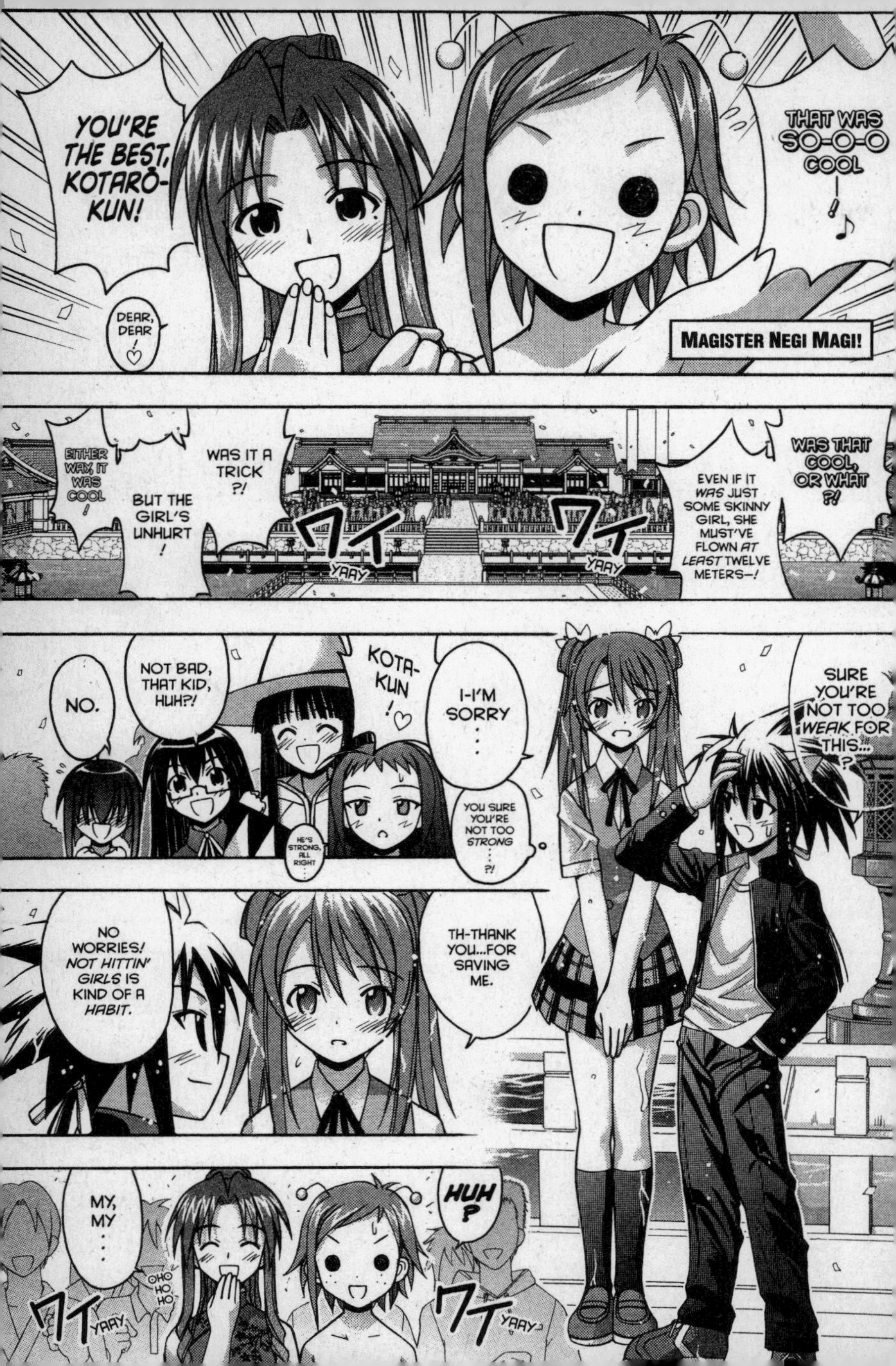
THAT WAS SO-O-O COOL!♪
MAGISTER NEGI MAGI!
YOU'RE THE BEST, KOTARŌ-KUN!
DEAR, DEAR!♡
WAS THAT COOL, OR WHAT?!
EVEN IF IT WAS JUST SOME SKINNY GIRL, SHE MUST'VE FLOWN AT LEAST TWELVE METERS—!
YAAY
YAAY
WAS IT A TRICK?!
BUT THE GIRL'S UNHURT!
EITHER WAY, IT WAS COOL!
SURE YOU'RE NOT TOO WEAK FOR THIS...?
I-I'M SORRY...
KOTA-KUN!♡
YOU SURE YOU'RE NOT TOO STRONG...?!
NOT BAD, THAT KID, HUH?!
HE'S STRONG, ALL RIGHT...
NO.
TH-THANK YOU...FOR SAVING ME.
NO WORRIES! NOT HITTIN' GIRLS IS KIND OF A HABIT.
HUH?
YAAY
MY, MY...
OHO HO HO
YAAY

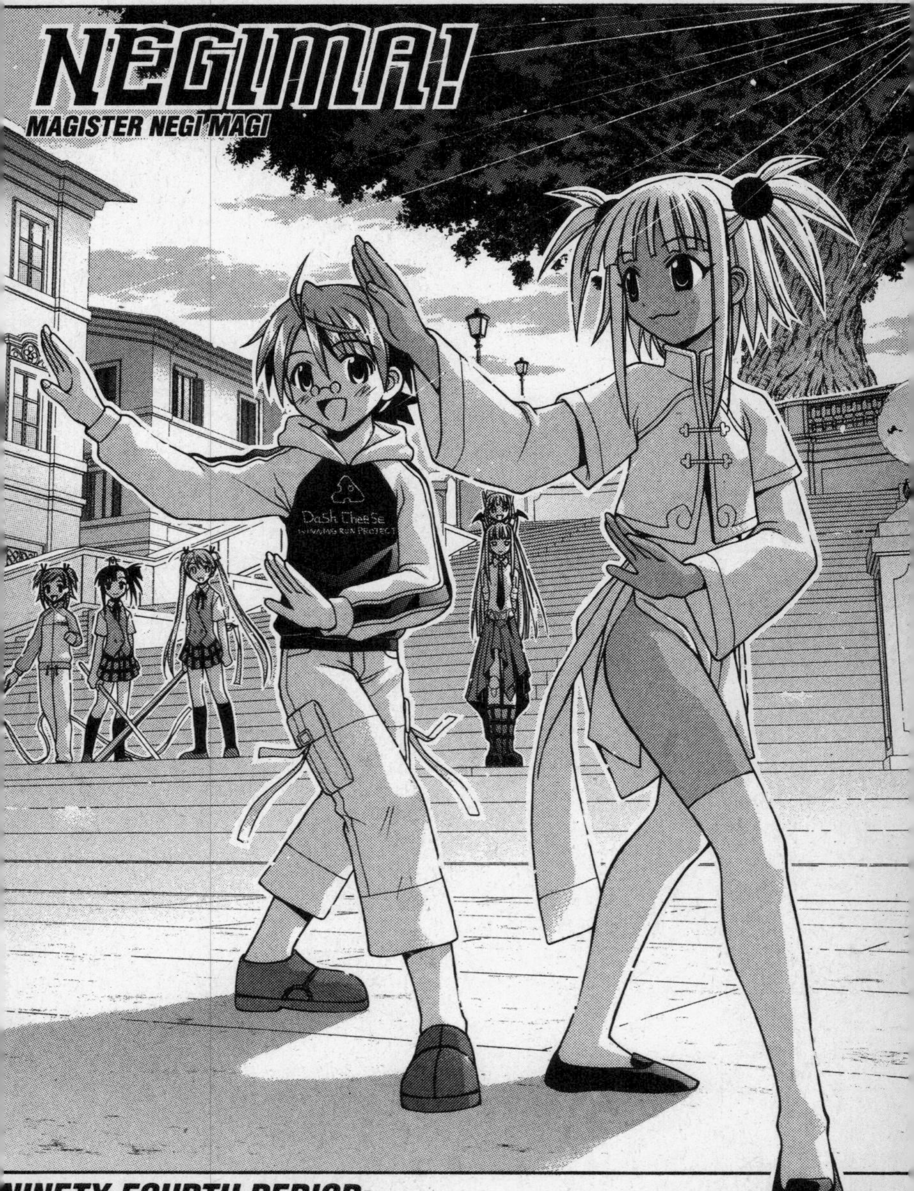
NEGIMA!
MAGISTER NEGI MAGI
DaSh CheeSe

NINETY-FOURTH PERIOD: EXTREME COMBAT! TATSUMIYA VS. KŪ FEI

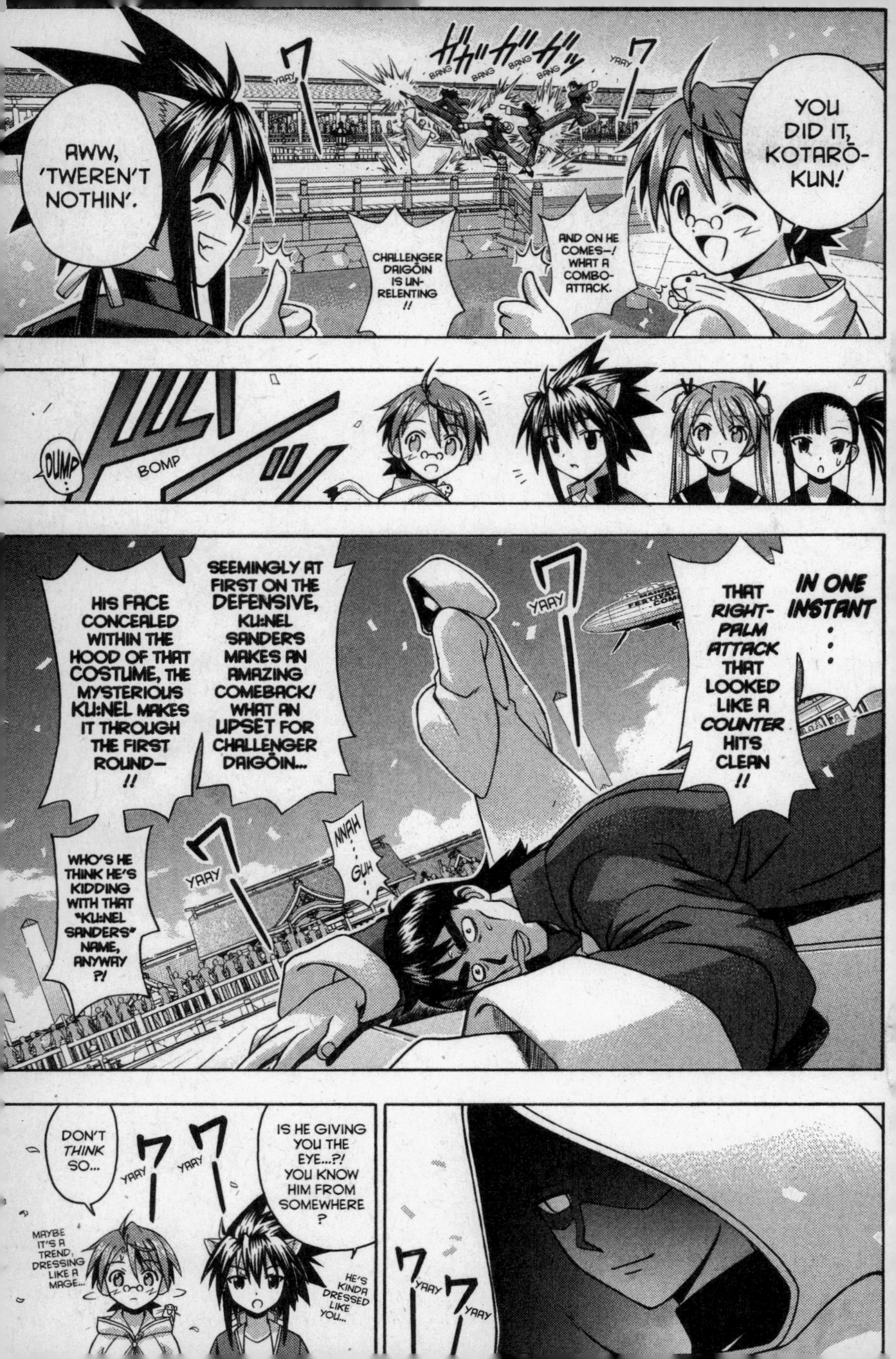
YOU DID IT, KOTARŌ-KUN!
YAAY
BANG BANG BANG BANG
AND ON HE COMES—! WHAT A COMBO-ATTACK.
CHALLENGER DAIGŌIN IS UN-RELENTING !!
YAAY
AWW, 'TWEREN'T NOTHIN'.
BOMP
DUMP
IN ONE INSTANT . . .
THAT RIGHT-PALM ATTACK THAT LOOKED LIKE A COUNTER HITS CLEAN !!
YAAY
SEEMINGLY AT FIRST ON THE DEFENSIVE, KU:NEL SANDERS MAKES AN AMAZING COMEBACK! WHAT AN UPSET FOR CHALLENGER DAIGŌIN...
HIS FACE CONCEALED WITHIN THE HOOD OF THAT COSTUME, THE MYSTERIOUS KU:NEL MAKES IT THROUGH THE FIRST ROUND— !!
NNAH... GUH
YAAY
WHO'S HE THINK HE'S KIDDING WITH THAT "KU:NEL SANDERS" NAME, ANYWAY ?!
YAAY
YAAY
IS HE GIVING YOU THE EYE...?! YOU KNOW HIM FROM SOMEWHERE ?
YAAY
YAAY
DON'T THINK SO...
HE'S KINDA DRESSED LIKE YOU...
MAYBE IT'S A TREND, DRESSING LIKE A MAGE...

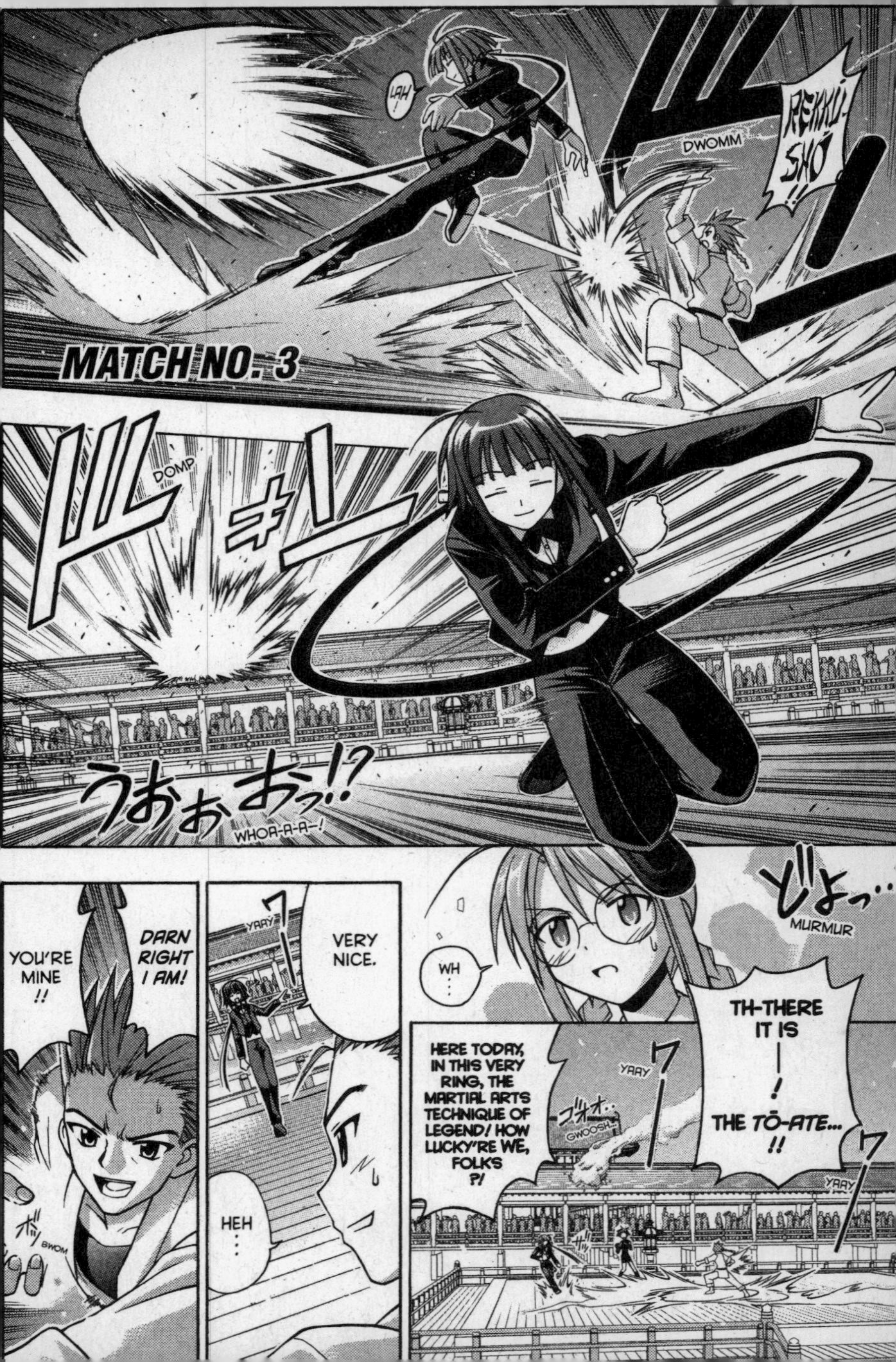
REKKŪ-SHŌ!!
DWOMM
LAH!
MATCH NO. 3
DOMP
うおぉおっ!?
WHOA-A-A-!
どよっ…
MURMUR
WH...
TH-THERE IT IS—! THE TŌ-ATE...!!
YAAY
HERE TODAY, IN THIS VERY RING, THE MARTIAL ARTS TECHNIQUE OF LEGEND! HOW LUCKY'RE WE, FOLKS?!
YAAY
GWOOSH
YAAY
VERY NICE.
HEH...
DARN RIGHT I AM!
YOU'RE MINE!!
BWOM

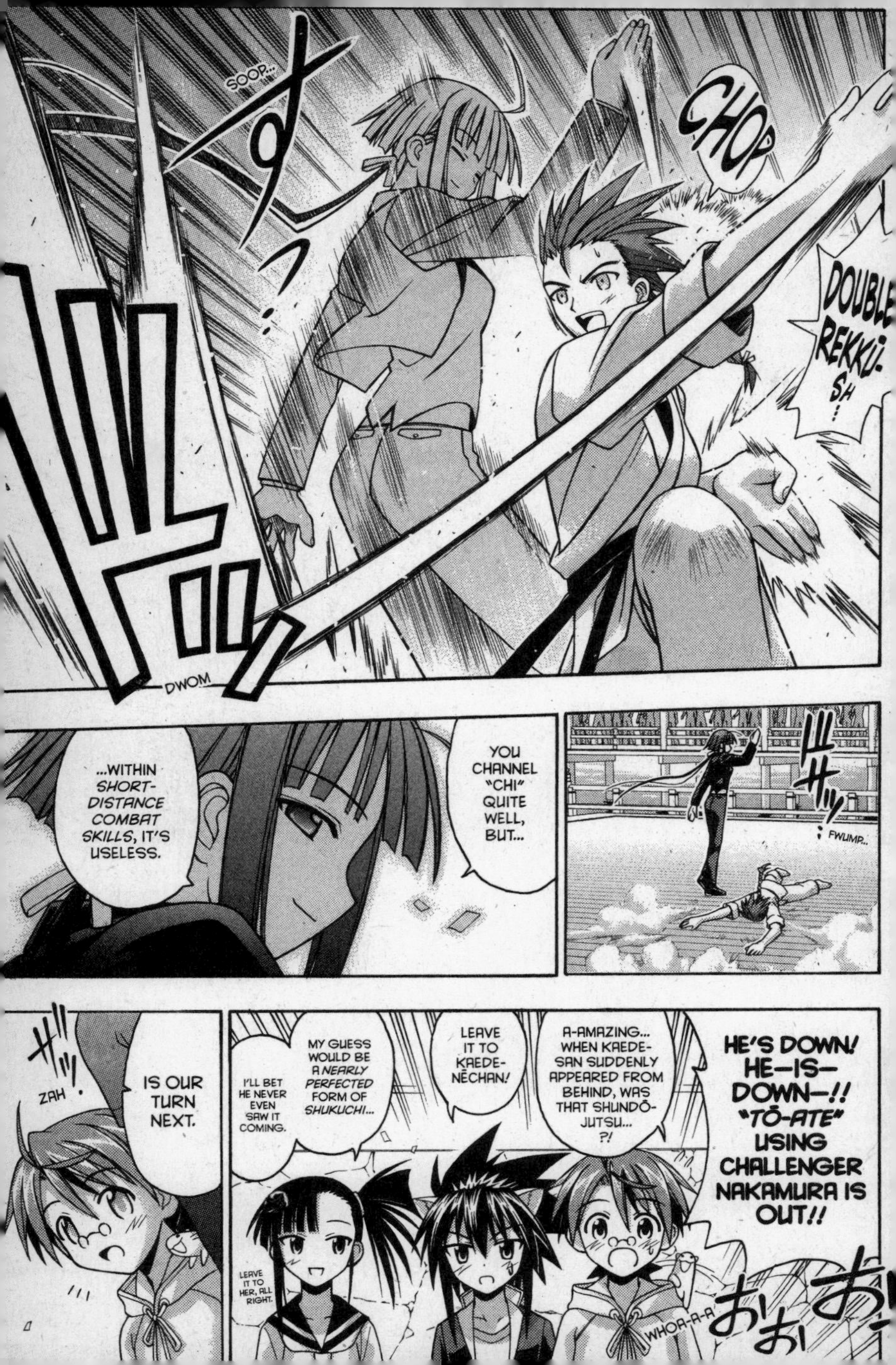

CHOP
SOOP...
DOUBLE REKKŪ-SH!
DWOM
FWUMP...
YOU CHANNEL "CHI" QUITE WELL, BUT...
...WITHIN SHORT-DISTANCE COMBAT SKILLS, IT'S USELESS.
HE'S DOWN! HE-IS-DOWN-!! "TŌ-ATE" USING CHALLENGER NAKAMURA IS OUT!!
A-AMAZING... WHEN KAEDE-SAN SUDDENLY APPEARED FROM BEHIND, WAS THAT SHUNDŌ-JUTSU...?!
LEAVE IT TO KAEDE-NĒCHAN!
MY GUESS WOULD BE A NEARLY PERFECTED FORM OF SHUKUCHI...
I'LL BET HE NEVER EVEN SAW IT COMING.
LEAVE IT TO HER, ALL RIGHT.
WHOA-A-A
ZAH
IS OUR TURN NEXT.

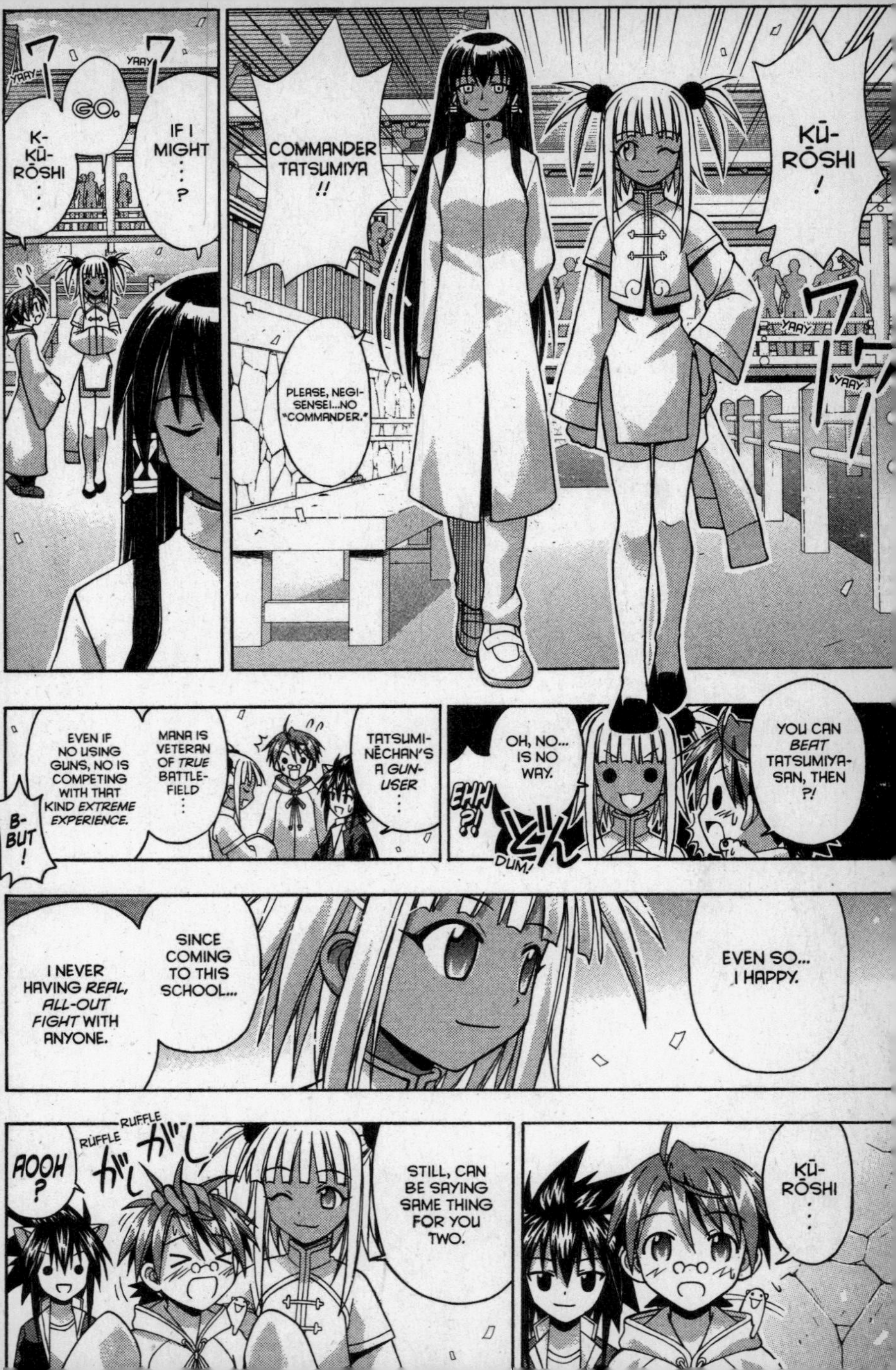
KŪ-RŌSHI!
COMMANDER TATSUMIYA!!
YAAY
YAAY
PLEASE, NEGI-SENSEI...NO "COMMANDER."
IF I MIGHT...?
YAAY
GO.
YAAY
K-KŪ-RŌSHI...
YOU CAN BEAT TATSUMIYA-SAN, THEN?!
OH, NO... IS NO WAY.
EHH?!
DUM!
TATSUMI-NĒCHAN'S A GUN-USER...
MANA IS VETERAN OF TRUE BATTLE-FIELD...
EVEN IF NO USING GUNS, NO IS COMPETING WITH THAT KIND EXTREME EXPERIENCE.
B-BUT!
EVEN SO... I HAPPY.
SINCE COMING TO THIS SCHOOL...
I NEVER HAVING REAL, ALL-OUT FIGHT WITH ANYONE.
KŪ-RŌSHI...
STILL, CAN BE SAYING SAME THING FOR YOU TWO.
RUFFLE
RUFFLE
AOOH?

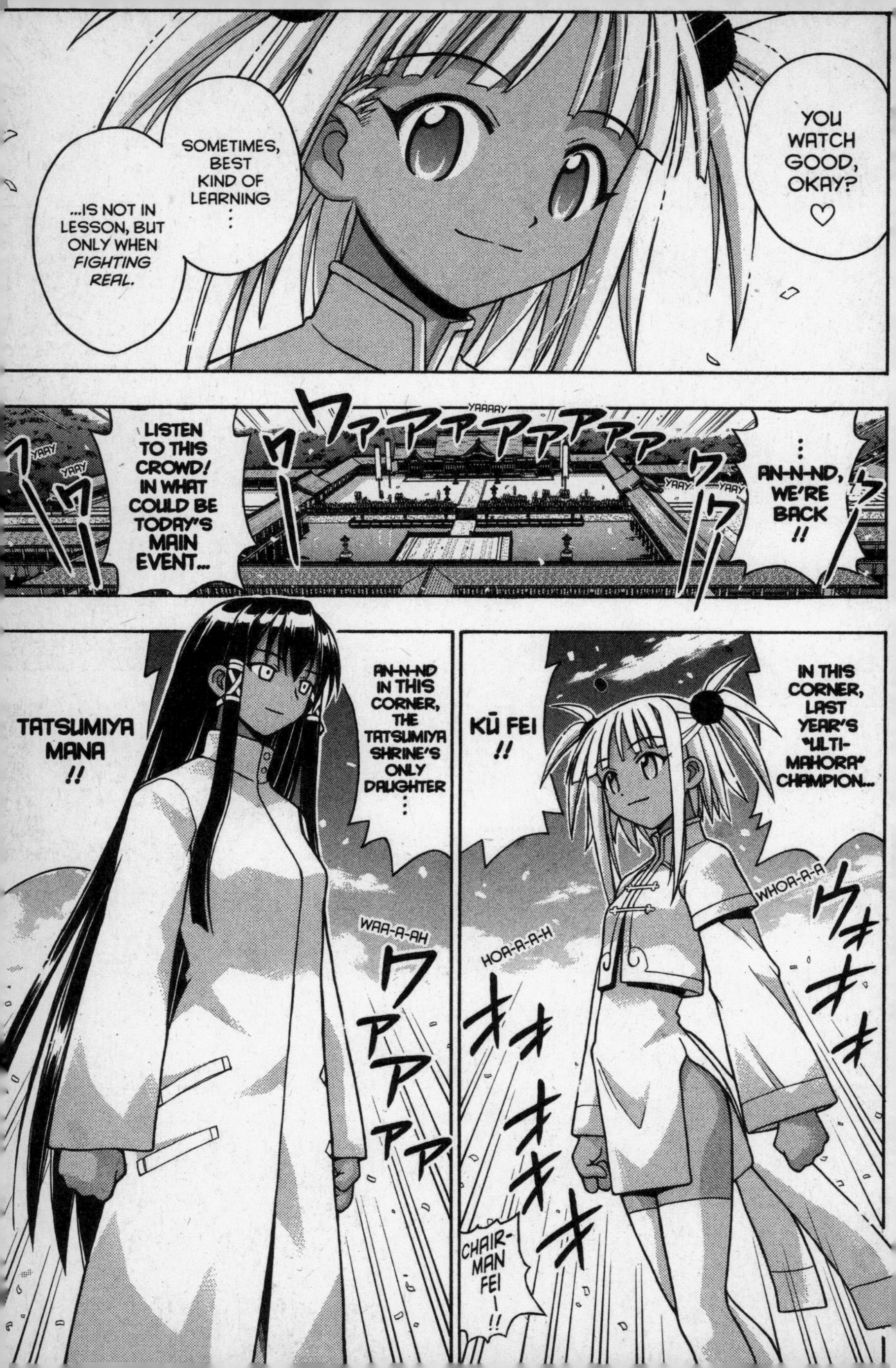
YOU WATCH GOOD, OKAY? ♡
SOMETIMES, BEST KIND OF LEARNING ...
...IS NOT IN LESSON, BUT ONLY WHEN *FIGHTING REAL.*
... AN-N-ND, WE'RE BACK !!
YAAAAY
YAAY
YAAY
YAAY
YAAY
LISTEN TO THIS CROWD! IN WHAT COULD BE TODAY'S MAIN EVENT...
IN THIS CORNER, LAST YEAR'S "ULTI-MAHORA" CHAMPION...
KŪ FEI !!
WHOA-A-A
HOA-A-A-H
CHAIR-MAN FEI !!
AN-N-ND IN THIS CORNER, THE TATSUMIYA SHRINE'S ONLY DAUGHTER ...
TATSUMIYA MANA !!
WAA-A-AH

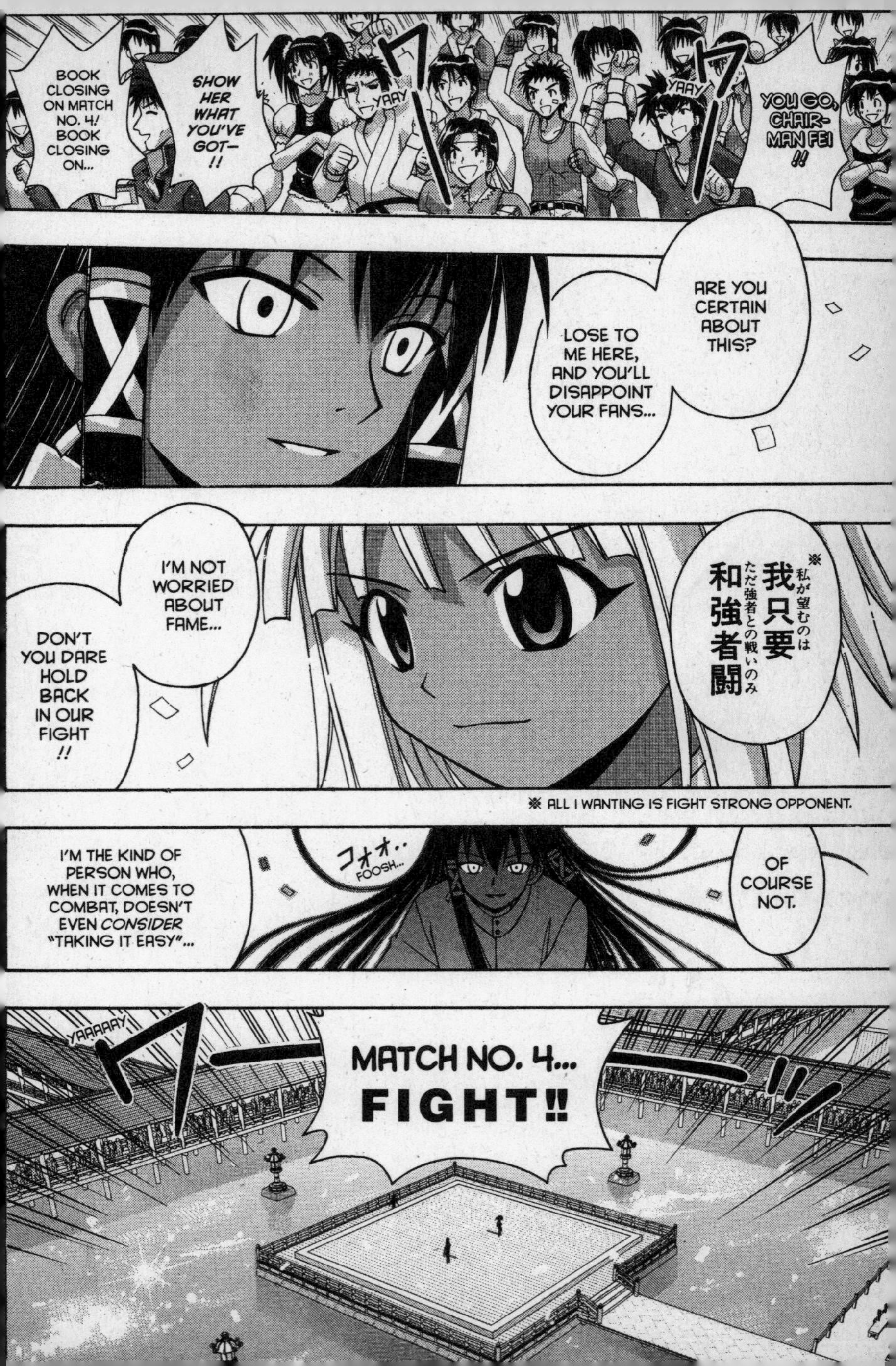
YOU GO, CHAIR-MAN FEI!!
YAAY
YAAY
SHOW HER WHAT YOU'VE GOT—!!
BOOK CLOSING ON MATCH NO. 4! BOOK CLOSING ON...
ARE YOU CERTAIN ABOUT THIS?
LOSE TO ME HERE, AND YOU'LL DISAPPOINT YOUR FANS...
※我只要和強者闘
私が望むのはただ強者との戦いのみ
I'M NOT WORRIED ABOUT FAME...
DON'T YOU DARE HOLD BACK IN OUR FIGHT!!
※ ALL I WANTING IS FIGHT STRONG OPPONENT.
OF COURSE NOT.
コォオ.. FOOSH...
I'M THE KIND OF PERSON WHO, WHEN IT COMES TO COMBAT, DOESN'T EVEN *CONSIDER* "TAKING IT EASY"...
YAAAAAY
MATCH NO. 4... **FIGHT!!**

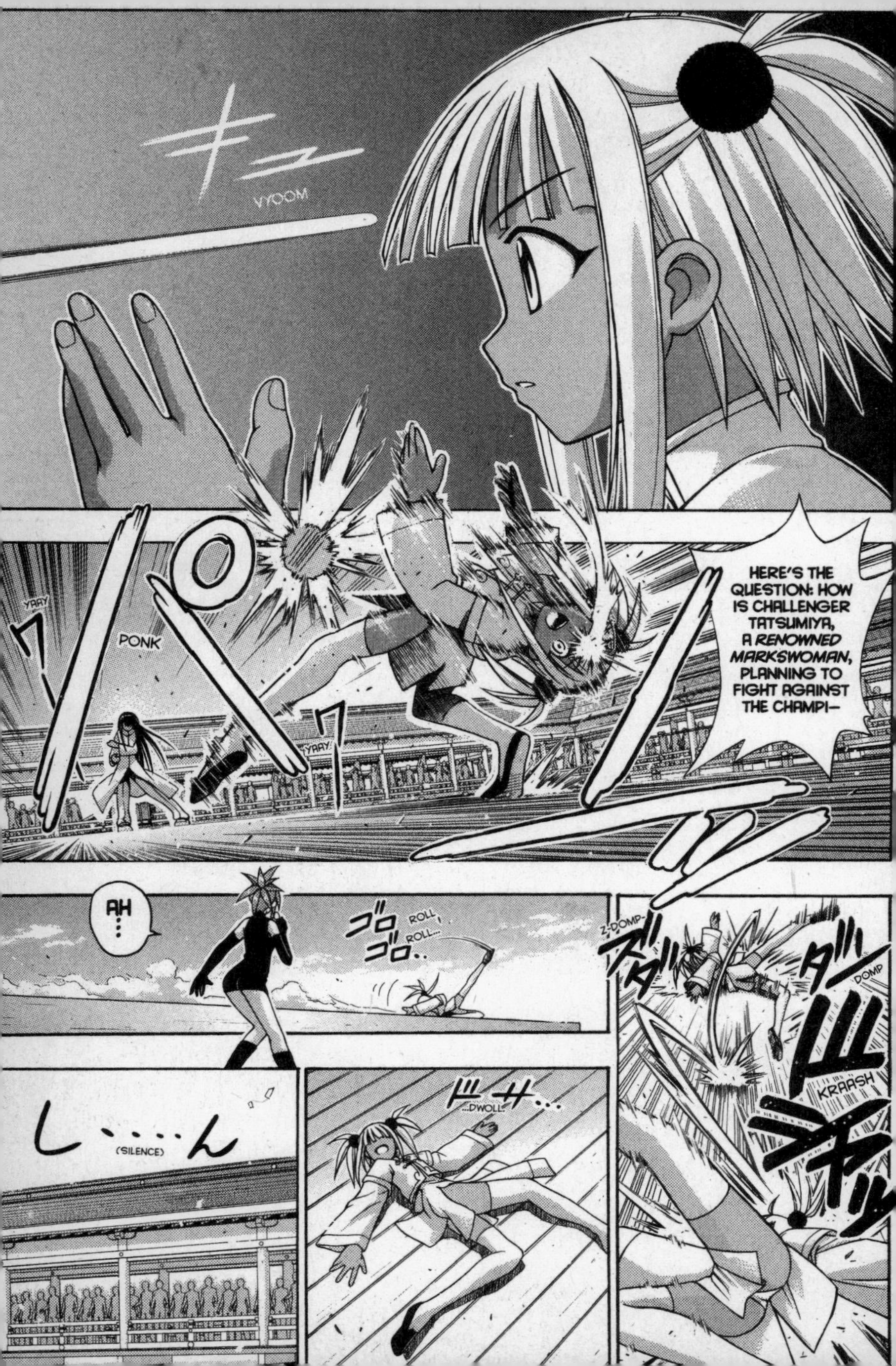

VYOOM
HERE'S THE QUESTION: HOW IS CHALLENGER TATSUMIYA, A *RENOWNED MARKSWOMAN*, PLANNING TO FIGHT AGAINST THE CHAMPI—
PONK
YAAY
YAAY!
Z-DOMP
DOMP
KRAASH
AH...
ゴロゴロ..
ROLL ROLL...
ドサ...
...DWOLL
し…ん
(SILENCE)

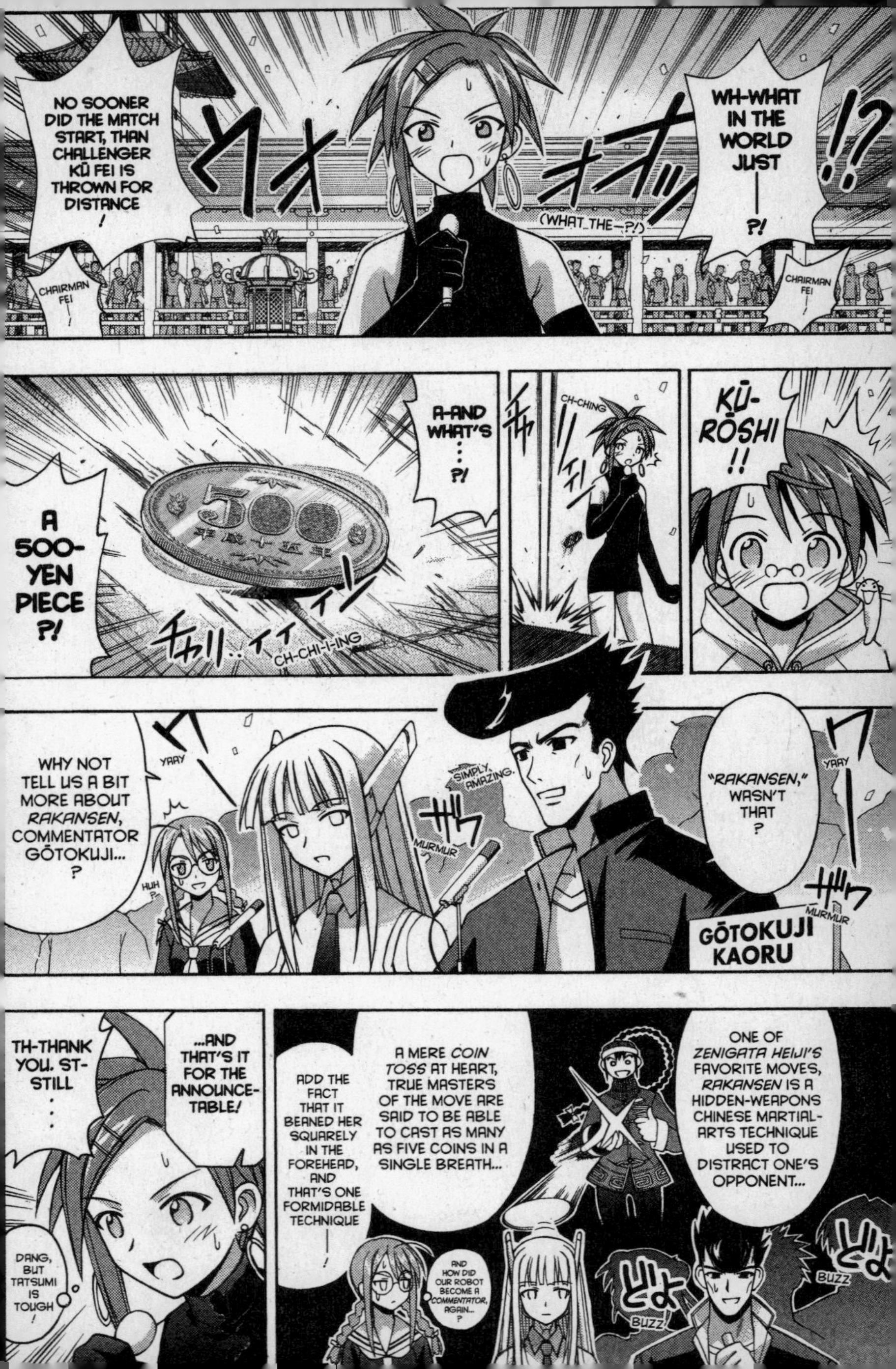
WH-WHAT IN THE WORLD JUST—?!
CHAIRMAN FEI—!
(WHAT THE—?!)
NO SOONER DID THE MATCH START, THAN CHALLENGER KŪ FEI IS THROWN FOR DISTANCE!
CHAIRMAN FEI—!
KŪ-RŌSHI!!
CH-CHING
A-AND WHAT'S...?!
A 500-YEN PIECE?!
CH-CHI-I-ING
YAAY
"RAKANSEN," WASN'T THAT?
MURMUR
GŌTOKUJI KAORU
SIMPLY, AMAZING.
MURMUR
YAAY
WHY NOT TELL US A BIT MORE ABOUT RAKANSEN, COMMENTATOR GŌTOKUJI...?
HUH?
ONE OF ZENIGATA HEIJI'S FAVORITE MOVES, RAKANSEN IS A HIDDEN-WEAPONS CHINESE MARTIAL-ARTS TECHNIQUE USED TO DISTRACT ONE'S OPPONENT...
A MERE COIN TOSS AT HEART, TRUE MASTERS OF THE MOVE ARE SAID TO BE ABLE TO CAST AS MANY AS FIVE COINS IN A SINGLE BREATH...
ADD THE FACT THAT IT BEANED HER SQUARELY IN THE FOREHEAD, AND THAT'S ONE FORMIDABLE TECHNIQUE—!
BUZZ
AND HOW DID OUR ROBOT BECOME A COMMENTATOR, AGAIN...?
BUZZ
...AND THAT'S IT FOR THE ANNOUNCE-TABLE!
TH-THANK YOU. ST-STILL...
DANG, BUT TATSUMI IS TOUGH!

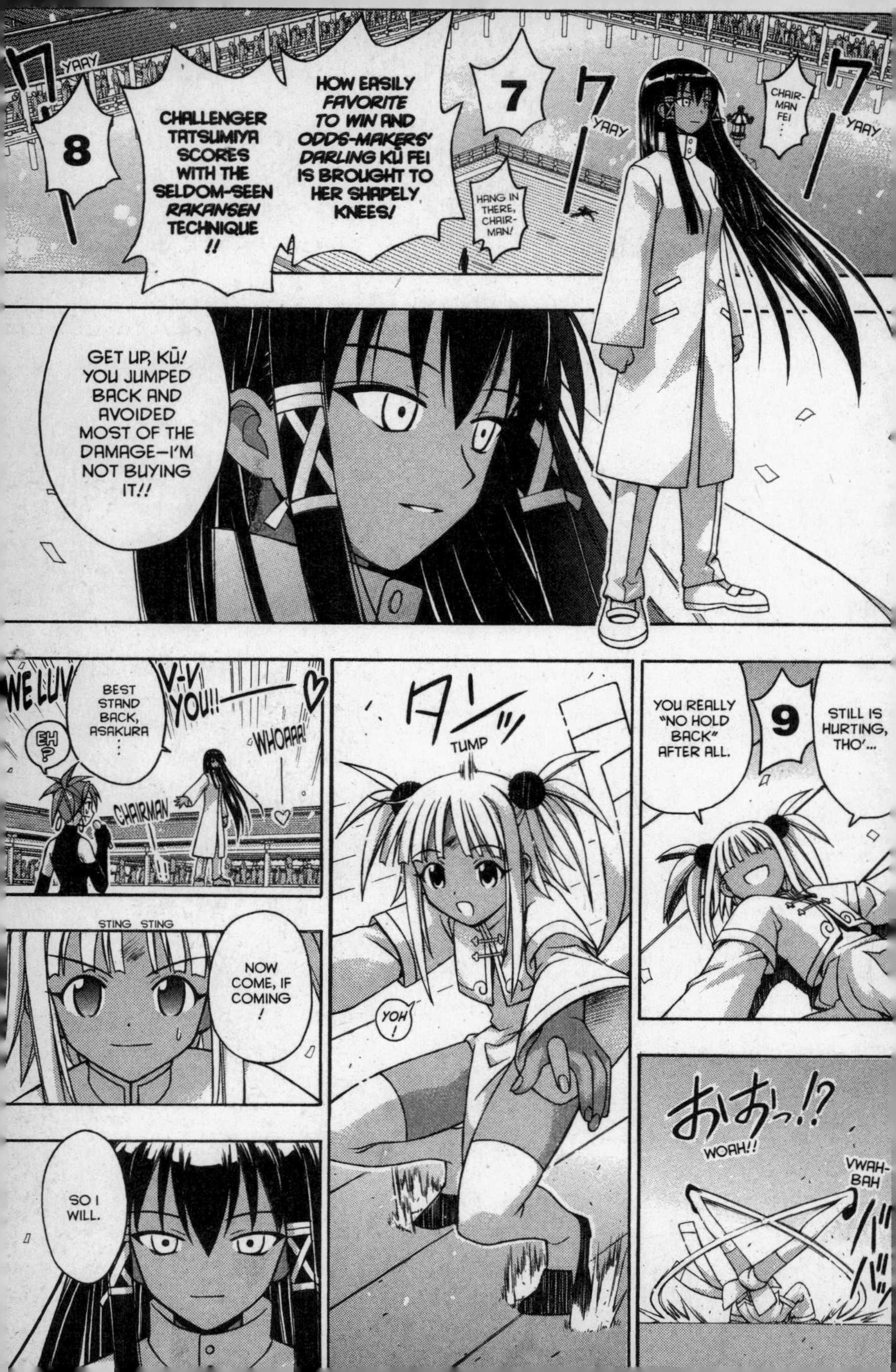
CHAIR-MAN FEI...
YAAY
7
HOW EASILY FAVORITE TO WIN AND ODDS-MAKERS' DARLING KŪ FEI IS BROUGHT TO HER SHAPELY KNEES!
HANG IN THERE, CHAIR-MAN!
CHALLENGER TATSUMIYA SCORES WITH THE SELDOM-SEEN RAKANSEN TECHNIQUE !!
8
YAAY
YAAY
GET UP, KŪ! YOU JUMPED BACK AND AVOIDED MOST OF THE DAMAGE—I'M NOT BUYING IT!!
STILL IS HURTING, THO'...
9
YOU REALLY "NO HOLD BACK" AFTER ALL.
おおっ!?
WOAH!!
VWAH-BAH
TUMP
YOH!
V-V YOU!!
WE LUV
BEST STAND BACK, ASAKURA...
WHOAAA!
CHAIRMAN
EH?
STING STING
NOW COME, IF COMING!
SO I WILL.

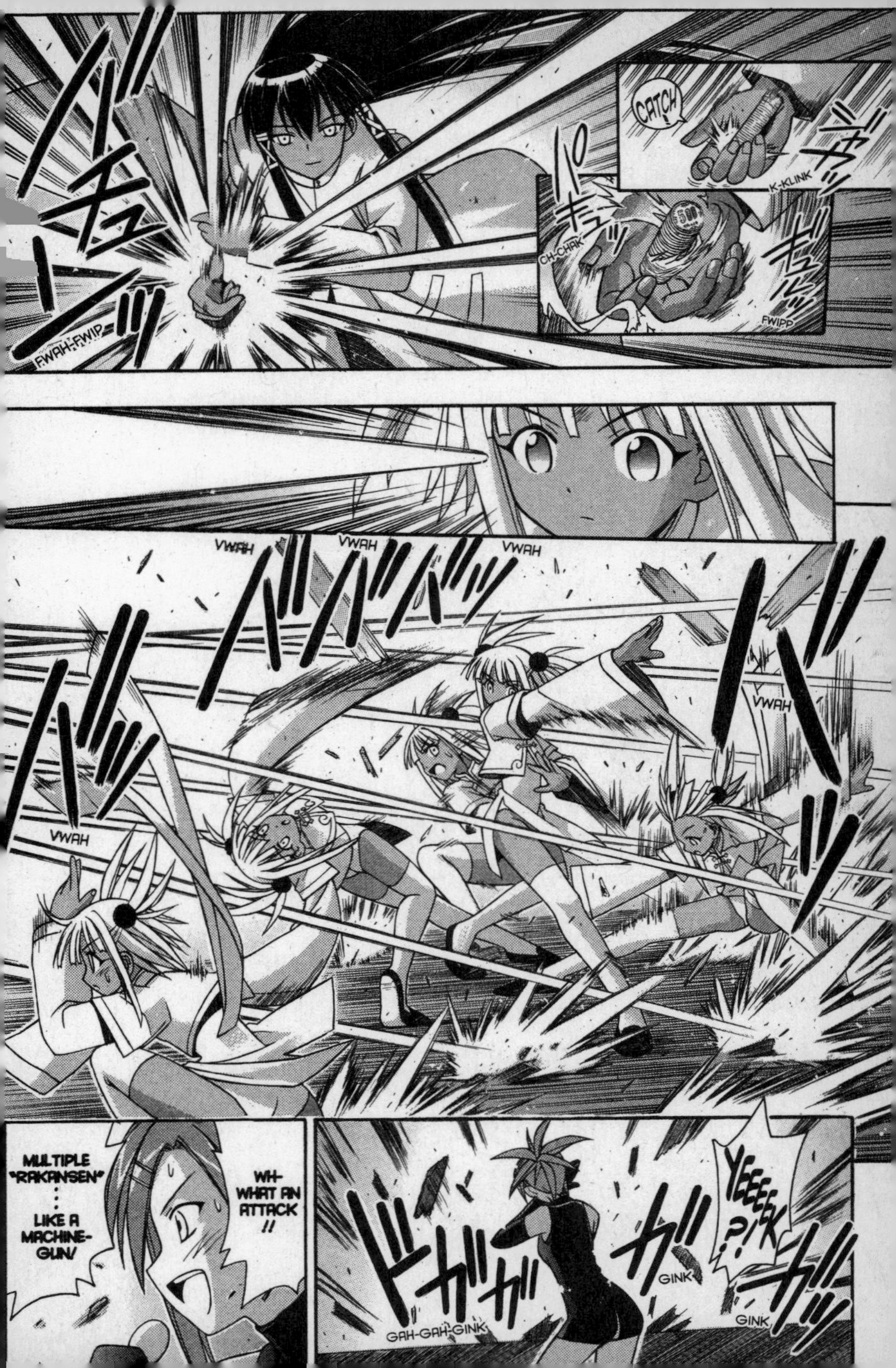
CATCH!
K-KLINK
CH-CHAK
FWIPP
FWAH-FWIP
VWAH
VWAH
VWAH
VWAH
VWAH
YEEEEEK?!
GINK
GINK
GAH-GAH-GINK
WH-WHAT AN ATTACK!!
MULTIPLE "RAKANSEN"... LIKE A MACHINE-GUN!

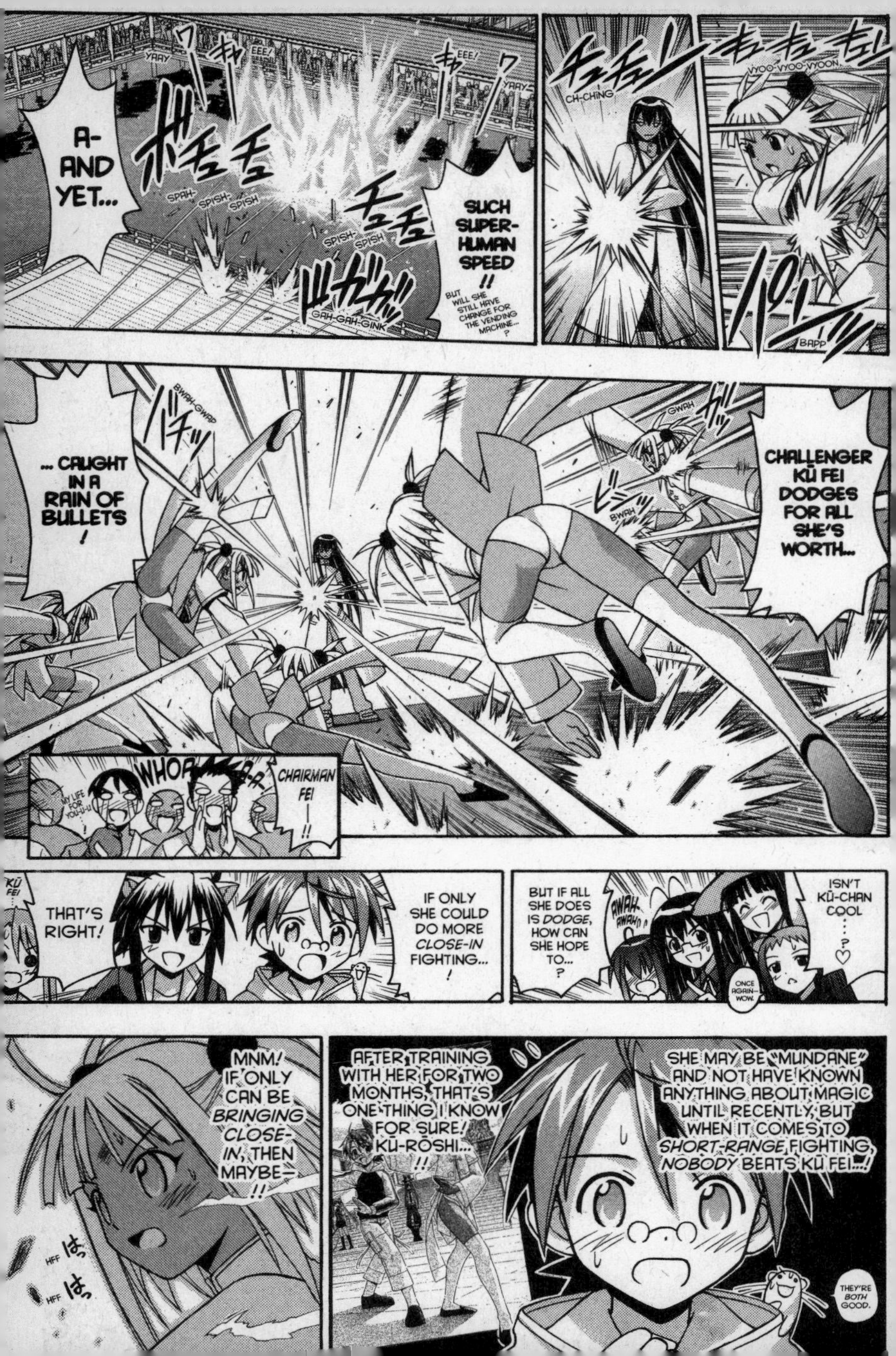
VYOO-VYOO-VYOON
BAPP
CH-CHING
YAAY
EEE!
EEE!
YAAY
A- AND YET...
SPAH- SPISH- SPISH
SPISH- SPISH
SUCH SUPER-HUMAN SPEED!!
BUT WILL SHE STILL HAVE CHANGE FOR THE VENDING MACHINE...?
GAH-GAH-GINK
CHALLENGER KŪ FEI DODGES FOR ALL SHE'S WORTH...
GWAH
BWAH
BWAH-GWAP
... CAUGHT IN A RAIN OF BULLETS!
CHAIRMAN FEI—!!
WHOA-A-R
MY LIFE FOR YOU-U-U!
ISN'T KŪ-CHAN COOL...?♡
AWAH AWAH
BUT IF ALL SHE DOES IS DODGE, HOW CAN SHE HOPE TO...?
ONCE AGAIN-WOW.
IF ONLY SHE COULD DO MORE CLOSE-IN FIGHTING...!
THAT'S RIGHT!
KŪ FEI...
SHE MAY BE "MUNDANE" AND NOT HAVE KNOWN ANYTHING ABOUT MAGIC UNTIL RECENTLY, BUT WHEN IT COMES TO SHORT-RANGE FIGHTING, NOBODY BEATS KŪ FEI...!
THEY'RE BOTH GOOD.
AFTER TRAINING WITH HER FOR TWO MONTHS, THAT'S ONE THING I KNOW FOR SURE! KŪ-RŌSHI...!!
MNM! IF ONLY CAN BE BRINGING CLOSE-IN, THEN MAYBE—!!
HFF
HFF

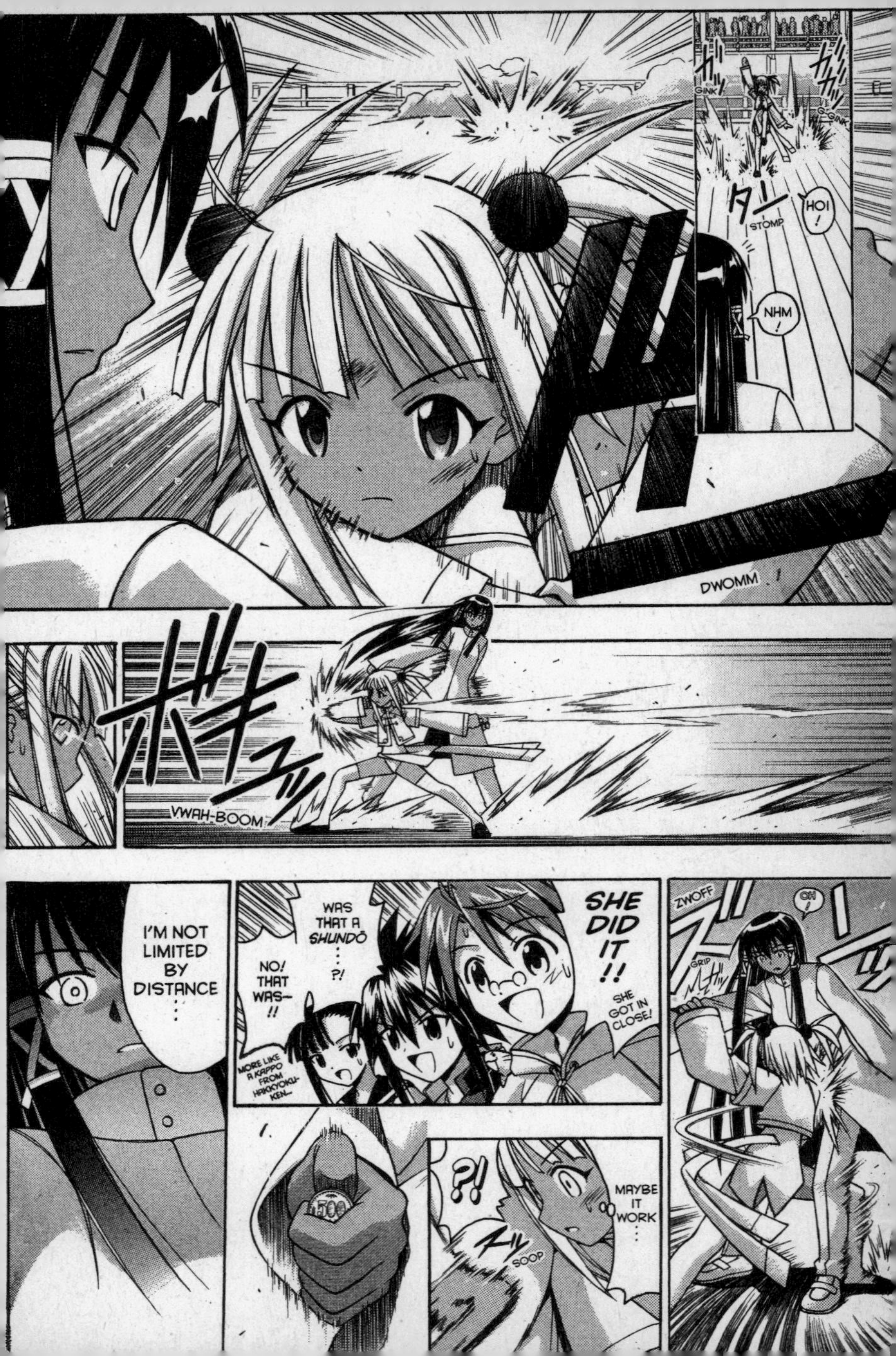
GINK
G'GINK
STOMP
HOI!
NHM!
DWOMM
VWAH-BOOM
ZWOFF
OH!
GRIP
SHE DID IT!!
SHE GOT IN CLOSE!
WAS THAT A SHUNDŌ...?!
NO! THAT WAS—!!
MORE LIKE A KAPPO FROM HAKKYOKUKEN...
?!
MAYBE IT WORK...
SOOP
I'M NOT LIMITED BY DISTANCE...

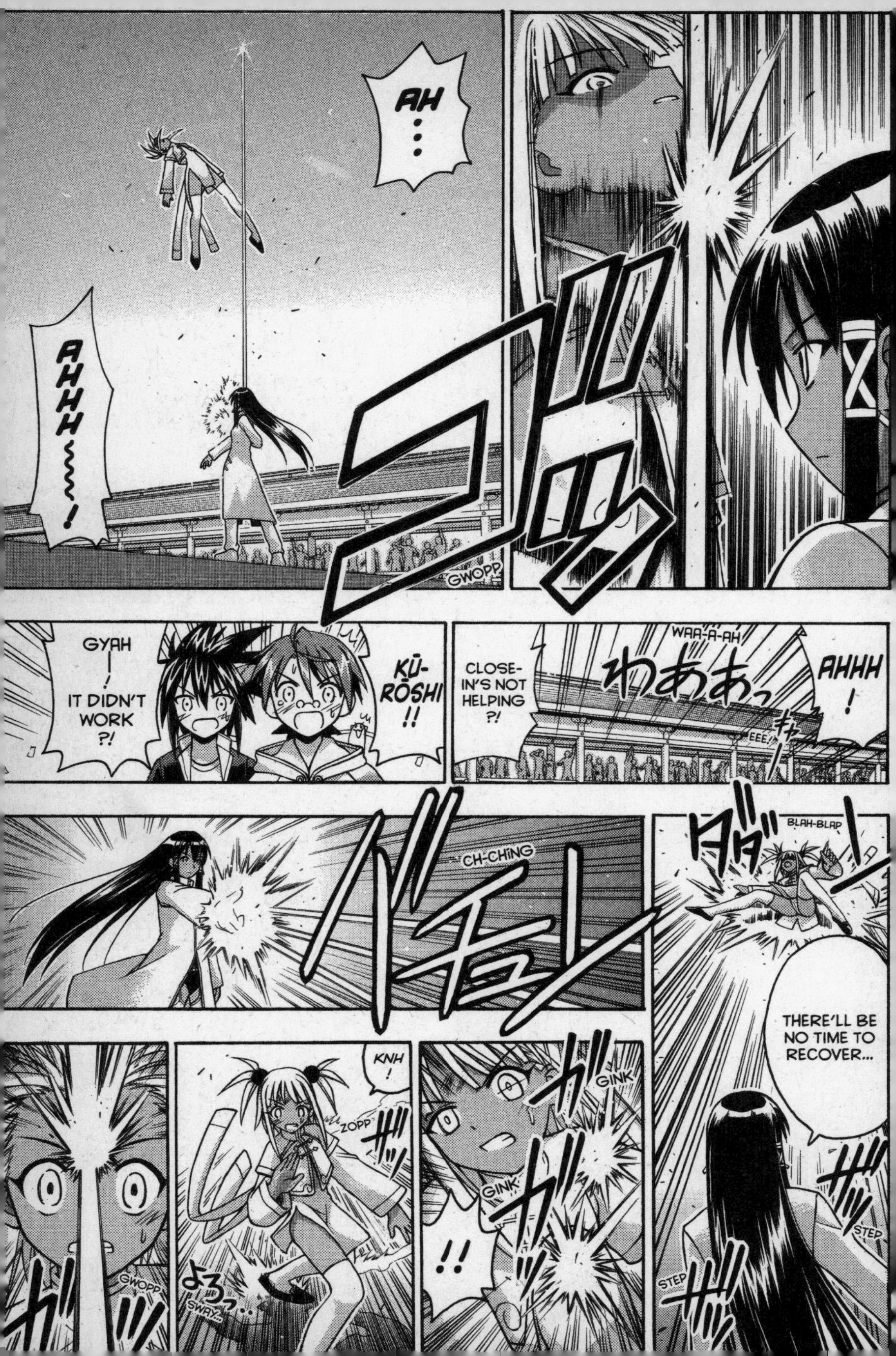
AH...
AHHHH~~~!
GWOPP
AHHH!
WAA-A-AH
わあああっ
EEE!!
CLOSE-IN'S NOT HELPING?!
KŪ-RŌSHI!!
GYAH! IT DIDN'T WORK?!
BLAH-BLAP
CH-CHING
THERE'LL BE NO TIME TO RECOVER...
STEP
STEP
GINK
GINK
!!
KNH!
ZOPP
よろっ..
SWAY...
GWOPP

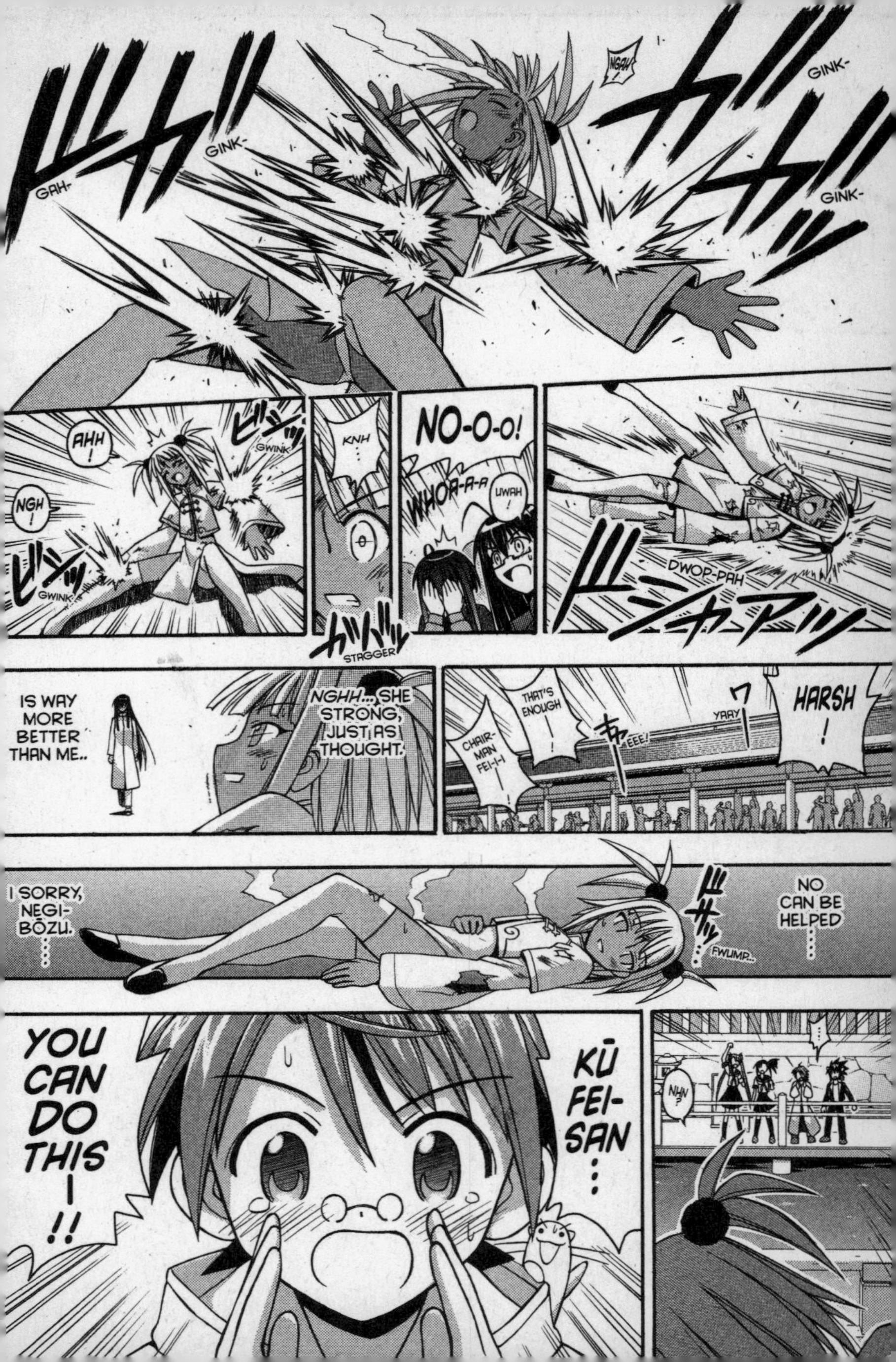
GINK-
NGAH!
GINK-
GINK-
GAH-
DWOP-PAH
NO-O-O!
UWAH!
WHOA-A-A
KNH...
STAGGER
AHH!
GWINK
NGH!
GWINK
HARSH!
YAAY
THAT'S ENOUGH!
EEE!
CHAIRMAN FEI-I-I!
NGHH... SHE STRONG, JUST AS THOUGHT.
IS WAY MORE BETTER THAN ME..
NO CAN BE HELPED...
FWUMP...
I SORRY, NEGI-BŌZU. ...
...
NHN?
KŪ FEI-SAN...
YOU CAN DO THIS-!!

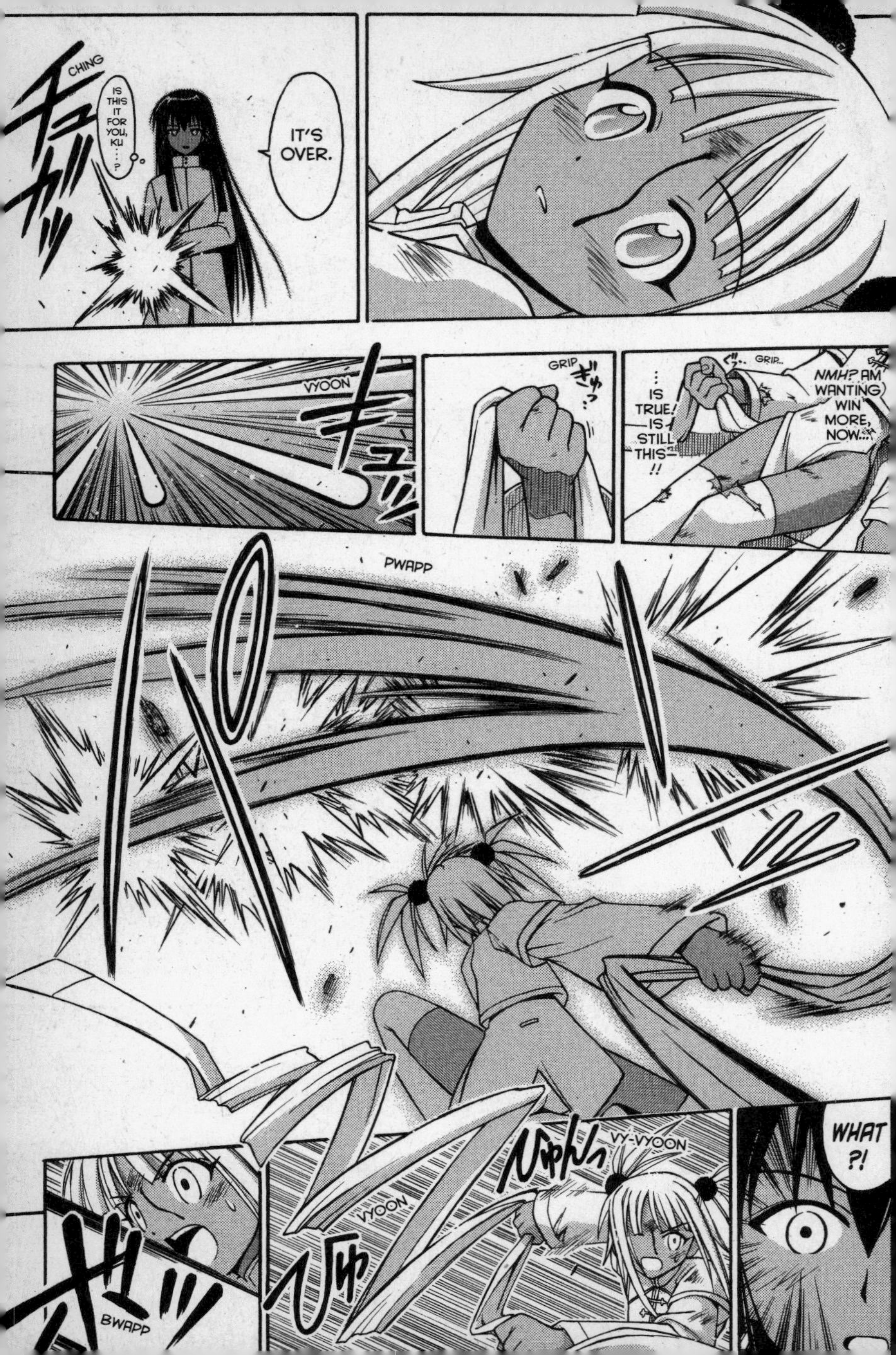
IT'S OVER.
IS THIS IT FOR YOU, KU...?
CHING
NMH? AM WANTING WIN MORE, NOW...
GRIP..
...IS TRUE! IS STILL THIS!!
GRIP
VYOON
PWAPP
WHAT?!
VY-VYOON
VYOON
BWAPP

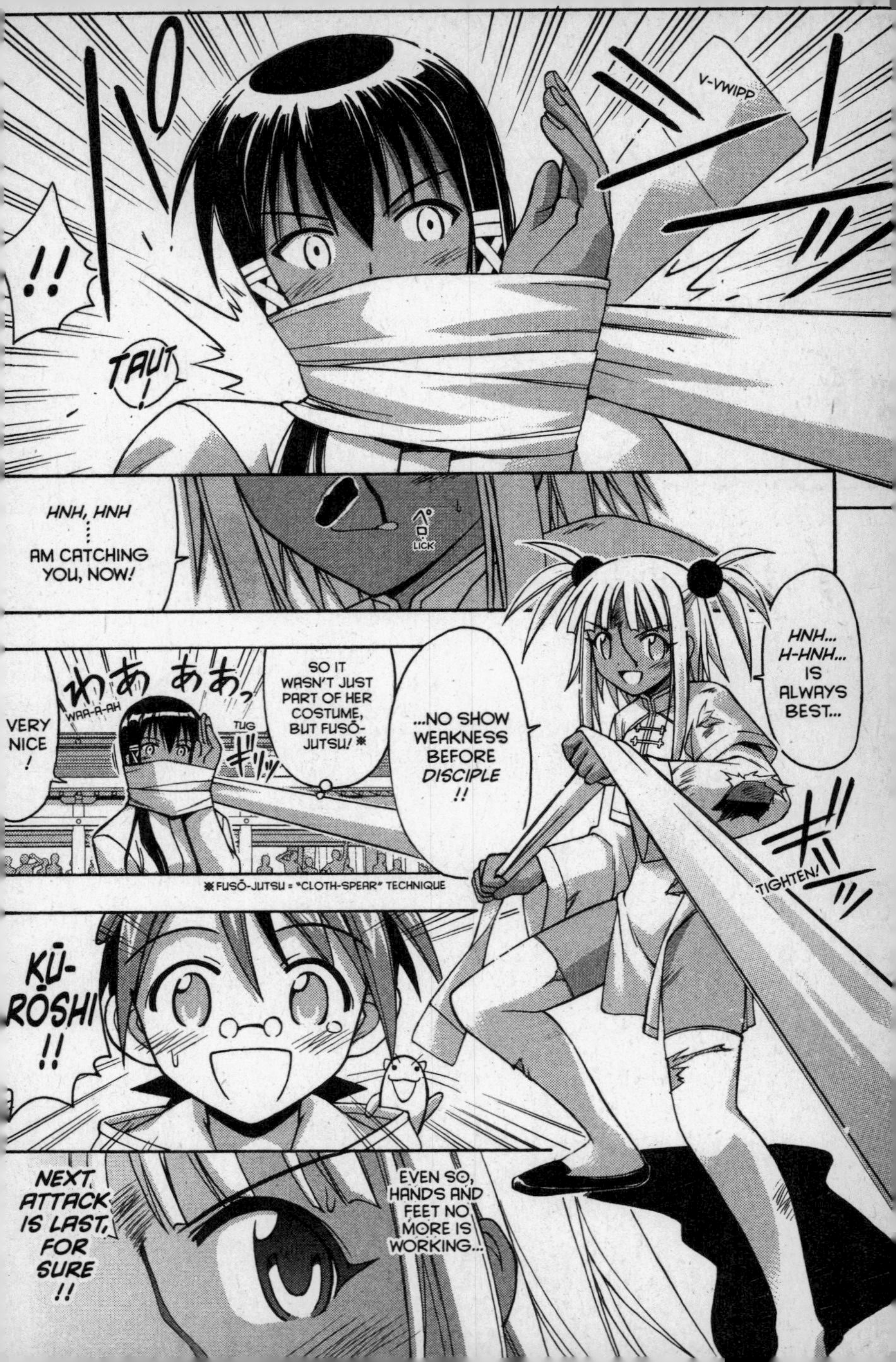
V-VWIPP
!!
TAUT!
ペロ
LICK
HNH, HNH... AM CATCHING YOU, NOW!
HNH... H-HNH... IS ALWAYS BEST...
...NO SHOW WEAKNESS BEFORE DISCIPLE!!
TIGHTEN!
SO IT WASN'T JUST PART OF HER COSTUME, BUT FUSŌ-JUTSU! ※
TUG
わあ ああっ
WAA-A-AH
VERY NICE!
※ FUSŌ-JUTSU = "CLOTH-SPEAR" TECHNIQUE
KŪ-RŌSHI!!
EVEN SO, HANDS AND FEET NO MORE IS WORKING...
NEXT ATTACK IS LAST, FOR SURE!!

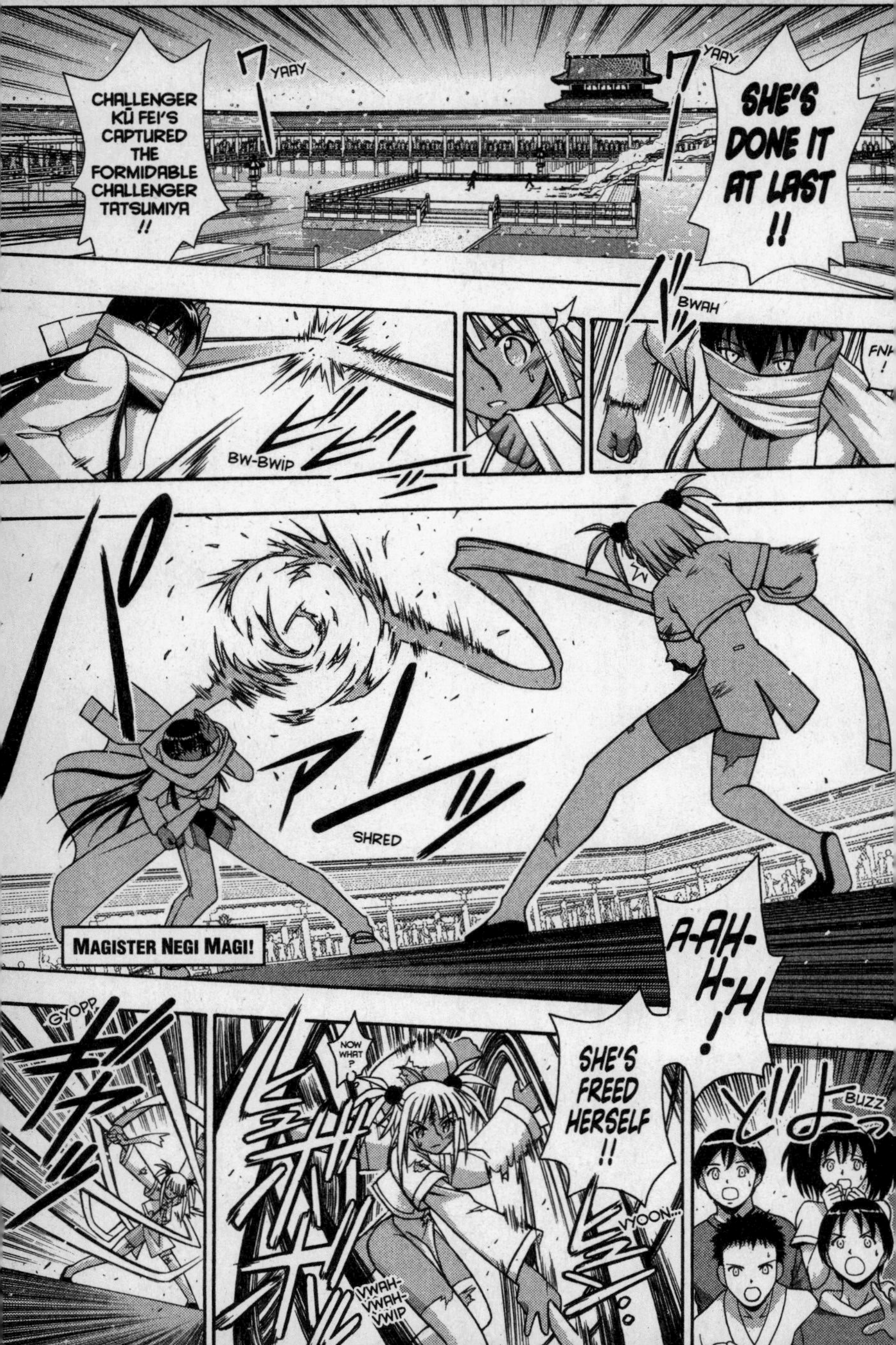
YAAY
SHE'S DONE IT AT LAST !!
YAAY
CHALLENGER KŪ FEI'S CAPTURED THE FORMIDABLE CHALLENGER TATSUMIYA !!
FNH !
BWAH
BW-BWIP
SHRED
MAGISTER NEGI MAGI!
A-AH-H-H !
SHE'S FREED HERSELF !!
BUZZ
NOW WHAT ?
VYOON...
VWAH-VWAH-VWIP
GYOPP

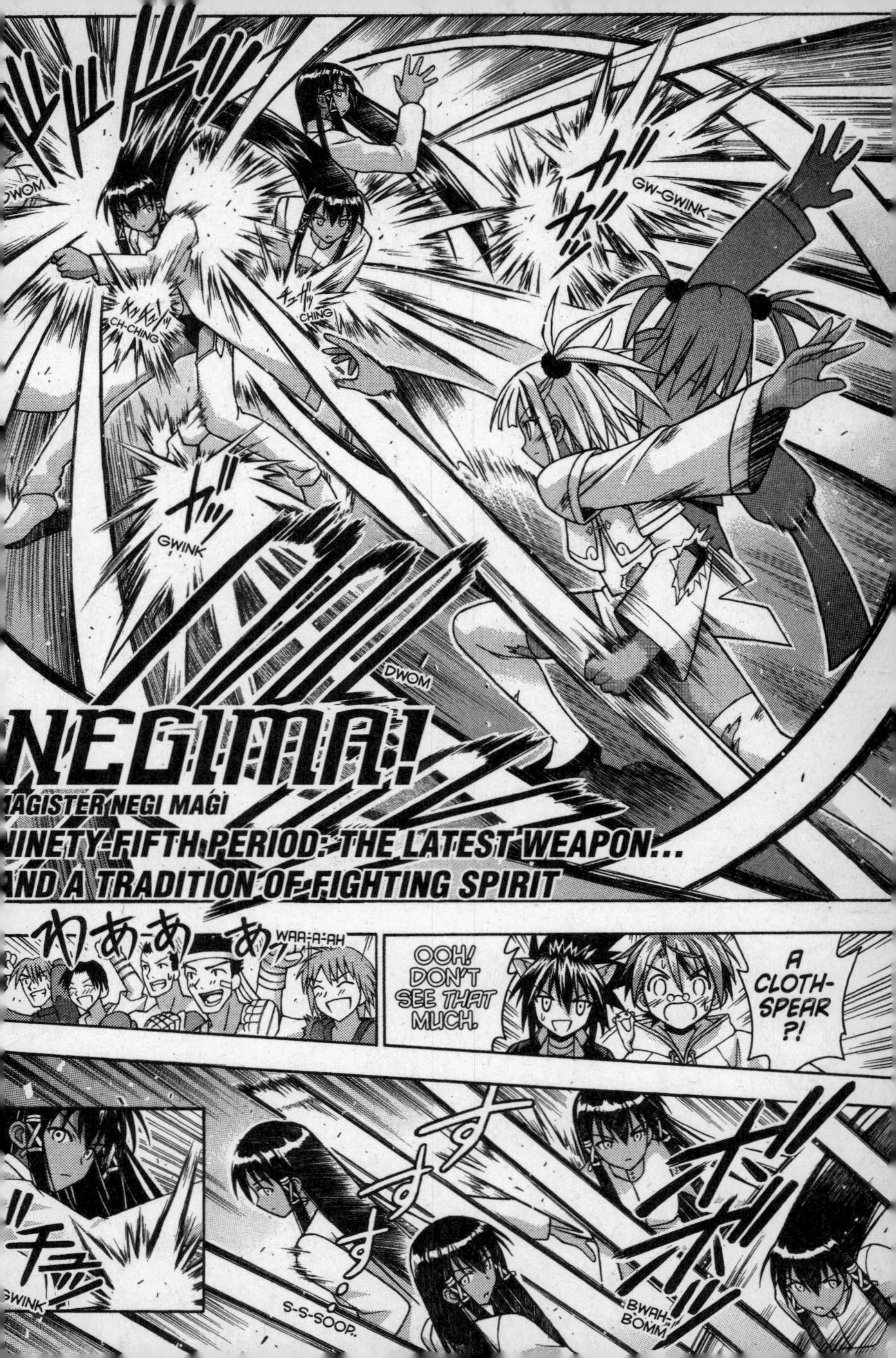
GW-GWINK
DWOM
CHING
CH-CHING
GWINK
DWOM
NEGIMA!
MAGISTER NEGI MAGI
NINETY-FIFTH PERIOD: THE LATEST WEAPON...
AND A TRADITION OF FIGHTING SPIRIT
A CLOTH-SPEAR?!
OOH! DON'T SEE THAT MUCH.
WAA-A-AH
BWAH-BOMM
S-S-SOOP..
GWINK

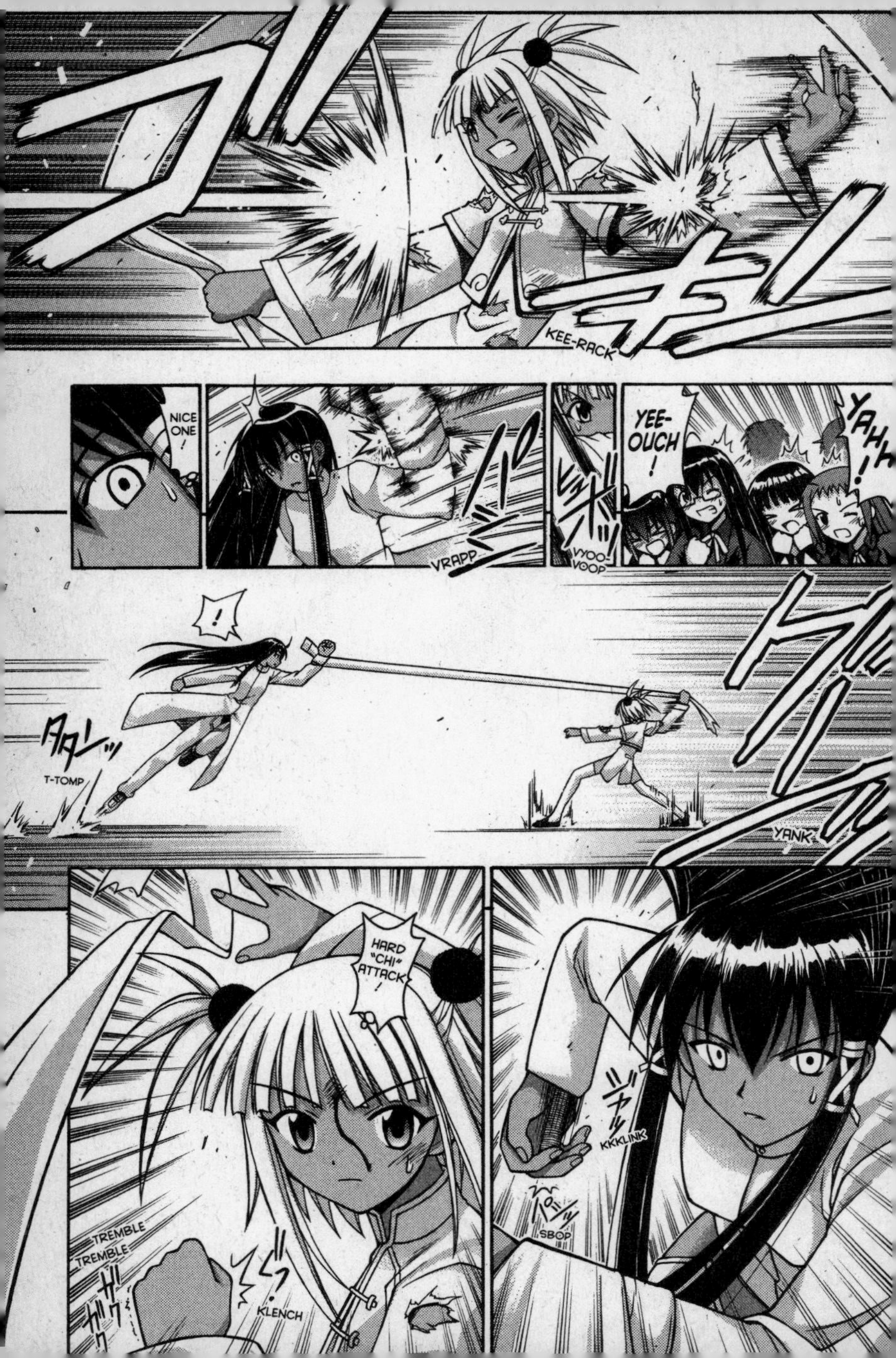

KEE-RACK
YEE-OUCH!
YAHH!
VYOO-VOOP
VRAPP
NICE ONE!
YANK
!
T-TOMP
KKKLINK
SBOP
HARD "CHI" ATTACK!
TREMBLE
TREMBLE
KLENCH

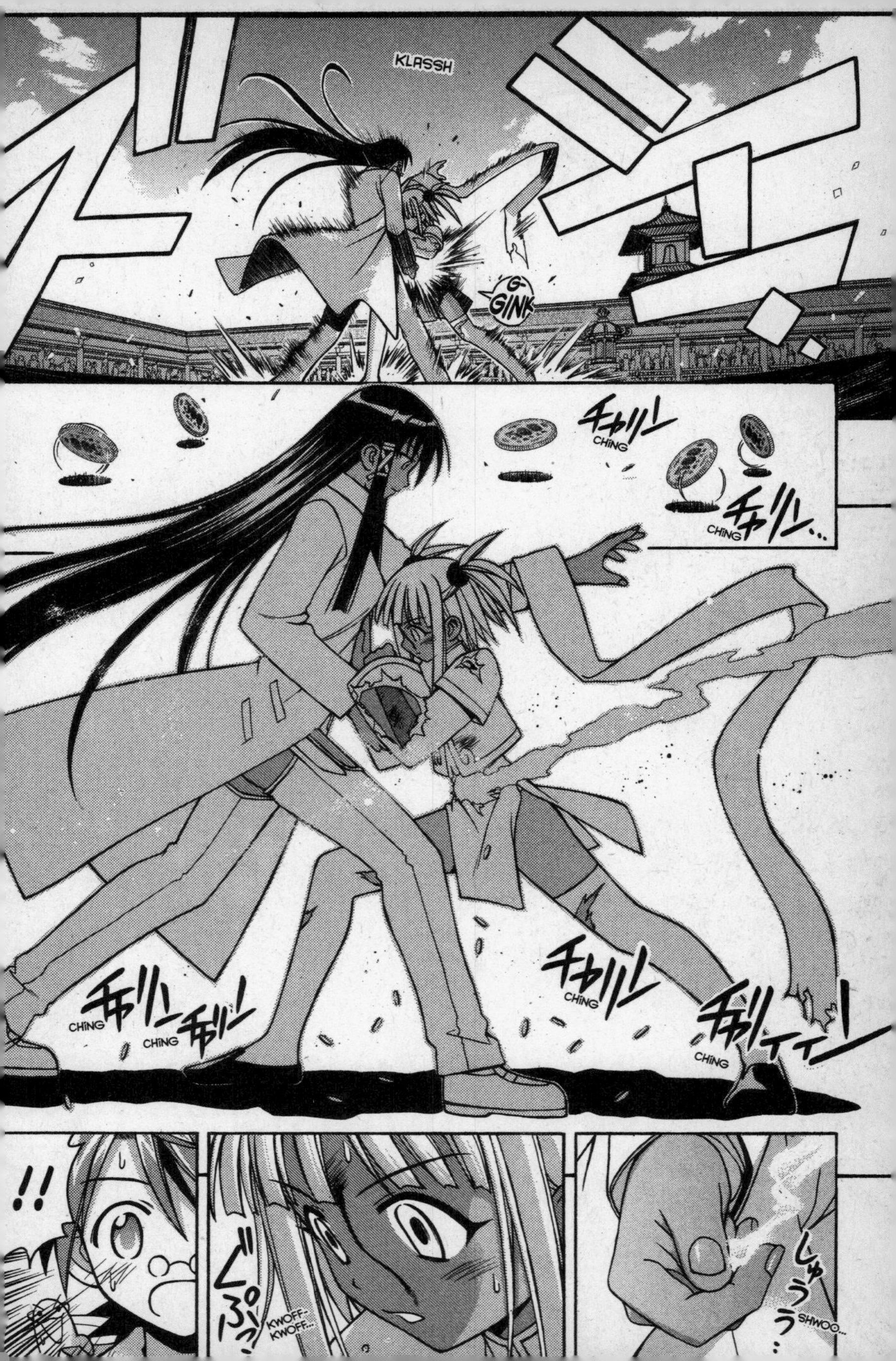
KLASSH
G-GINK
チャリン
CHING
チャリン…
CHING
チャリン
CHING
CHING
CHING
CHING
SHWOO...
KWOFF-KWOFF...
!!

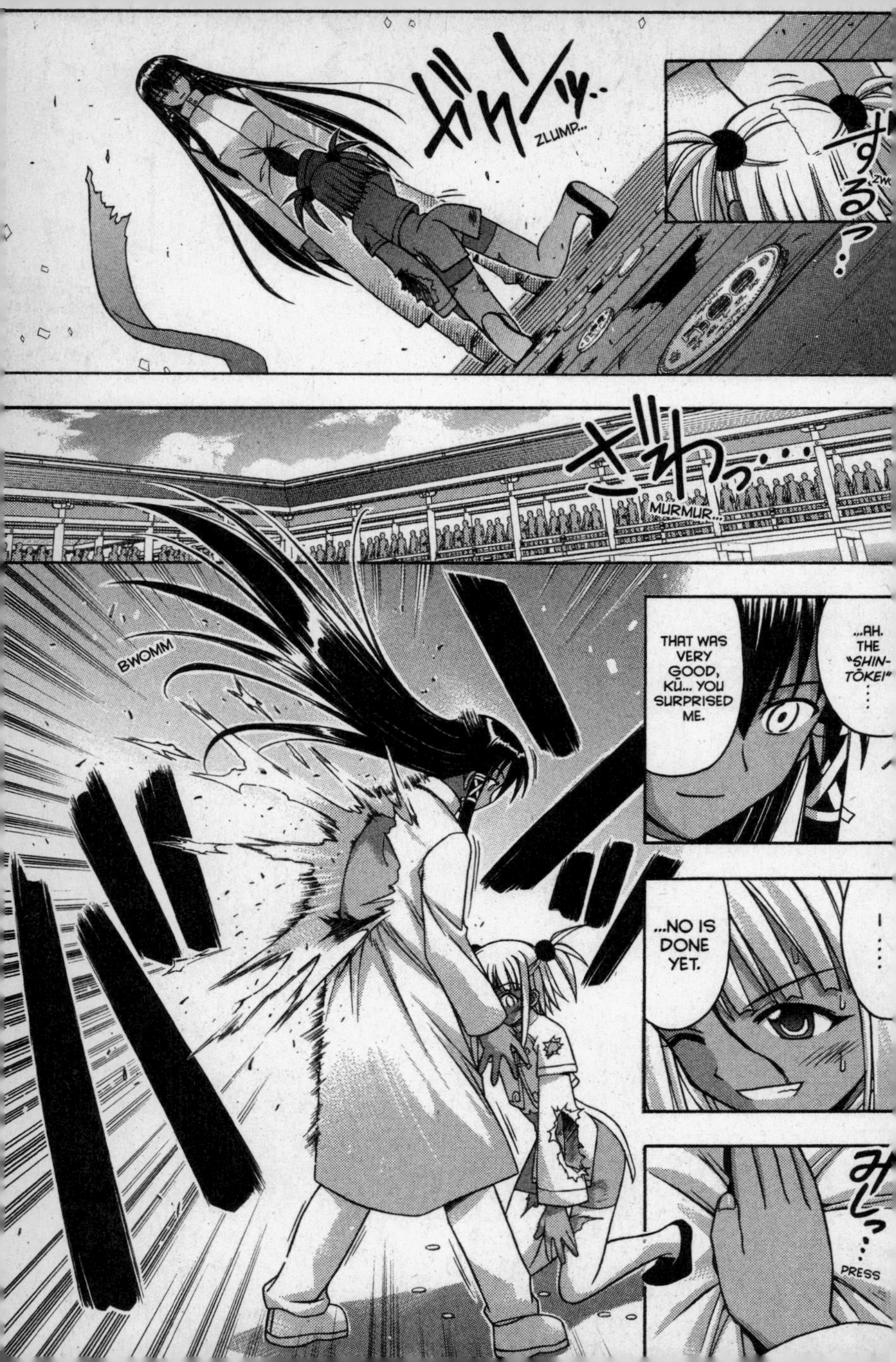

ずるっ..
ドサッ..
ZLUMP...
ざわっ...
MURMUR...
...AH. THE "SHIN-TŌKEI"....
THAT WAS VERY GOOD, KŪ... YOU SURPRISED ME.
I....
...NO IS DONE YET.
みしっ..
PRESS
BWOMM

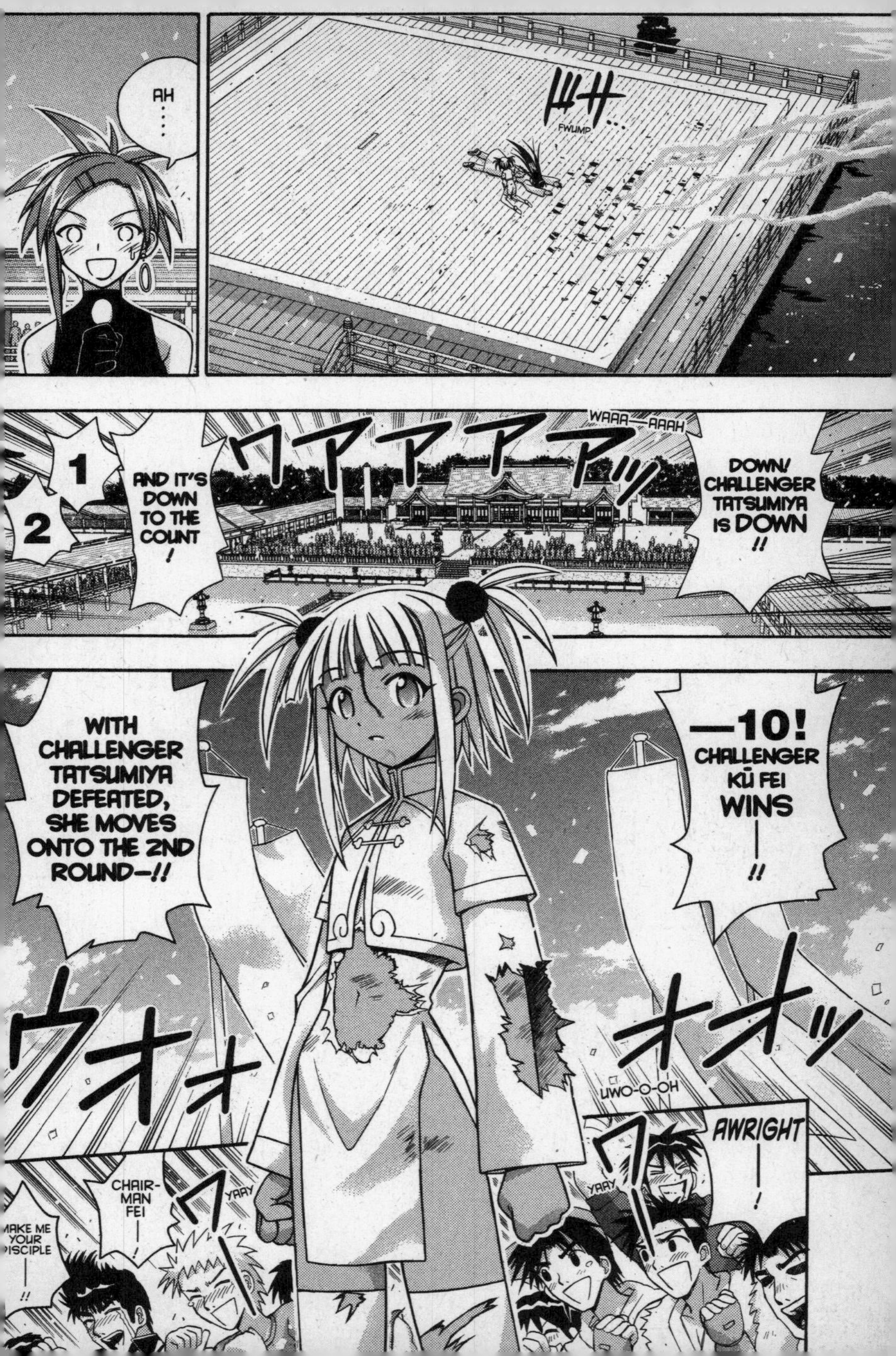
FWUMP...
AH......
WAAA—AAAH
DOWN! CHALLENGER TATSUMIYA IS DOWN!!
AND IT'S DOWN TO THE COUNT!
1
2
—10! CHALLENGER KŪ FEI WINS—!!
WITH CHALLENGER TATSUMIYA DEFEATED, SHE MOVES ONTO THE 2ND ROUND–!!
UWO-O-OH
AWRIGHT—!
YAAY
YAAY
CHAIR-MAN FEI—!
MAKE ME YOUR DISCIPLE—!!

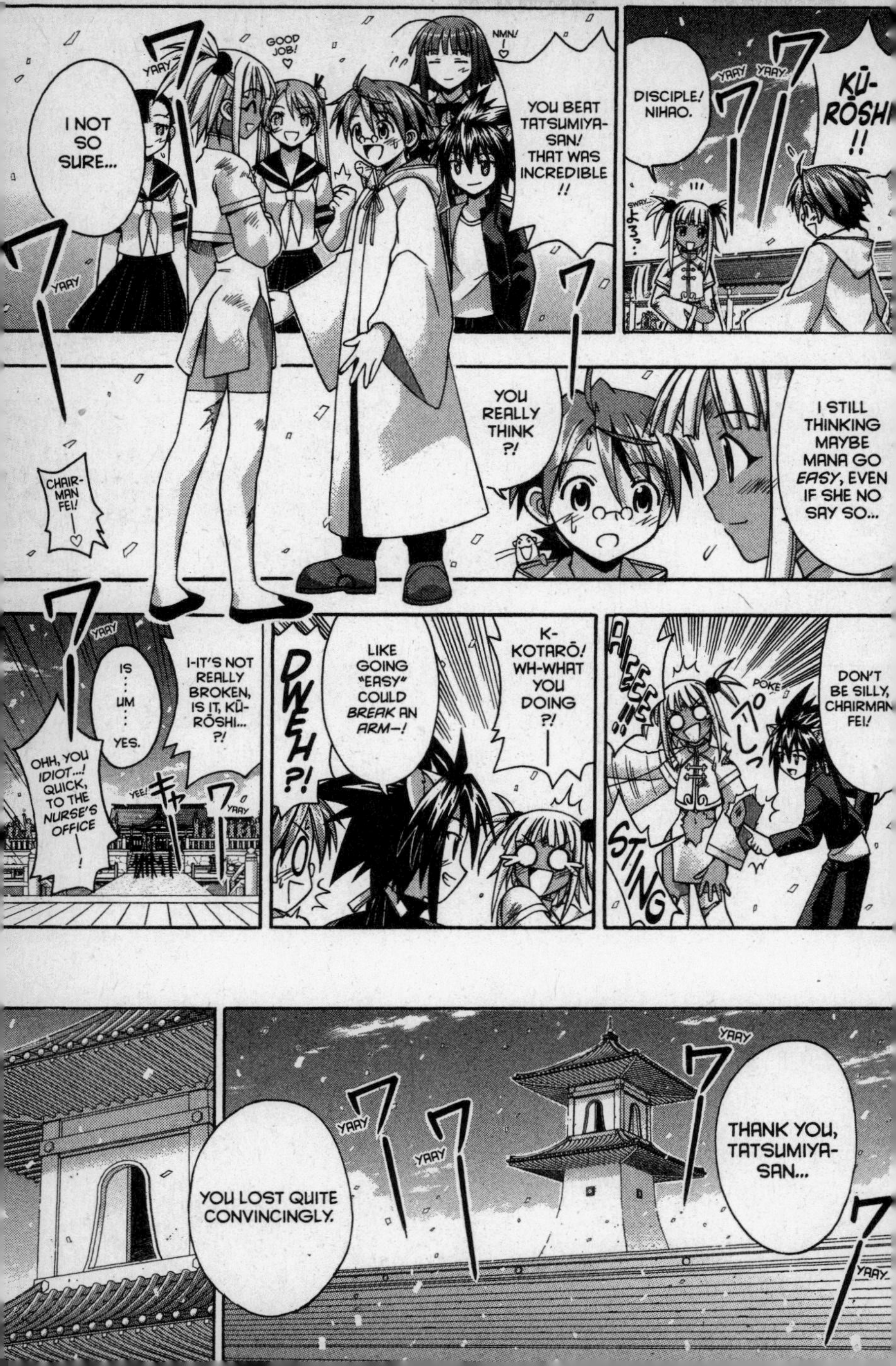
KŪ-RŌSHI!!
YAAY YAAY
DISCIPLE! NIHAO.
SWAY...
NMN! ♡
YOU BEAT TATSUMIYA-SAN! THAT WAS INCREDIBLE!!
GOOD JOB! ♡
YAAY
I NOT SO SURE...
YAAY
I STILL THINKING MAYBE MANA GO EASY, EVEN IF SHE NO SAY SO...
YOU REALLY THINK?!
CHAIRMAN FEI! ♡
DON'T BE SILLY, CHAIRMAN FEI!
POKE
AIEEEE!!
STING
K-KOTARŌ! WH-WHAT YOU DOING?!
LIKE GOING "EASY" COULD BREAK AN ARM—!
DWEH?!
I-IT'S NOT REALLY BROKEN, IS IT, KŪRŌSHI...?!
IS... UM... YES.
YAAY
OHH, YOU IDIOT...! QUICK, TO THE NURSE'S OFFICE!
YEE!
YAAY
YAAY
THANK YOU, TATSUMIYA-SAN...
YAAY
YAAY
YOU LOST QUITE CONVINCINGLY.
YAAY

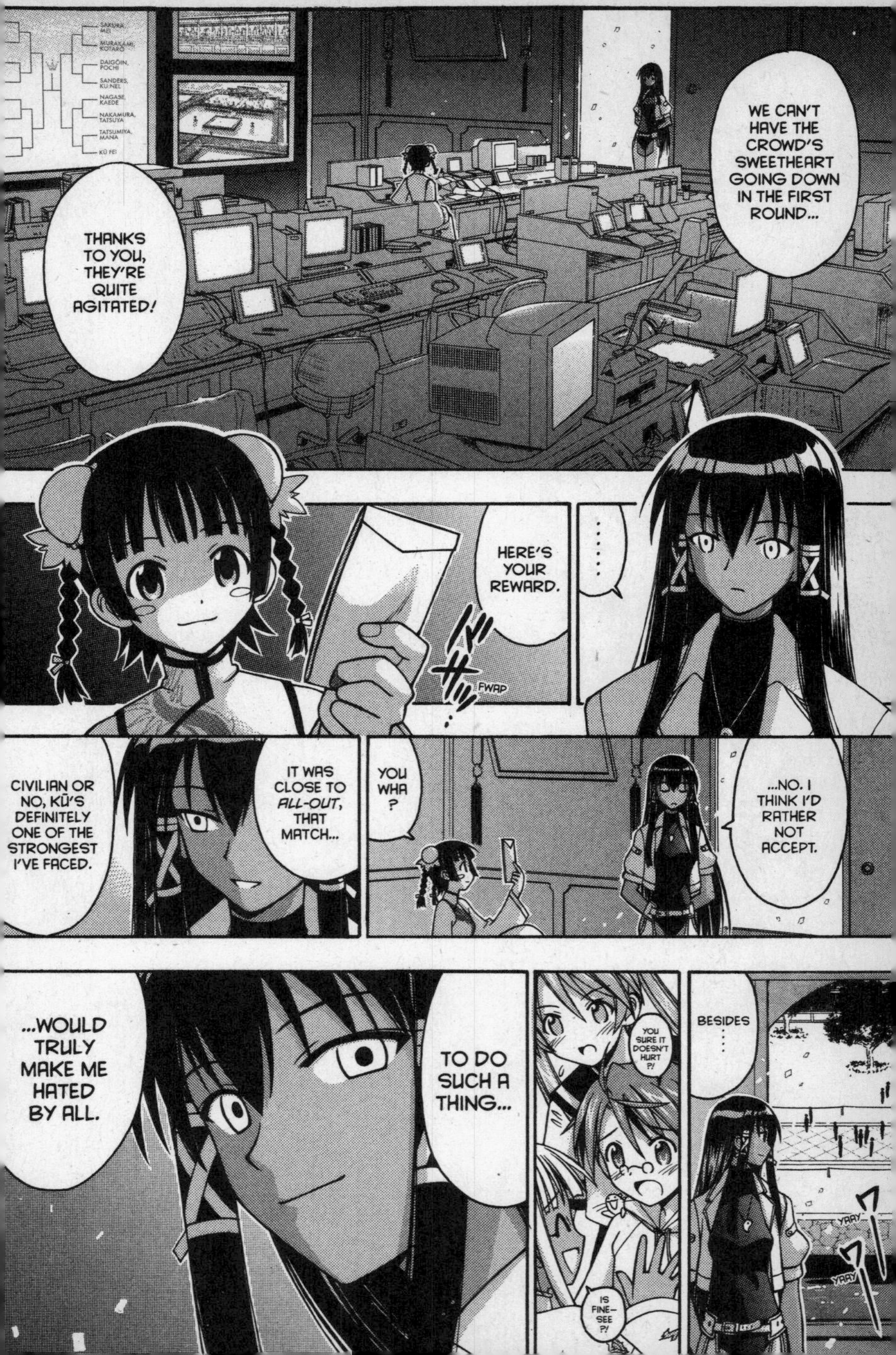

WE CAN'T HAVE THE CROWD'S SWEETHEART GOING DOWN IN THE FIRST ROUND...
SAKURA, MEI
MURAKAMI, KOTARO
DAIGŌIN, POCHI
SANDERS, KU:NEL
NAGASE, KAEDE
NAKAMURA, TATSUYA
TATSUMIYA, MANA
KŪ FEI
THANKS TO YOU, THEY'RE QUITE AGITATED!
......
HERE'S YOUR REWARD.
FWAP
...NO. I THINK I'D RATHER NOT ACCEPT.
YOU WHA ?
IT WAS CLOSE TO *ALL-OUT*, THAT MATCH...
CIVILIAN OR NO, KŪ'S DEFINITELY ONE OF THE STRONGEST I'VE FACED.
BESIDES .....
YAAY
YAAY
YOU SURE IT DOESN'T HURT?!
IS FINE-SEE?!
TO DO SUCH A THING...
...WOULD TRULY MAKE ME HATED BY ALL.

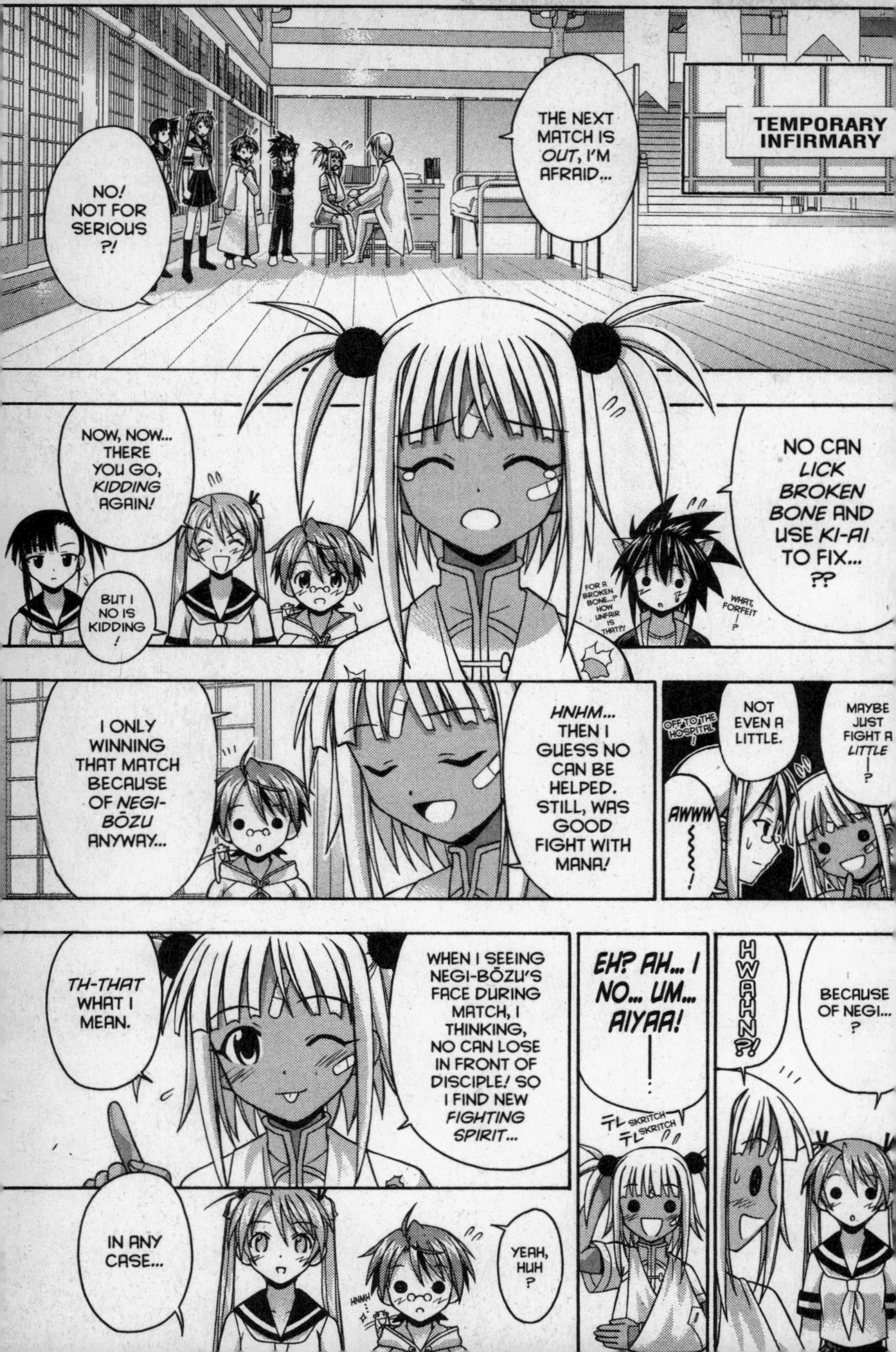
TEMPORARY INFIRMARY
THE NEXT MATCH IS OUT, I'M AFRAID...
NO! NOT FOR SERIOUS ?!
NO CAN LICK BROKEN BONE AND USE KI-AI TO FIX... ??
WHAT, FORFEIT ?
FOR A BROKEN BONE...? HOW UNFAIR IS THAT?!
NOW, NOW... THERE YOU GO, KIDDING AGAIN!
BUT I NO IS KIDDING !
MAYBE JUST FIGHT A LITTLE ?
NOT EVEN A LITTLE.
OFF TO THE HOSPITAL!
AWWW~!
HNHM... THEN I GUESS NO CAN BE HELPED. STILL, WAS GOOD FIGHT WITH MANA!
I ONLY WINNING THAT MATCH BECAUSE OF NEGI-BŌZU ANYWAY...
BECAUSE OF NEGI... ?
HWAHN?!
EH? AH... I NO... UM... AIYAA!
テレ SKRITCH
テレ SKRITCH
WHEN I SEEING NEGI-BŌZU'S FACE DURING MATCH, I THINKING, NO CAN LOSE IN FRONT OF DISCIPLE! SO I FIND NEW FIGHTING SPIRIT...
TH-THAT WHAT I MEAN.
YEAH, HUH ?
HNMH
IN ANY CASE...

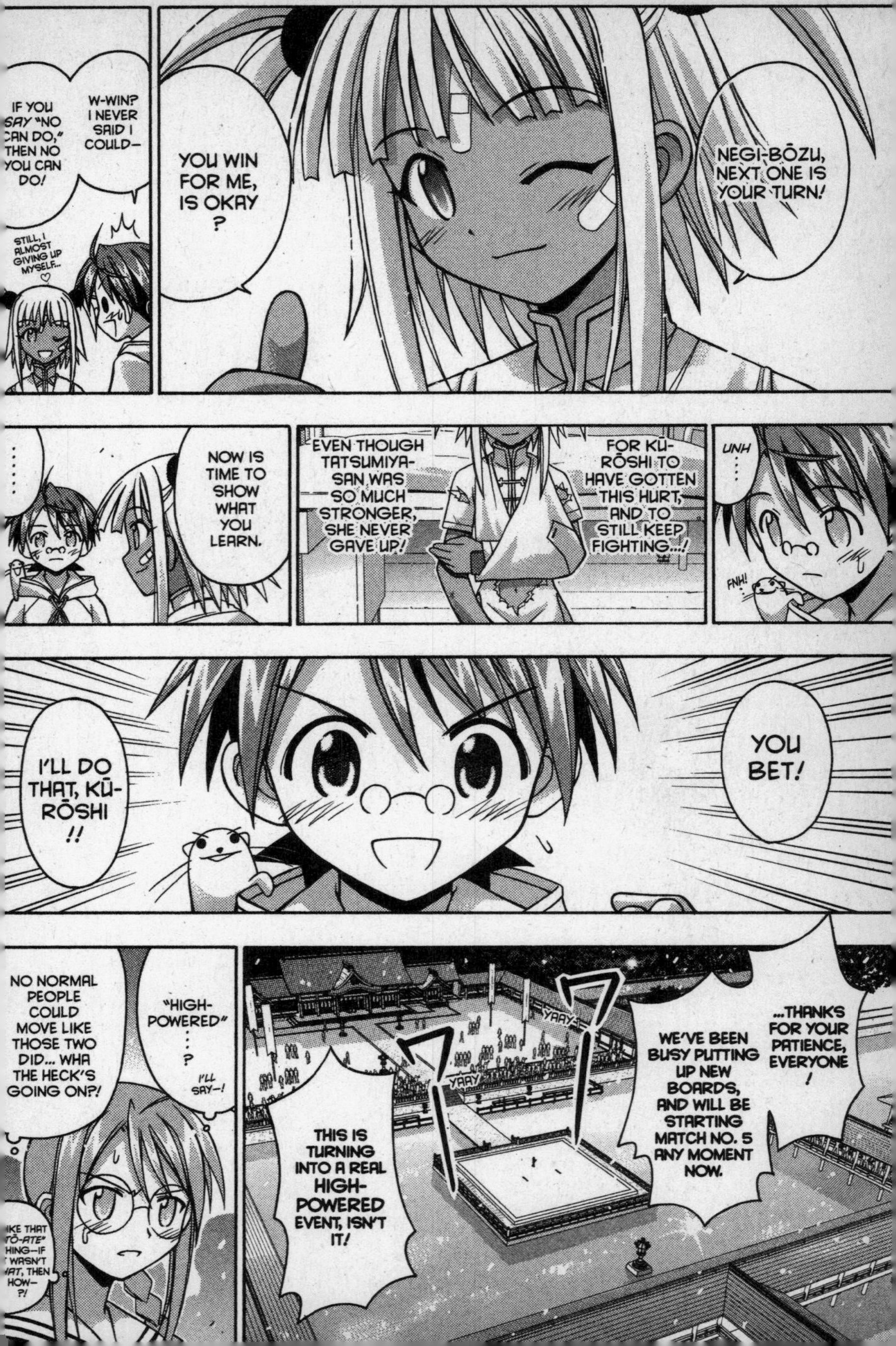

NEGI-BŌZU, NEXT ONE IS YOUR TURN!
YOU WIN FOR ME, IS OKAY ?
W-WIN? I NEVER SAID I COULD—
IF YOU SAY "NO CAN DO," THEN NO YOU CAN DO!
STILL, I ALMOST GIVING UP MYSELF... ♡
UNH ...
FNH!
FOR KŪ-RŌSHI TO HAVE GOTTEN THIS HURT, AND TO STILL KEEP FIGHTING...!
EVEN THOUGH TATSUMIYA-SAN WAS SO MUCH STRONGER, SHE NEVER GAVE UP!
NOW IS TIME TO SHOW WHAT YOU LEARN.
......
YOU BET!
I'LL DO THAT, KŪ-RŌSHI !!
...THANKS FOR YOUR PATIENCE, EVERYONE!
WE'VE BEEN BUSY PUTTING UP NEW BOARDS, AND WILL BE STARTING MATCH NO. 5 ANY MOMENT NOW.
YAAY
YAAY
THIS IS TURNING INTO A REAL HIGH-POWERED EVENT, ISN'T IT!
"HIGH-POWERED" . . . ?
I'LL SAY—!
NO NORMAL PEOPLE COULD MOVE LIKE THOSE TWO DID... WHA THE HECK'S GOING ON?!
IKE THAT "TŌ-ATE" HING—IF WASN'T HAT, THEN HOW—?!

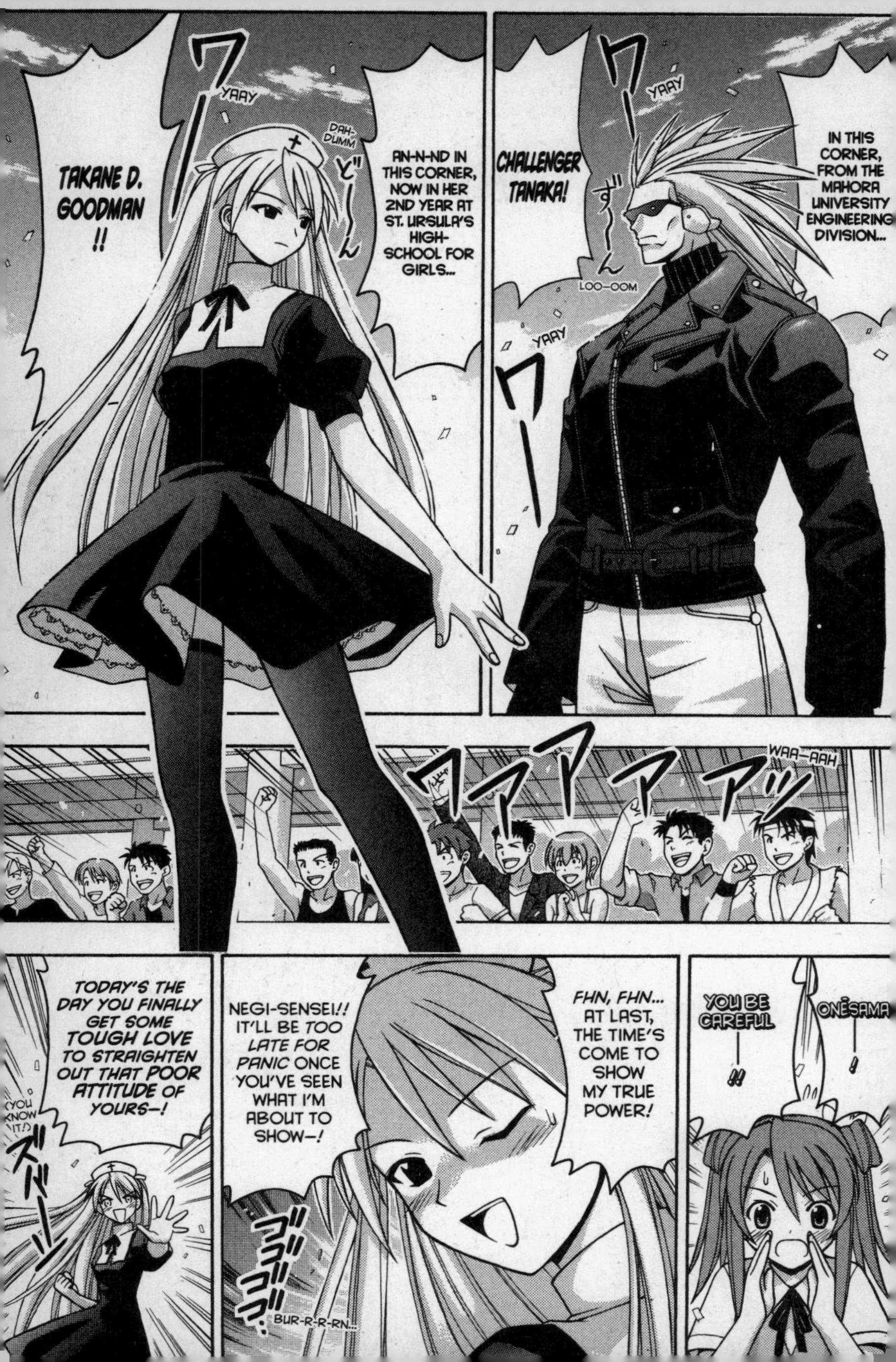

IN THIS CORNER, FROM THE MAHORA UNIVERSITY ENGINEERING DIVISION...
YAAY
LOO—OOM
CHALLENGER TANAKA!
YAAY
AN-N-ND IN THIS CORNER, NOW IN HER 2ND YEAR AT ST. URSULA'S HIGH-SCHOOL FOR GIRLS...
DAH-DUMM
YAAY
TAKANE D. GOODMAN!!
WAA—AAH
ONĒSAMA—!
YOU BE CAREFUL—!!
FHN, FHN... AT LAST, THE TIME'S COME TO SHOW MY TRUE POWER!
NEGI-SENSEI!! IT'LL BE TOO LATE FOR PANIC ONCE YOU'VE SEEN WHAT I'M ABOUT TO SHOW—!
BUR-R-R-RN...
TODAY'S THE DAY YOU FINALLY GET SOME TOUGH LOVE TO STRAIGHTEN OUT THAT POOR ATTITUDE OF YOURS—!
(YOU KNOW IT!♪)

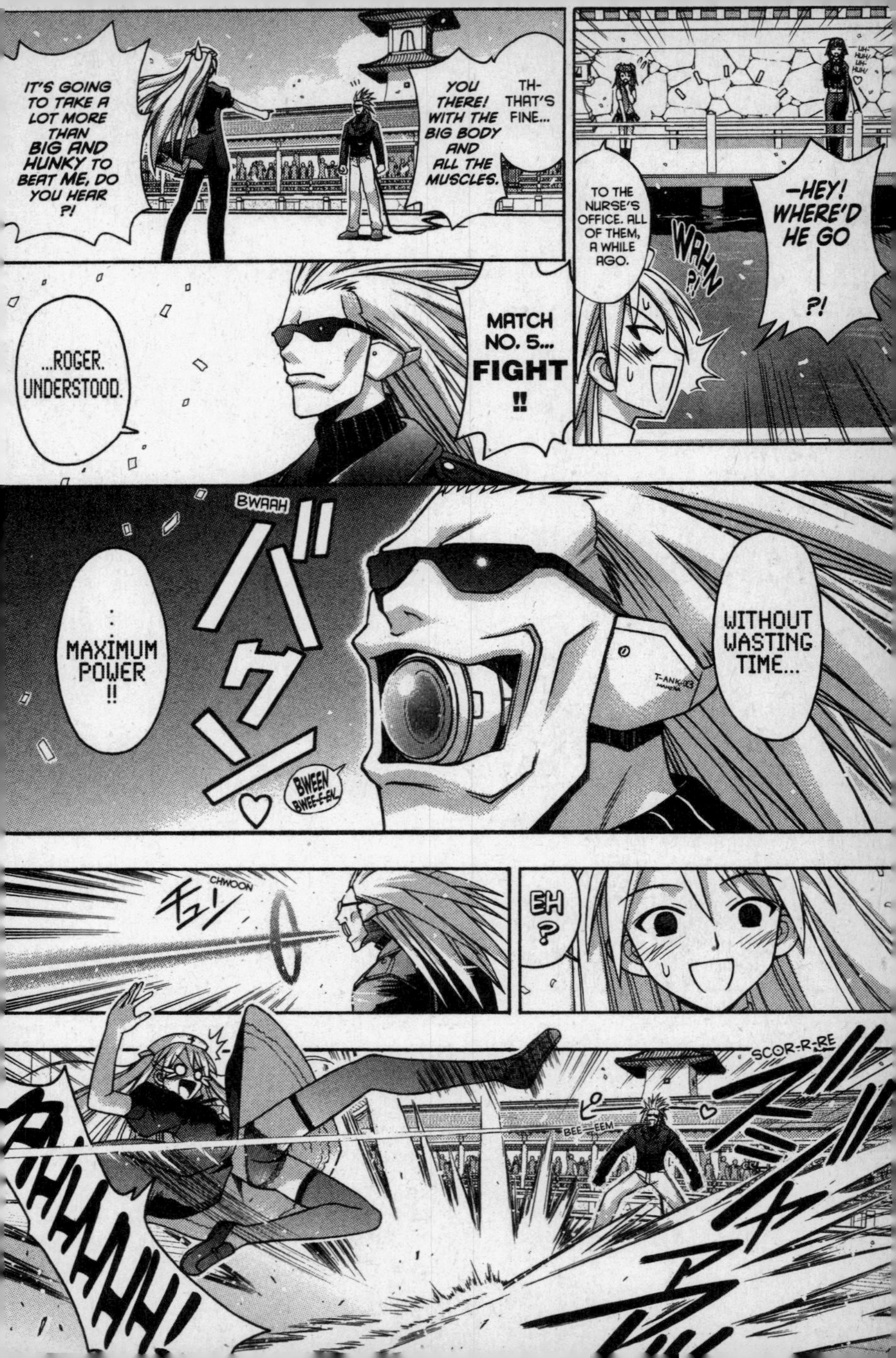
UH-HUH/ UH-HUH/ ♡
—HEY! WHERE'D HE GO —?!
TO THE NURSE'S OFFICE. ALL OF THEM, A WHILE AGO.
WAHN ?!
TH-THAT'S FINE...
YOU THERE! WITH THE BIG BODY AND ALL THE MUSCLES.
IT'S GOING TO TAKE A LOT MORE THAN BIG AND HUNKY TO BEAT ME, DO YOU HEAR ?!
MATCH NO. 5... FIGHT !!
...ROGER. UNDERSTOOD.
WITHOUT WASTING TIME...
BWAAH
...MAXIMUM POWER !!
BWEEN BWEE-E-EN
EH ?
CHWOON
SCOR-R-RE
BEE EEM
AHHHHHH!

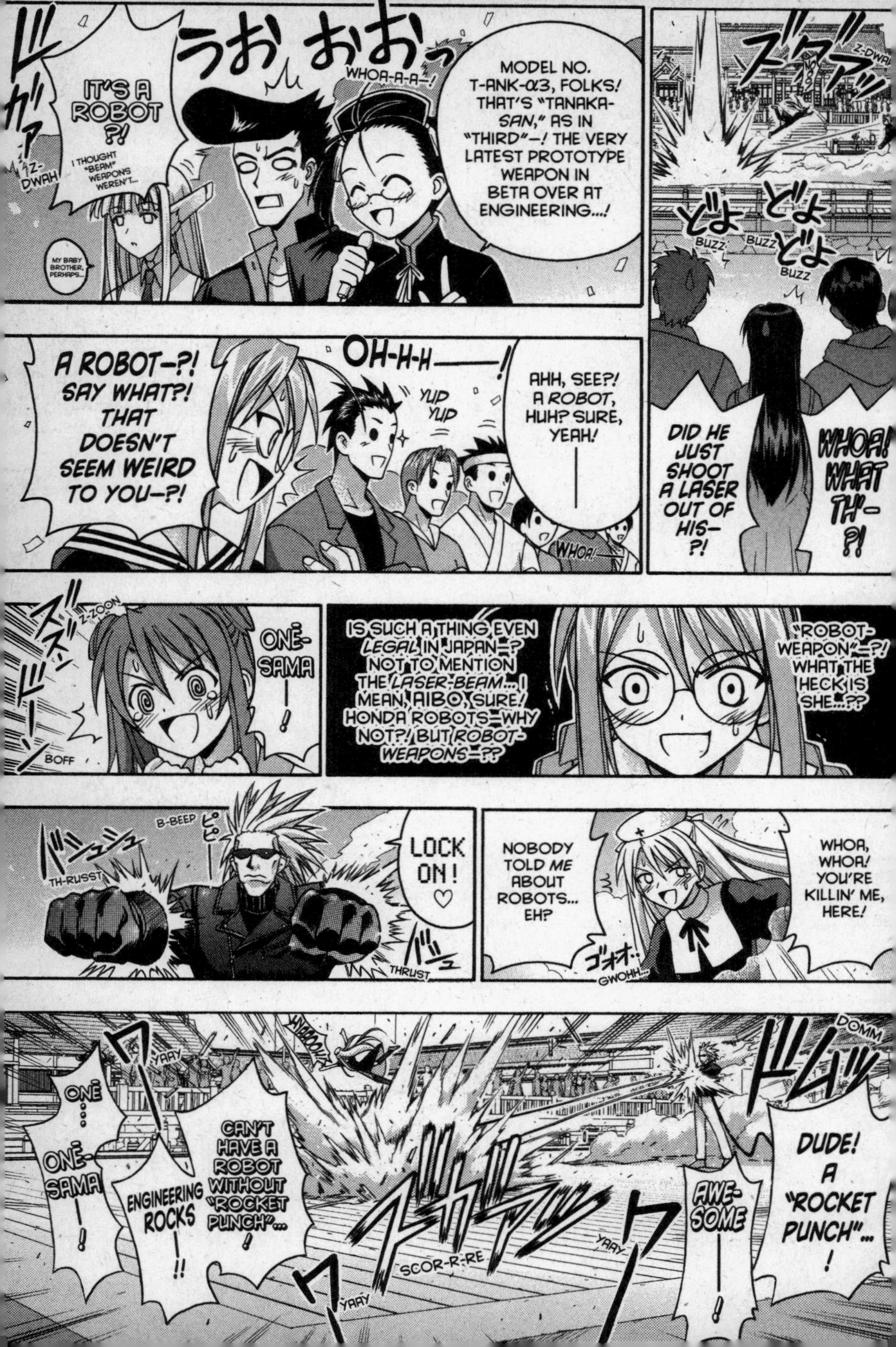
ズガァ
Z-DWAH
どよどよどよ
BUZZ
BUZZ
BUZZ
WHOA! WHAT TH—?!
DID HE JUST SHOOT A LASER OUT OF HIS—?!
MODEL NO. T-ANK-α3, FOLKS! THAT'S "TANAKA-SAN," AS IN "THIRD"—! THE VERY LATEST PROTOTYPE WEAPON IN BETA OVER AT ENGINEERING...!
うおおおっ
WHOA-A-A—!
IT'S A ROBOT?!
I THOUGHT "BEAM" WEAPONS WEREN'T...
ドガァ
Z-DWAH
MY BABY BROTHER, PERHAPS...
AHH, SEE?! A ROBOT, HUH? SURE, YEAH! —
OH-H-H——!
YUP YUP
WHOA!
A ROBOT—?! SAY WHAT?! THAT DOESN'T SEEM WEIRD TO YOU—?!
"ROBOT-WEAPON"—?! WHAT THE HECK IS SHE...??
IS SUCH A THING EVEN LEGAL IN JAPAN—? NOT TO MENTION THE LASER-BEAM... I MEAN, AIBO, SURE! HONDA ROBOTS—WHY NOT?! BUT ROBOT-WEAPONS—??
ONĒ-SAMA—!
Z-ZOON
BOFF
WHOA, WHOA! YOU'RE KILLIN' ME, HERE!
NOBODY TOLD ME ABOUT ROBOTS... EH?
ゴオオ
GWOHH...
LOCK ON! ♡
ピピ
B-BEEP
バシュ
THRUST
TH-RUSST
DOMM
ドム
DUDE! A "ROCKET PUNCH"...!
AWESOME—!
YAAY
HYAAAAA!?
CAN'T HAVE A ROBOT WITHOUT "ROCKET PUNCH"...!
ENGINEERING ROCKS—!!
SCOR-R-RE
YAAY
ONĒ... ONĒ-SAMA—!
YAAY
YAAY

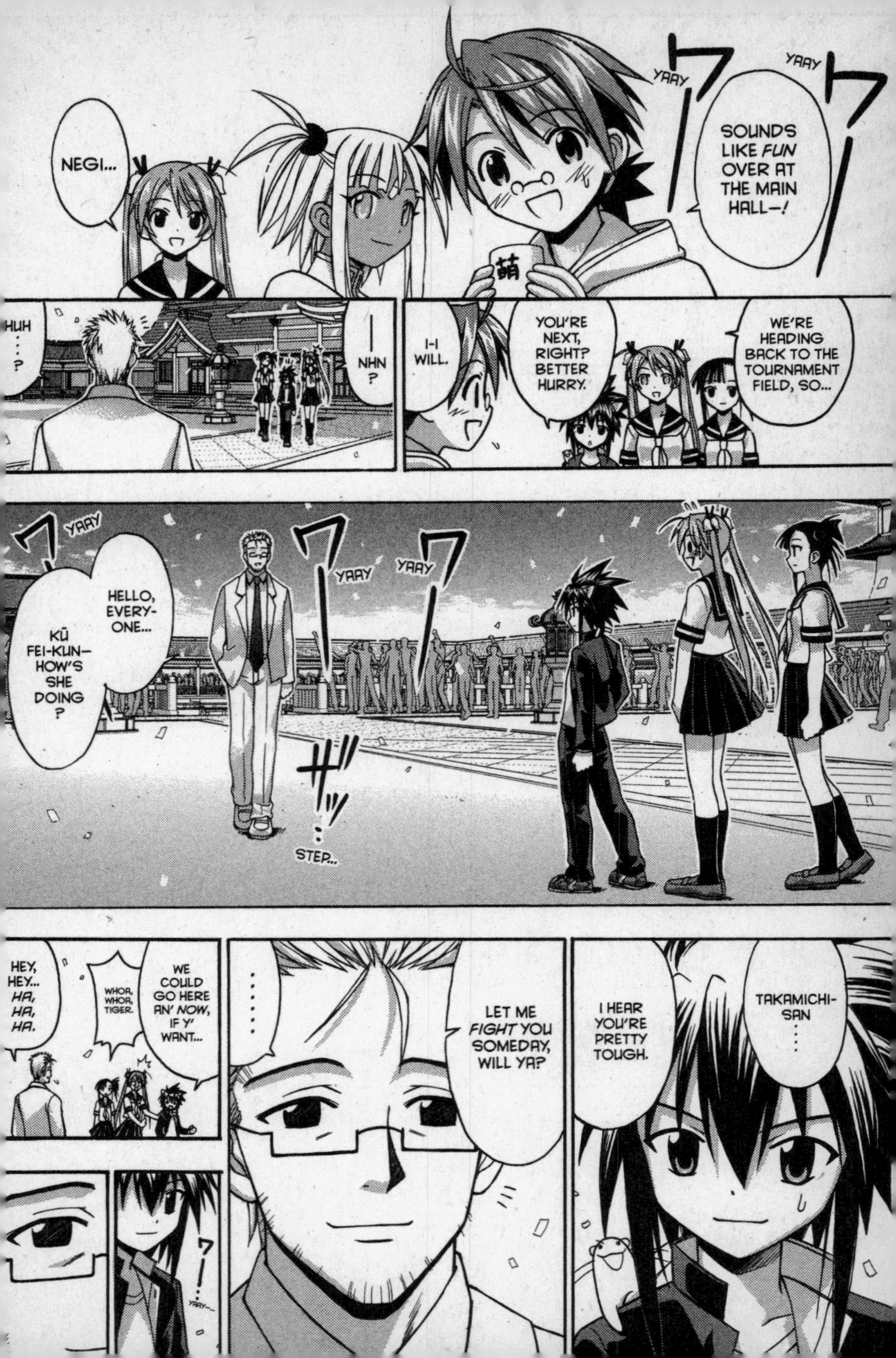

YAAY
SOUNDS LIKE *FUN* OVER AT THE MAIN HALL—!
YAAY
NEGI...
WE'RE HEADING BACK TO THE TOURNAMENT FIELD, SO...
YOU'RE NEXT, RIGHT? BETTER HURRY.
I-I WILL.
NHN ?
HUH . . . ?
YAAY
YAAY
HELLO, EVERYONE...
KŪ FEI-KUN—HOW'S SHE DOING ?
YAAY
STEP...
TAKAMICHI-SAN . . .
I HEAR YOU'RE PRETTY TOUGH.
LET ME *FIGHT* YOU SOMEDAY, WILL YA?
......
WE COULD GO HERE AN' *NOW*, IF Y' WANT...
WHOA, WHOA, TIGER.
HEY, HEY... *HA, HA, HA.*
YAAY~

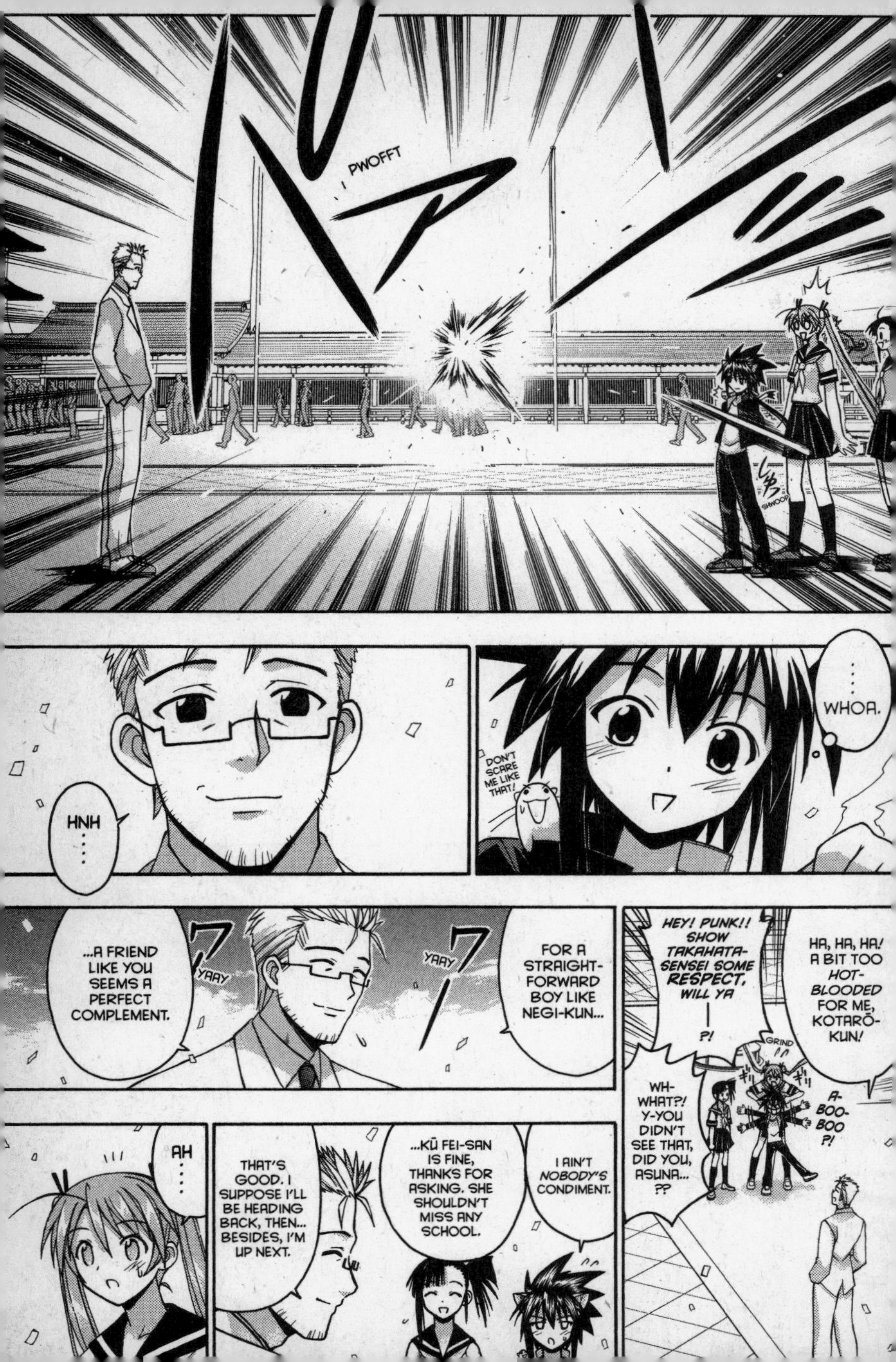

PWOFFT
SHWOOP
...WHOA.
DON'T SCARE ME LIKE THAT!
HNH...
HEY! PUNK!! SHOW TAKAHATA-SENSEI SOME RESPECT, WILL YA—?!
HA, HA, HA! A BIT TOO HOT-BLOODED FOR ME, KOTARŌ-KUN!
GRIND
A-BOO-BOO?!
WH-WHAT?! Y-YOU DIDN'T SEE THAT, DID YOU, ASUNA...??
FOR A STRAIGHT-FORWARD BOY LIKE NEGI-KUN...
YAAY
YAAY
...A FRIEND LIKE YOU SEEMS A PERFECT COMPLEMENT.
I AIN'T NOBODY'S CONDIMENT.
...KŪ FEI-SAN IS FINE, THANKS FOR ASKING. SHE SHOULDN'T MISS ANY SCHOOL.
THAT'S GOOD. I SUPPOSE I'LL BE HEADING BACK, THEN... BESIDES, I'M UP NEXT.
AH...

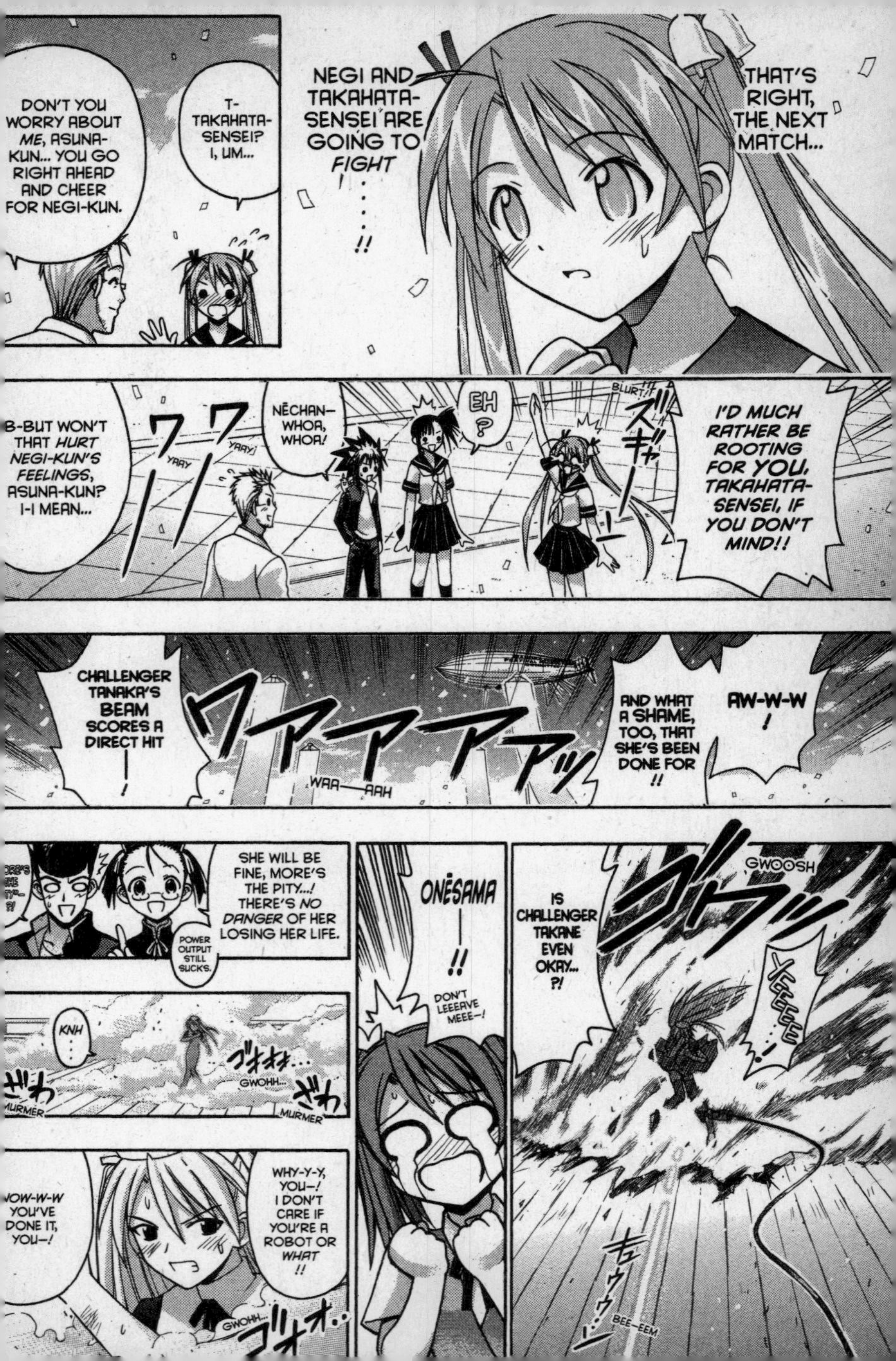

THAT'S RIGHT, THE NEXT MATCH...
NEGI AND TAKAHATA-SENSEI ARE GOING TO FIGHT ......!!
T-TAKAHATA-SENSEI? I, UM...
DON'T YOU WORRY ABOUT ME, ASUNA-KUN... YOU GO RIGHT AHEAD AND CHEER FOR NEGI-KUN.
I'D MUCH RATHER BE ROOTING FOR YOU, TAKAHATA-SENSEI, IF YOU DON'T MIND!!
BLURT!
EH?
NĒCHAN— WHOA, WHOA!
YAAY!
YAAY
B-BUT WON'T THAT HURT NEGI-KUN'S FEELINGS, ASUNA-KUN? I-I MEAN...
AW-W-W!
AND WHAT A SHAME, TOO, THAT SHE'S BEEN DONE FOR!!
WAA—AAH
CHALLENGER TANAKA'S BEAM SCORES A DIRECT HIT—!
GWOOSH
YEEEEE...!
IS CHALLENGER TAKANE EVEN OKAY...?!
BEE—EEM
ONĒSAMA—!!
DON'T LEEEAVE MEEE—!
SHE WILL BE FINE, MORE'S THE PITY...! THERE'S NO DANGER OF HER LOSING HER LIFE.
POWER OUTPUT STILL SUCKS.
KNH...
GWOHH...
MURMER
MURMER
WHY-Y-Y, YOU—! I DON'T CARE IF YOU'RE A ROBOT OR WHAT!!
OW-W-W YOU'VE DONE IT, YOU—!
GWOHH...

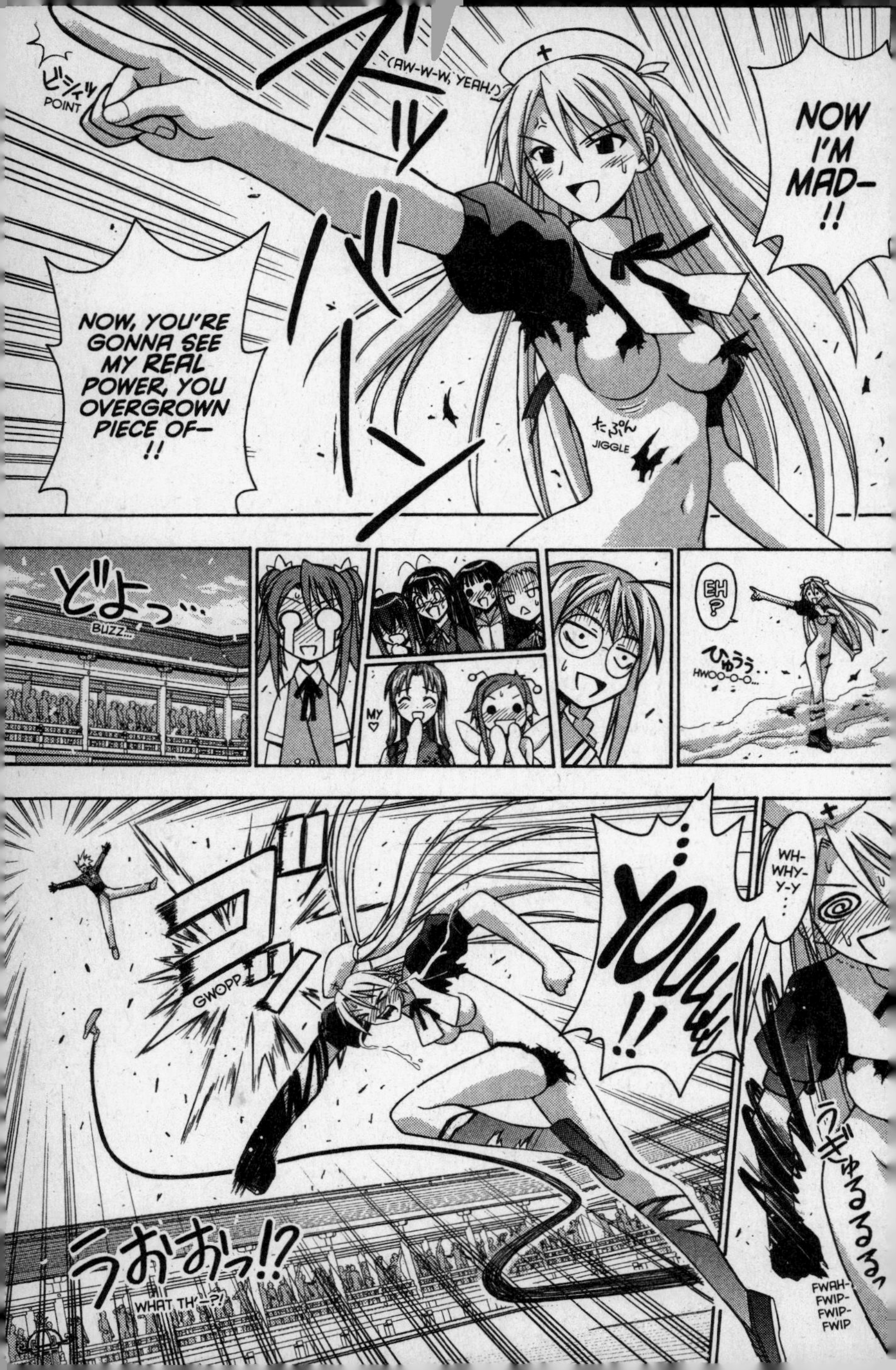
NOW I'M MAD—!!
(AW-W-W, YEAH!)
たぷん
JIGGLE
NOW, YOU'RE GONNA SEE MY REAL POWER, YOU OVERGROWN PIECE OF—!!
ビシッ
POINT
EH?
ひゅうう…
HWOO-O-O…
MY ♡
どよっ…
BUZZ…
WH-WHY-Y-Y…
うぎゅるるる
FWAH-FWIP-FWIP-FWIP
…YOU!!
GWOPP
うおおっ!?
WHAT TH—?!

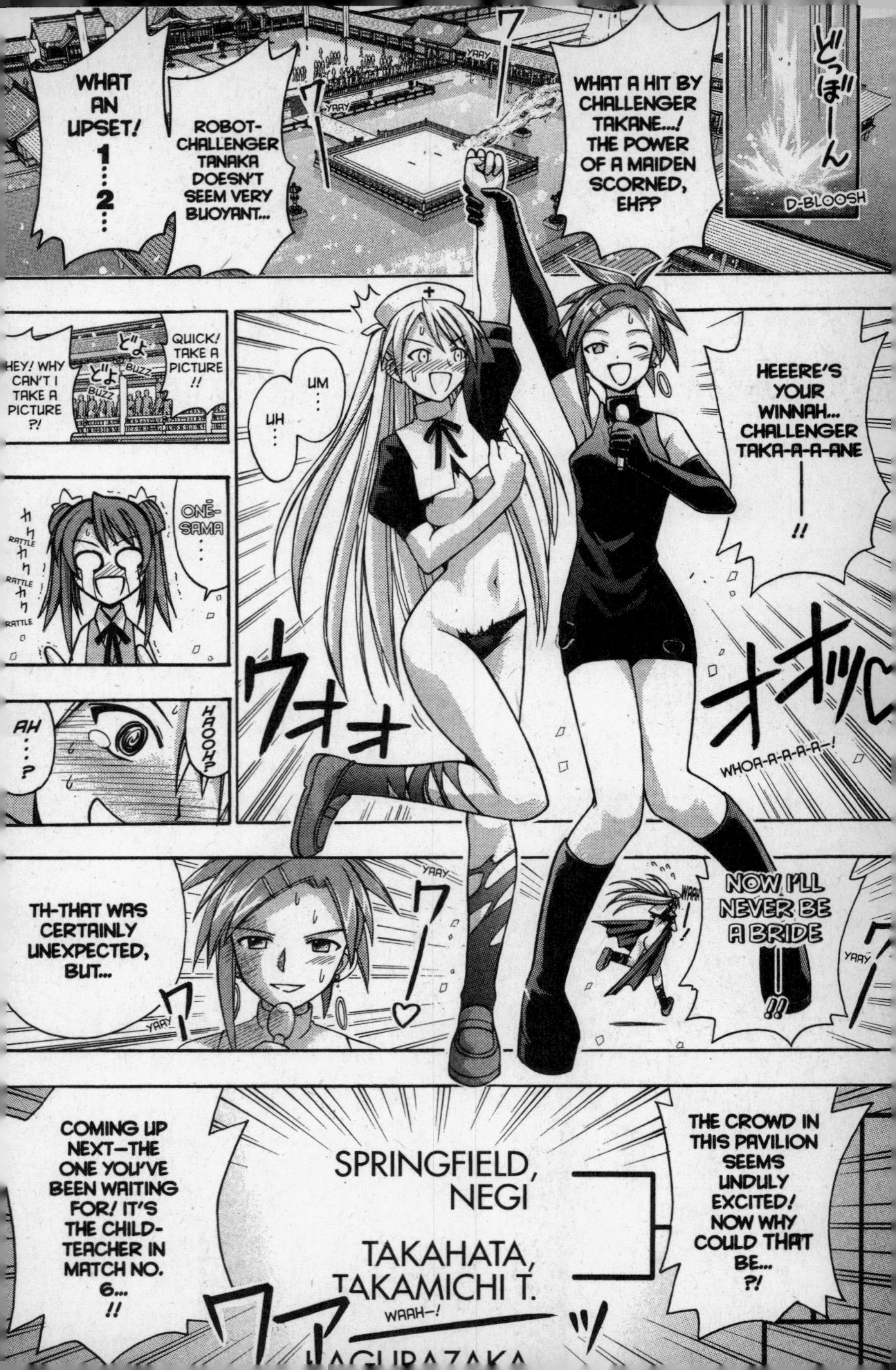

どっぽーん
D-BLOOSH
WHAT A HIT BY CHALLENGER TAKANE...! THE POWER OF A MAIDEN SCORNED, EH??
ワー
YAAY
ワー
YAAY
ROBOT-CHALLENGER TANAKA DOESN'T SEEM VERY BUOYANT...
WHAT AN UPSET! 1...2...
HEEERE'S YOUR WINNAH... CHALLENGER TAKA-A-A-ANE—!!
UM...
UH...
ウォォオオッ
WHOA-A-A-A-A-!
QUICK! TAKE A PICTURE!!
どよどよ
BUZZ BUZZ
HEY! WHY CAN'T I TAKE A PICTURE?!
ONĒ-SAMA...
RATTLE RATTLE RATTLE
HAOOH?
AH...?
ワー
YAAY
NOW I'LL NEVER BE A BRIDE—!!
WAAH!
ワー
YAAY
ワー
YAAY
TH-THAT WAS CERTAINLY UNEXPECTED, BUT...
THE CROWD IN THIS PAVILION SEEMS UNDULY EXCITED! NOW WHY COULD THAT BE...?!
SPRINGFIELD, NEGI
TAKAHATA, TAKAMICHI T.
COMING UP NEXT—THE ONE YOU'VE BEEN WAITING FOR! IT'S THE CHILD-TEACHER IN MATCH NO. 6...!!
ワァッ
WAAH—!

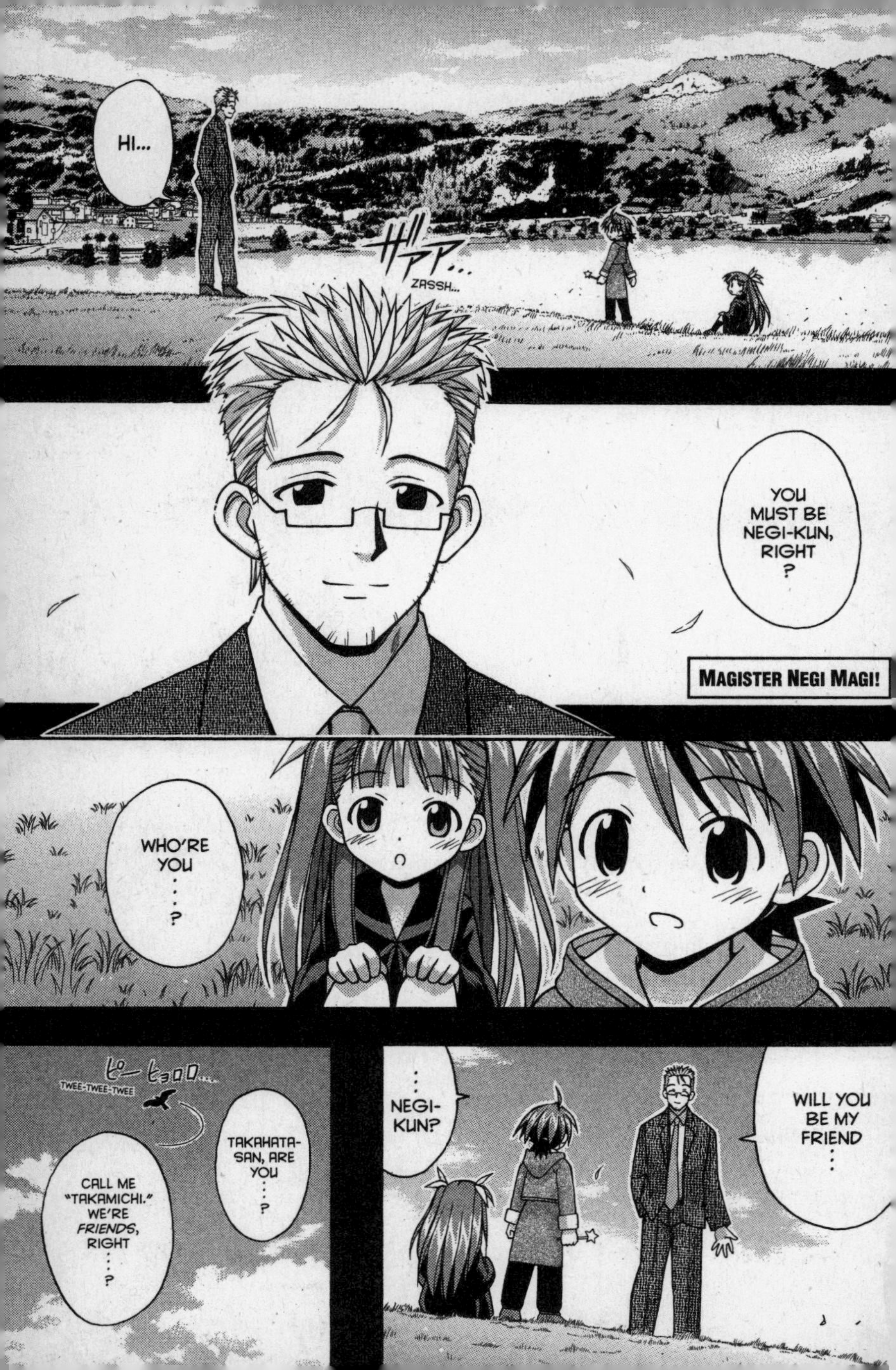
ザァァ...
ZASSH...
HI...
YOU MUST BE NEGI-KUN, RIGHT?
MAGISTER NEGI MAGI!
WHO'RE YOU...?
WILL YOU BE MY FRIEND...
...NEGI-KUN?
ピー ヒョロロ...
TWEE-TWEE-TWEE
TAKAHATA-SAN, ARE YOU...?
CALL ME "TAKAMICHI." WE'RE *FRIENDS*, RIGHT...?

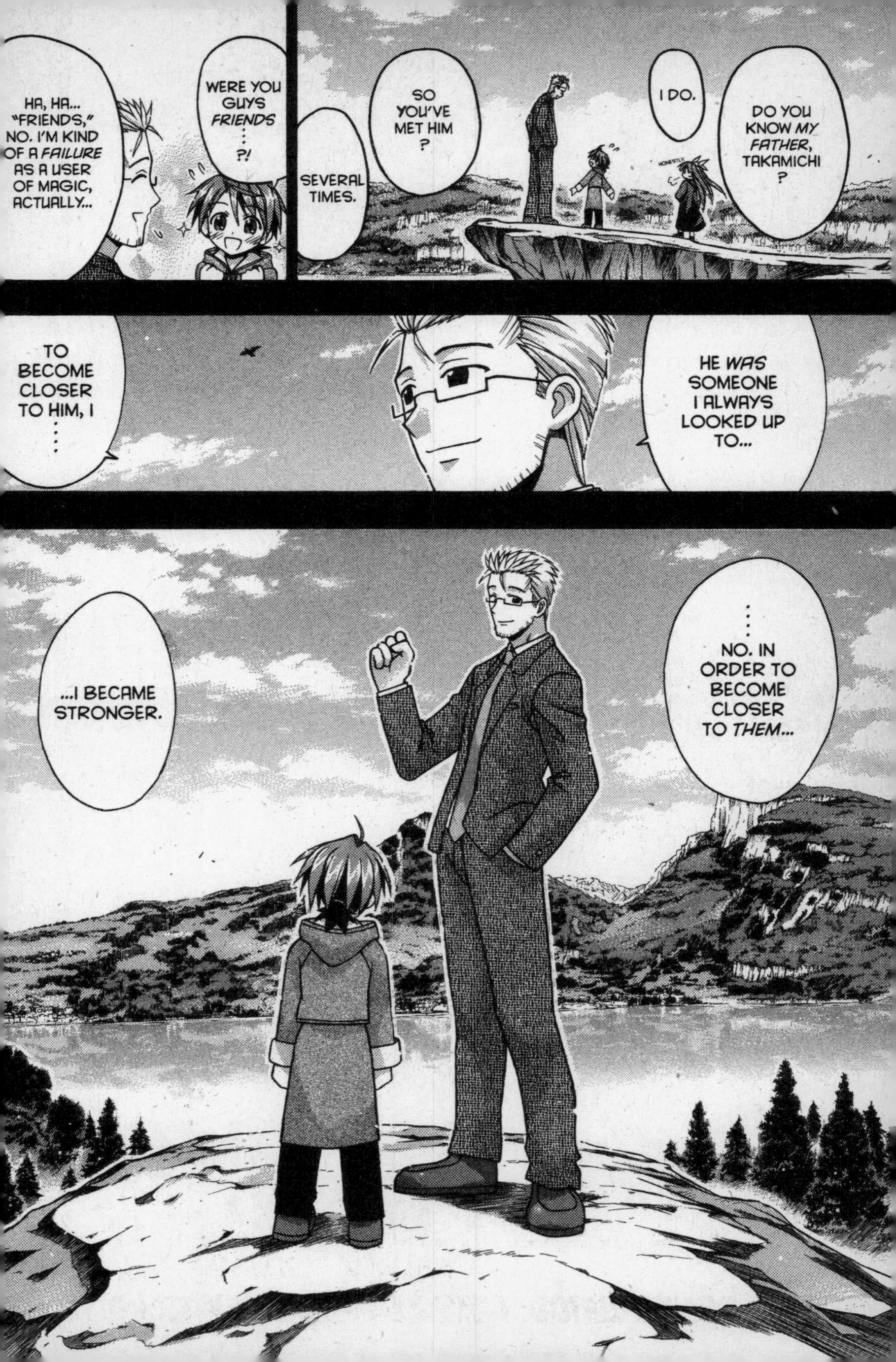
DO YOU KNOW MY FATHER, TAKAMICHI?
I DO.
HONESTLY.
SO YOU'VE MET HIM?
SEVERAL TIMES.
WERE YOU GUYS FRIENDS...?!
HA, HA... "FRIENDS," NO. I'M KIND OF A FAILURE AS A USER OF MAGIC, ACTUALLY...
HE WAS SOMEONE I ALWAYS LOOKED UP TO...
TO BECOME CLOSER TO HIM, I...
...NO. IN ORDER TO BECOME CLOSER TO THEM...
...I BECAME STRONGER.

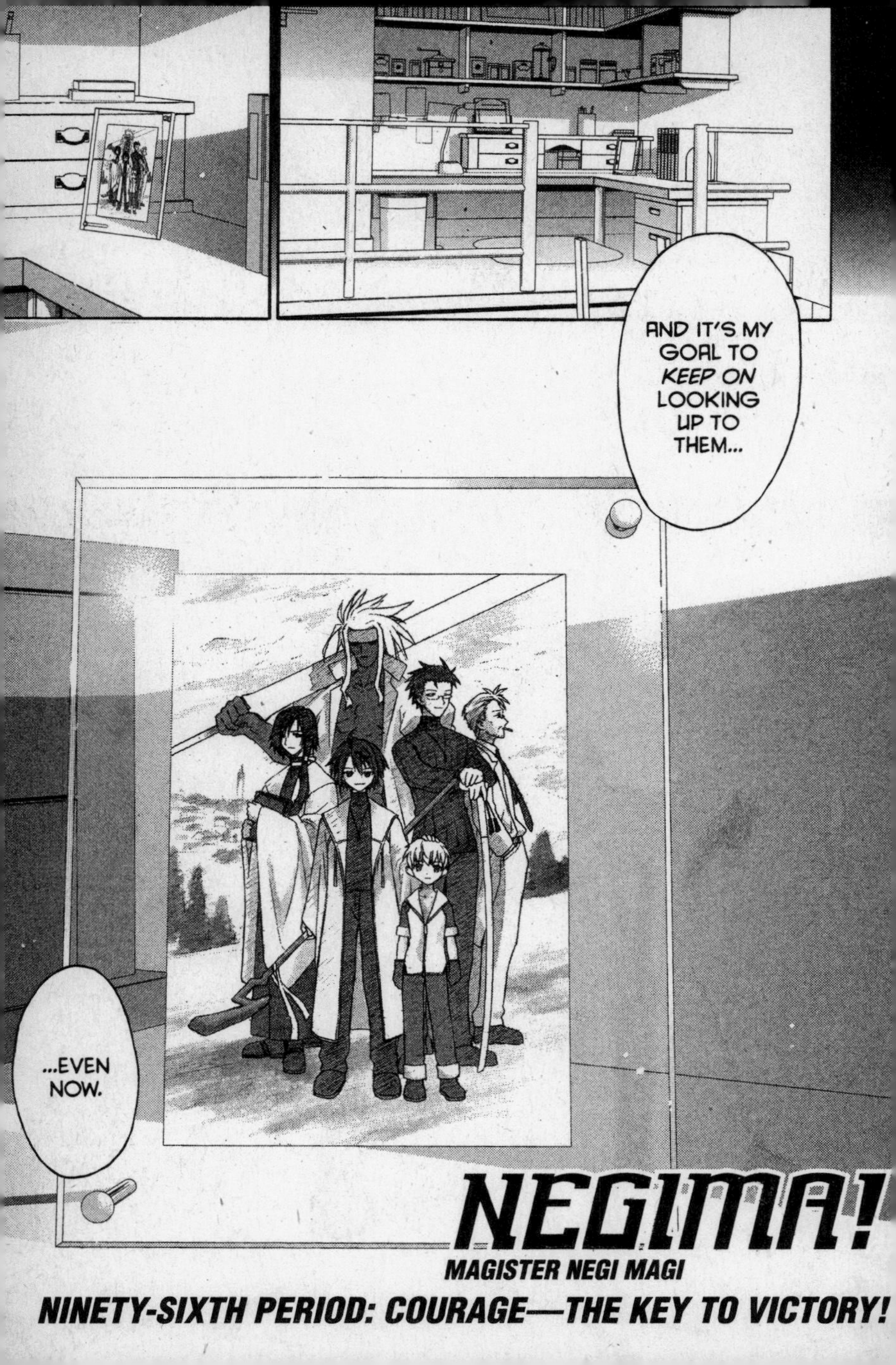
AND IT'S MY GOAL TO KEEP ON LOOKING UP TO THEM...
...EVEN NOW.
NEGIMA!
MAGISTER NEGI MAGI
NINETY-SIXTH PERIOD: COURAGE—THE KEY TO VICTORY!

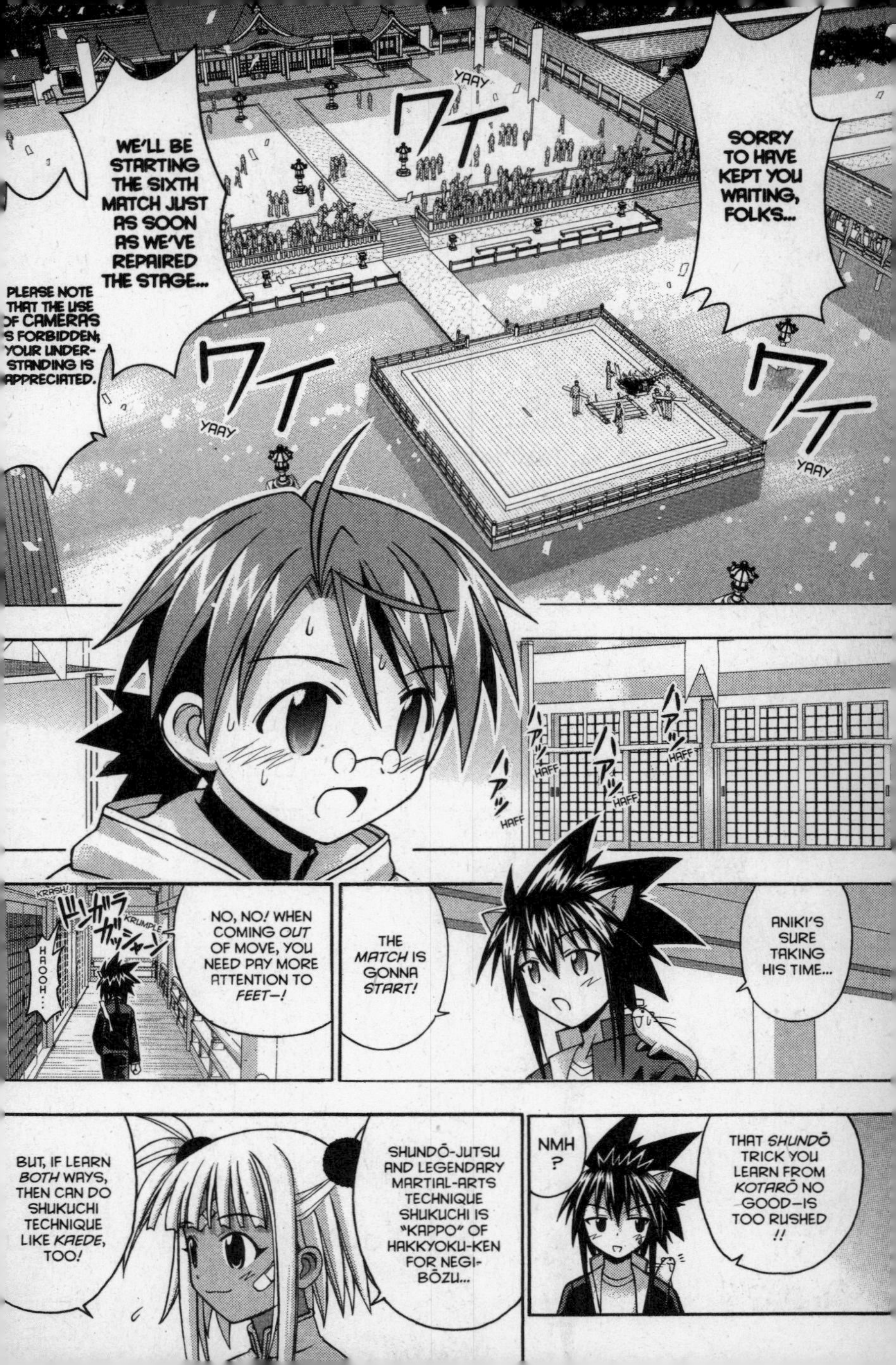
SORRY TO HAVE KEPT YOU WAITING, FOLKS...
WE'LL BE STARTING THE SIXTH MATCH JUST AS SOON AS WE'VE REPAIRED THE STAGE...
PLEASE NOTE THAT THE USE OF CAMERAS IS FORBIDDEN; YOUR UNDERSTANDING IS APPRECIATED.
ワイ
YAAY
ワイ
YAAY
ワイ
YAAY
ハァッ
HAFF
ハァッ
HAFF
ハァッ
HAFF
ハァッ
HAFF
ANIKI'S SURE TAKING HIS TIME...
THE *MATCH* IS GONNA *START!*
NO, NO! WHEN COMING *OUT* OF MOVE, YOU NEED PAY MORE ATTENTION TO *FEET*—!
ドンガラガッシャーン
KRASH!
KRUMPLE
HAOOH...
THAT *SHUNDŌ* TRICK YOU LEARN FROM *KOTARŌ* NO GOOD—IS TOO RUSHED !!
NMH ?
SHUNDŌ-JUTSU AND LEGENDARY MARTIAL-ARTS TECHNIQUE SHUKUCHI IS "KAPPO" OF HAKKYOKU-KEN FOR NEGI-BŌZU...
BUT, IF LEARN *BOTH* WAYS, THEN CAN DO SHUKUCHI TECHNIQUE LIKE *KAEDE*, TOO!

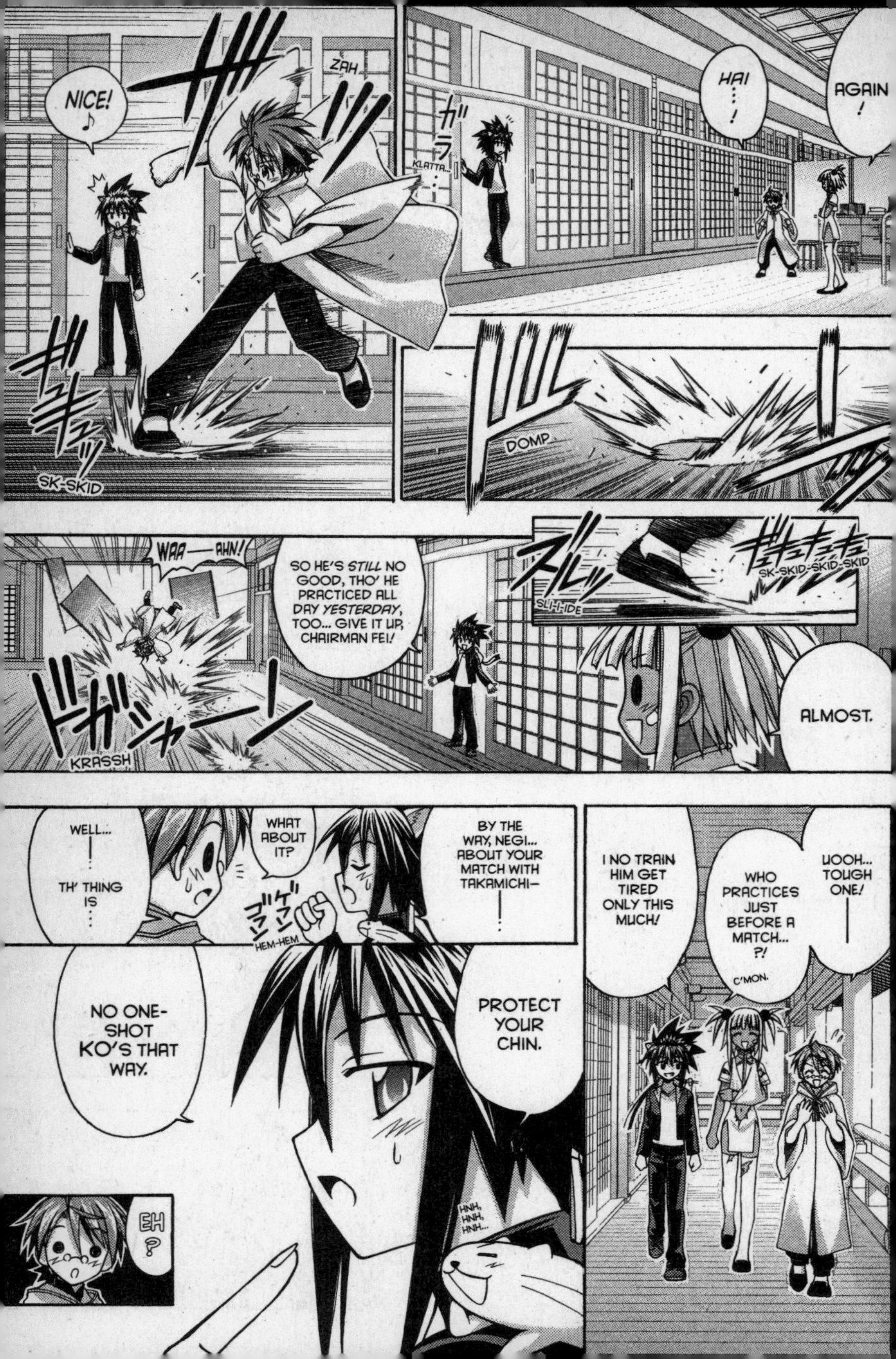
AGAIN!
HAI...!
KLATTA...
DOMP
ZAH
NICE! ♪
SK-SKID
SK-SKID-SKID-SKID
SLIH-IDE
ALMOST.
SO HE'S *STILL* NO GOOD, THO' HE PRACTICED ALL DAY *YESTERDAY*, TOO... GIVE IT UP, CHAIRMAN FEI!
WAA—AHN!
KRASSH
UOOH... TOUGH ONE!
WHO PRACTICES JUST BEFORE A MATCH...?!
C'MON.
I NO TRAIN HIM GET TIRED ONLY THIS MUCH!
BY THE WAY, NEGI... ABOUT YOUR MATCH WITH TAKAMICHI—!
WHAT ABOUT IT?
HEM-HEM
WELL...! TH' THING IS...
PROTECT YOUR CHIN.
NO ONE-SHOT KO'S THAT WAY.
HNH, HNH, HNH...
EH?

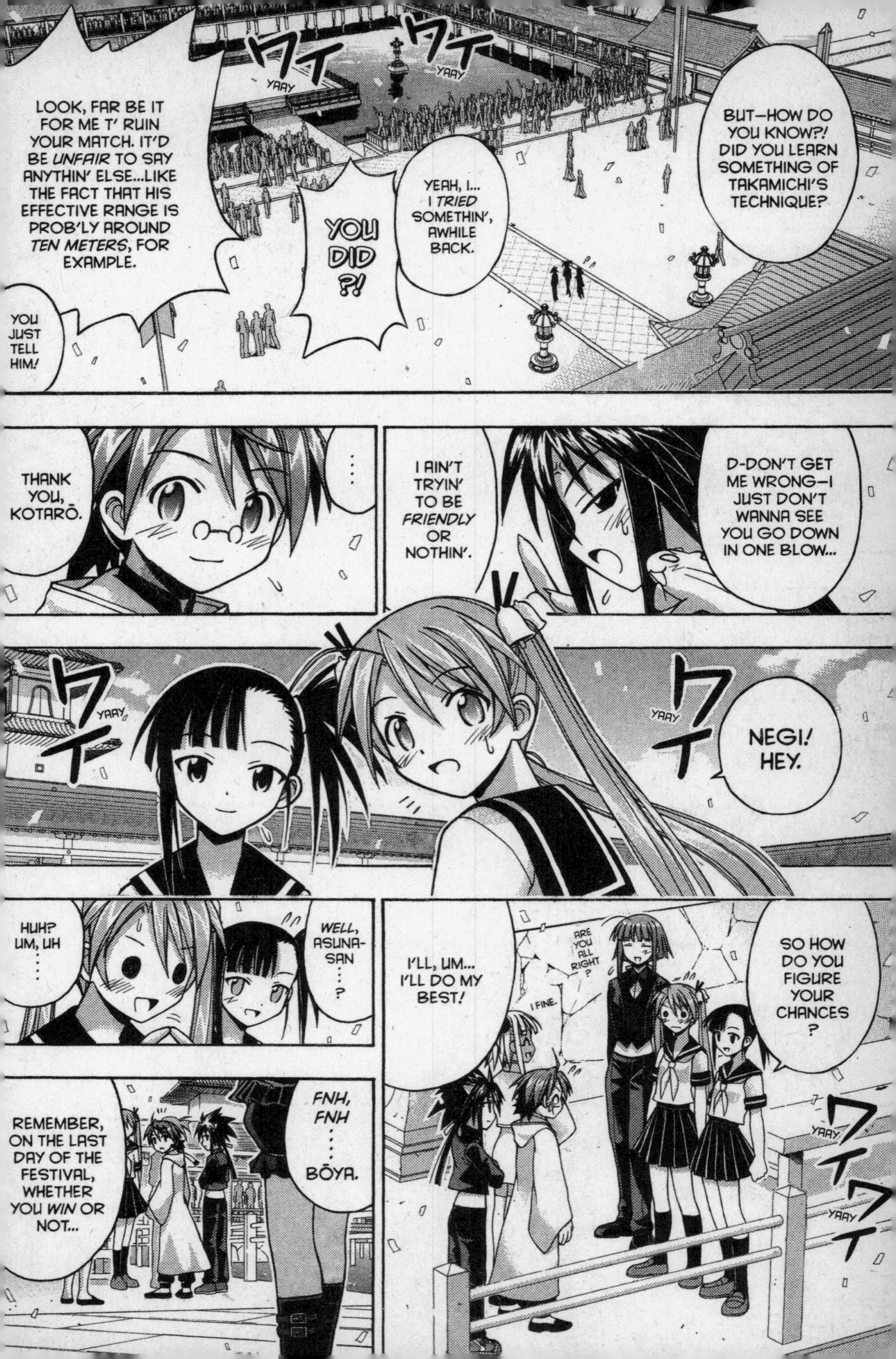

YAAY
YAAY
BUT—HOW DO YOU KNOW?! DID YOU LEARN SOMETHING OF TAKAMICHI'S TECHNIQUE?
YEAH, I... I *TRIED* SOMETHIN', AWHILE BACK.
YOU DID ?!
LOOK, FAR BE IT FOR ME T' RUIN YOUR MATCH. IT'D BE *UNFAIR* TO SAY ANYTHIN' ELSE...LIKE THE FACT THAT HIS EFFECTIVE RANGE IS PROB'LY AROUND *TEN METERS*, FOR EXAMPLE.
YOU JUST TELL HIM!
D-DON'T GET ME WRONG—I JUST DON'T WANNA SEE YOU GO DOWN IN ONE BLOW...
I AIN'T TRYIN' TO BE *FRIENDLY* OR NOTHIN'.
...
THANK YOU, KOTARŌ.
YAAY
NEGI! HEY.
YAAY
SO HOW DO YOU FIGURE YOUR CHANCES?
ARE YOU ALL RIGHT?
I FINE.
I'LL, UM... I'LL DO MY BEST!
YAAY
YAAY
WELL, ASUNA-SAN...?
HUH? UM, UH ....
FNH, FNH .... BŌYA.
REMEMBER, ON THE LAST DAY OF THE FESTIVAL, WHETHER YOU *WIN* OR NOT...

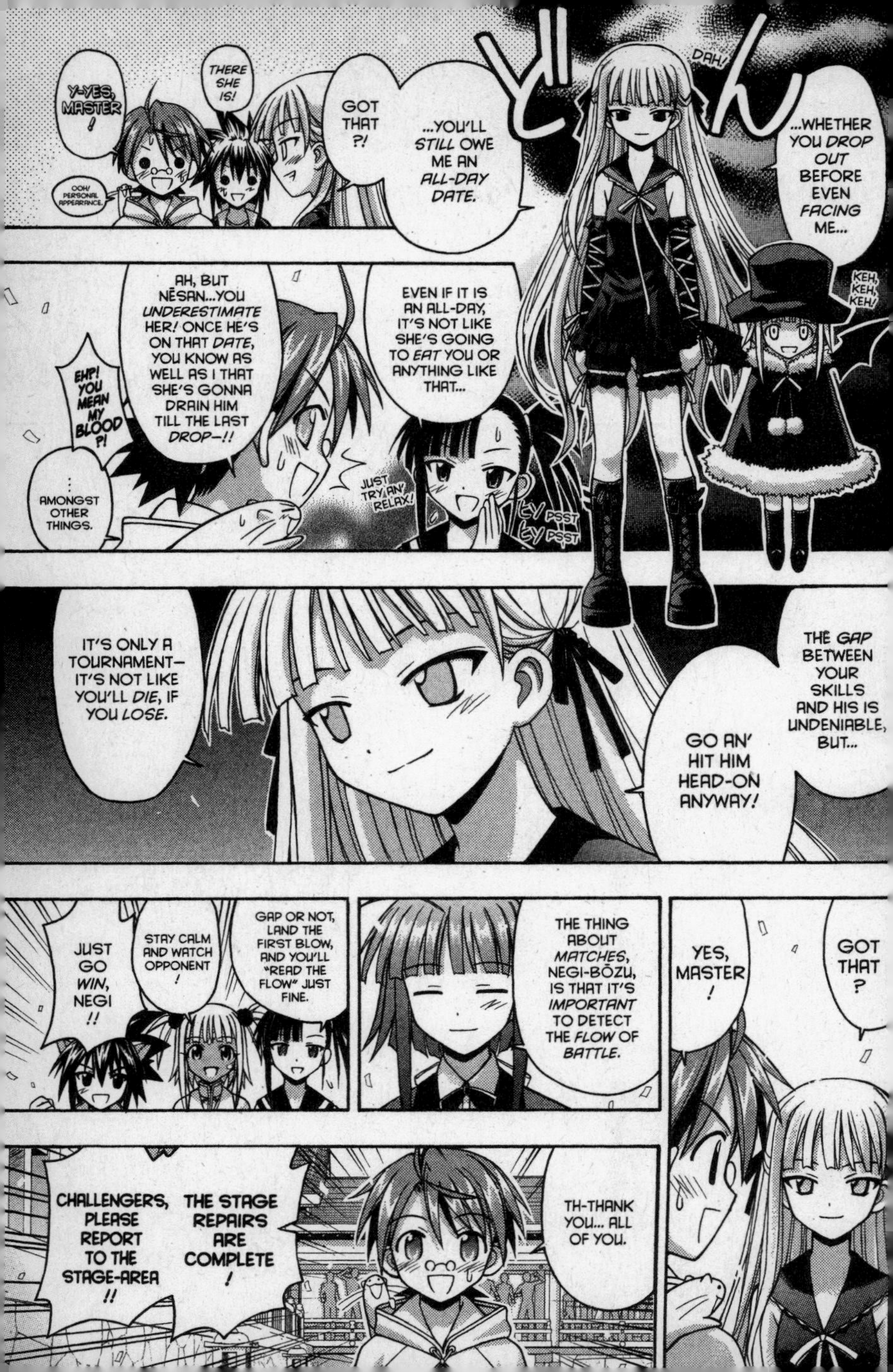
DAH!
...WHETHER YOU DROP OUT BEFORE EVEN FACING ME...
KEH, KEH, KEH!
...YOU'LL STILL OWE ME AN ALL-DAY DATE.
GOT THAT?!
THERE SHE IS!
Y-YES, MASTER!
OOH! PERSONAL APPEARANCE.
EVEN IF IT IS AN ALL-DAY, IT'S NOT LIKE SHE'S GOING TO EAT YOU OR ANYTHING LIKE THAT...
JUST TRY AN' RELAX!
PSST PSST
AH, BUT NĒSAN...YOU UNDERESTIMATE HER! ONCE HE'S ON THAT DATE, YOU KNOW AS WELL AS I THAT SHE'S GONNA DRAIN HIM TILL THE LAST DROP—!!
EHP! YOU MEAN MY BLOOD?!
... AMONGST OTHER THINGS.
THE GAP BETWEEN YOUR SKILLS AND HIS IS UNDENIABLE, BUT...
GO AN' HIT HIM HEAD-ON ANYWAY!
IT'S ONLY A TOURNAMENT— IT'S NOT LIKE YOU'LL DIE, IF YOU LOSE.
GOT THAT?
YES, MASTER!
THE THING ABOUT MATCHES, NEGI-BŌZU, IS THAT IT'S IMPORTANT TO DETECT THE FLOW OF BATTLE.
GAP OR NOT, LAND THE FIRST BLOW, AND YOU'LL "READ THE FLOW" JUST FINE.
STAY CALM AND WATCH OPPONENT!
JUST GO WIN, NEGI!!
TH-THANK YOU... ALL OF YOU.
THE STAGE REPAIRS ARE COMPLETE!
CHALLENGERS, PLEASE REPORT TO THE STAGE-AREA!!

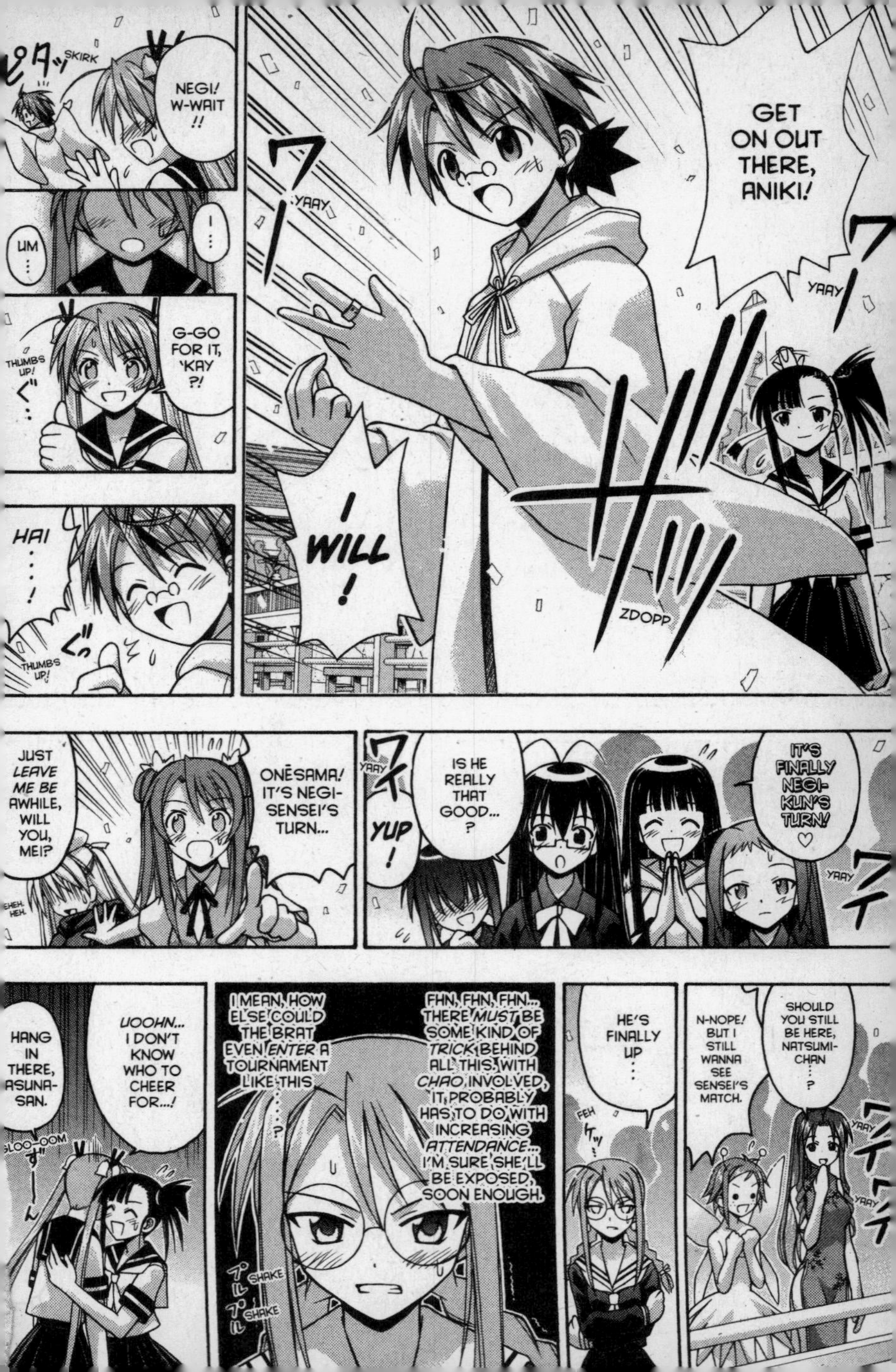
GET ON OUT THERE, ANIKI!
YAAY
YAAY
ZDOPP
I WILL!
SKIRK
NEGI! W-WAIT!!
I...
UM...
G-GO FOR IT, 'KAY?!
THUMBS UP!
HAI...!
THUMBS UP!
IT'S FINALLY NEGI-KUN'S TURN! ♡
YAAY
IS HE REALLY THAT GOOD...?
YUP!
YAAY
ONĒSAMA! IT'S NEGI-SENSEI'S TURN...
JUST LEAVE ME BE AWHILE, WILL YOU, MEI?
HEH. HEH.
SHOULD YOU STILL BE HERE, NATSUMI-CHAN...?
N-NOPE! BUT I STILL WANNA SEE SENSEI'S MATCH.
YAAY
YAAY
HE'S FINALLY UP...
FEH
FHN, FHN, FHN... THERE MUST BE SOME KIND OF TRICK BEHIND ALL THIS. WITH CHAO INVOLVED, IT PROBABLY HAS TO DO WITH INCREASING ATTENDANCE... I'M SURE SHE'LL BE EXPOSED SOON ENOUGH.
I MEAN, HOW ELSE COULD THE BRAT EVEN ENTER A TOURNAMENT LIKE THIS...?
SHAKE
SHAKE
UOOHN... I DON'T KNOW WHO TO CHEER FOR...!
HANG IN THERE, ASUNA-SAN.
GLOO-OOM

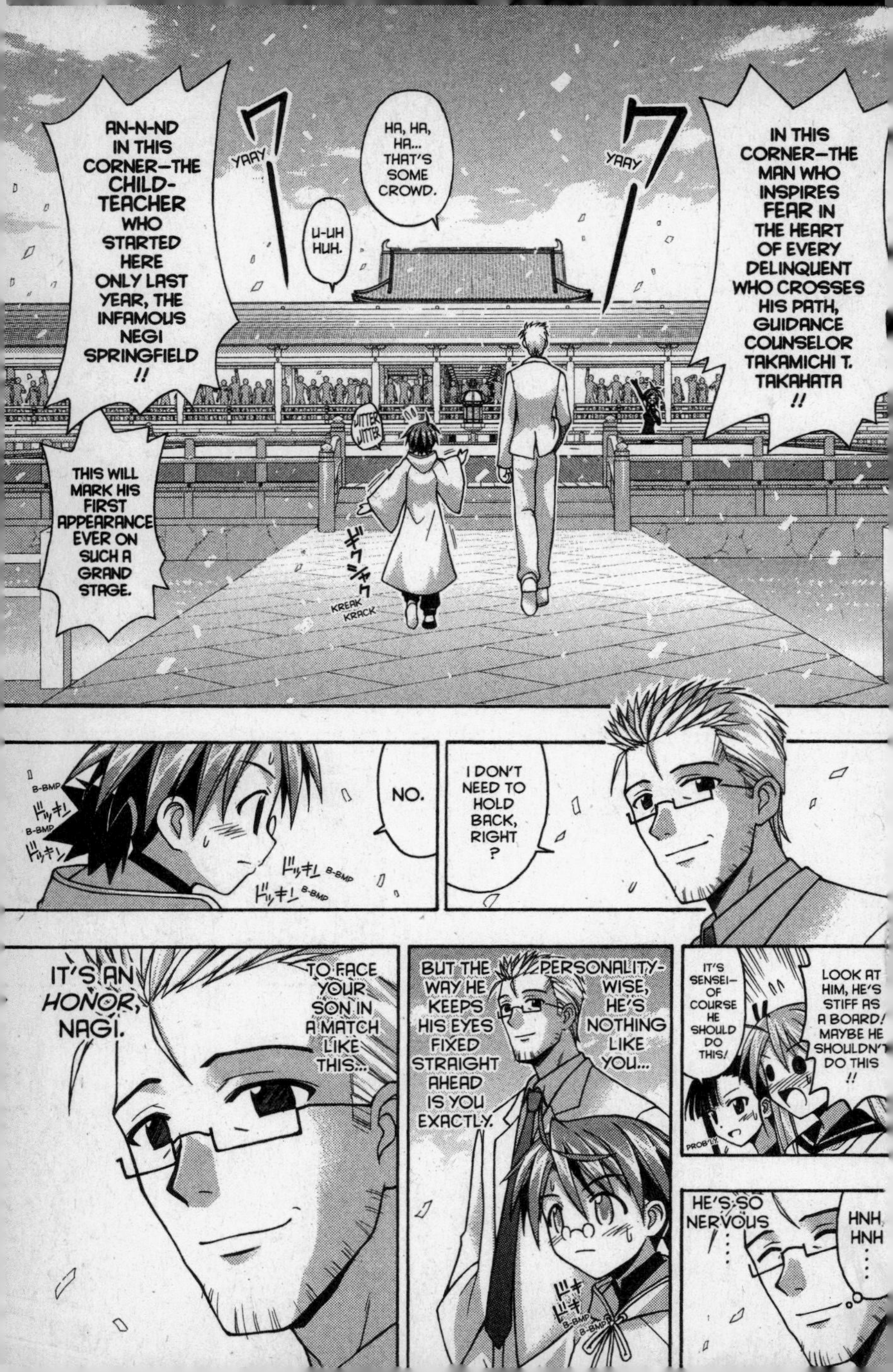
IN THIS CORNER—THE MAN WHO INSPIRES FEAR IN THE HEART OF EVERY DELINQUENT WHO CROSSES HIS PATH, GUIDANCE COUNSELOR TAKAMICHI T. TAKAHATA !!
YAAY
HA, HA, HA... THAT'S SOME CROWD.
U-UH HUH.
YAAY
AN-N-ND IN THIS CORNER—THE CHILD-TEACHER WHO STARTED HERE ONLY LAST YEAR, THE INFAMOUS NEGI SPRINGFIELD !!
JITTER JITTER
THIS WILL MARK HIS FIRST APPEARANCE EVER ON SUCH A GRAND STAGE.
KREAK KRACK
I DON'T NEED TO HOLD BACK, RIGHT?
NO.
B-BMP
B-BMP
B-BMP
B-BMP
LOOK AT HIM, HE'S STIFF AS A BOARD! MAYBE HE SHOULDN'T DO THIS !!
IT'S SENSEI—OF COURSE HE SHOULD DO THIS!
PROBLY
HNH HNH ...
HE'S SO NERVOUS ...
PERSONALITY-WISE, HE'S NOTHING LIKE YOU...
BUT THE WAY HE KEEPS HIS EYES FIXED STRAIGHT AHEAD IS YOU EXACTLY.
B-BMP
B-BMP
TO FACE YOUR SON IN A MATCH LIKE THIS...
IT'S AN HONOR, NAGI.

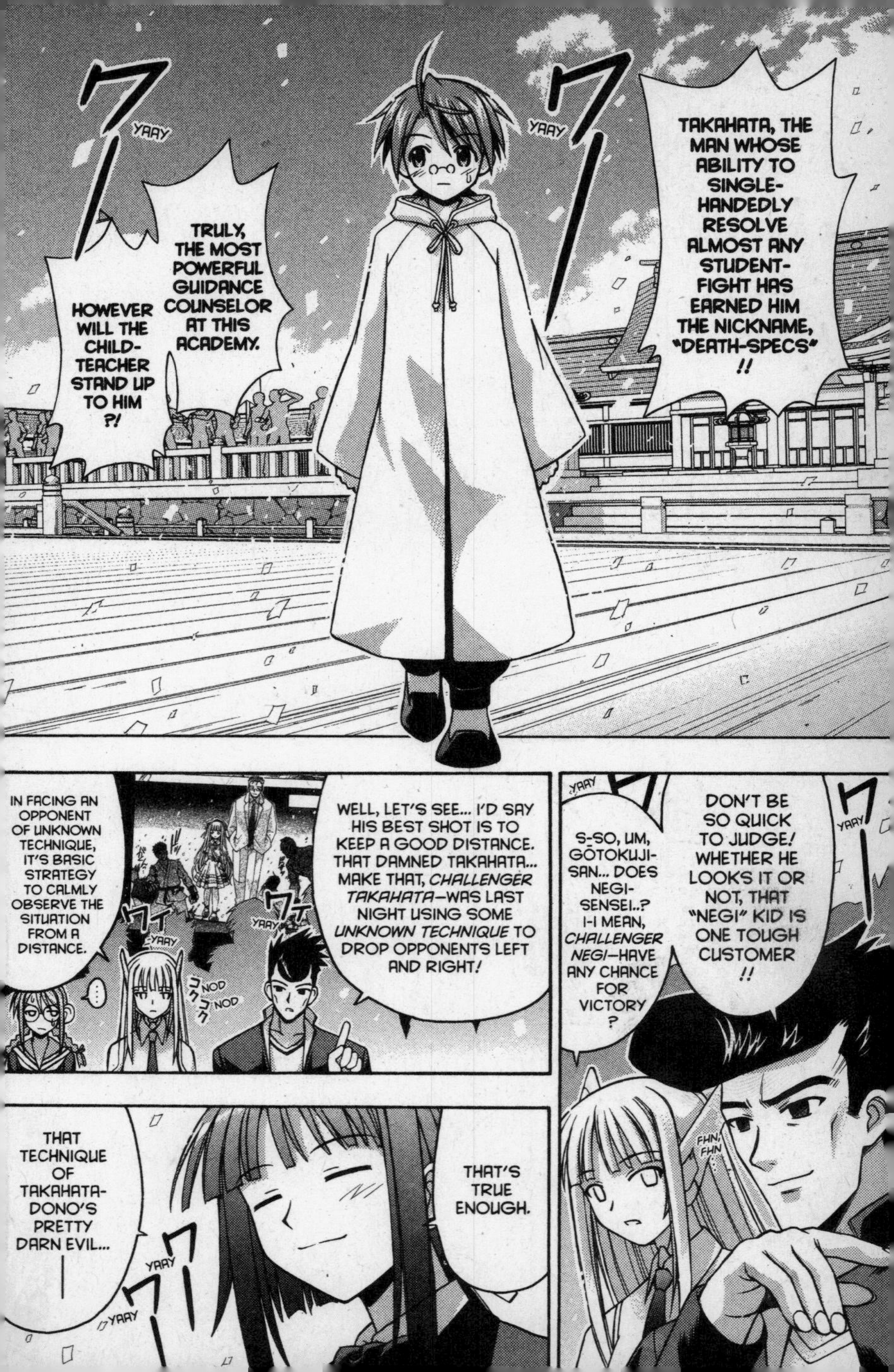
YAAY
YAAY
TAKAHATA, THE MAN WHOSE ABILITY TO SINGLE-HANDEDLY RESOLVE ALMOST ANY STUDENT-FIGHT HAS EARNED HIM THE NICKNAME, "DEATH-SPECS" !!
TRULY, THE MOST POWERFUL GUIDANCE COUNSELOR AT THIS ACADEMY.
HOWEVER WILL THE CHILD-TEACHER STAND UP TO HIM ?!
YAAY
YAAY
S-SO, UM, GŌTOKUJI-SAN... DOES NEGI-SENSEI..? I-I MEAN, CHALLENGER NEGI—HAVE ANY CHANCE FOR VICTORY ?
DON'T BE SO QUICK TO JUDGE! WHETHER HE LOOKS IT OR NOT, THAT "NEGI" KID IS ONE TOUGH CUSTOMER !!
YAAY
WELL, LET'S SEE... I'D SAY HIS BEST SHOT IS TO KEEP A GOOD DISTANCE. THAT DAMNED TAKAHATA... MAKE THAT, CHALLENGER TAKAHATA—WAS LAST NIGHT USING SOME UNKNOWN TECHNIQUE TO DROP OPPONENTS LEFT AND RIGHT!
YAAY
NOD NOD
IN FACING AN OPPONENT OF UNKNOWN TECHNIQUE, IT'S BASIC STRATEGY TO CALMLY OBSERVE THE SITUATION FROM A DISTANCE.
...
FHN, FHN
THAT TECHNIQUE OF TAKAHATA-DONO'S PRETTY DARN EVIL...
THAT'S TRUE ENOUGH.
YAAY
YAAY

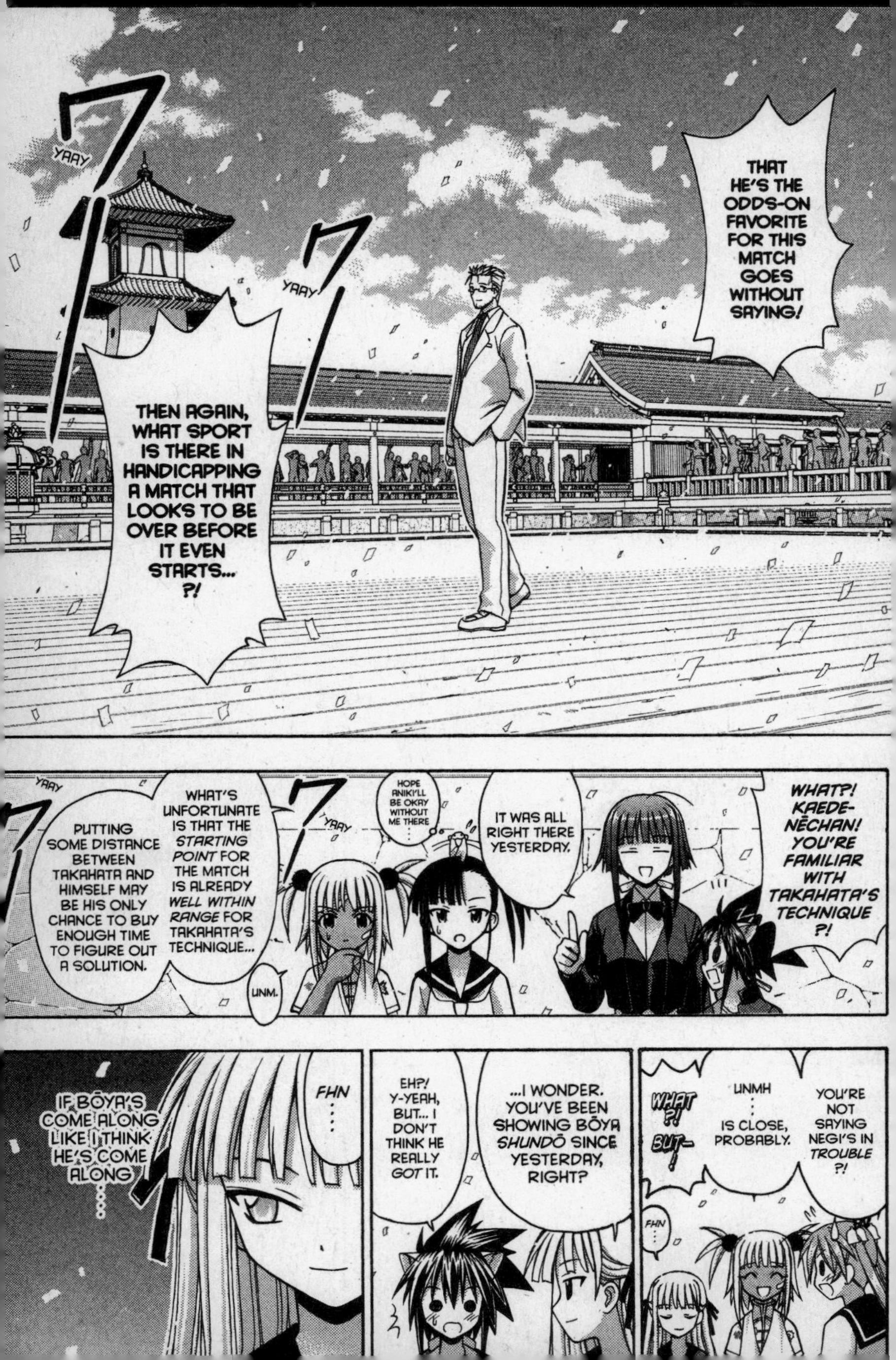
YAAY
THAT HE'S THE ODDS-ON FAVORITE FOR THIS MATCH GOES WITHOUT SAYING!
YAAY
THEN AGAIN, WHAT SPORT IS THERE IN HANDICAPPING A MATCH THAT LOOKS TO BE OVER BEFORE IT EVEN STARTS... ?!
WHAT?! KAEDE-NĒCHAN! YOU'RE FAMILIAR WITH TAKAHATA'S TECHNIQUE ?!
IT WAS ALL RIGHT THERE YESTERDAY.
HOPE ANIKI'LL BE OKAY WITHOUT ME THERE . . .
YAAY
WHAT'S UNFORTUNATE IS THAT THE STARTING POINT FOR THE MATCH IS ALREADY WELL WITHIN RANGE FOR TAKAHATA'S TECHNIQUE...
YAAY
PUTTING SOME DISTANCE BETWEEN TAKAHATA AND HIMSELF MAY BE HIS ONLY CHANCE TO BUY ENOUGH TIME TO FIGURE OUT A SOLUTION.
UNM.
YOU'RE NOT SAYING NEGI'S IN TROUBLE ?!
UNMH . . . IS CLOSE, PROBABLY.
WHAT ?! BUT- !
FHN . . .
...I WONDER. YOU'VE BEEN SHOWING BŌYA SHUNDŌ SINCE YESTERDAY, RIGHT?
EH?! Y-YEAH, BUT... I DON'T THINK HE REALLY GOT IT.
FHN . . .
IF BŌYA'S COME ALONG LIKE I THINK HE'S COME ALONG . . .

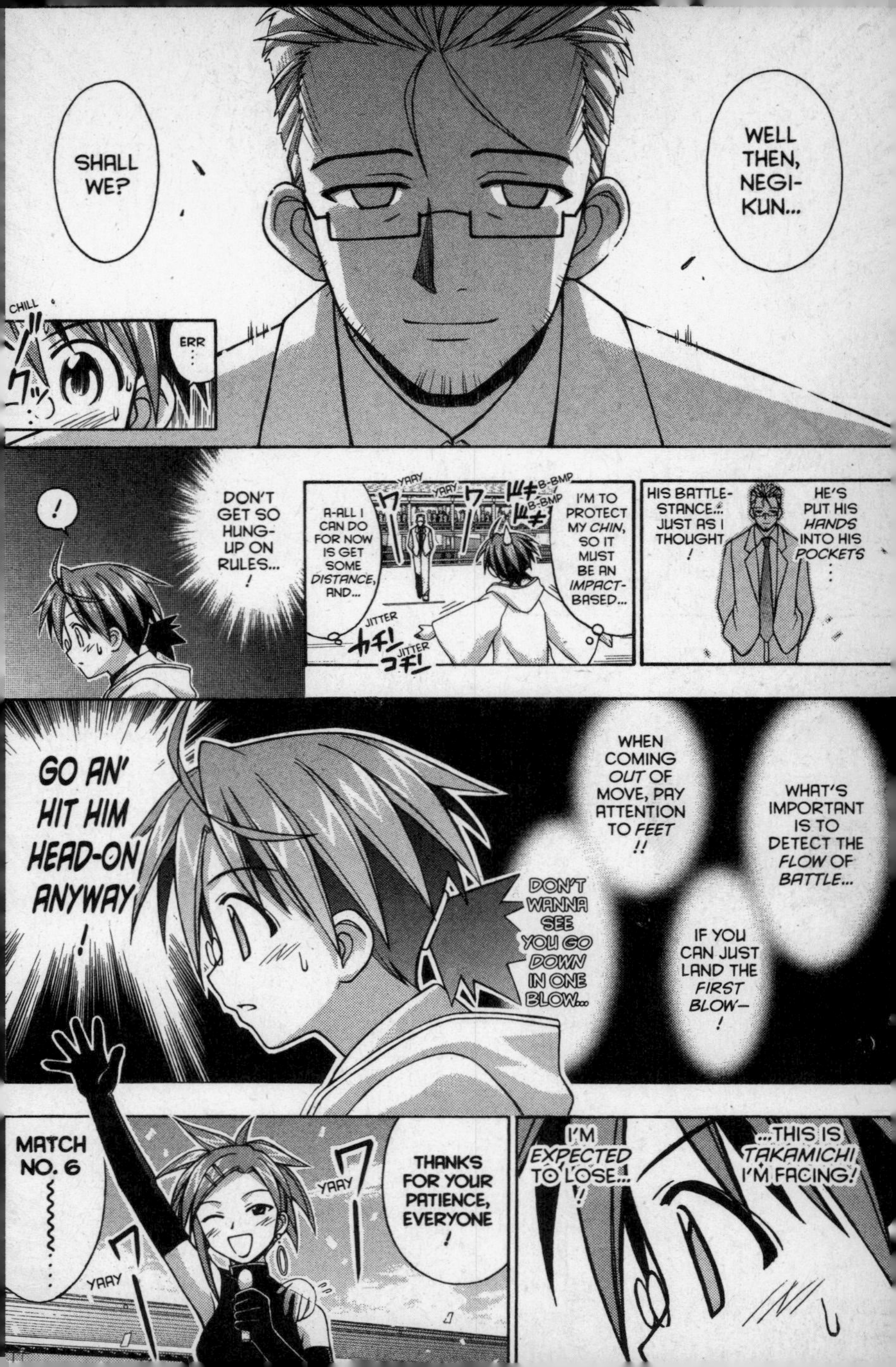
WELL THEN, NEGI-KUN...
SHALL WE?
CHILL
ERR...
HE'S PUT HIS HANDS INTO HIS POCKETS...
HIS BATTLE-STANCE... JUST AS I THOUGHT!
B-BMP
B-BMP
I'M TO PROTECT MY CHIN, SO IT MUST BE AN IMPACT-BASED...
YAAY
YAAY
A-ALL I CAN DO FOR NOW IS GET SOME DISTANCE, AND...
JITTER
JITTER
DON'T GET SO HUNG-UP ON RULES...!
!
WHAT'S IMPORTANT IS TO DETECT THE FLOW OF BATTLE...
WHEN COMING OUT OF MOVE, PAY ATTENTION TO FEET!!
IF YOU CAN JUST LAND THE FIRST BLOW—!
DON'T WANNA SEE YOU GO DOWN IN ONE BLOW...
GO AN' HIT HIM HEAD-ON ANYWAY!
...THIS IS TAKAMICHI I'M FACING!
I'M EXPECTED TO LOSE...!
THANKS FOR YOUR PATIENCE, EVERYONE!
YAAY
MATCH NO. 6...
YAAY

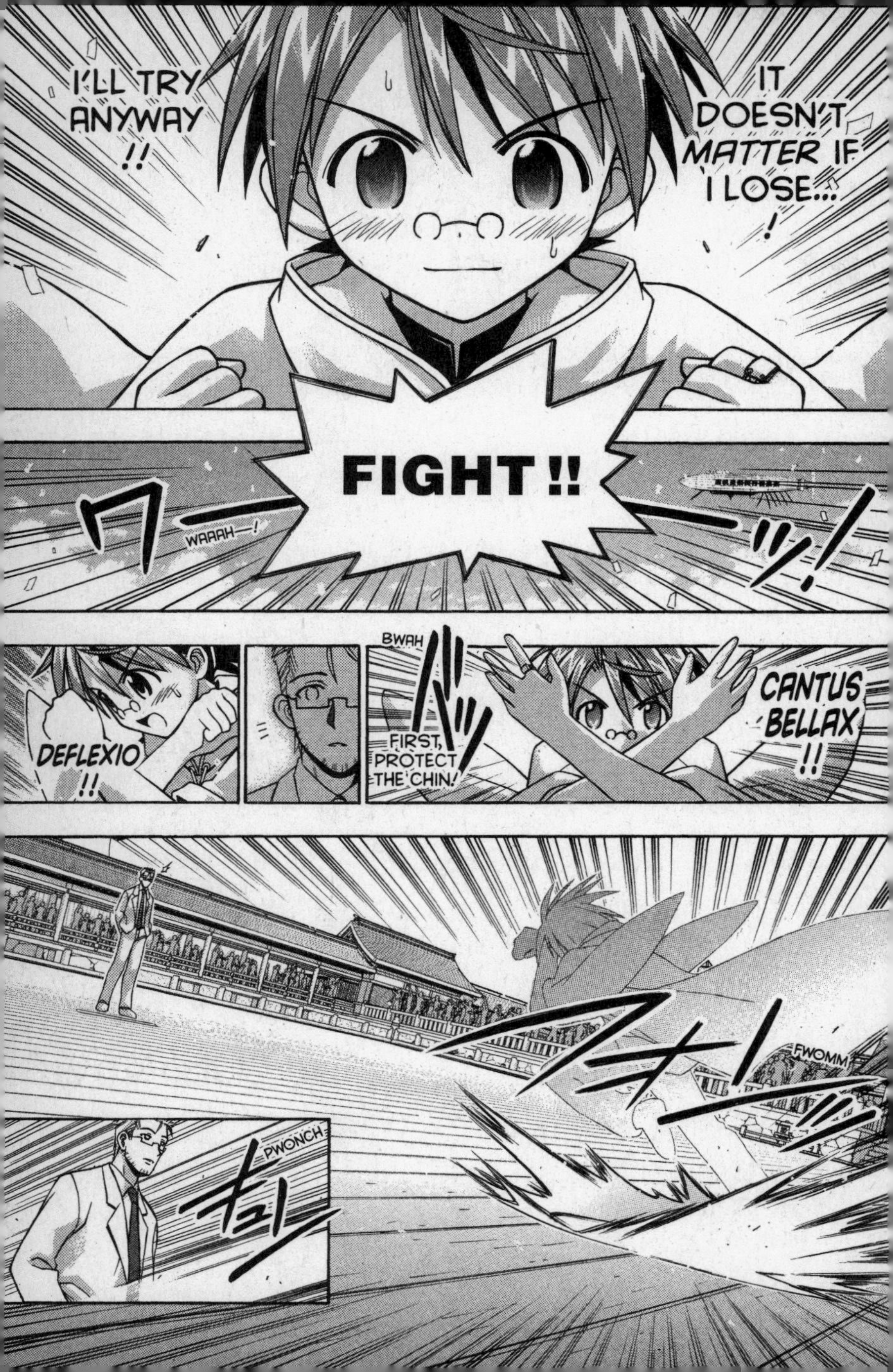
IT DOESN'T MATTER IF I LOSE...!
I'LL TRY ANYWAY!!
FIGHT!!
WAAAH—!
CANTUS BELLAX!!
BWAH
FIRST, PROTECT THE CHIN!
DEFLEXIO!!
FWOMM
PWONCH

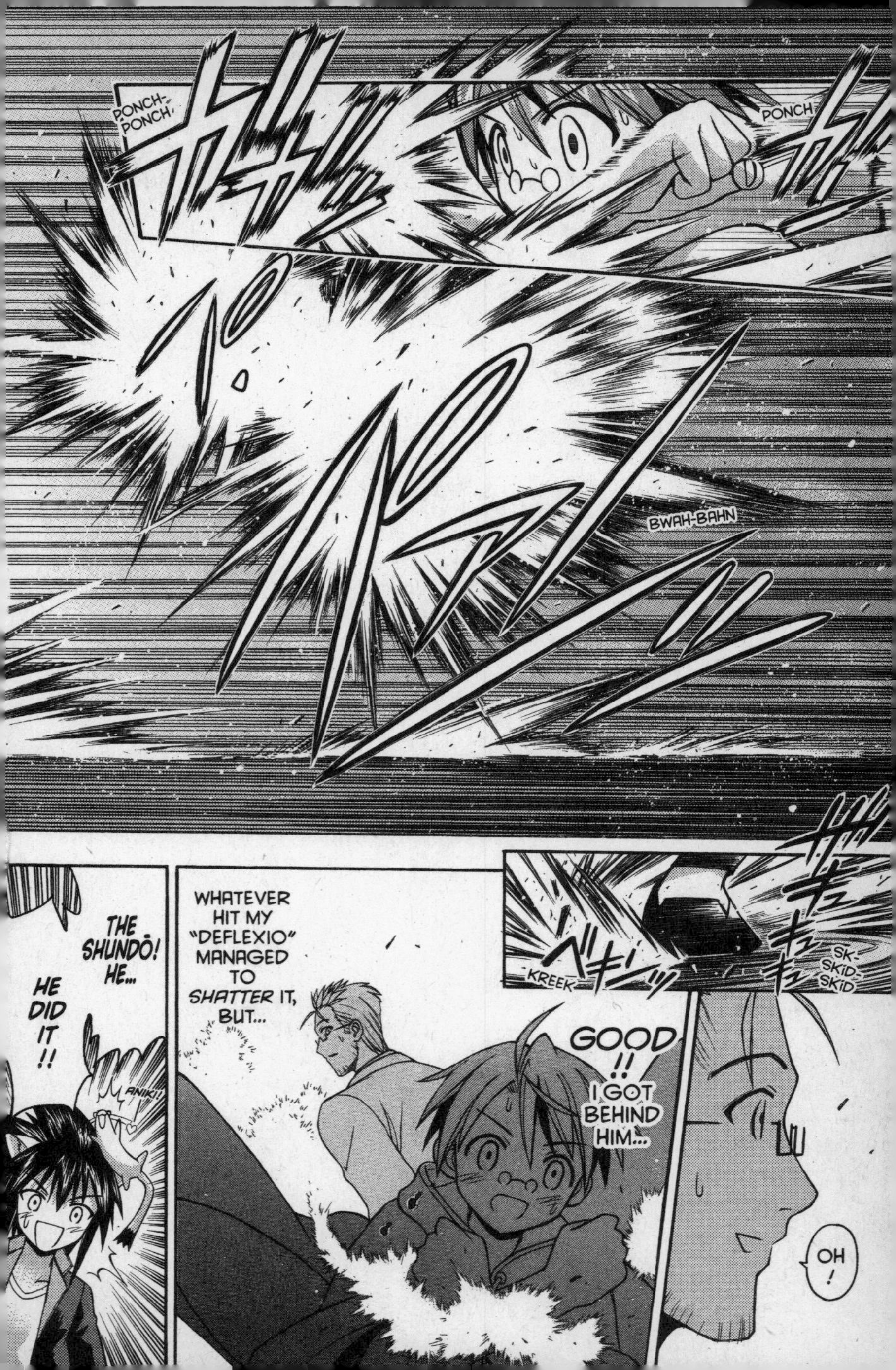
PONCH
PONCH-PONCH
BWAH-BAHN
SK-SKID-SKID
KREEK
OH!
GOOD!! I GOT BEHIND HIM...
WHATEVER HIT MY "DEFLEXIO" MANAGED TO SHATTER IT, BUT...
THE SHUNDŌ! HE...
HE DID IT!!
ANIKI!!

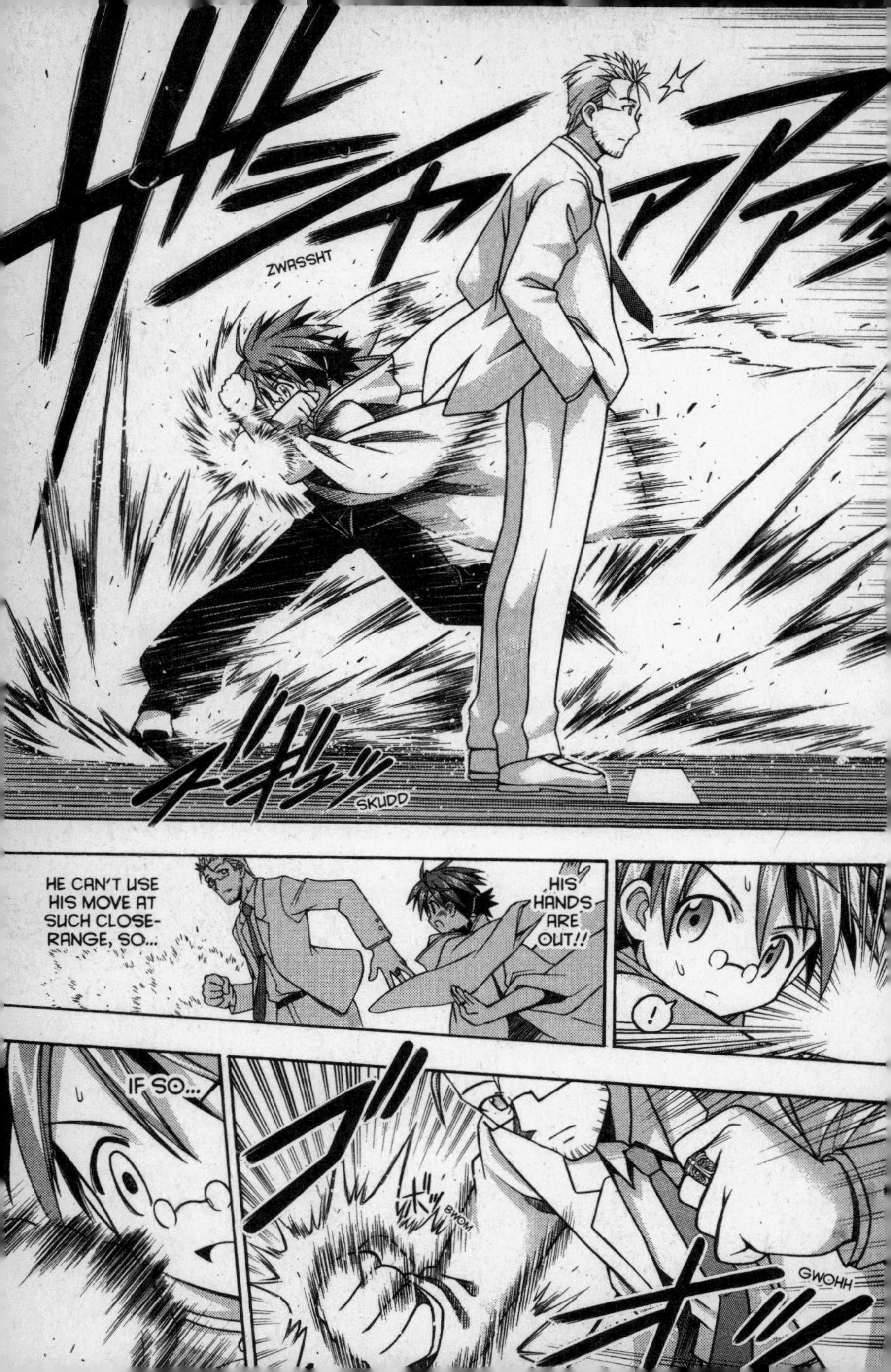
ZWASSHT
SKUDD
!
HIS HANDS ARE OUT!!
HE CAN'T USE HIS MOVE AT SUCH CLOSE-RANGE, SO...
BWOM
GWOHH
IF SO...

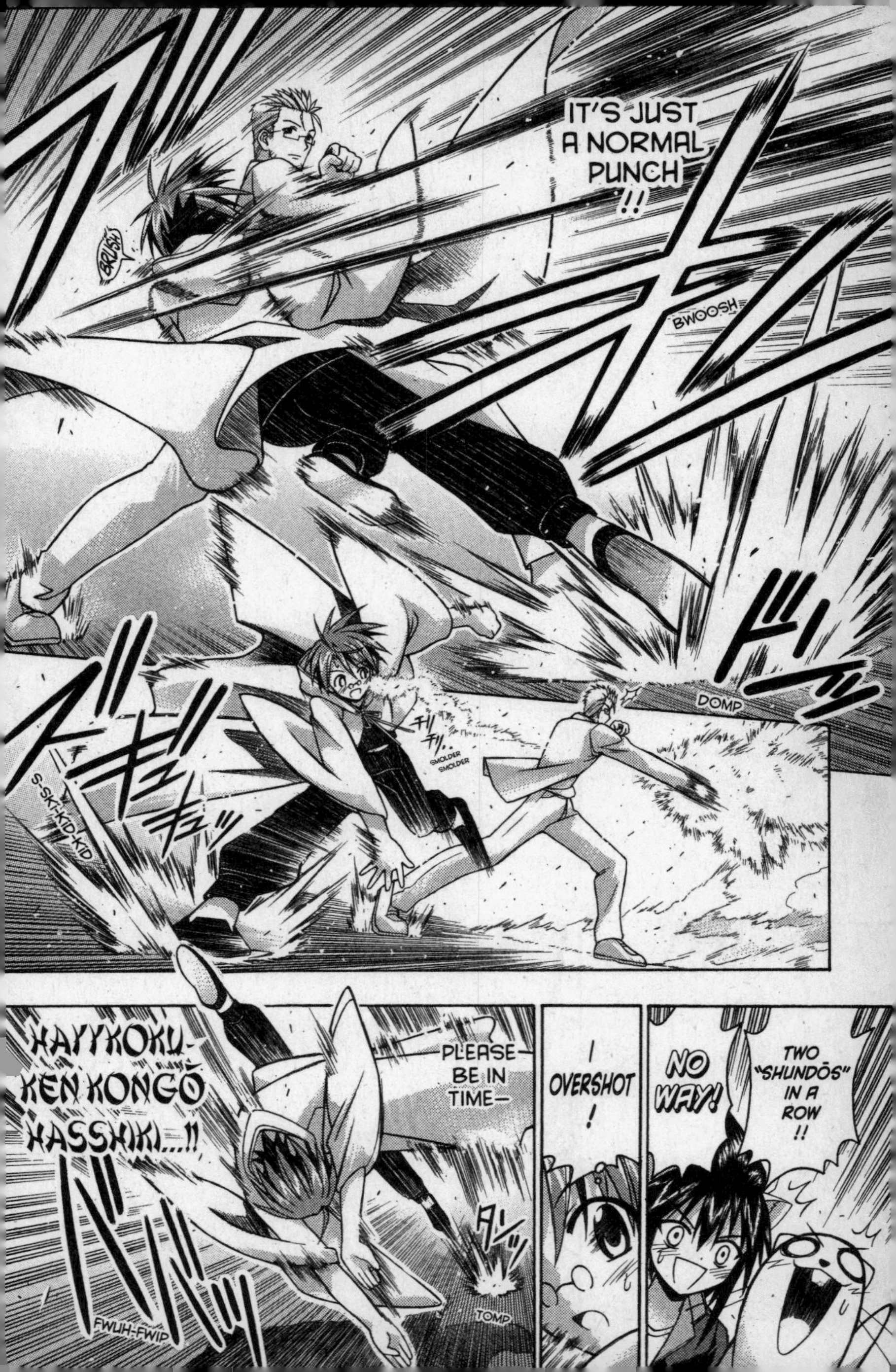
IT'S JUST A NORMAL PUNCH !!
BWOOSH
BRUSH
DOMP
SMOLDER SMOLDER
S-SKI-KID-KID
TWO "SHUNDŌS" IN A ROW !!
NO WAY!
I OVERSHOT !
PLEASE BE IN TIME—
HAYYKOKU-KEN KONGŌ HASSHIKI...!!
TOMP
FWUH-FWIP

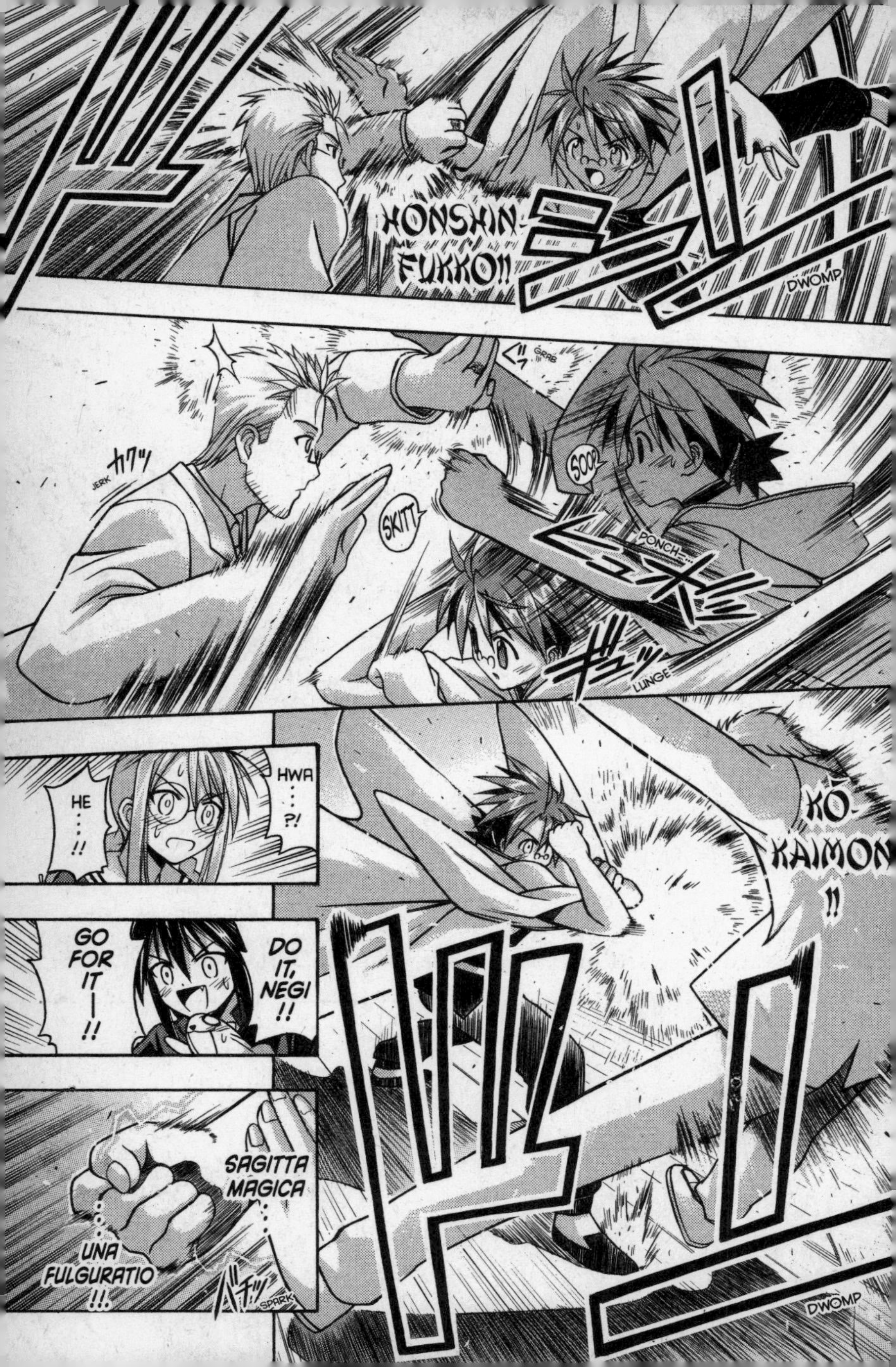
HONSHIN FUKKO!!
DWOMP
GRAB
SOOP
PONCH
JERK
SKITT
LUNGE
KŌ-KAIMON!!
DWOMP
HWA...?!
HE...!!
DO IT, NEGI!!
GO FOR IT—!!
SAGITTA MAGICA...
UNA FULGURATIO!!
SPARK

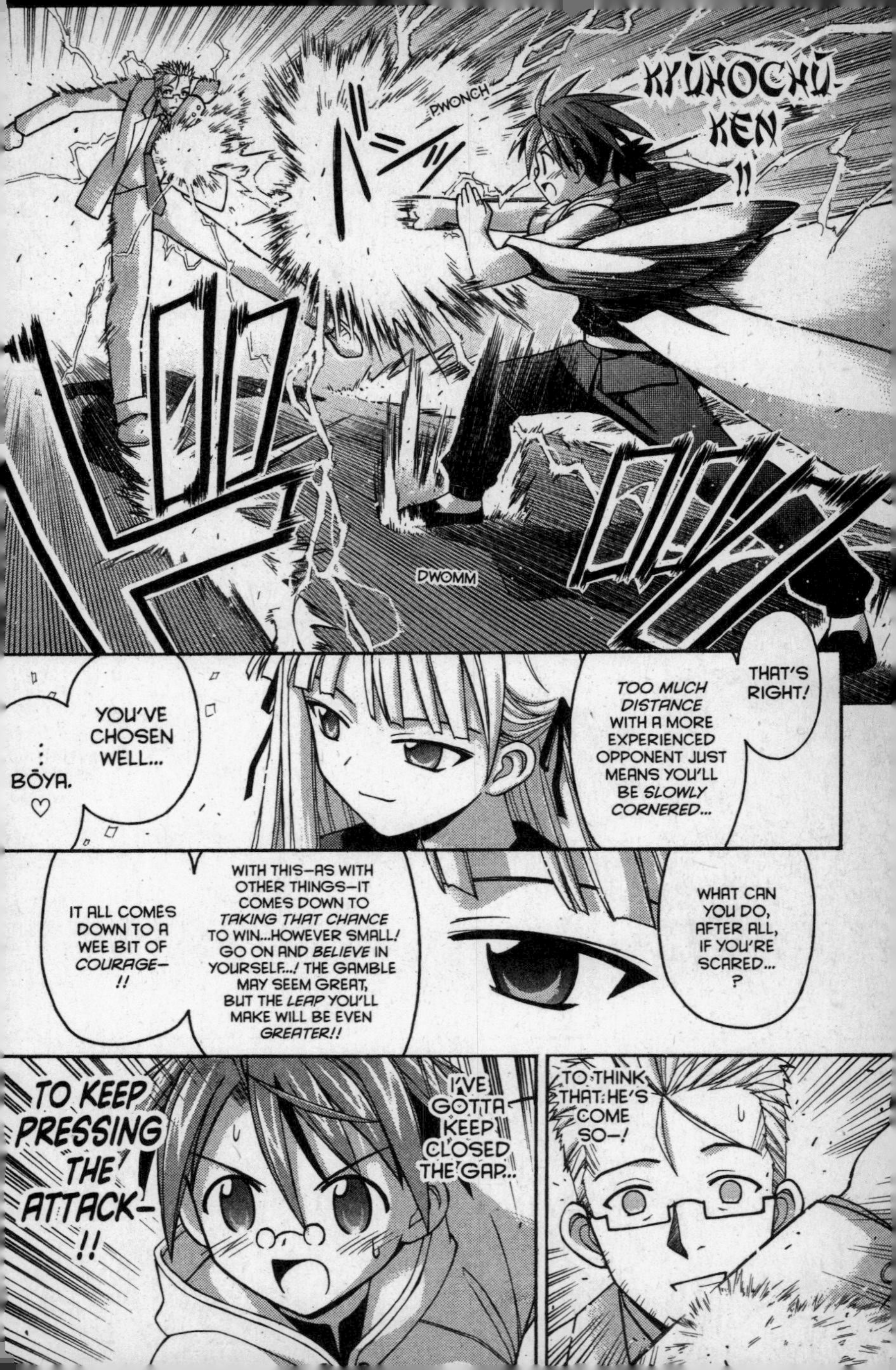
KYŪHOCHŪ KEN!!
PWONCH
DWOMM
THAT'S RIGHT! *TOO MUCH DISTANCE* WITH A MORE EXPERIENCED OPPONENT JUST MEANS YOU'LL BE *SLOWLY CORNERED...*
YOU'VE CHOSEN WELL...
...BŌYA. ♡
WHAT CAN YOU DO, AFTER ALL, IF YOU'RE SCARED...?
WITH THIS—AS WITH OTHER THINGS—IT COMES DOWN TO *TAKING THAT CHANCE* TO WIN...HOWEVER SMALL! GO ON AND *BELIEVE* IN YOURSELF...! THE GAMBLE MAY SEEM GREAT, BUT THE *LEAP* YOU'LL MAKE WILL BE EVEN *GREATER!!*
IT ALL COMES DOWN TO A WEE BIT OF *COURAGE—!!*
TO THINK THAT HE'S COME SO—!
I'VE GOTTA KEEP CLOSED THE GAP...
TO KEEP PRESSING THE ATTACK—!!

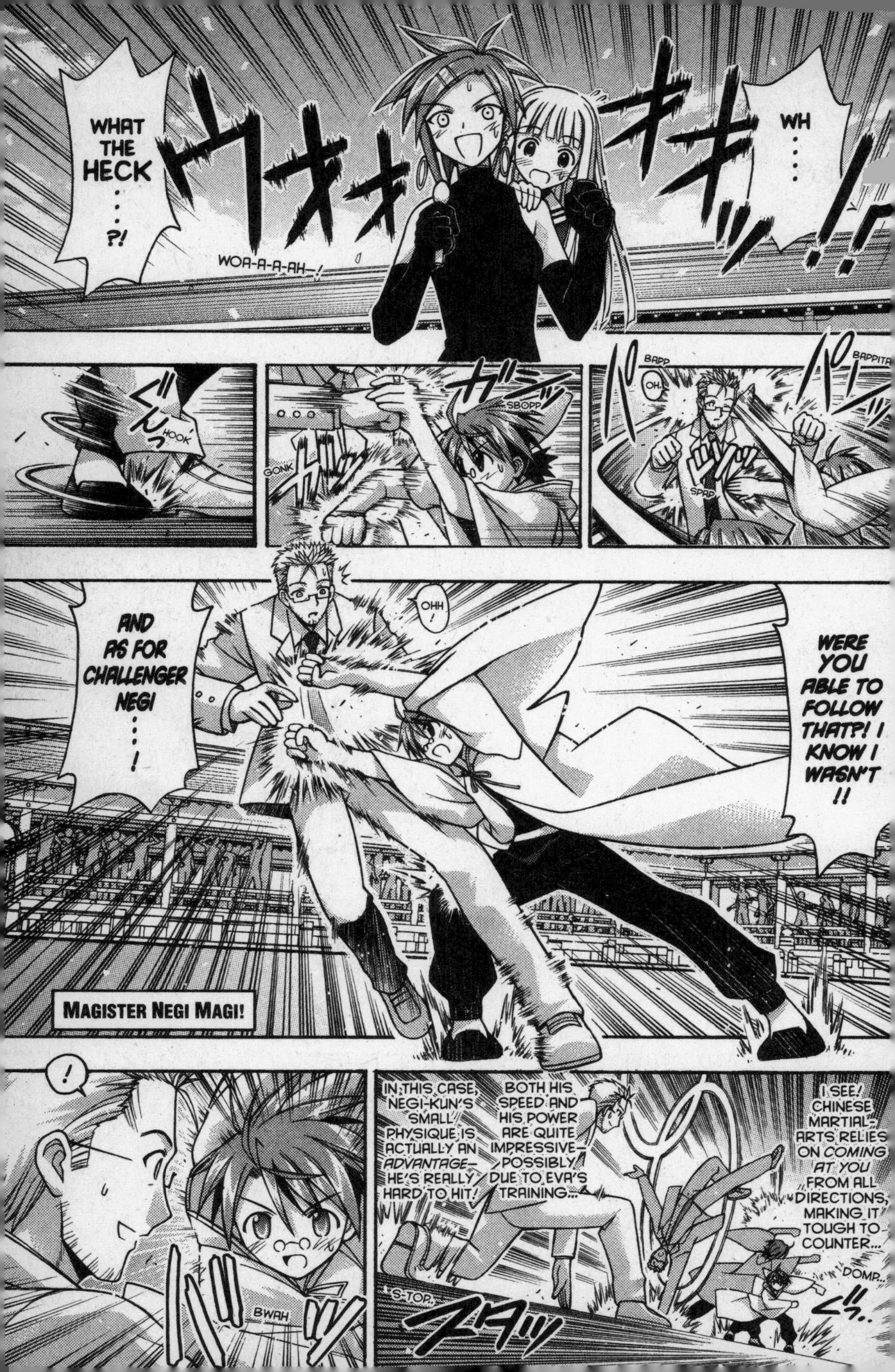

WH......!!
WHAT THE HECK...?!
WOA-A-A-AH—!
BAPP
OH.
BAPPITA
SPAP
SBOPP
GONK
HOOK
WERE YOU ABLE TO FOLLOW THAT?! I KNOW I WASN'T!!
OHH!
AND AS FOR CHALLENGER NEGI...!
MAGISTER NEGI MAGI!
I SEE! CHINESE MARTIAL-ARTS RELIES ON *COMING AT YOU* FROM ALL DIRECTIONS, MAKING IT TOUGH TO COUNTER...
BOTH HIS SPEED AND HIS POWER ARE QUITE IMPRESSIVE—POSSIBLY DUE TO EVA'S TRAINING...
IN THIS CASE, NEGI-KUN'S SMALL PHYSIQUE IS ACTUALLY AN *ADVANTAGE*—HE'S REALLY HARD TO HIT!
DOMP...
S-TOP...
!
BWAH

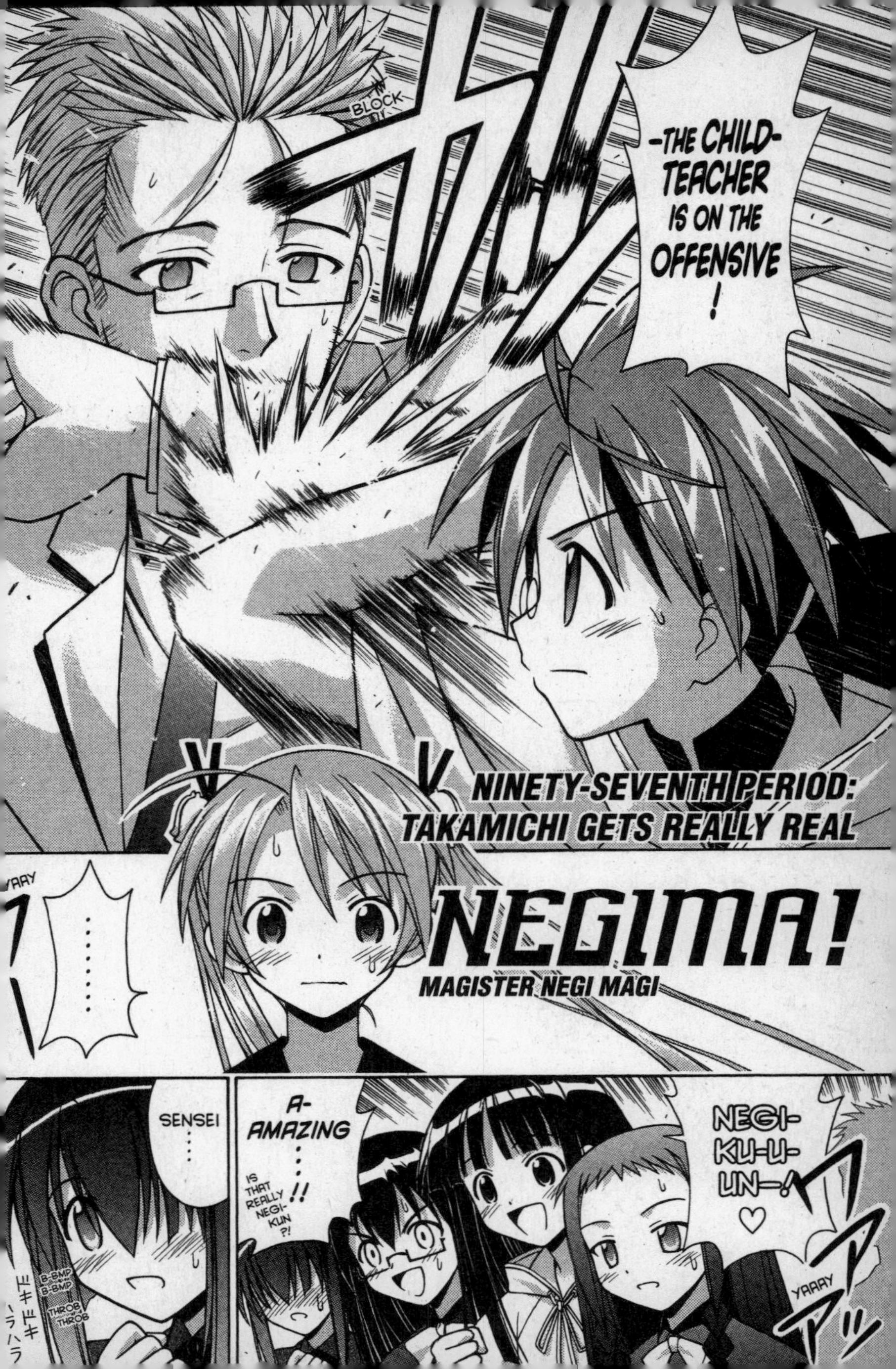

-THE CHILD-TEACHER IS ON THE OFFENSIVE!
BLOCK
NINETY-SEVENTH PERIOD: TAKAMICHI GETS REALLY REAL
NEGIMA!
MAGISTER NEGI MAGI
......
YAAY
NEGI-KU-U-UN-! ♡
YAAAY
A-AMAZING......!!
IS THAT REALLY NEGI-KUN?!
SENSEI......
B-BMP B-BMP
THROB THROB
ドキドキ
ハラハラ

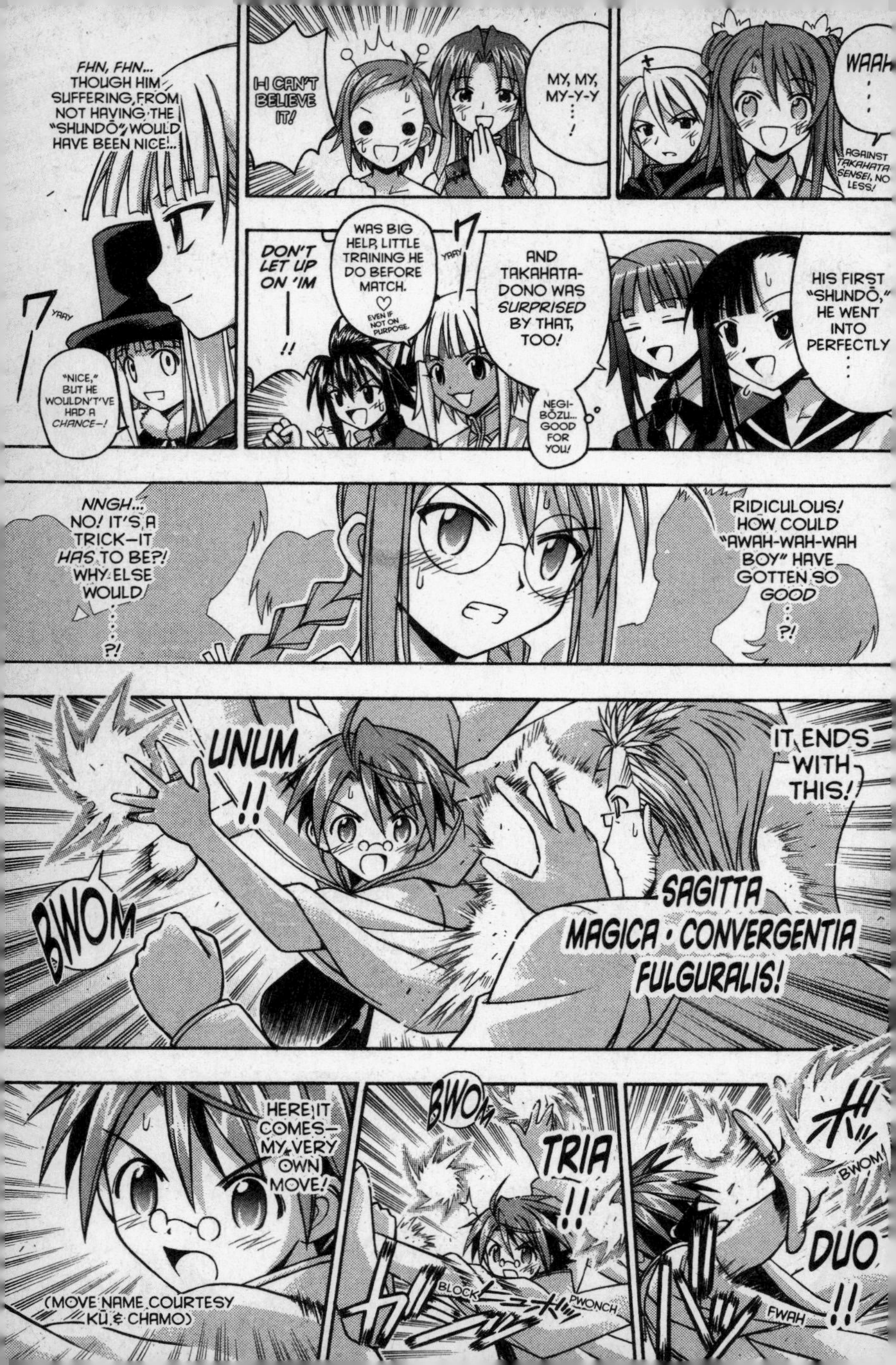
WAAH...!
AGAINST TAKAHATA-SENSEI, NO LESS!
MY, MY, MY-Y-Y...!
I-I CAN'T BELIEVE IT!
HIS FIRST "SHUNDŌ," HE WENT INTO PERFECTLY...
AND TAKAHATA-DONO WAS SURPRISED BY THAT, TOO!
NEGI-BŌZU... GOOD FOR YOU!
YAAY
WAS BIG HELP, LITTLE TRAINING HE DO BEFORE MATCH. ♡
EVEN IF NOT ON PURPOSE.
DON'T LET UP ON 'IM—!!
FHN, FHN... THOUGH HIM SUFFERING FROM NOT HAVING THE "SHUNDŌ" WOULD HAVE BEEN NICE!...
"NICE," BUT HE WOULDN'T'VE HAD A CHANCE—!
YAAY
RIDICULOUS! HOW COULD "AWAH-WAH-WAH BOY" HAVE GOTTEN SO GOOD...?!
NNGH... NO! IT'S A TRICK—IT HAS TO BE?! WHY ELSE WOULD...?!
IT ENDS WITH THIS!
SAGITTA MAGICA · CONVERGENTIA FULGURALIS!
UNUM!!
BWOM
BWOM!
DUO!!
FWAH
BWOM
TRIA!!
PWONCH
BLOCK
HERE IT COMES—MY VERY OWN MOVE!
(MOVE NAME COURTESY KŪ & CHAMO)

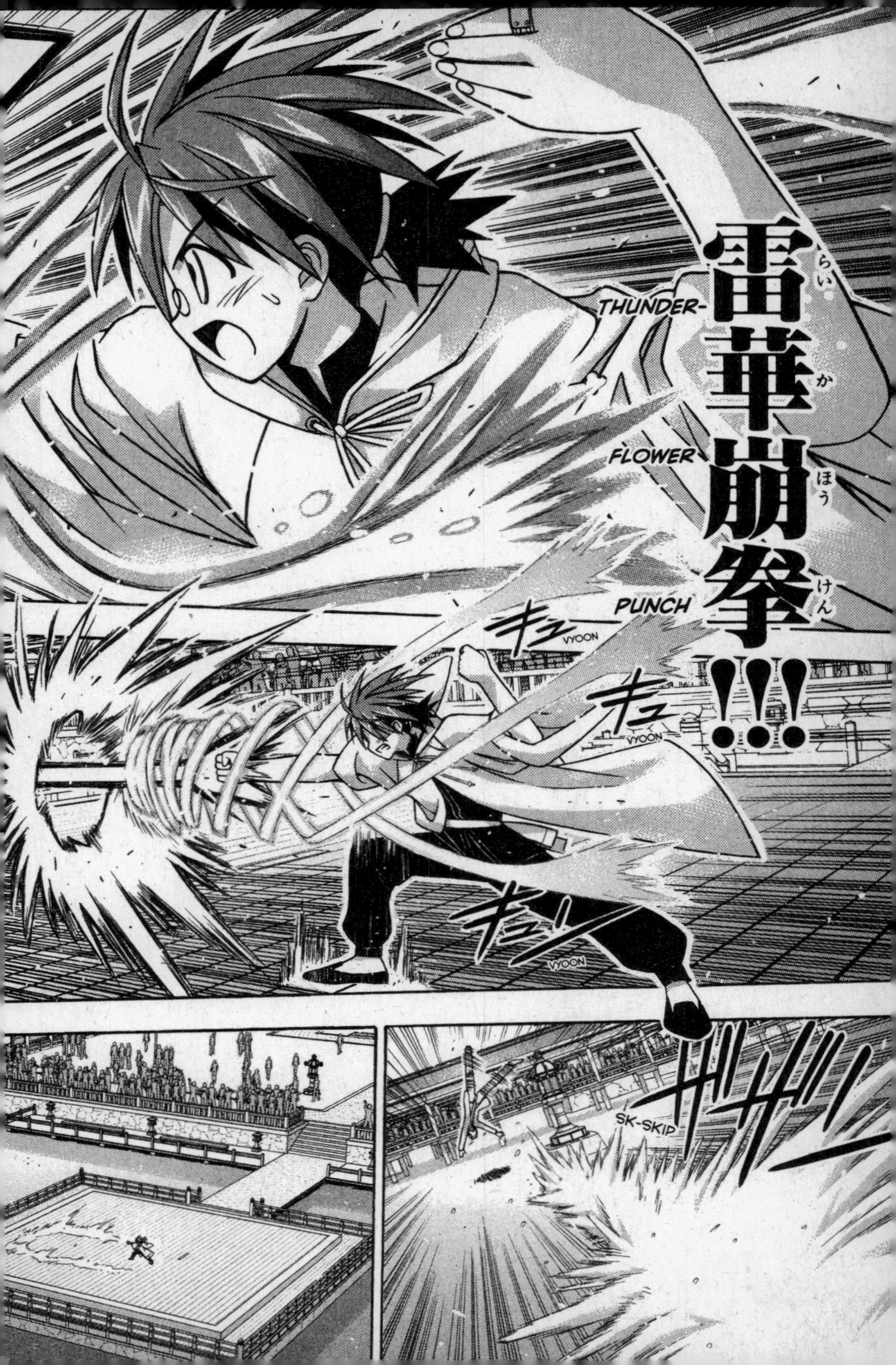

雷華崩拳!!!
THUNDER-
FLOWER
PUNCH
VYOON
VYOON
VYOON
SK-SKIP

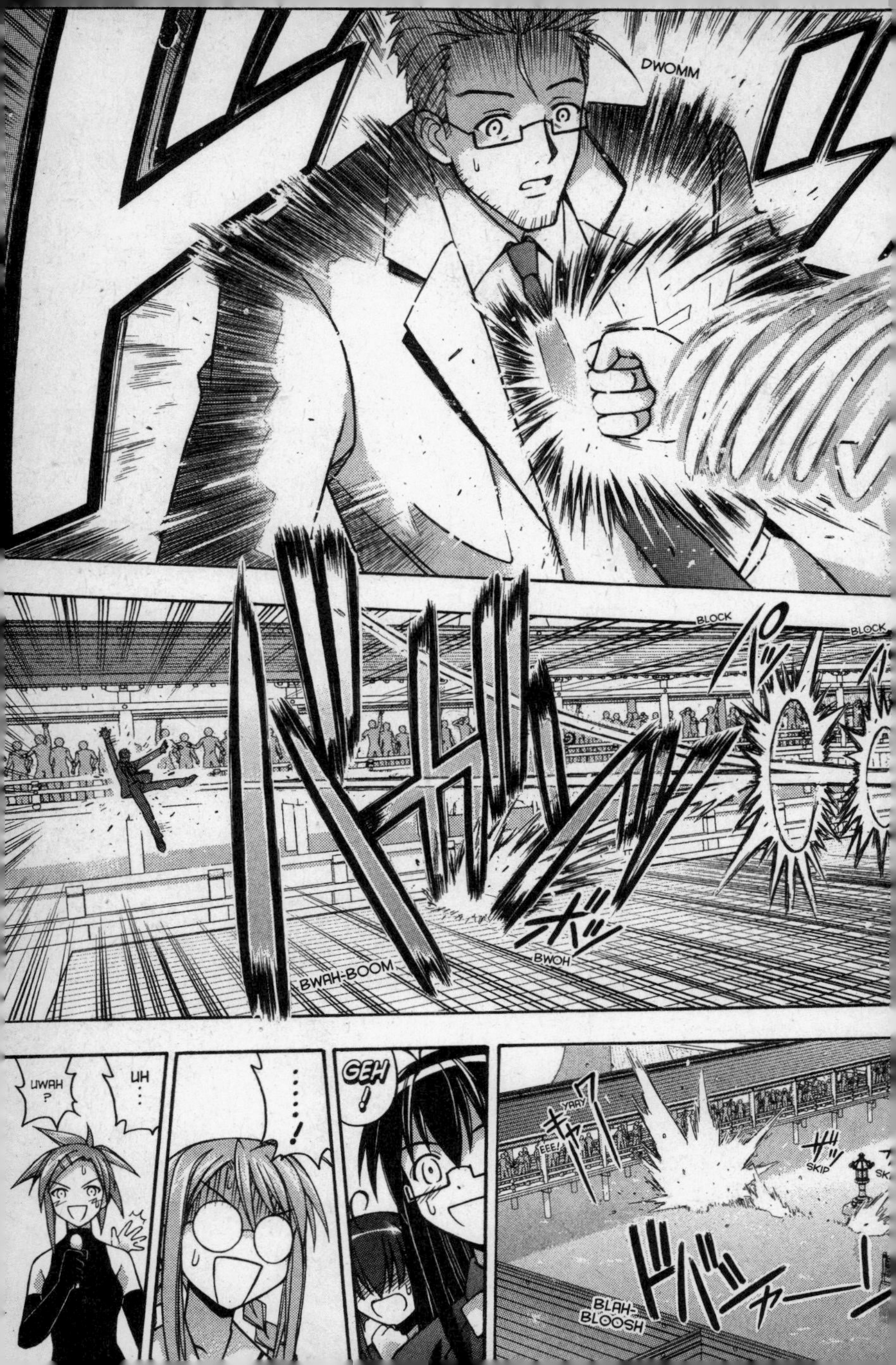
DWOMM
BLOCK
BLOCK
BWOH
BWAH-BOOM
SKIP
YAAY
EEE!
BLAH-BLOOSH
GEH!
.....!
UH...
UWAH?

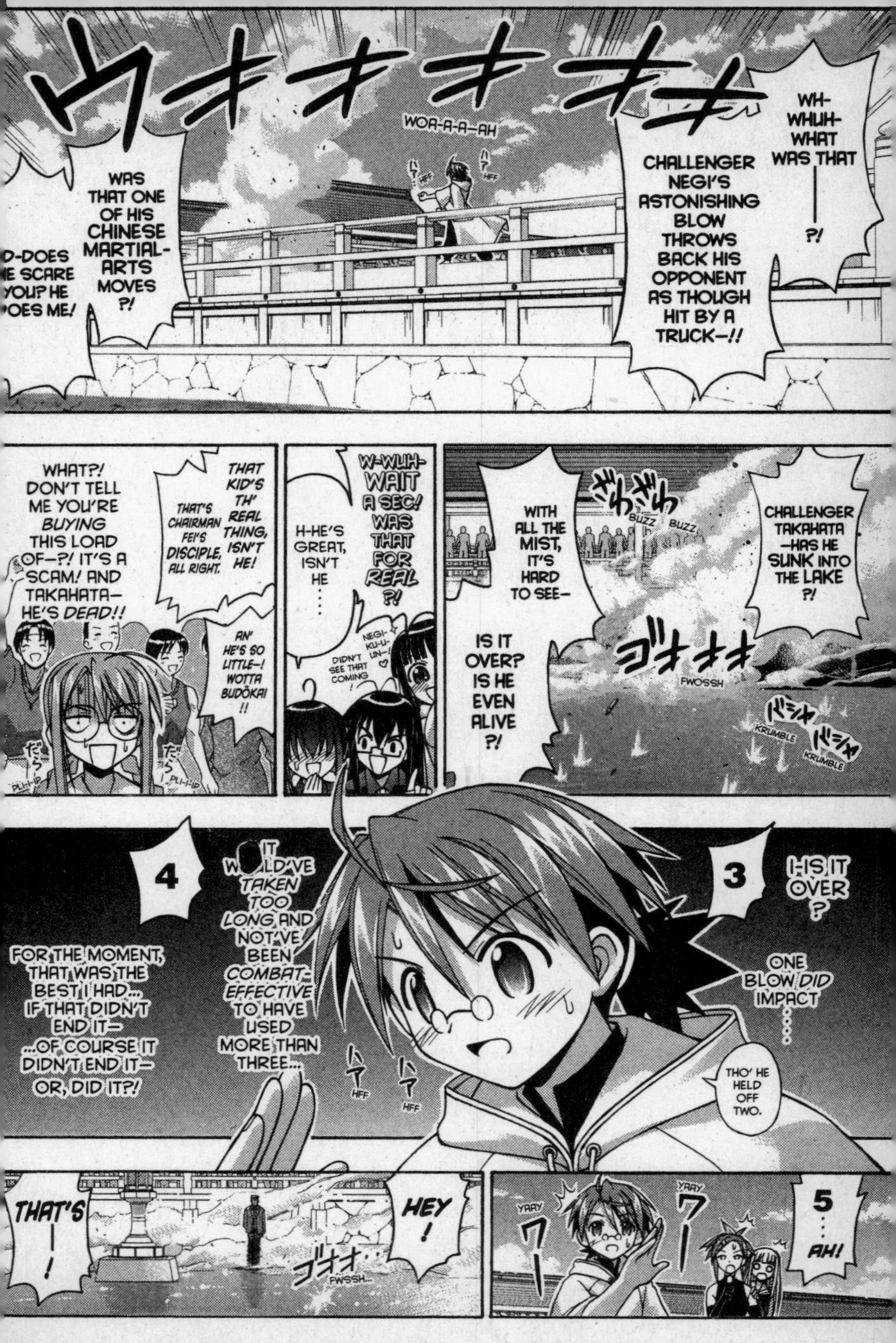

WH-WHUH-WHAT WAS THAT —— ?!
CHALLENGER NEGI'S ASTONISHING BLOW THROWS BACK HIS OPPONENT AS THOUGH HIT BY A TRUCK—!!
WOA-A-A—AH
HFF HFF
WAS THAT ONE OF HIS CHINESE MARTIAL-ARTS MOVES ?!
D-DOES E SCARE YOU? HE OES ME!
CHALLENGER TAKAHATA —HAS HE SUNK INTO THE LAKE ?!
BUZZ BUZZ
WITH ALL THE MIST, IT'S HARD TO SEE—
IS IT OVER? IS HE EVEN ALIVE ?!
FWOSSH
KRUMBLE KRUMBLE
W-WUH-WAIT A SEC! WAS THAT FOR REAL ?!
H-HE'S GREAT, ISN'T HE ....
NEGI-KU-U-UN—!
DIDN'T SEE THAT COMING!
THAT KID'S TH' REAL THING, ISN'T HE!
THAT'S CHAIRMAN FEI'S DISCIPLE, ALL RIGHT.
WHAT?! DON'T TELL ME YOU'RE BUYING THIS LOAD OF—?! IT'S A SCAM! AND TAKAHATA—HE'S DEAD!!
AN' HE'S SO LITTLE—! WOTTA BUDŌKAI !!
PLI-I-IP PLI-I-IP
3
I-IS IT OVER ?
ONE BLOW DID IMPACT ......
THO' HE HELD OFF TWO.
HFF HFF
4
IT WOULD'VE TAKEN TOO LONG AND NOT'VE BEEN COMBAT-EFFECTIVE TO HAVE USED MORE THAN THREE...
FOR THE MOMENT, THAT WAS THE BEST I HAD... IF THAT DIDN'T END IT— ...OF COURSE IT DIDN'T END IT— OR, DID IT?!
5 ... AH!
YAAY YAAY
HEY !
FWSSH...
THAT'S — !

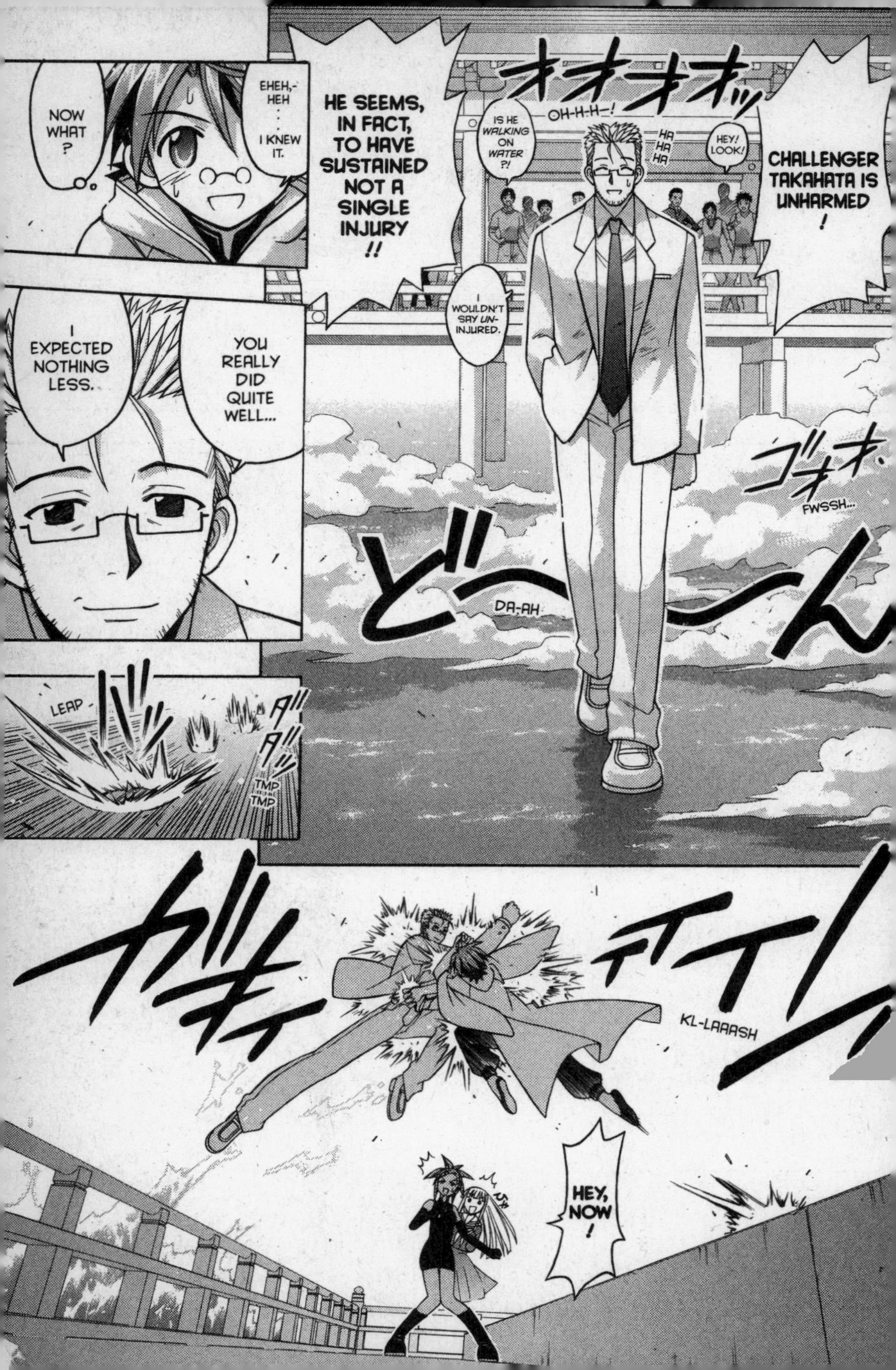
CHALLENGER TAKAHATA IS UNHARMED!
オオオオッ
OH-H-H-!
HEY! LOOK!
HA HA HA
IS HE WALKING ON WATER ?!
HE SEEMS, IN FACT, TO HAVE SUSTAINED NOT A SINGLE INJURY!!
I WOULDN'T SAY UN-INJURED.
FWSSH...
DA-AH
EHEH,-HEH . . . I KNEW IT.
NOW WHAT ?
YOU REALLY DID QUITE WELL...
I EXPECTED NOTHING LESS.
TMP TMP
LEAP
KL-LAAASH
HEY, NOW!

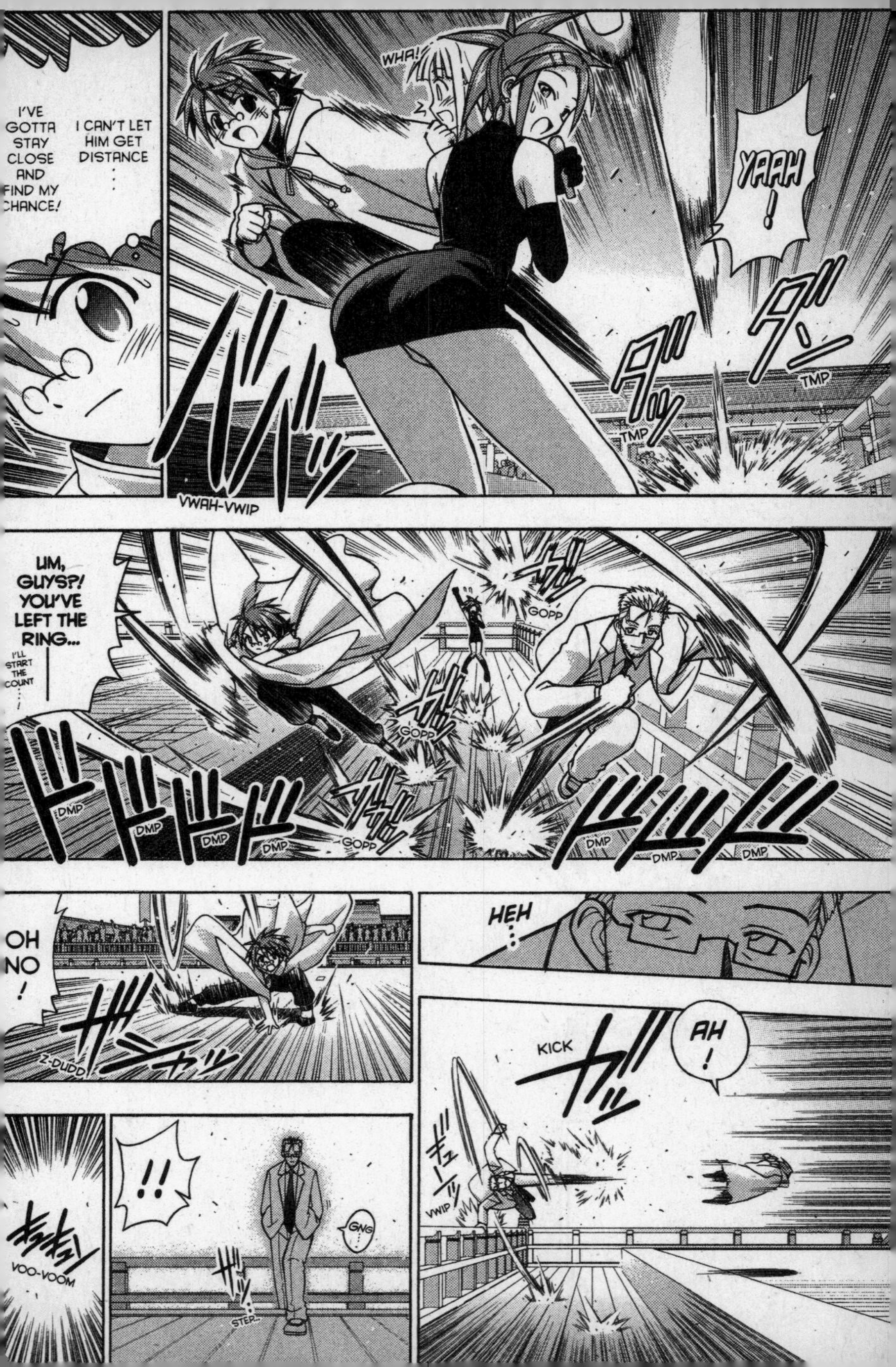
YAAH!
WHA!
TMP
TMP
VWAH-VWIP
I CAN'T LET HIM GET DISTANCE...
I'VE GOTTA STAY CLOSE AND FIND MY CHANCE!
GOPP
GOPP
GOPP
UM, GUYS?! YOU'VE LEFT THE RING...
I'LL START THE COUNT...
DMP
DMP
DMP
DMP
DMP
DMP
DMP
HEH...
AH!
KICK
VWIP
OH NO!
Z-DUDD
!!
GNG...
STEP...
VOO-VOOM

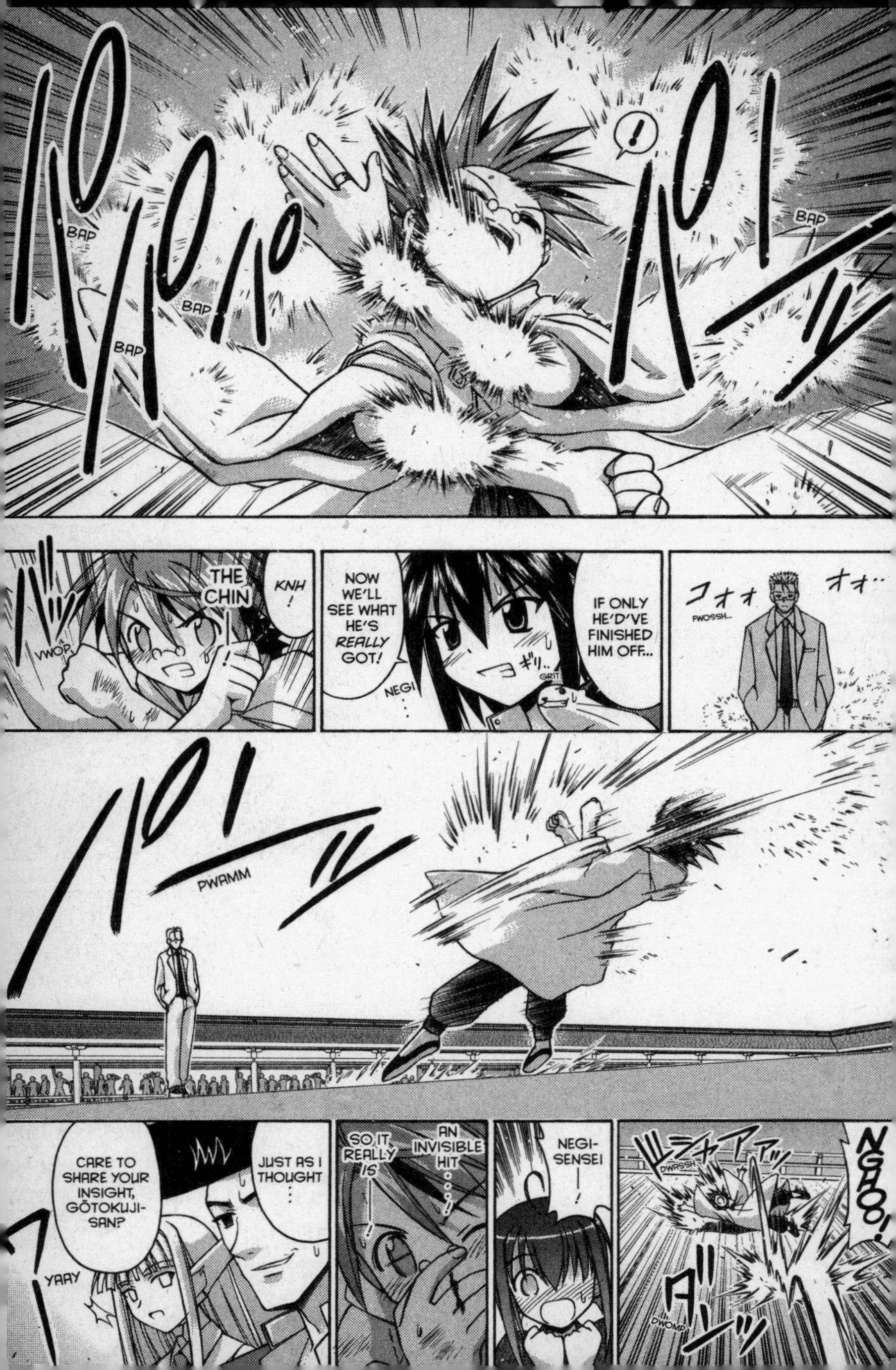

!
BAP
BAP
BAP
BAP
コォオ
オオ…
PWOSSH...
IF ONLY HE'D'VE FINISHED HIM OFF...
ギリ..
GRIT
NOW WE'LL SEE WHAT HE'S *REALLY* GOT!
NEGI...
KNH!
THE CHIN!
VWOP
PWAMM
NGHOO!
ドシャアッ
DWASSH
DWOMP
NEGI-SENSEI!
AN INVISIBLE HIT...!?
SO IT REALLY IS...!
JUST AS I THOUGHT...
CARE TO SHARE YOUR INSIGHT, GŌTOKUJI-SAN?
YAAY

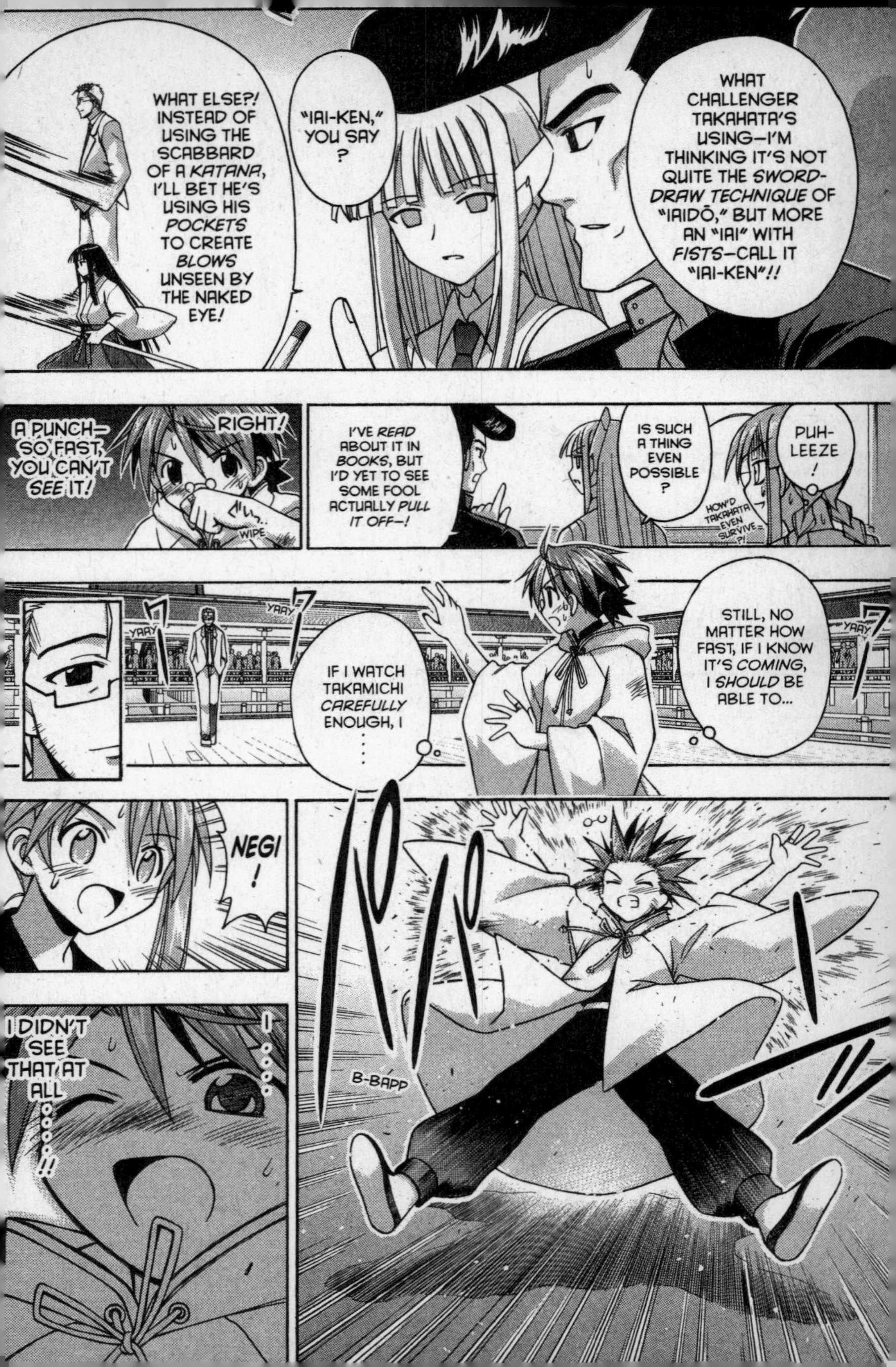
WHAT CHALLENGER TAKAHATA'S USING—I'M THINKING IT'S NOT QUITE THE *SWORD-DRAW TECHNIQUE* OF "IAIDŌ," BUT MORE AN "IAI" WITH *FISTS*—CALL IT "IAI-KEN"!!
"IAI-KEN," YOU SAY?
WHAT ELSE?! INSTEAD OF USING THE SCABBARD OF A *KATANA*, I'LL BET HE'S USING HIS *POCKETS* TO CREATE *BLOWS* UNSEEN BY THE NAKED EYE!
PUH-LEEZE!
HOW'D TAKAHATA EVEN SURVIVE?!
IS SUCH A THING EVEN POSSIBLE?
I'VE *READ* ABOUT IT IN *BOOKS*, BUT I'D YET TO SEE SOME FOOL ACTUALLY *PULL IT OFF*—!
RIGHT!
A PUNCH—SO FAST, YOU CAN'T *SEE* IT!
WIPE
YAAY
STILL, NO MATTER HOW FAST, IF I KNOW IT'S *COMING*, I *SHOULD* BE ABLE TO...
IF I WATCH TAKAMICHI *CAREFULLY* ENOUGH, I . . .
YAAY
YAAY
B-BAPP
NEGI!
I....
I DIDN'T SEE THAT AT ALL.....!!

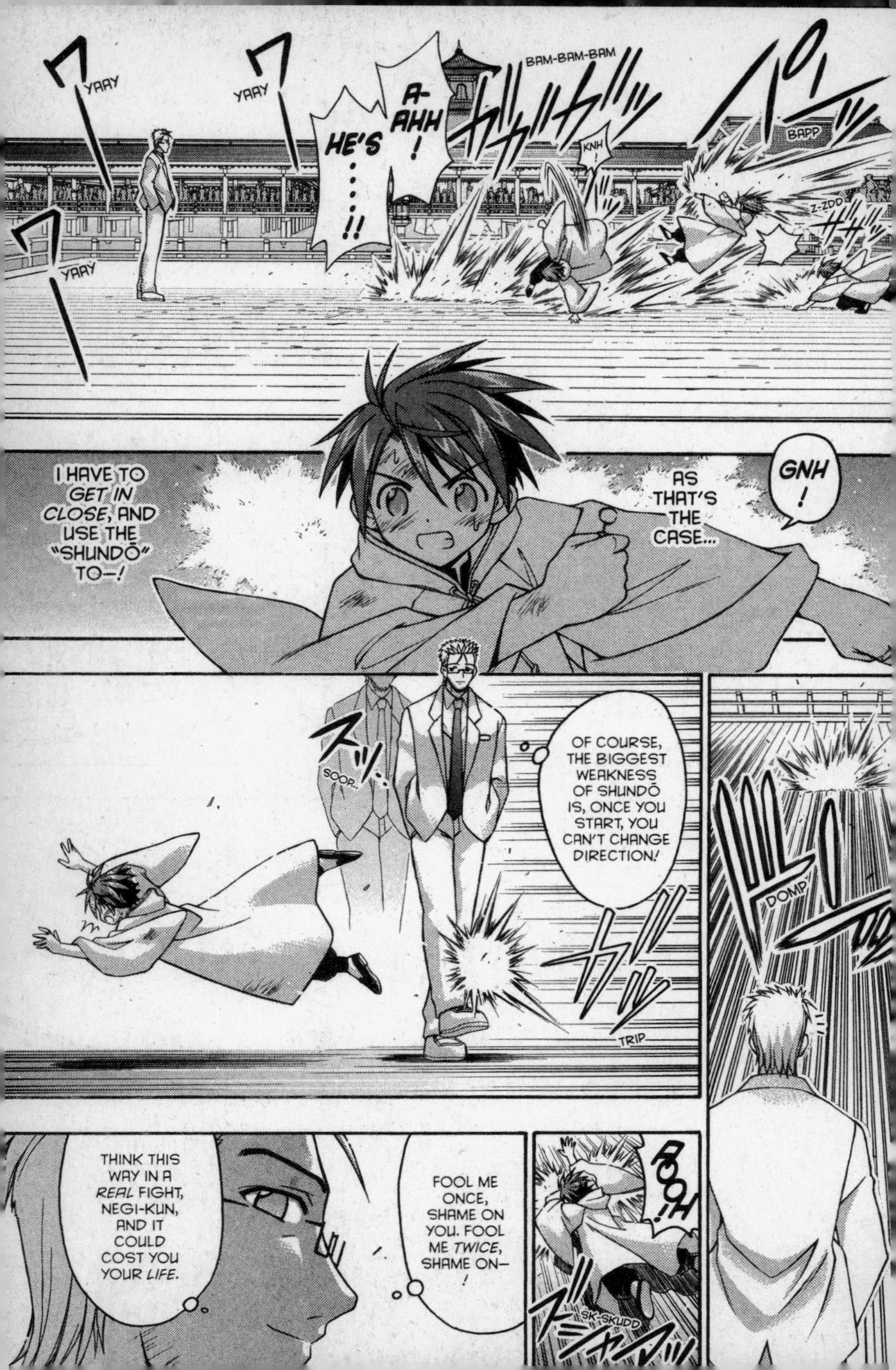
BAPP
KNH!
Z-ZDD
BAM-BAM-BAM
A-AHH!
HE'S......!!
YAAY
YAAY
YAAY
GNH!
AS THAT'S THE CASE...
I HAVE TO *GET IN CLOSE*, AND USE THE "SHUNDŌ" TO—!
DOMP
OF COURSE, THE BIGGEST WEAKNESS OF SHUNDŌ IS, ONCE YOU START, YOU CAN'T CHANGE DIRECTION!
SOOP..
TRIP
ROOH!!
SK-SKUDD
FOOL ME ONCE, SHAME ON YOU. FOOL ME *TWICE*, SHAME ON—!
THINK THIS WAY IN A *REAL* FIGHT, NEGI-KUN, AND IT COULD COST YOU YOUR *LIFE*.

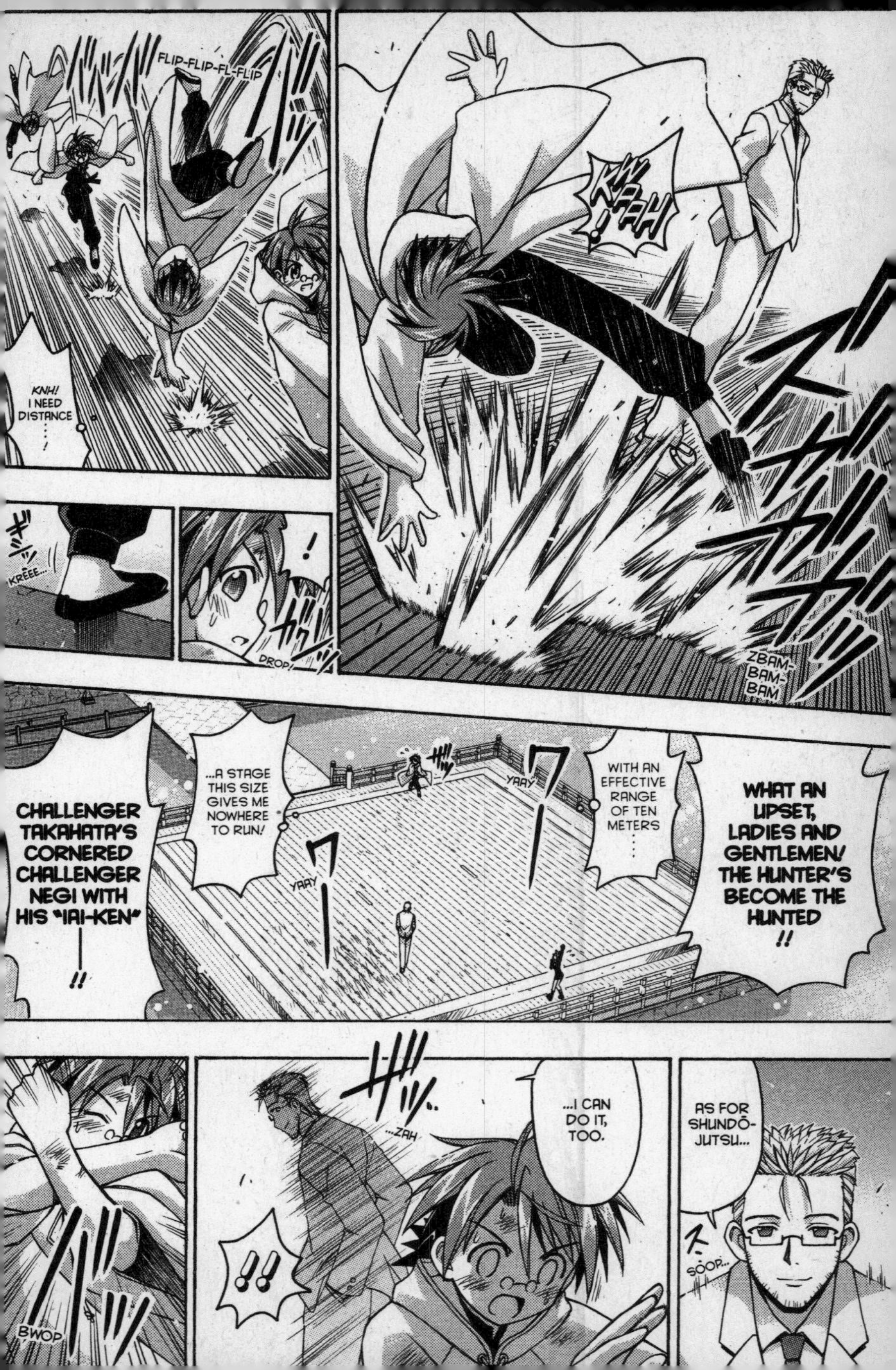

KWAAH!
ZBAM-BAM-BAM
FLIP-FLIP-FL-FLIP
KNH! I NEED DISTANCE...!
!
DROP!
KREEE...
WHAT AN UPSET, LADIES AND GENTLEMEN! THE HUNTER'S BECOME THE HUNTED!!
WITH AN EFFECTIVE RANGE OF TEN METERS...
YAAY
...A STAGE THIS SIZE GIVES ME NOWHERE TO RUN!
YAAY
CHALLENGER TAKAHATA'S CORNERED CHALLENGER NEGI WITH HIS "IAI-KEN"—!!
AS FOR SHUNDŌ-JUTSU...
SOOP...
...I CAN DO IT, TOO.
...ZAH
!!
BWOP

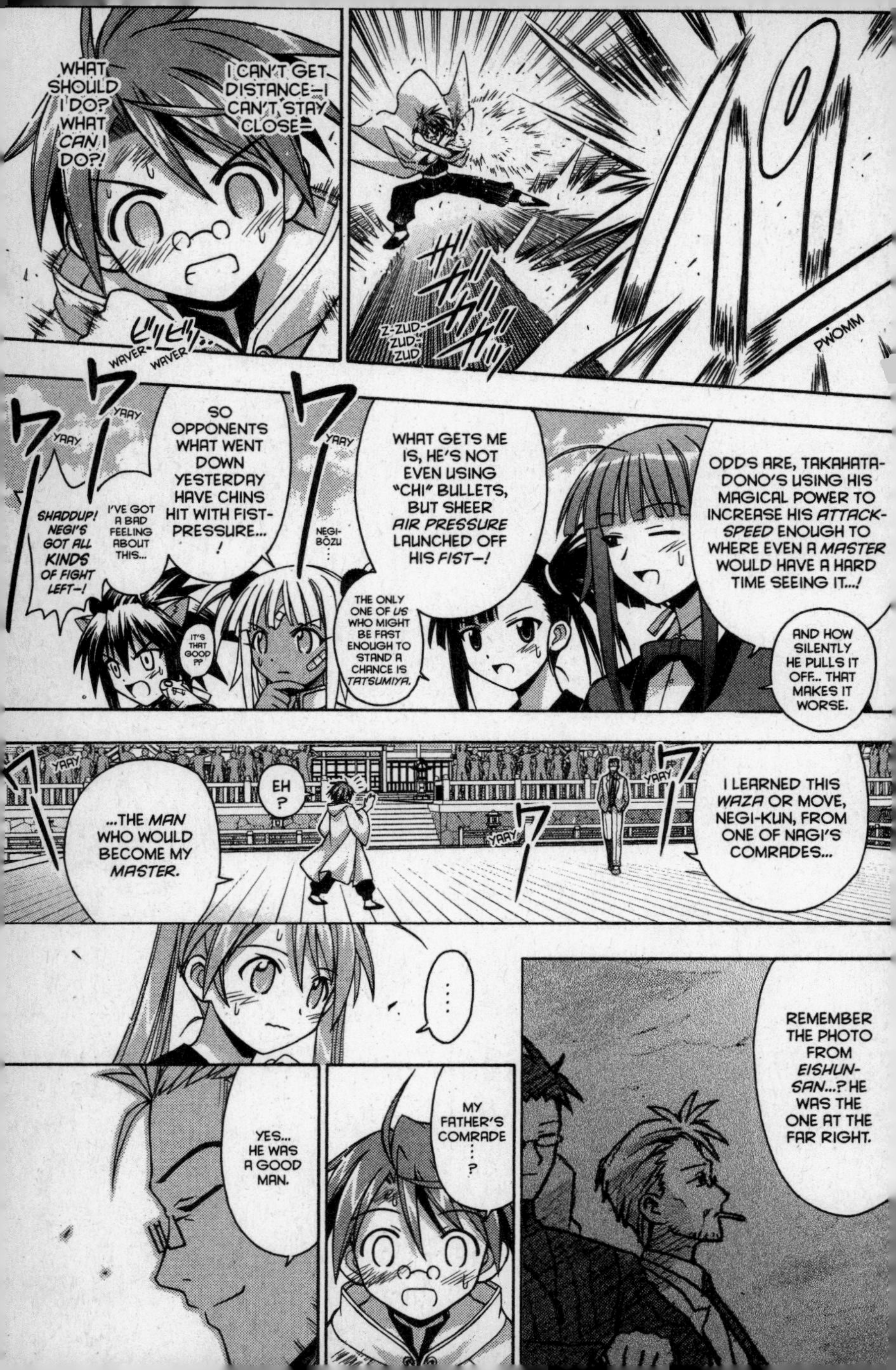
PWOMM
Z-ZUD-ZUD ZUD
I CAN'T GET DISTANCE—I CAN'T STAY CLOSE—
WHAT SHOULD I DO? WHAT CAN I DO?!
WAVER WAVER
ODDS ARE, TAKAHATA-DONO'S USING HIS MAGICAL POWER TO INCREASE HIS ATTACK-SPEED ENOUGH TO WHERE EVEN A MASTER WOULD HAVE A HARD TIME SEEING IT...!
AND HOW SILENTLY HE PULLS IT OFF... THAT MAKES IT WORSE.
WHAT GETS ME IS, HE'S NOT EVEN USING "CHI" BULLETS, BUT SHEER AIR PRESSURE LAUNCHED OFF HIS FIST—!
THE ONLY ONE OF US WHO MIGHT BE FAST ENOUGH TO STAND A CHANCE IS TATSUMIYA.
YAARY
NEGI-BŌZU...
SO OPPONENTS WHAT WENT DOWN YESTERDAY HAVE CHINS HIT WITH FIST-PRESSURE...!
YAARY
I'VE GOT A BAD FEELING ABOUT THIS...
IT'S THAT GOOD??
SHADDUP! NEGI'S GOT ALL KINDS OF FIGHT LEFT—!
YAARY
I LEARNED THIS WAZA OR MOVE, NEGI-KUN, FROM ONE OF NAGI'S COMRADES...
YAARY
YAARY
EH?
YAARY
...THE MAN WHO WOULD BECOME MY MASTER.
REMEMBER THE PHOTO FROM EISHUN-SAN...? HE WAS THE ONE AT THE FAR RIGHT.
...
MY FATHER'S COMRADE...?
YES... HE WAS A GOOD MAN.

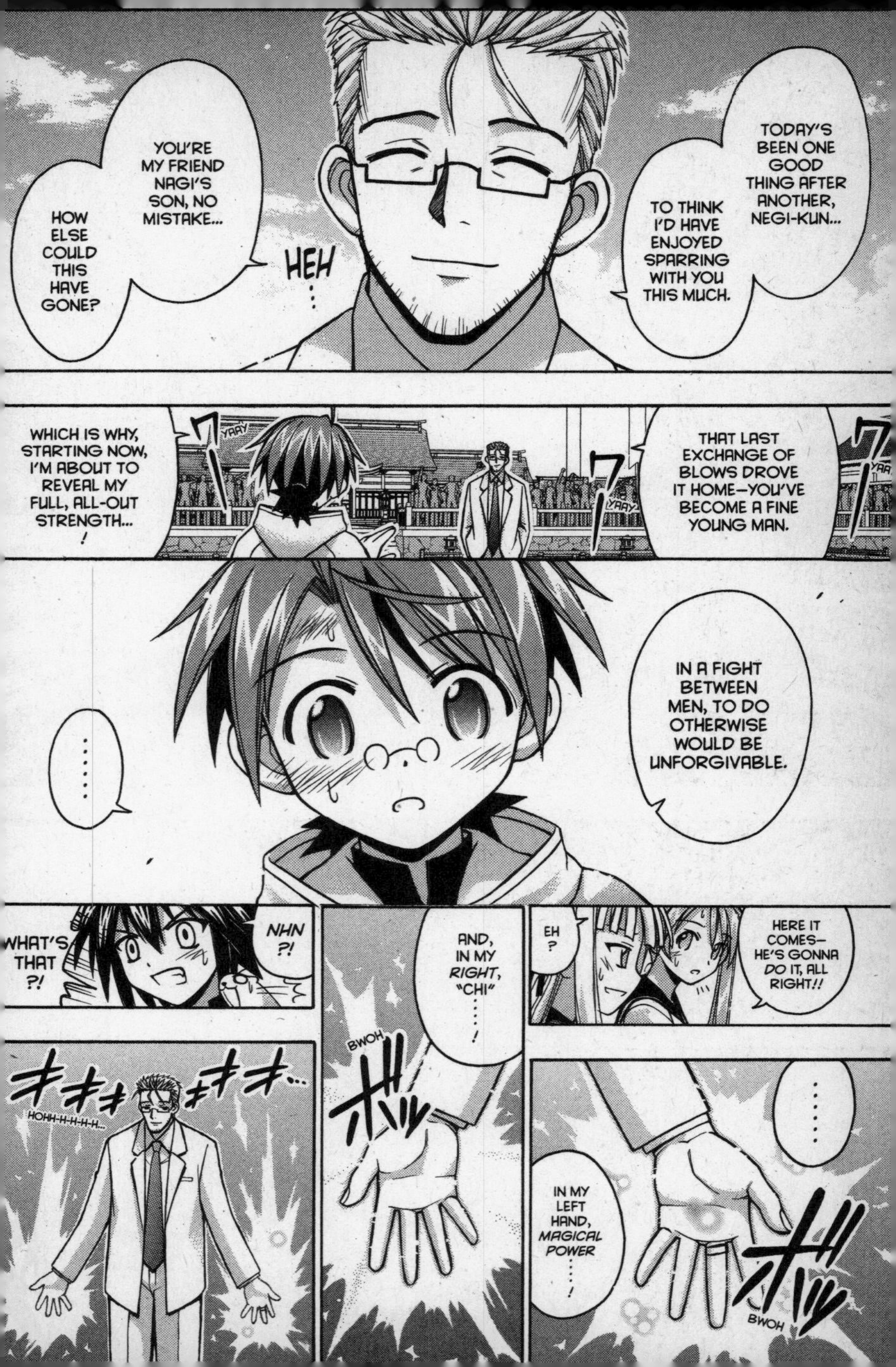
TODAY'S BEEN ONE GOOD THING AFTER ANOTHER, NEGI-KUN...
TO THINK I'D HAVE ENJOYED SPARRING WITH YOU THIS MUCH.
HEH...
YOU'RE MY FRIEND NAGI'S SON, NO MISTAKE...
HOW ELSE COULD THIS HAVE GONE?
THAT LAST EXCHANGE OF BLOWS DROVE IT HOME—YOU'VE BECOME A FINE YOUNG MAN.
YAAY
YAAY
YAAY
WHICH IS WHY, STARTING NOW, I'M ABOUT TO REVEAL MY FULL, ALL-OUT STRENGTH...!
IN A FIGHT BETWEEN MEN, TO DO OTHERWISE WOULD BE UNFORGIVABLE.
......
HERE IT COMES—HE'S GONNA DO IT, ALL RIGHT!!
EH?
......
IN MY LEFT HAND, MAGICAL POWER......!
BWOH
AND, IN MY RIGHT, "CHI"......!
BWOH
NHN?!
WHAT'S THAT?!
HOHH-H-H-H-H...

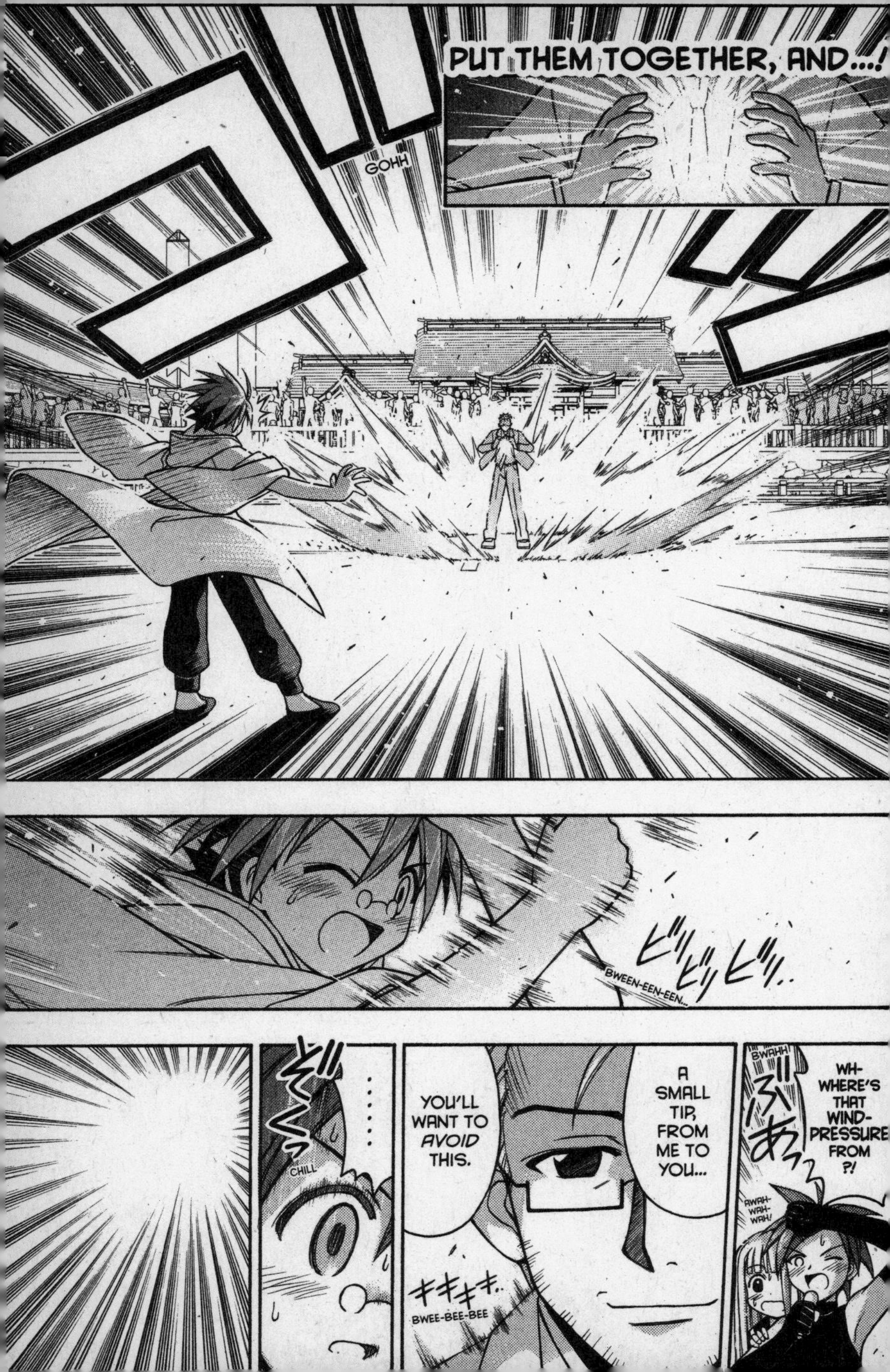

PUT THEM TOGETHER, AND...!
GOHH
BWEEN-EEN-EEN...
WH-WHERE'S THAT WIND-PRESSURE FROM?!
BWAHH
AWAH-WAH-WAH!
A SMALL TIP, FROM ME TO YOU...
YOU'LL WANT TO *AVOID* THIS.
......
CHILL
BWEE-BEE-BEE

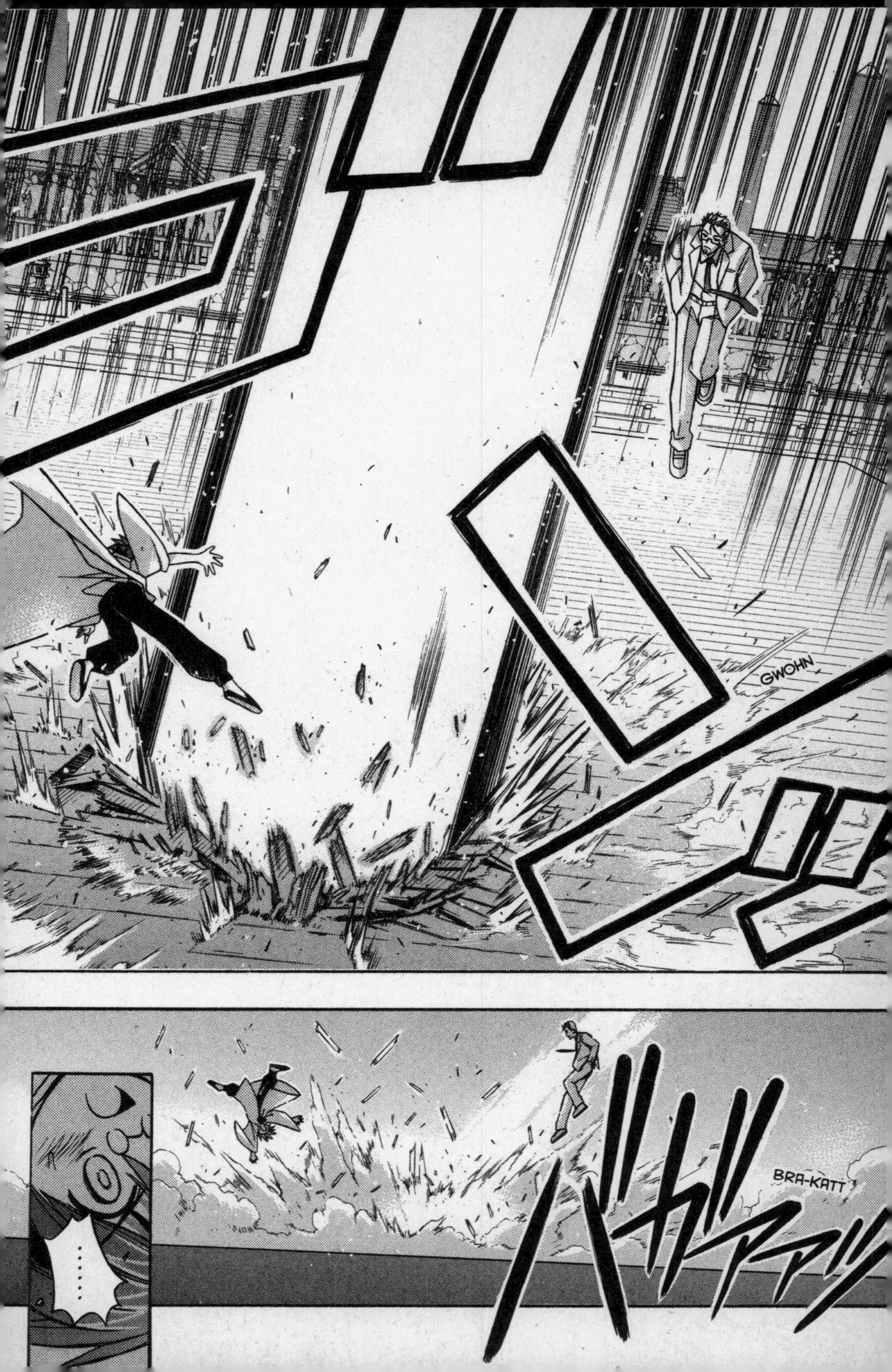
GWOHN
BRA-KATT
......

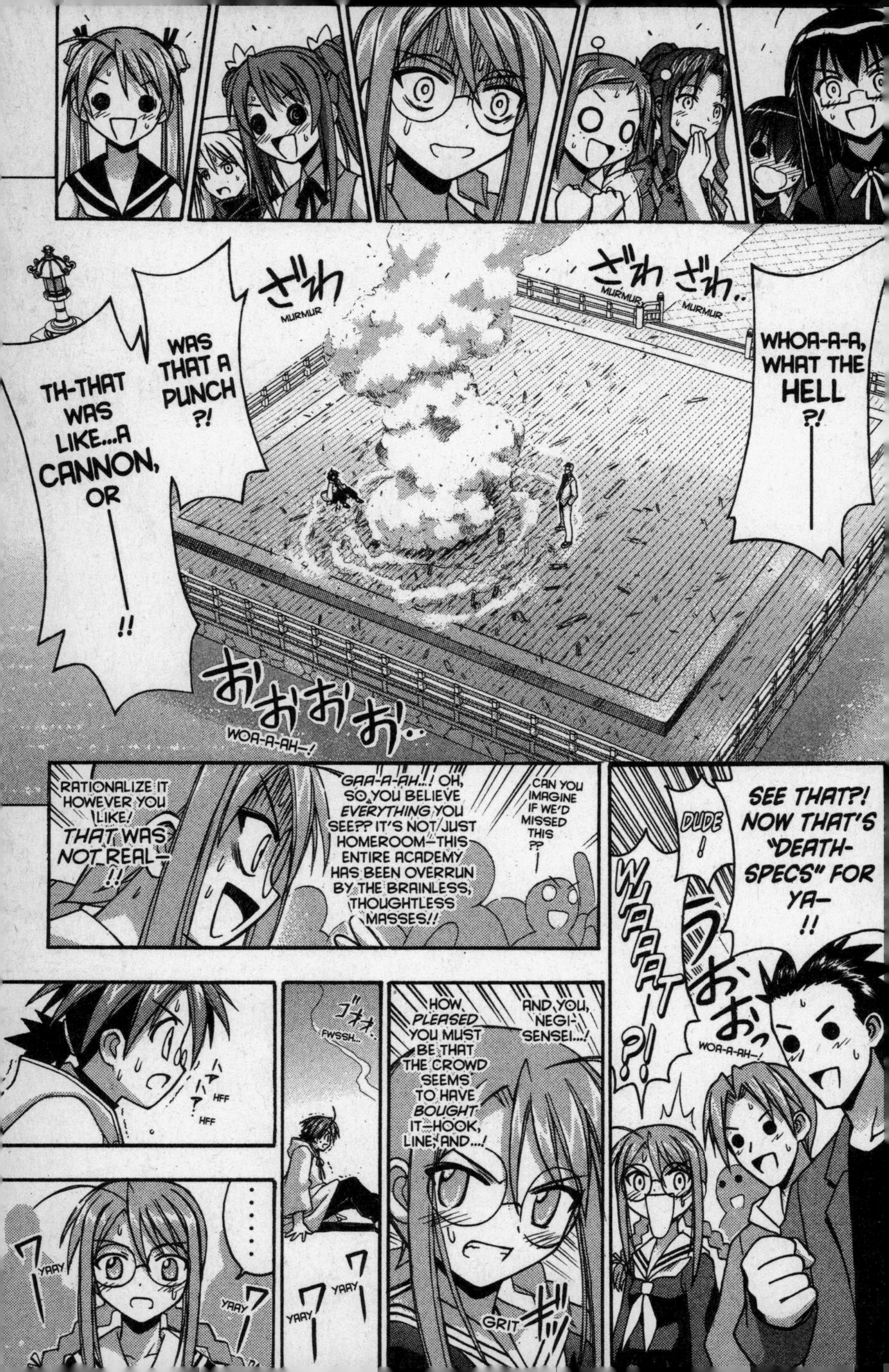

WHOA-A-A, WHAT THE HELL?!—
ざわざわ..
MURMUR
MURMUR
ざわ
MURMUR
WAS THAT A PUNCH?!
TH-THAT WAS LIKE...A CANNON, OR——!!
おおおお..
WOA-A-AH—!
SEE THAT?! NOW THAT'S "DEATH-SPECS" FOR YA—!!
うおっ
WOA-A-AH—!
DUDE!
WHAAAT—?!
CAN YOU IMAGINE IF WE'D MISSED THIS??—
GAA-A-AH...! OH, SO YOU BELIEVE EVERYTHING YOU SEE?? IT'S NOT JUST HOMEROOM—THIS ENTIRE ACADEMY HAS BEEN OVERRUN BY THE BRAINLESS, THOUGHTLESS MASSES!!
RATIONALIZE IT HOWEVER YOU LIKE! THAT WAS NOT REAL—!!
AND YOU, NEGI-SENSEI...!
HOW PLEASED YOU MUST BE THAT THE CROWD SEEMS TO HAVE BOUGHT IT—HOOK, LINE, AND...!
GRIT
ゴオオ..
FWSSH..
ハァ
HFF
ハァ
HFF
......
ワー
YAAY
ワー
YAAY
ワー
YAAY
ワー
YAAY

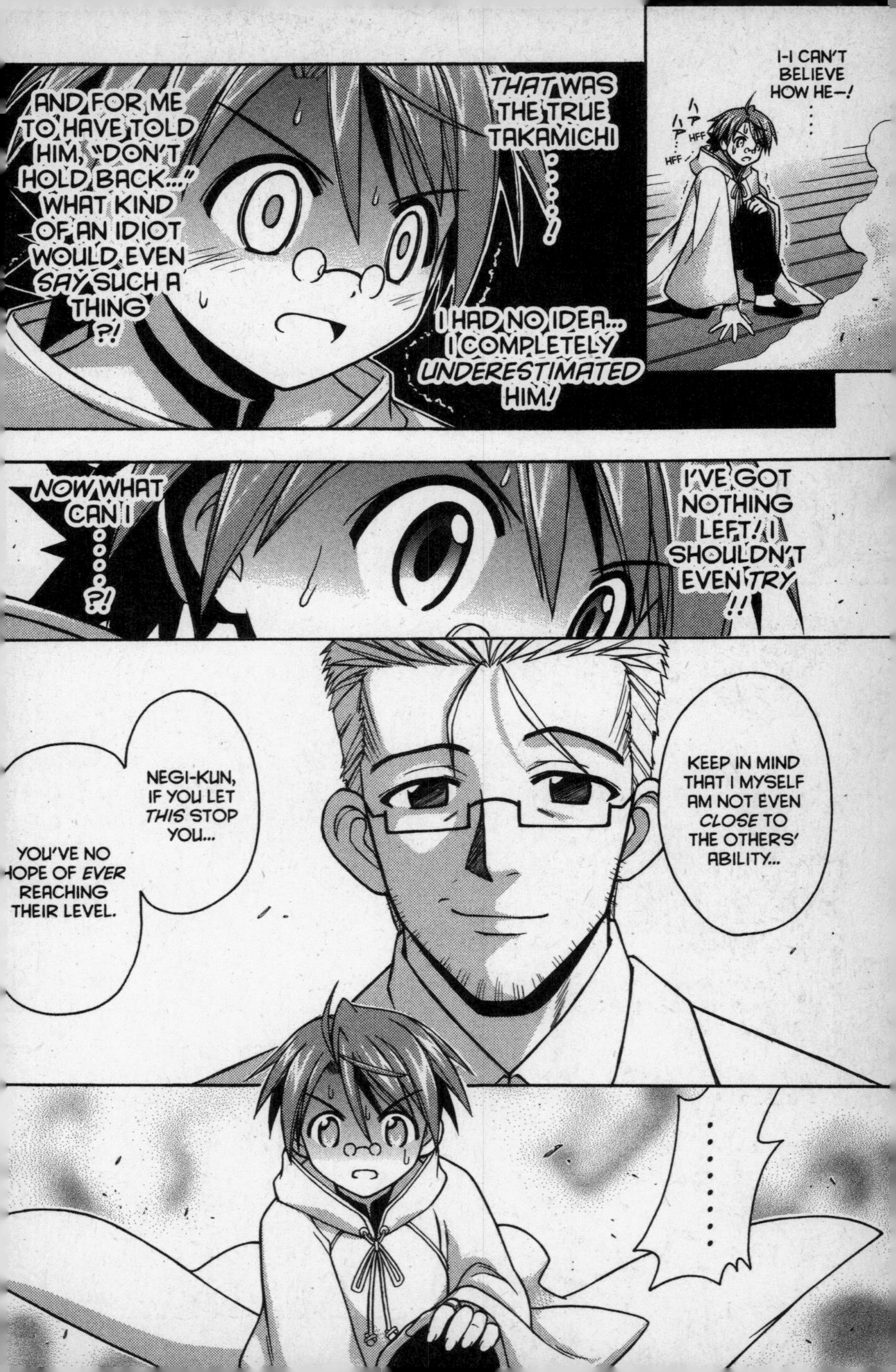

I-I CAN'T BELIEVE HOW HE—! ....
ハァ ハァ
HFF HFF
THAT WAS THE TRUE TAKAMICHI ....!
AND FOR ME TO HAVE TOLD HIM, "DON'T HOLD BACK..." WHAT KIND OF AN IDIOT WOULD EVEN *SAY* SUCH A THING ?!
I HAD NO IDEA... I COMPLETELY *UNDERESTIMATED* HIM!
I'VE GOT NOTHING LEFT! I SHOULDN'T EVEN *TRY* !!
NOW WHAT CAN I ......?!
KEEP IN MIND THAT I MYSELF AM NOT EVEN *CLOSE* TO THE OTHERS' ABILITY...
NEGI-KUN, IF YOU LET *THIS* STOP YOU...
YOU'VE NO HOPE OF *EVER* REACHING THEIR LEVEL.
......

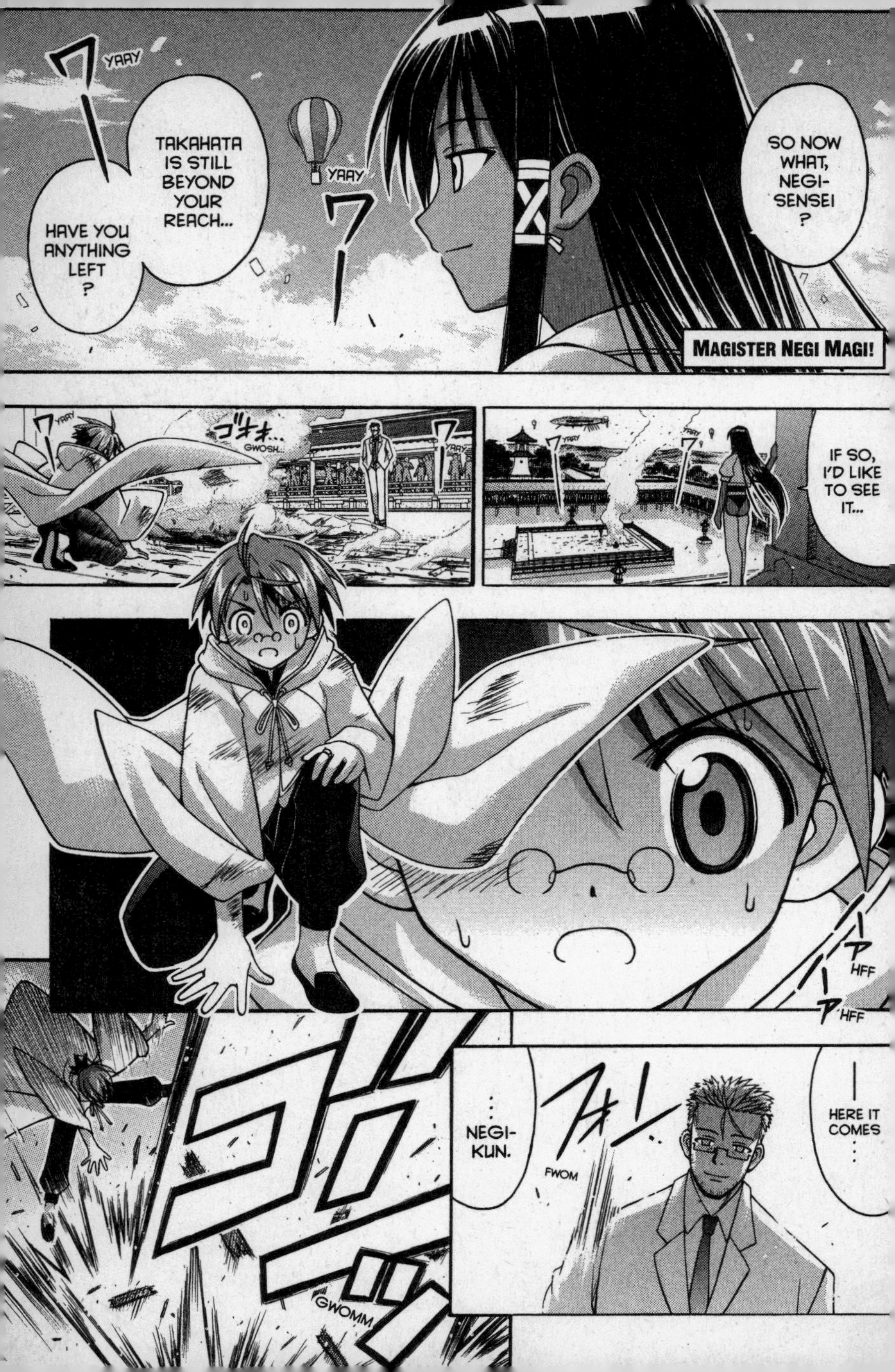
SO NOW WHAT, NEGI-SENSEI?
TAKAHATA IS STILL BEYOND YOUR REACH...
HAVE YOU ANYTHING LEFT?
YAAY
YAAY
MAGISTER NEGI MAGI!
IF SO, I'D LIKE TO SEE IT...
YAAY
GWOSH...
YAAY
HFF
HFF
HERE IT COMES...
...NEGI-KUN.
FWOM
GWOMM

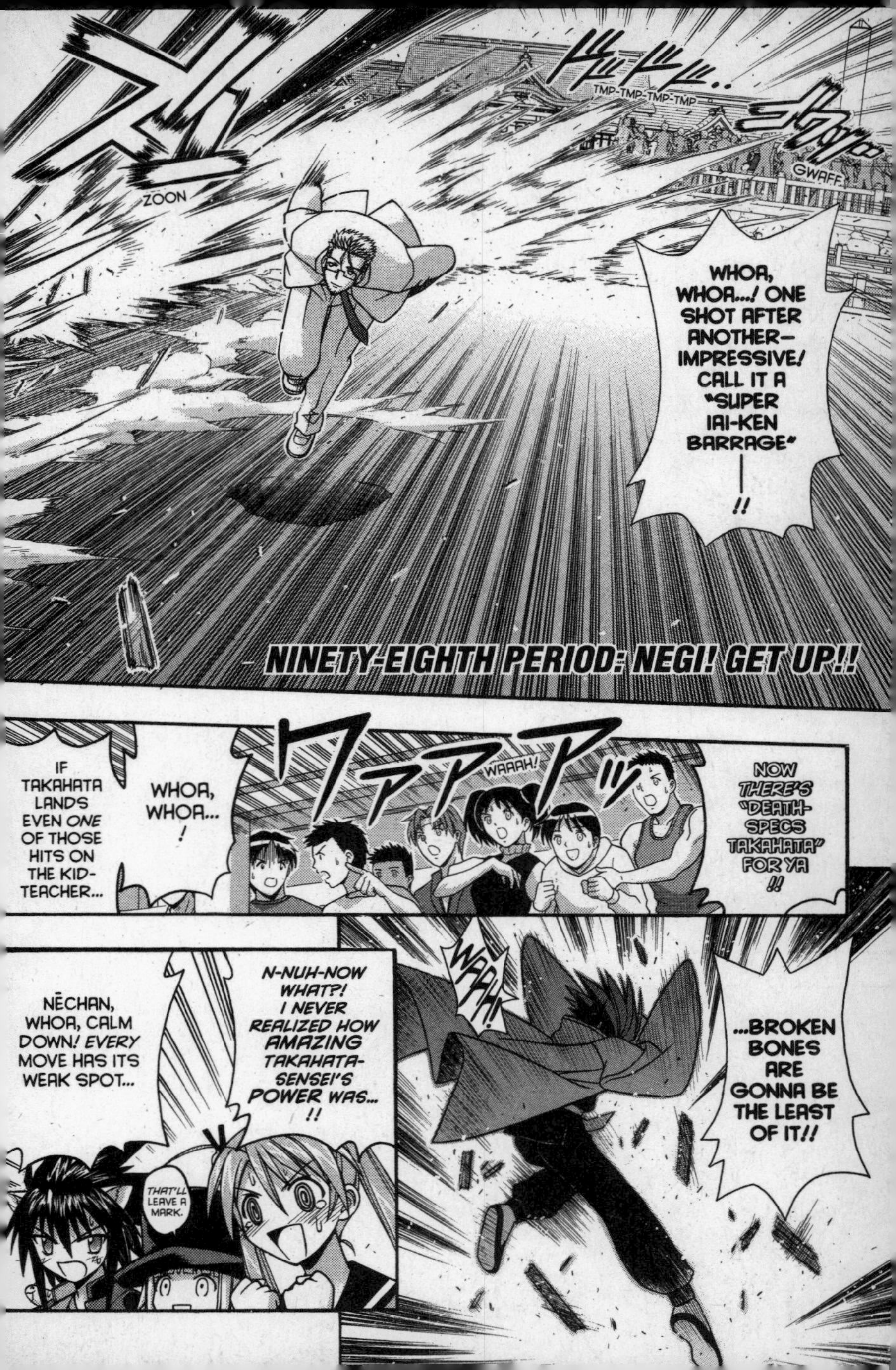

TMP-TMP-TMP-TMP
GWAFF
WHOA, WHOA...! ONE SHOT AFTER ANOTHER—IMPRESSIVE! CALL IT A "SUPER IAI-KEN BARRAGE"—!!
ZOON
NINETY-EIGHTH PERIOD: NEGI! GET UP!!
NOW THERE'S "DEATH-SPECS TAKAHATA" FOR YA!!
WAAAH!
WHOA, WHOA...!
IF TAKAHATA LANDS EVEN ONE OF THOSE HITS ON THE KID-TEACHER...
...BROKEN BONES ARE GONNA BE THE LEAST OF IT!!
N-NUH-NOW WHAT?! I NEVER REALIZED HOW AMAZING TAKAHATA-SENSEI'S POWER WAS...!!
NĒCHAN, WHOA, CALM DOWN! EVERY MOVE HAS ITS WEAK SPOT...
THAT'LL LEAVE A MARK.

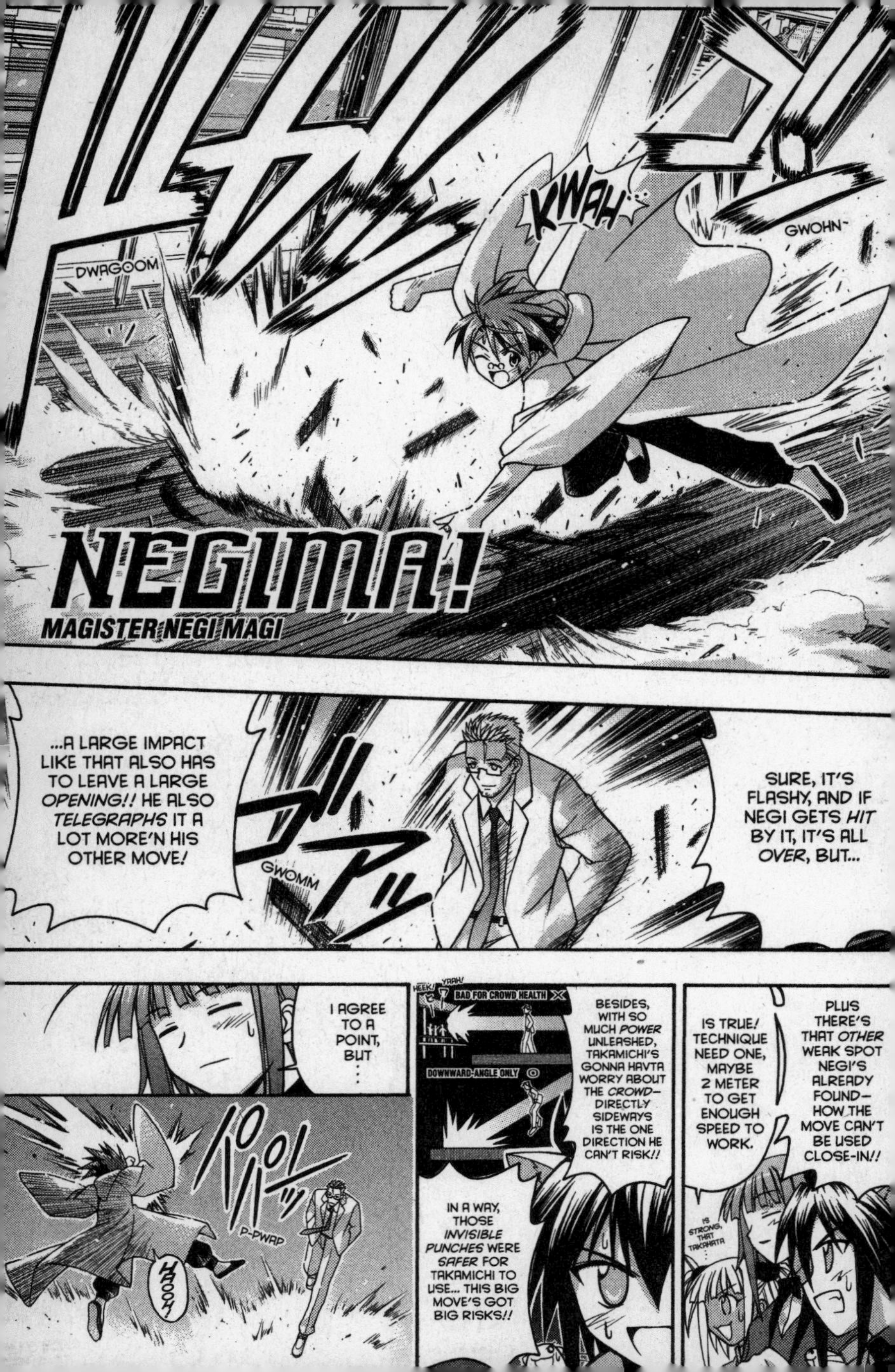

GWOHN
KWAH
DWAGOOM
NEGIMA!
MAGISTER NEGI MAGI
SURE, IT'S FLASHY, AND IF NEGI GETS *HIT* BY IT, IT'S ALL *OVER*, BUT...
...A LARGE IMPACT LIKE THAT ALSO HAS TO LEAVE A LARGE *OPENING!!* HE ALSO *TELEGRAPHS* IT A LOT MORE'N HIS OTHER MOVE!
GWOMM
PLUS THERE'S THAT *OTHER* WEAK SPOT NEGI'S ALREADY FOUND—HOW THE MOVE CAN'T BE USED CLOSE-IN!!
IS TRUE! TECHNIQUE NEED ONE, MAYBE 2 METER TO GET ENOUGH SPEED TO WORK.
IS STRONG, THAT TAKAHATA
BESIDES, WITH SO MUCH *POWER* UNLEASHED, TAKAMICHI'S GONNA HAVTA WORRY ABOUT THE *CROWD*—DIRECTLY SIDEWAYS IS THE ONE DIRECTION HE CAN'T RISK!!
HEEK!
YAAH!
BAD FOR CROWD HEALTH X
DOWNWARD-ANGLE ONLY O
IN A WAY, THOSE *INVISIBLE PUNCHES* WERE *SAFER* FOR TAKAMICHI TO USE... THIS BIG MOVE'S GOT BIG RISKS!!
I AGREE TO A POINT, BUT ...
P-PWAP
HROOH!

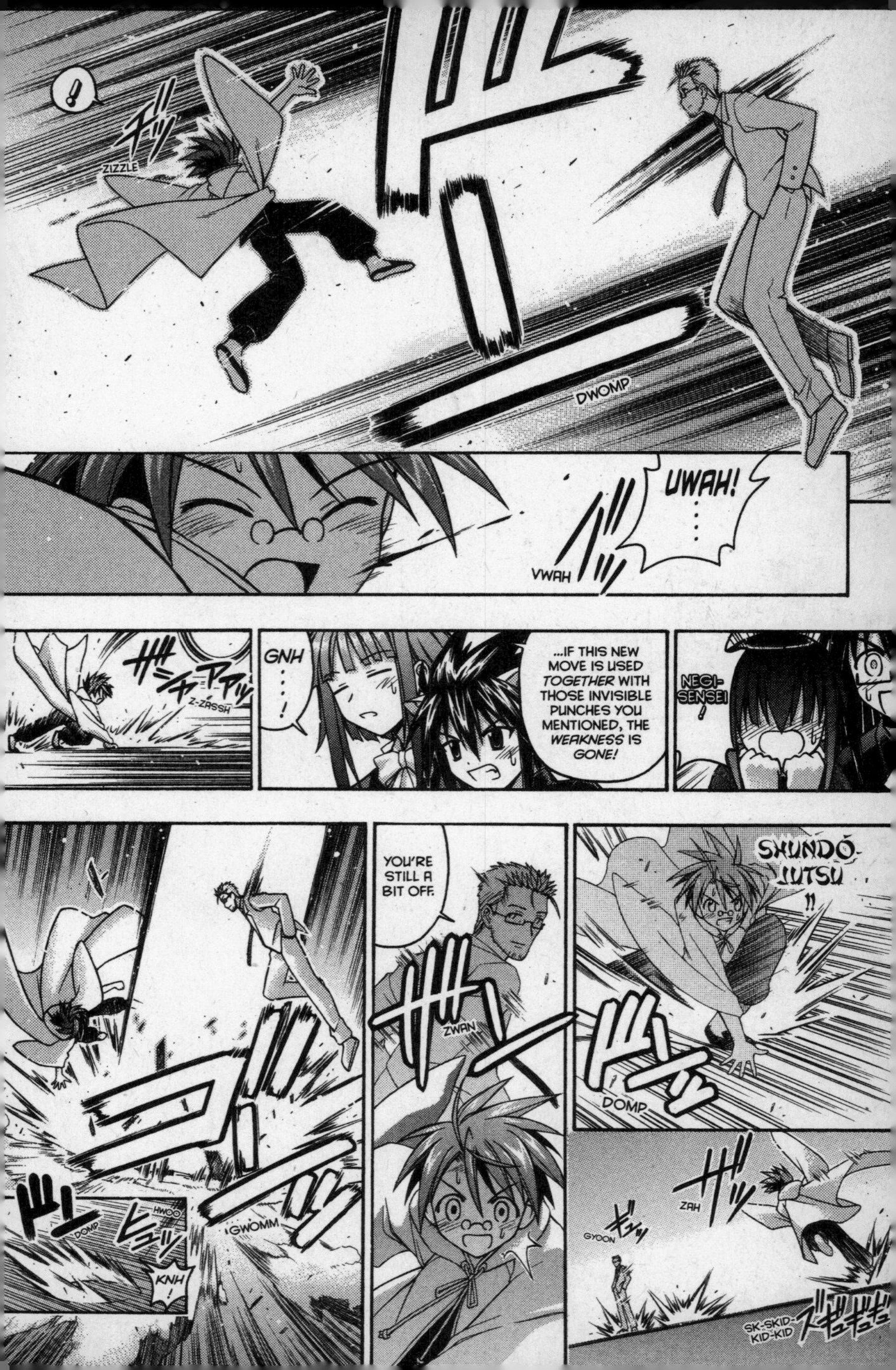
!
ZIZZLE
DWOMP
UWAH!
...
VWAH
NEGI-SENSEI!
...IF THIS NEW MOVE IS USED *TOGETHER* WITH THOSE INVISIBLE PUNCHES YOU MENTIONED, THE *WEAKNESS* IS GONE!
GNH...!
Z-ZASSH
SHUNDŌ-JUTSU!!
DOMP
YOU'RE STILL A BIT OFF.
ZWAN
HWOO
DOMP
GWOMM
KNH!
ZAH
GYOON
SK-SKID-KID-KID

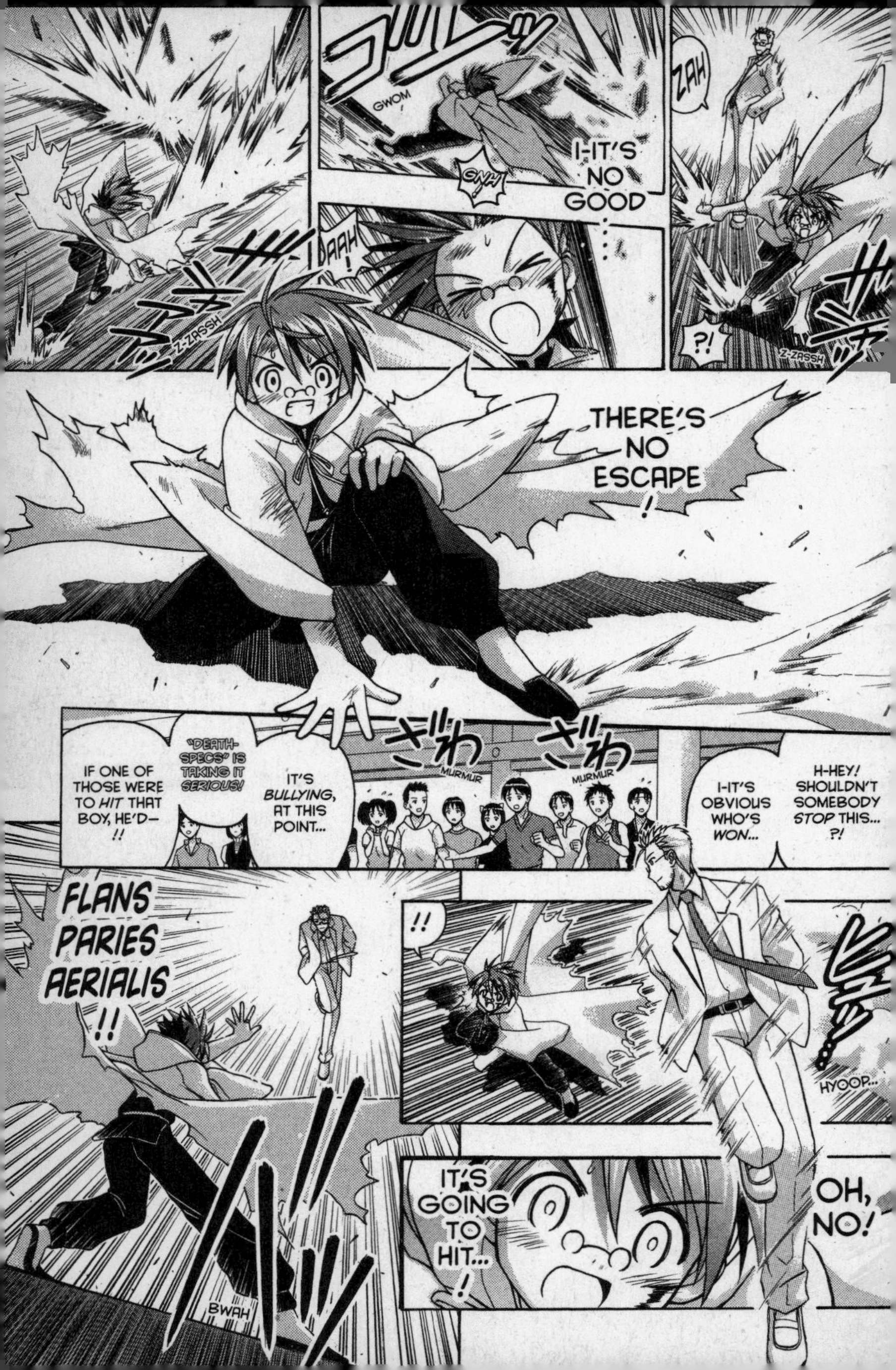
ZAH
?!
Z-ZASSH
GWOM
GNH
I-IT'S NO GOOD...
AAAH!
Z-ZASSH
THERE'S NO ESCAPE!
H-HEY! SHOULDN'T SOMEBODY *STOP* THIS...?!
I-IT'S OBVIOUS WHO'S *WON*...
MURMUR
MURMUR
IT'S *BULLYING*, AT THIS POINT...
"DEATH-SPECS" IS TAKING IT *SERIOUS!*
IF ONE OF THOSE WERE TO *HIT* THAT BOY, HE'D—!!
HYOOP...
!!
OH, NO!
IT'S GOING TO HIT...!
FLANS PARIES AERIALIS!!
BWAH

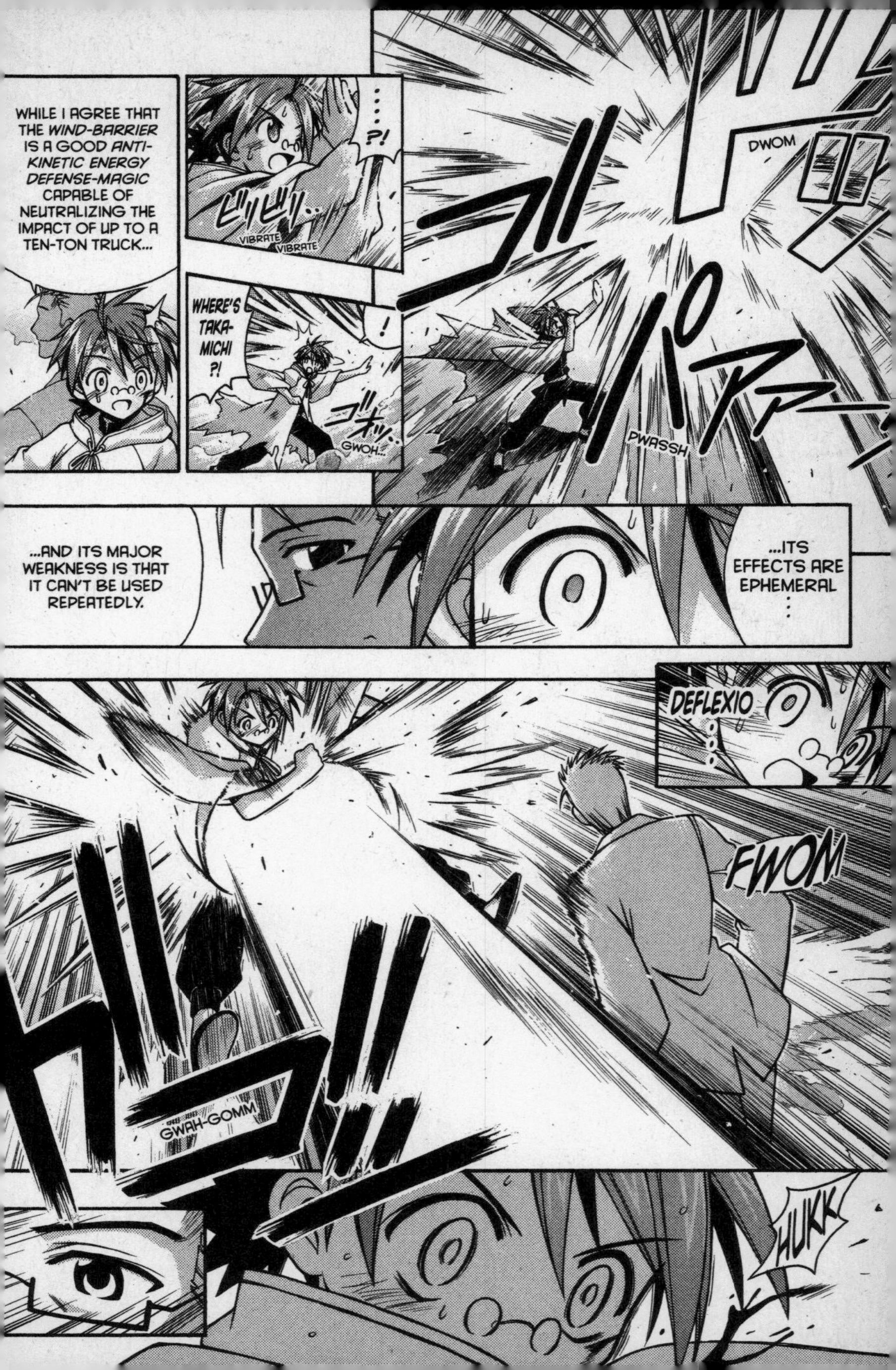
DWOM
PWASSH
...?!
VIBRATE
VIBRATE
!
WHERE'S TAKA-MICHI ?!
GWOH...
WHILE I AGREE THAT THE *WIND-BARRIER* IS A GOOD *ANTI-KINETIC ENERGY DEFENSE-MAGIC* CAPABLE OF NEUTRALIZING THE IMPACT OF UP TO A TEN-TON TRUCK...
...ITS EFFECTS ARE EPHEMERAL ...
...AND ITS MAJOR WEAKNESS IS THAT IT CAN'T BE USED REPEATEDLY.
DEFLEXIO ...
FWOM
GWAH-GOMM
HUKK

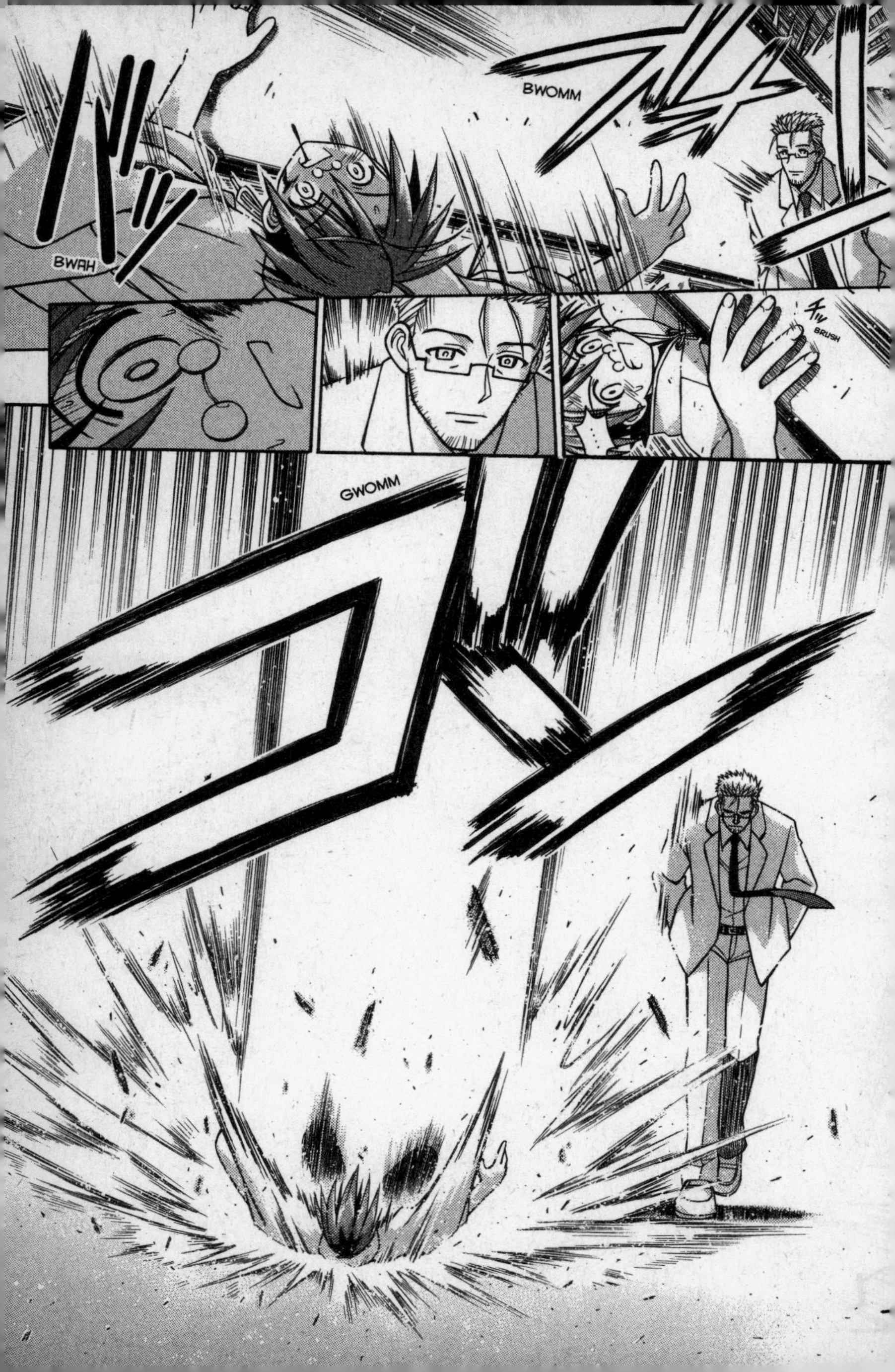
BWOMM
BWAH
BRUSH
GWOMM

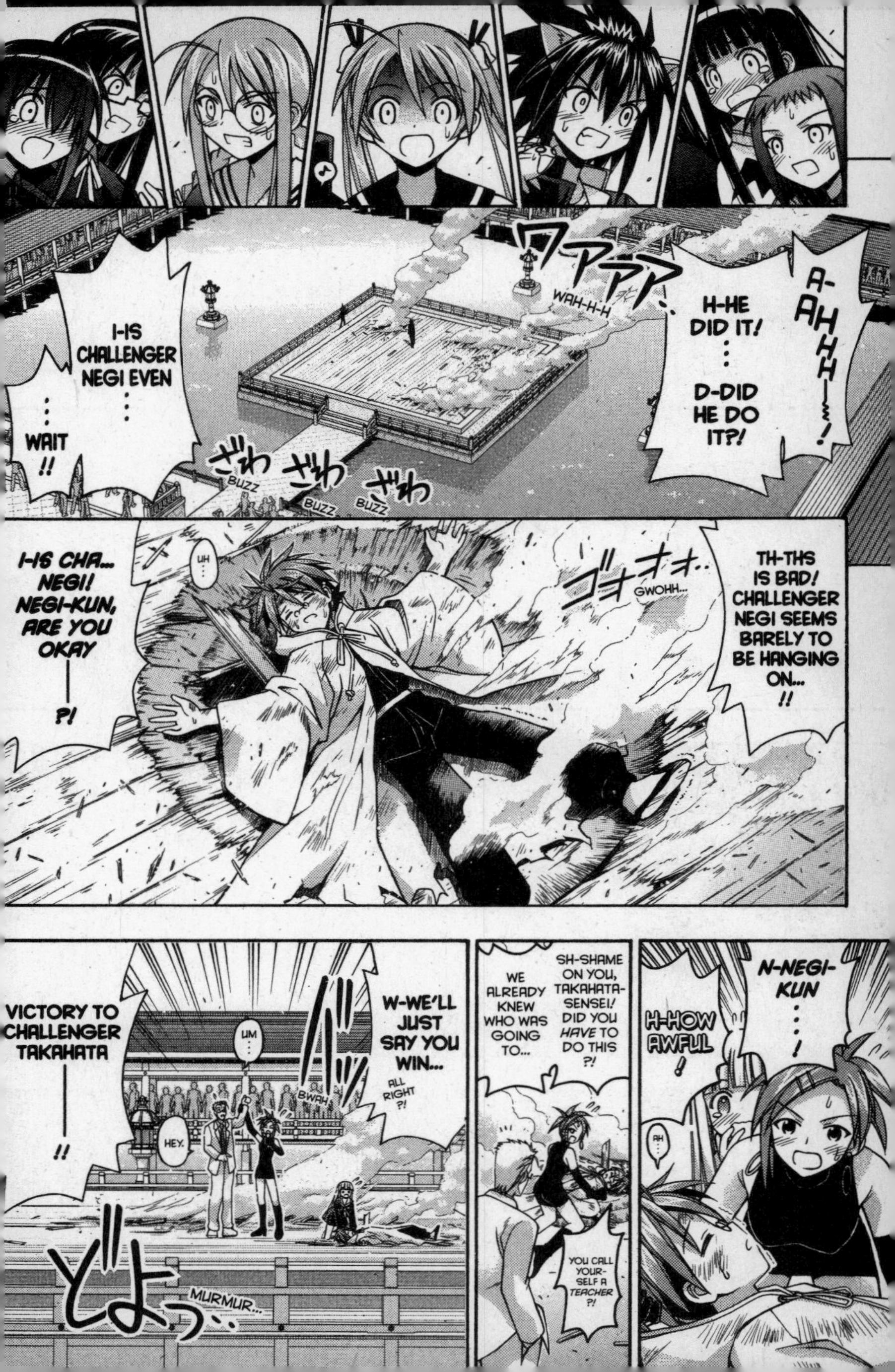
A-AHHH~!
H-HE DID IT! ... D-DID HE DO IT?!
WAH-H-H
I-IS CHALLENGER NEGI EVEN ...
... WAIT !!
BUZZ
BUZZ
BUZZ
TH-THS IS BAD! CHALLENGER NEGI SEEMS BARELY TO BE HANGING ON... !!
GWOHH...
UH ...
I-IS CHA... NEGI! NEGI-KUN, ARE YOU OKAY —?!
N-NEGI-KUN ... !
H-HOW AWFUL !
AH ...
SH-SHAME ON YOU, TAKAHATA-SENSEI! DID YOU *HAVE* TO DO THIS ?!
WE ALREADY KNEW WHO WAS GOING TO...
YOU CALL YOUR-SELF A *TEACHER* ?!
W-WE'LL JUST SAY YOU WIN...
ALL RIGHT ?!
BWAH
UM ...
VICTORY TO CHALLENGER TAKAHATA — !!
HEY.
MURMUR...

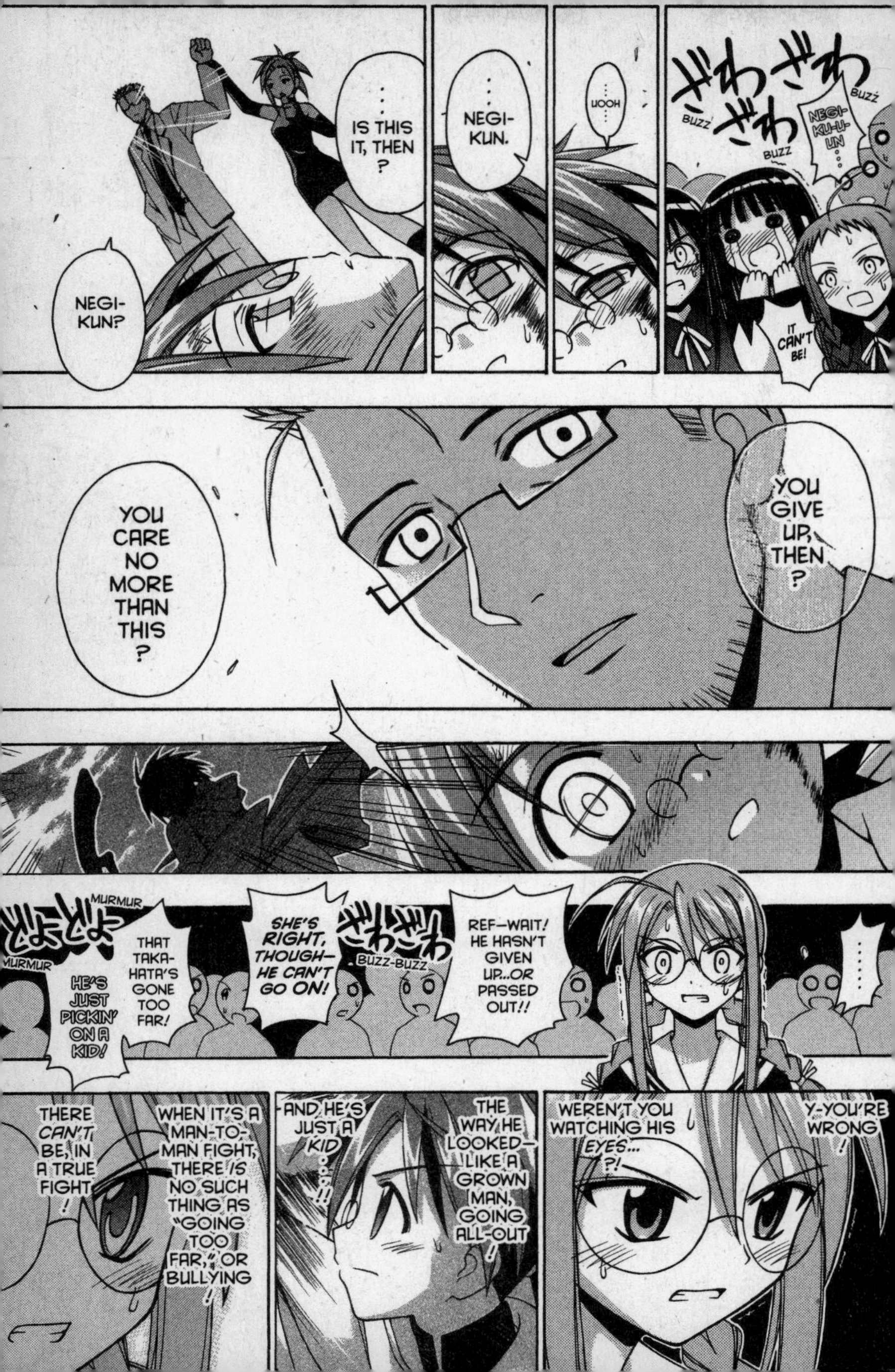
ざわざわ ざわ
BUZZ BUZZ BUZZ
NEGI-KU-U-UN...
IT CAN'T BE!
...UOOH...
...NEGI-KUN.
...IS THIS IT, THEN?
NEGI-KUN?
YOU GIVE UP, THEN?
YOU CARE NO MORE THAN THIS?
......
REF—WAIT! HE HASN'T GIVEN UP...OR PASSED OUT!!
ざわざわ BUZZ-BUZZ
SHE'S RIGHT, THOUGH—HE CAN'T GO ON!
THAT TAKAHATA'S GONE TOO FAR!
HE'S JUST PICKIN' ON A KID!
どよどよ MURMUR MURMUR
Y-YOU'RE WRONG!
WEREN'T YOU WATCHING HIS EYES...?!
THE WAY HE LOOKED—LIKE A GROWN MAN, GOING ALL-OUT!
AND HE'S JUST A KID...!!
WHEN IT'S A MAN-TO-MAN FIGHT, THERE IS NO SUCH THING AS "GOING TOO FAR," OR BULLYING!
THERE CAN'T BE, IN A TRUE FIGHT!

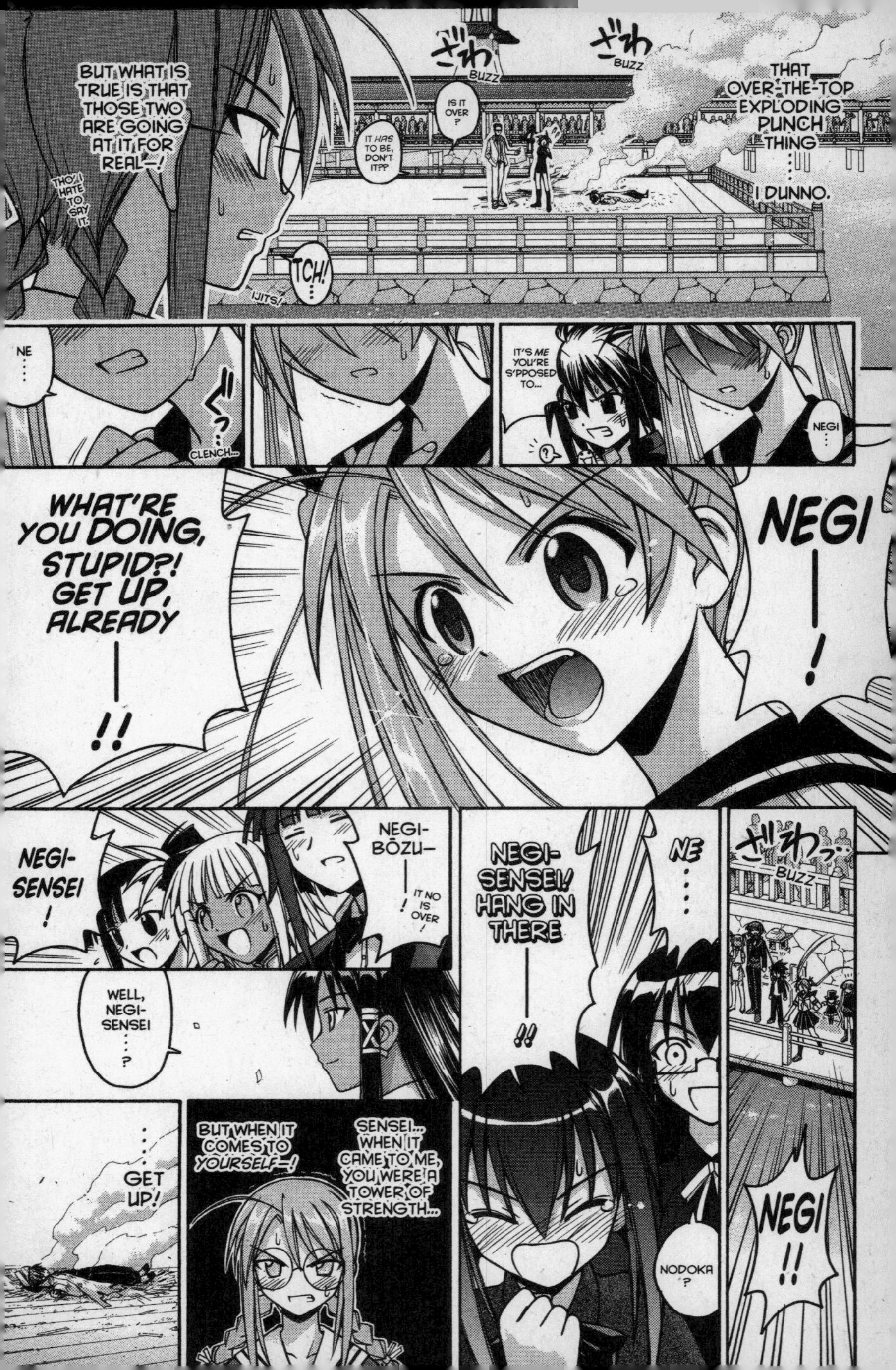

THAT OVER-THE-TOP EXPLODING PUNCH THING... I DUNNO.
ざわ BUZZ
ざわ BUZZ
IS IT OVER?
IT HAS TO BE, DON'T IT??
BUT WHAT IS TRUE IS THAT THOSE TWO ARE GOING AT IT FOR REAL—!
THO' I HATE TO SAY IT.
TCH!...
IJITS!
NEGI...
IT'S ME YOU'RE S'PPOSED TO...
?
NE...
ぐっ CLENCH...
NEGI—!
WHAT'RE YOU DOING, STUPID?! GET UP, ALREADY—!!
ざわっ BUZZ
NE....
NEGI-SENSEI! HANG IN THERE—!!
NEGI-BŌZU—!
IT NO IS OVER!
NEGI-SENSEI!
WELL, NEGI-SENSEI...?
NEGI!!
NODOKA?
SENSEI... WHEN IT CAME TO ME, YOU WERE A TOWER OF STRENGTH...
BUT WHEN IT COMES TO YOURSELF—!
...GET UP!

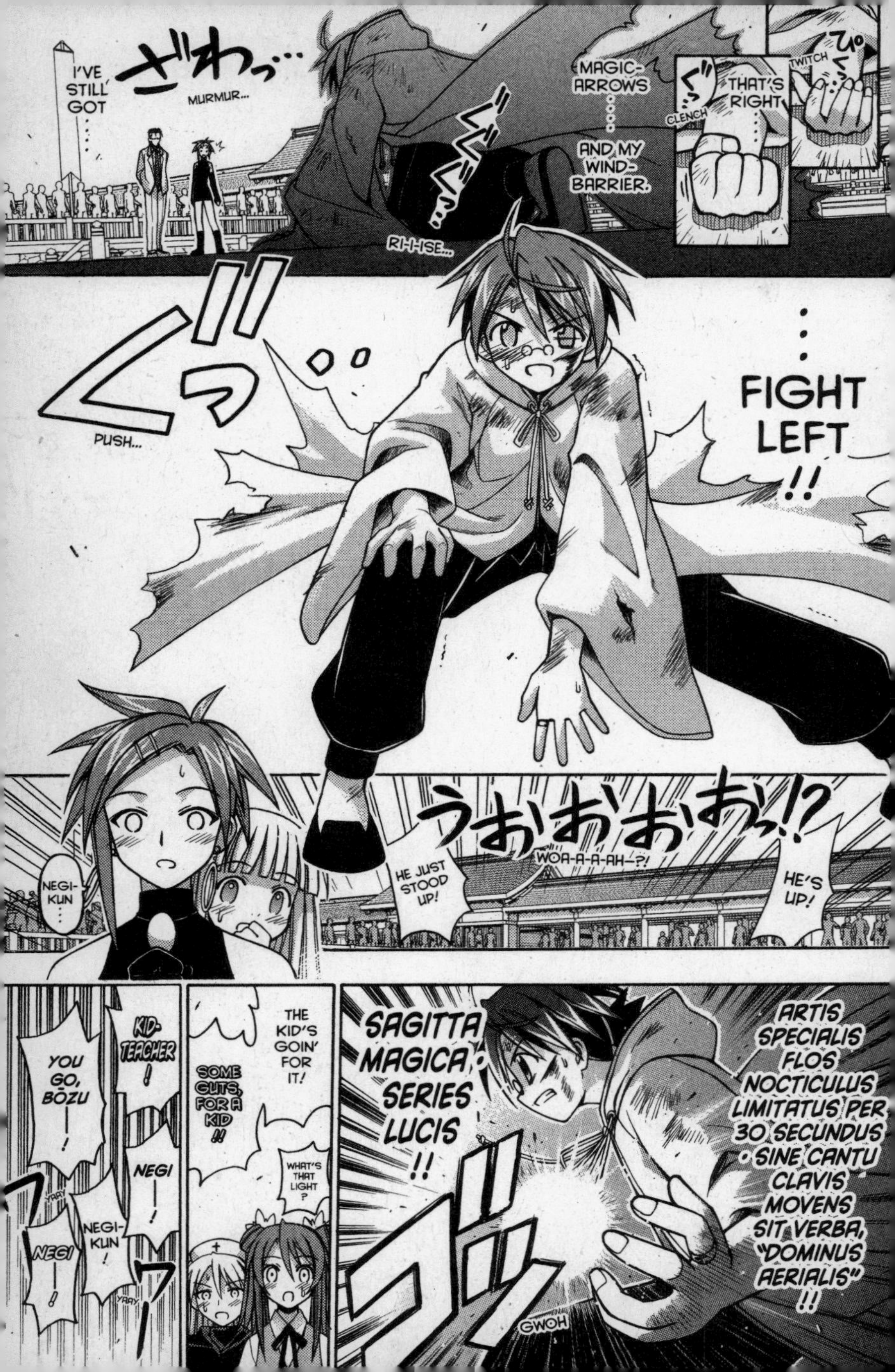
ぴくっ
TWITCH
ぐっ
CLENCH
THAT'S RIGHT...
MAGIC-ARROWS.....
AND MY WIND-BARRIER.
RI-I-ISE...
ざわっ…
MURMUR...
I'VE STILL GOT...
...FIGHT LEFT!!
ぐぐっ
PUSH...
HE'S UP!
うおおおおっ!?
WOA-A-A-AH-?!
HE JUST STOOD UP!
NEGI-KUN...
ARTIS SPECIALIS FLOS NOCTICULUS LIMITATUS PER 30 SECUNDUS. SINE CANTU CLAVIS MOVENS SIT VERBA, "DOMINUS AERIALIS"!!
SAGITTA MAGICA, SERIES LUCIS!!
GWOH
THE KID'S GOIN' FOR IT!
SOME GUTS, FOR A KID!!
WHAT'S THAT LIGHT?
KID-TEACHER!
YOU GO, BŌZU--!
NEGI--!
NEGI-KUN!
NEGI--!
YAAY
YAAY

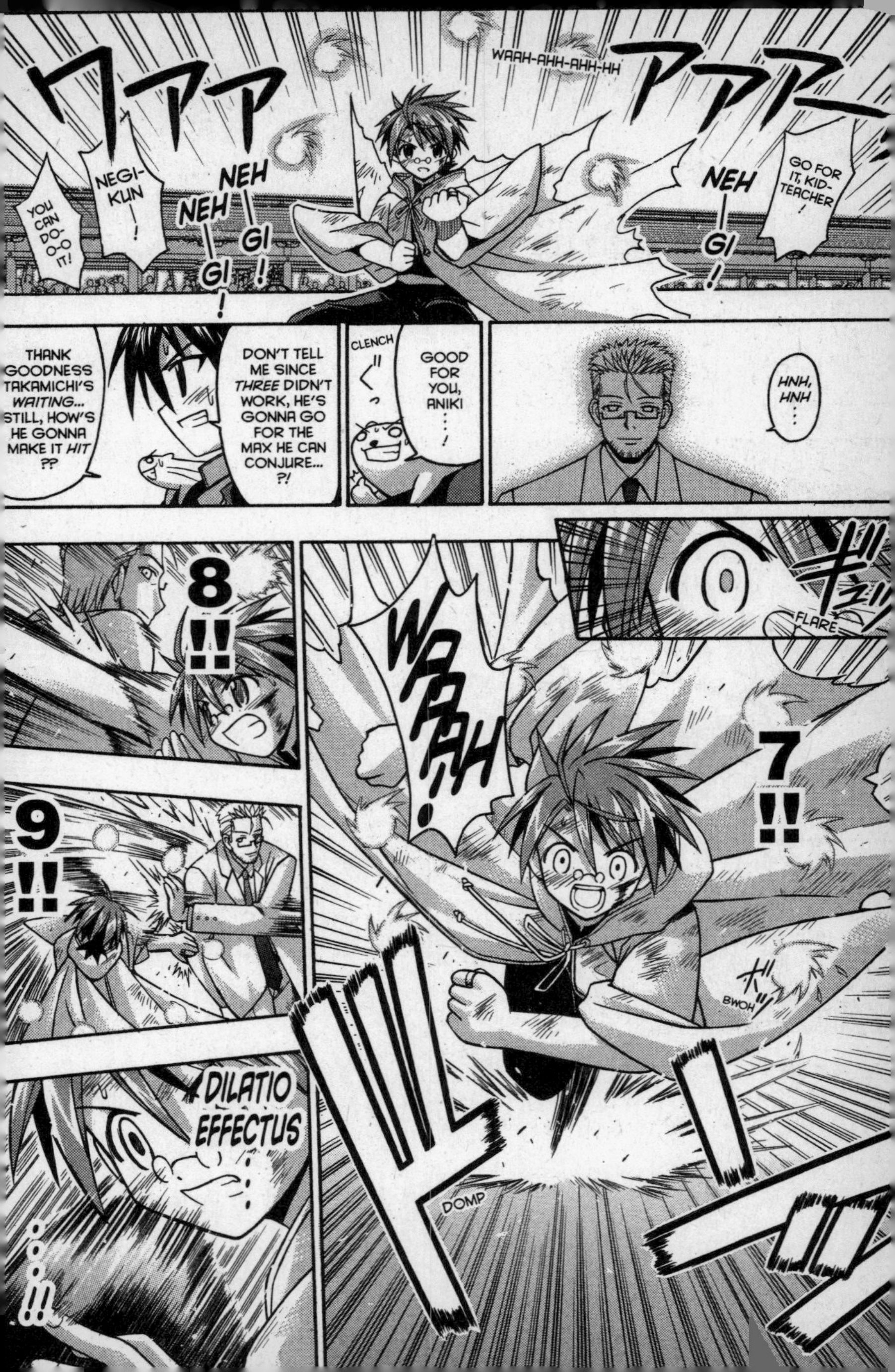

GO FOR IT, KID-TEACHER!
NEH-GI!
WAAH-AHH-AHH-HH
NEH-GI!
NEGI-KUN!
NEH-GI!
YOU CAN DO-O-O IT!
HNH, HNH...
CLENCH
GOOD FOR YOU, ANIKI...!
DON'T TELL ME SINCE *THREE* DIDN'T WORK, HE'S GONNA GO FOR THE MAX HE CAN CONJURE...?!
THANK GOODNESS TAKAMICHI'S *WAITING*... STILL, HOW'S HE GONNA MAKE IT *HIT*??
FLARE
WAAAH!!
7!!
BWOH
DOMP
8!!
9!!
DILATIO EFFECTUS
...!!

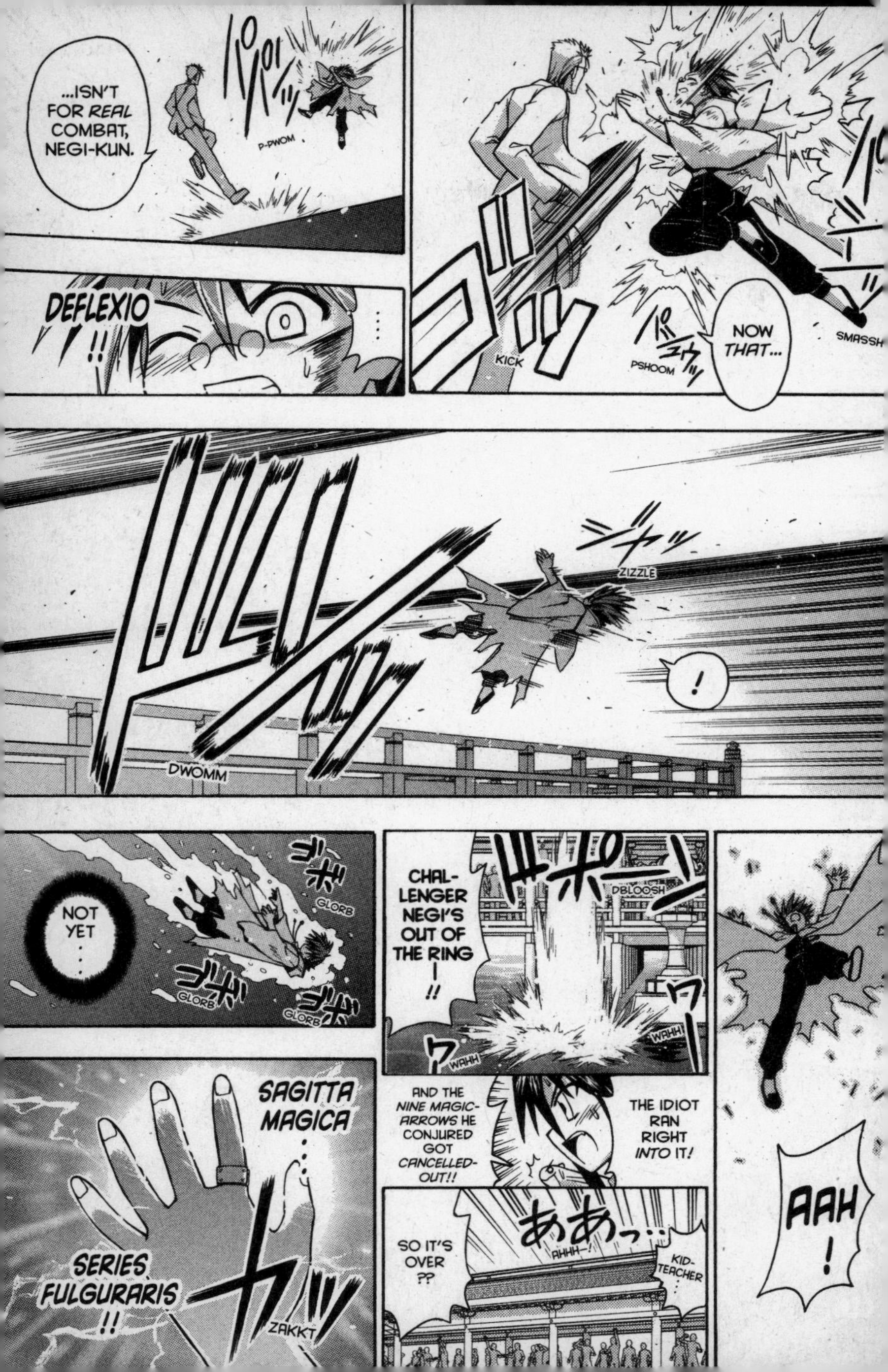
SMASSH
NOW THAT...
PSHOOM
KICK
...ISN'T FOR *REAL* COMBAT, NEGI-KUN.
P-PWOM
...
DEFLEXIO !!
ZIZZLE
!
DWOMM
AAH !
DBLOOSH
CHAL-LENGER NEGI'S OUT OF THE RING — !!
WAHH
WAHH
THE IDIOT RAN RIGHT *INTO IT!*
AND THE *NINE MAGIC-ARROWS* HE CONJURED GOT *CANCELLED-OUT!!*
AHHH—!
KID-TEACHER
SO IT'S OVER ??
GLORB
NOT YET ...
GLORB
GLORB
SAGITTA MAGICA ...
SERIES FULGURARIS !!
ZAKKT

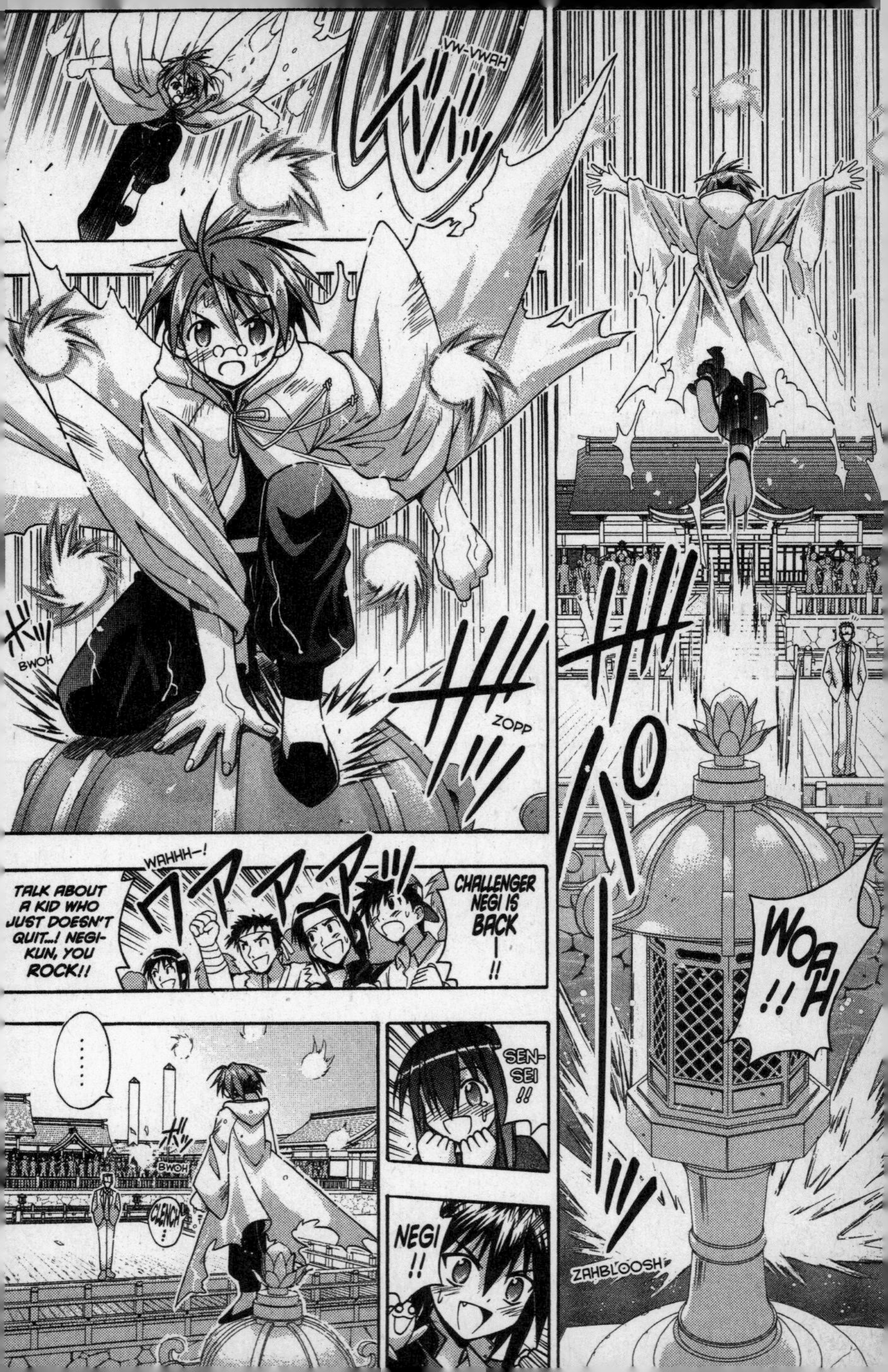
WOAH!!
ZAHBLOOSH
VW-VWAH
BWOH
ZOPP
CHALLENGER NEGI IS BACK!!
WAHHH-!
TALK ABOUT A KID WHO JUST DOESN'T QUIT...! NEGI-KUN, YOU ROCK!!
SEN-SEI!!
NEGI!!
......
BWOH
CLENCH...

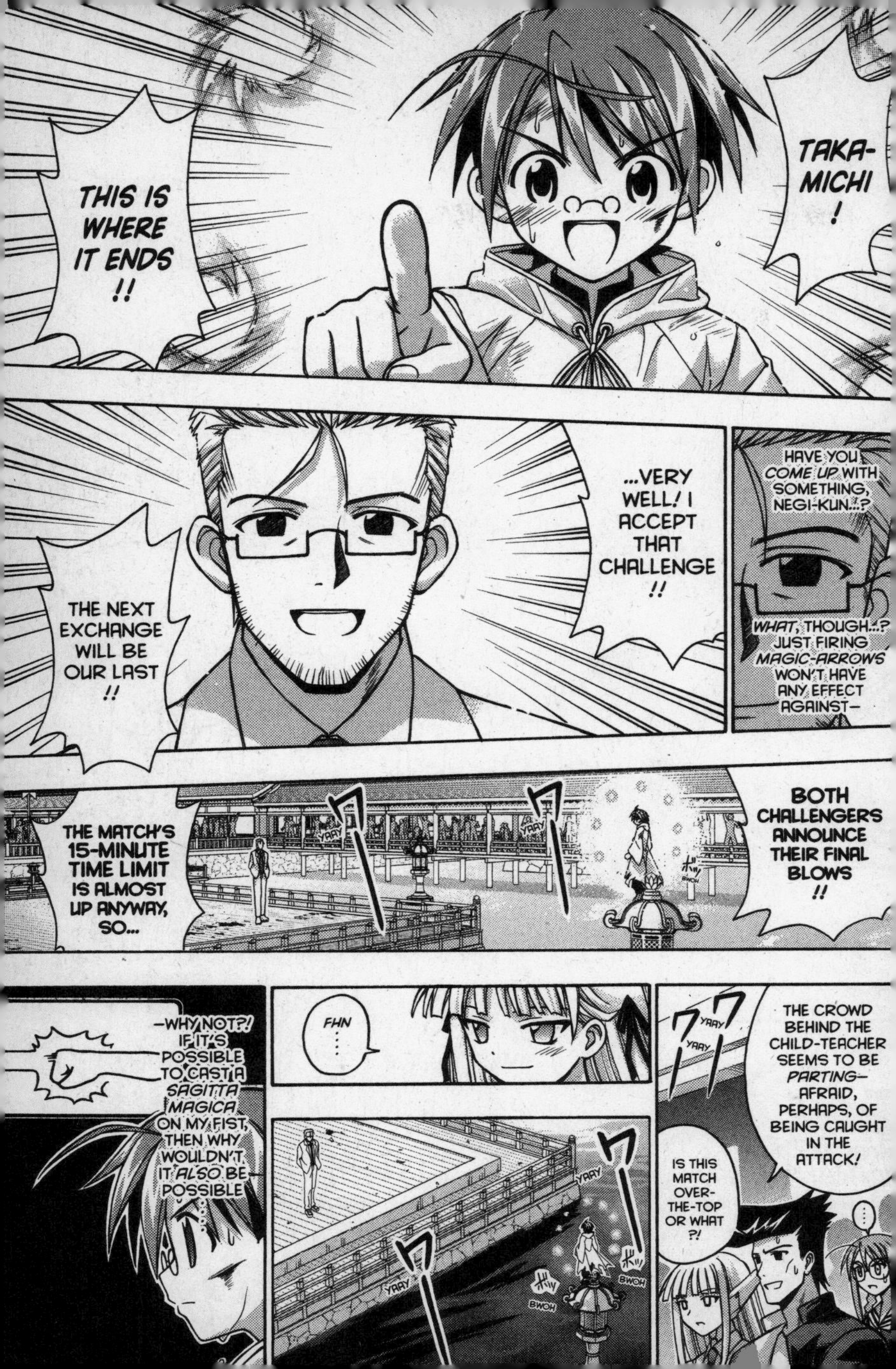
TAKA-MICHI!
THIS IS WHERE IT ENDS!!
HAVE YOU COME UP WITH SOMETHING, NEGI-KUN...?
WHAT, THOUGH...? JUST FIRING MAGIC-ARROWS WON'T HAVE ANY EFFECT AGAINST—
...VERY WELL! I ACCEPT THAT CHALLENGE!!
THE NEXT EXCHANGE WILL BE OUR LAST!!
BOTH CHALLENGERS ANNOUNCE THEIR FINAL BLOWS!!
YAAY
YAAY
BWOH
THE MATCH'S 15-MINUTE TIME LIMIT IS ALMOST UP ANYWAY, SO...
THE CROWD BEHIND THE CHILD-TEACHER SEEMS TO BE PARTING—AFRAID, PERHAPS, OF BEING CAUGHT IN THE ATTACK!
YAAY
YAAY
IS THIS MATCH OVER-THE-TOP OR WHAT?!
...
FHN ......
YAAY
YAAY
BWOH
BWOH
—WHY NOT?! IF IT'S POSSIBLE TO CAST A SAGITTA MAGICA ON MY FIST, THEN WHY WOULDN'T IT ALSO BE POSSIBLE ......

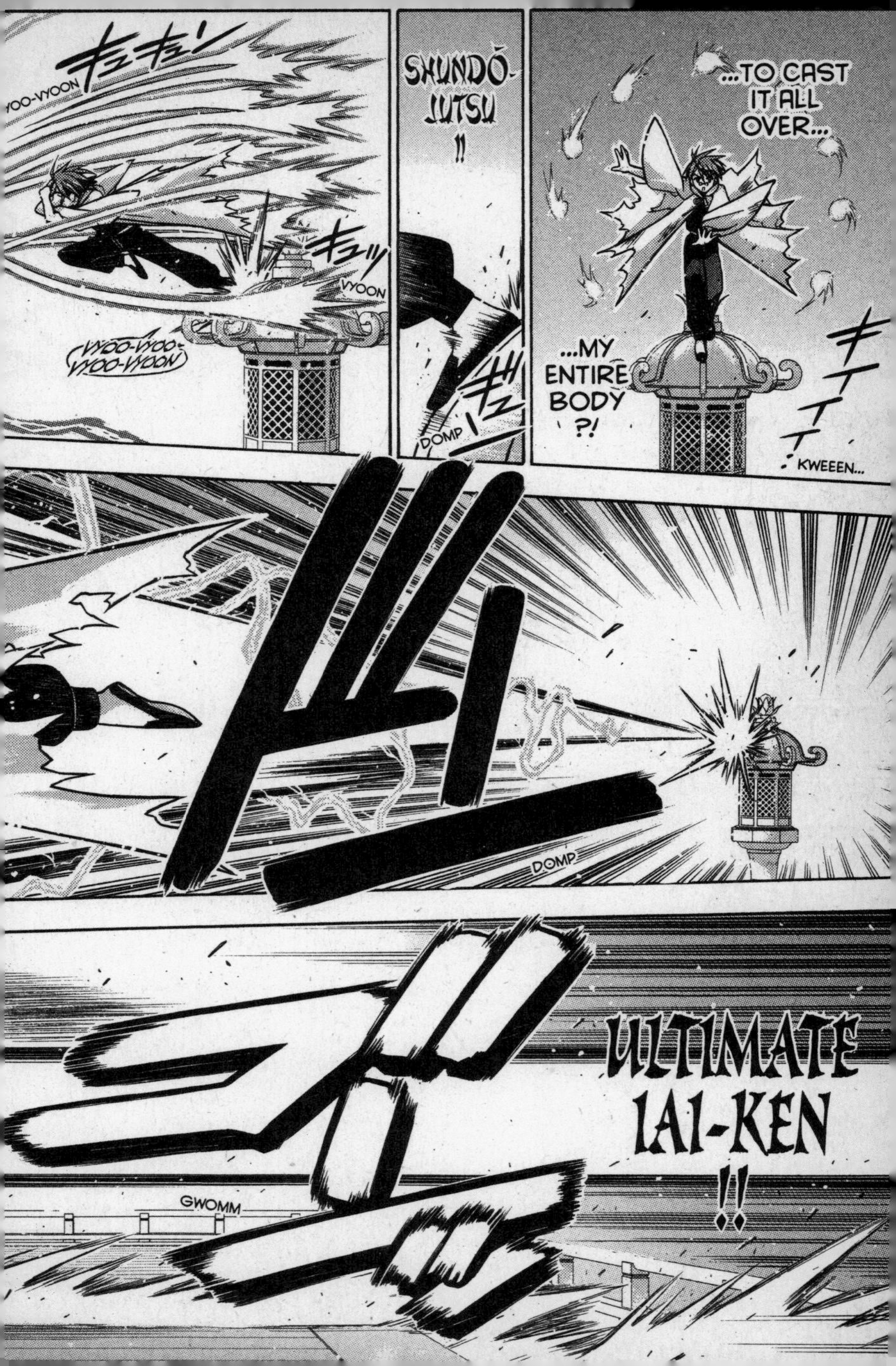
...TO CAST IT ALL OVER...
...MY ENTIRE BODY ?!
KWEEEN...
SHUNDŌ-JUTSU !!
DOMP
VYOO-VYOON
VYOON
VYOO-VYOO-VYOO-VYOON
DOMP
ULTIMATE IAI-KEN !!
GWOMM

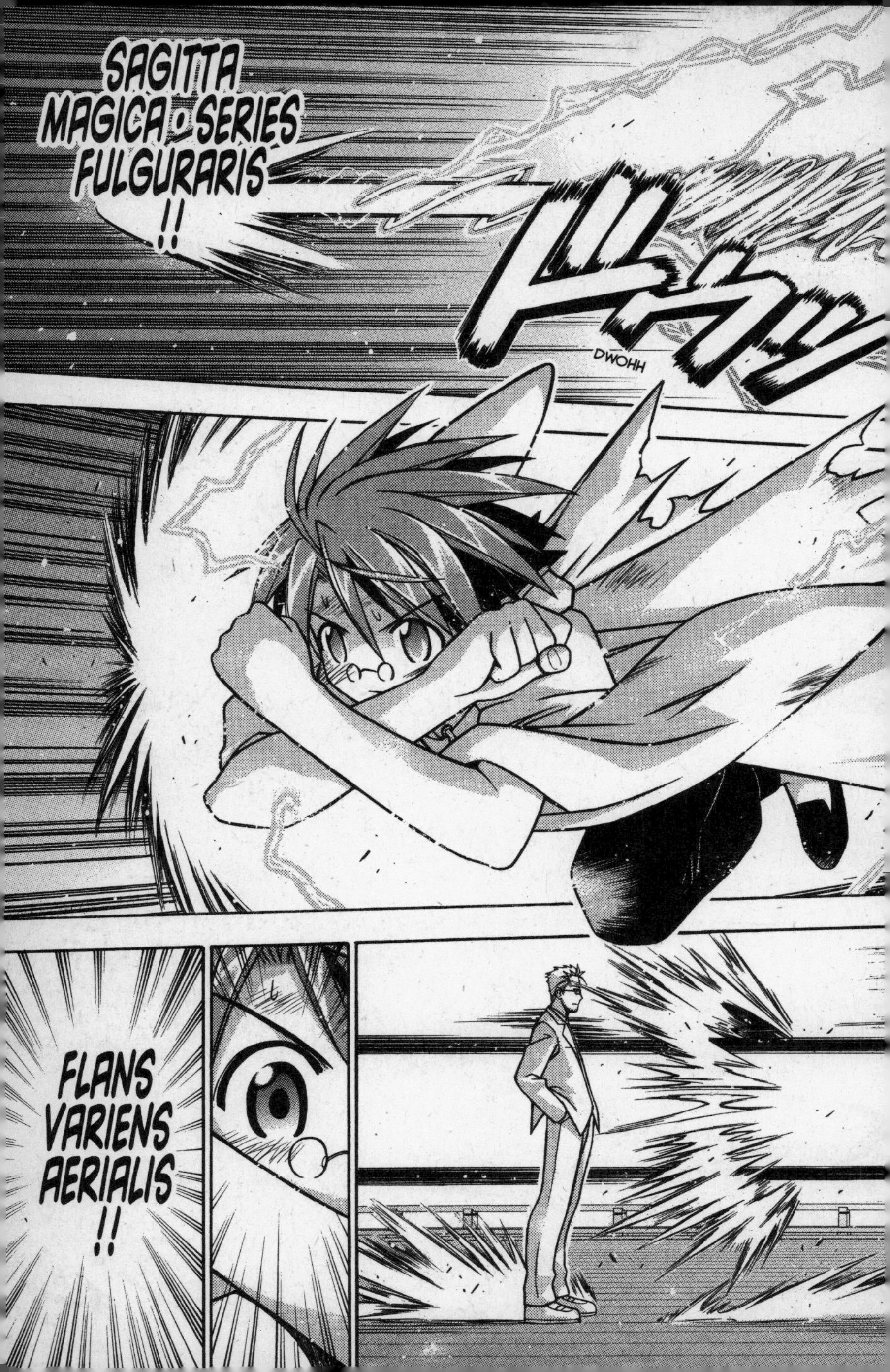
DWOHH
SAGITTA MAGICA · SERIES FULGURARIS !!
FLANS VARIENS AERIALIS !!

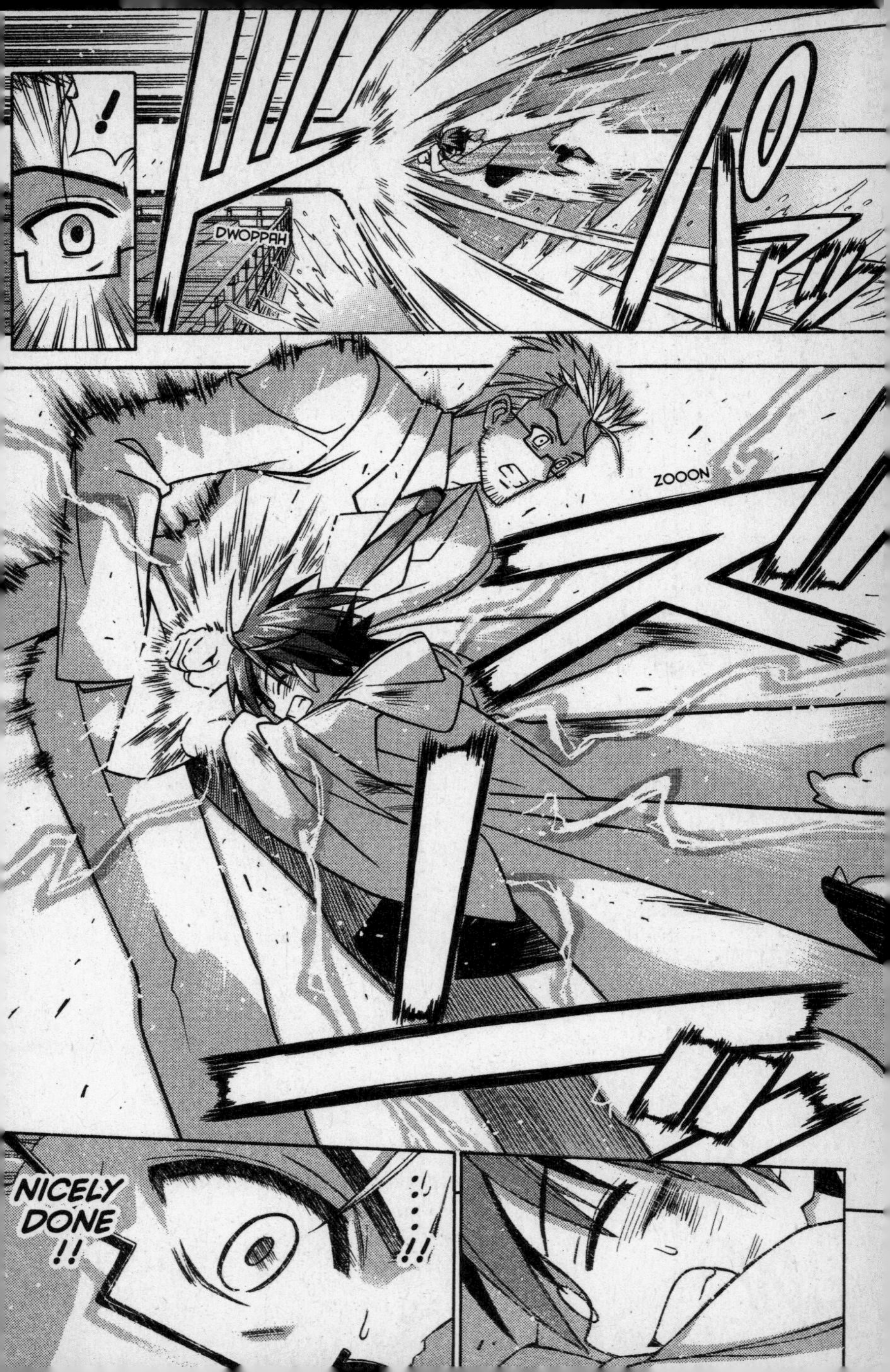
DWOPPAH
!
ZOOON
NICELY DONE !!
......!!

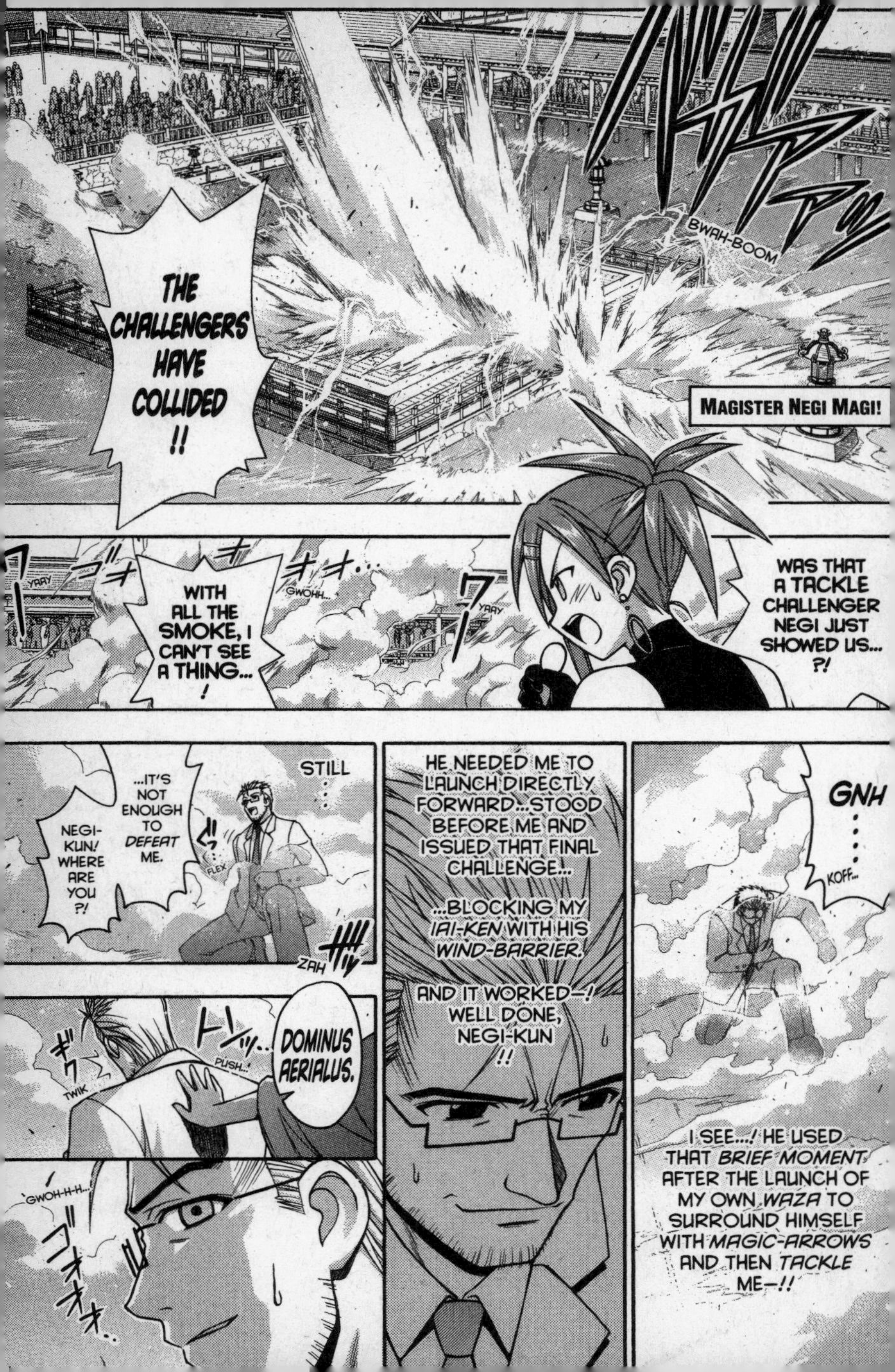
BWAH-BOOM
MAGISTER NEGI MAGI!
THE CHALLENGERS HAVE COLLIDED !!
WAS THAT A TACKLE CHALLENGER NEGI JUST SHOWED US...?!
YAAY
GWOHH...
WITH ALL THE SMOKE, I CAN'T SEE A THING...!
YAAY
GNH...
KOFF...
I SEE...! HE USED THAT BRIEF MOMENT AFTER THE LAUNCH OF MY OWN WAZA TO SURROUND HIMSELF WITH MAGIC-ARROWS AND THEN TACKLE ME—!!
HE NEEDED ME TO LAUNCH DIRECTLY FORWARD...STOOD BEFORE ME AND ISSUED THAT FINAL CHALLENGE...
...BLOCKING MY IAI-KEN WITH HIS WIND-BARRIER.
AND IT WORKED—! WELL DONE, NEGI-KUN!!
STILL...
...IT'S NOT ENOUGH TO DEFEAT ME.
FLEX
NEGI-KUN! WHERE ARE YOU?!
ZAH
DOMINUS AERIALUS.
PUSH...
TWIK
GWOH-H-H...

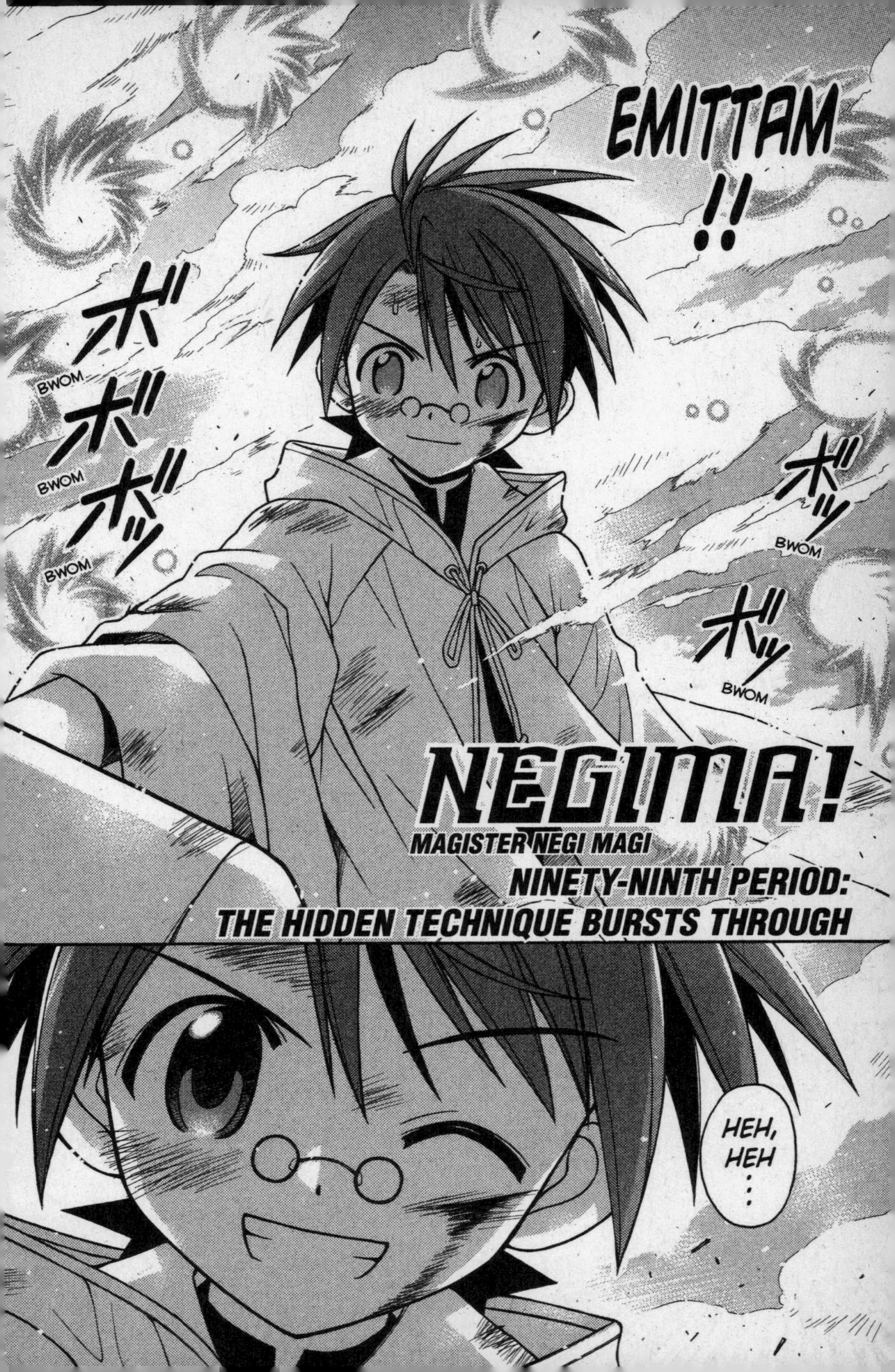
EMITTAM !!
ボッ
BWOM
ボッ
BWOM
ボボボッ
BWOM
BWOM
BWOM
NEGIMA!
MAGISTER NEGI MAGI
NINETY-NINTH PERIOD:
THE HIDDEN TECHNIQUE BURSTS THROUGH
HEH, HEH . . .

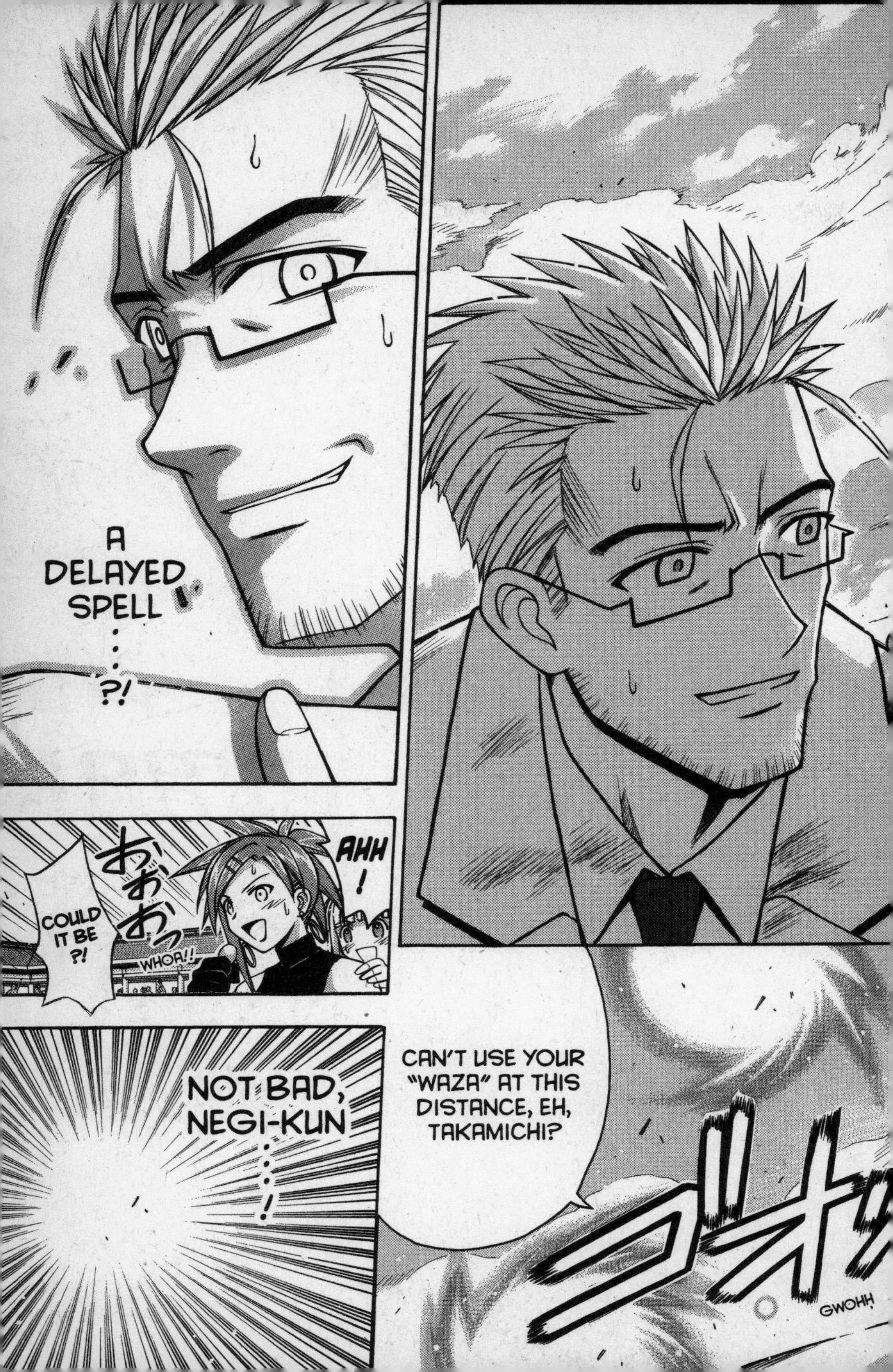

A DELAYED SPELL...?!
AHH!
あおおっ
WHOA!!
COULD IT BE ?!
CAN'T USE YOUR "WAZA" AT THIS DISTANCE, EH, TAKAMICHI?
ゴオッ
GWOHH
NOT BAD, NEGI-KUN...!

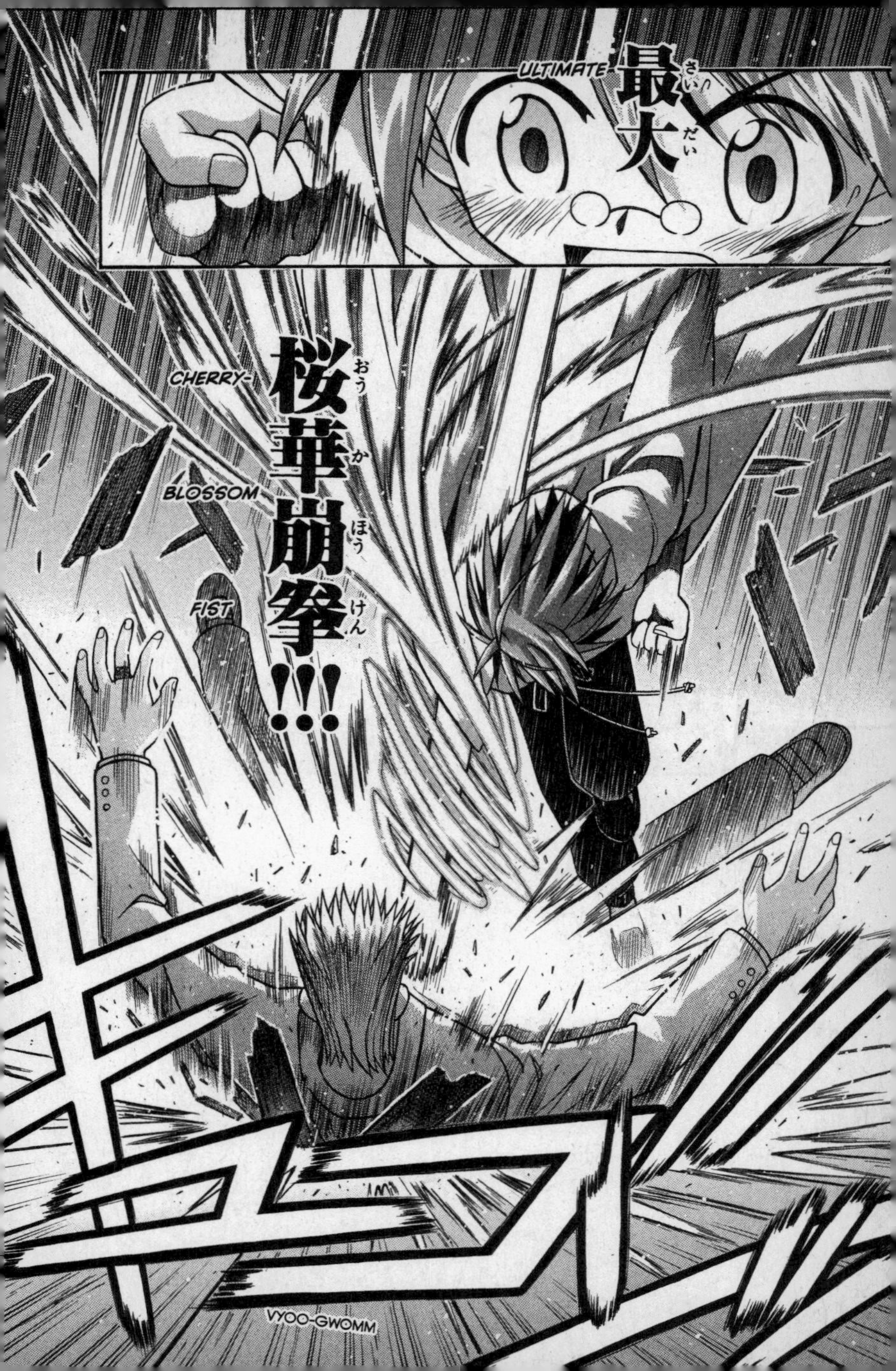
ULTIMATE
最大
CHERRY-
BLOSSOM
FIST
桜華崩拳!!!
VYOO-GWOMM

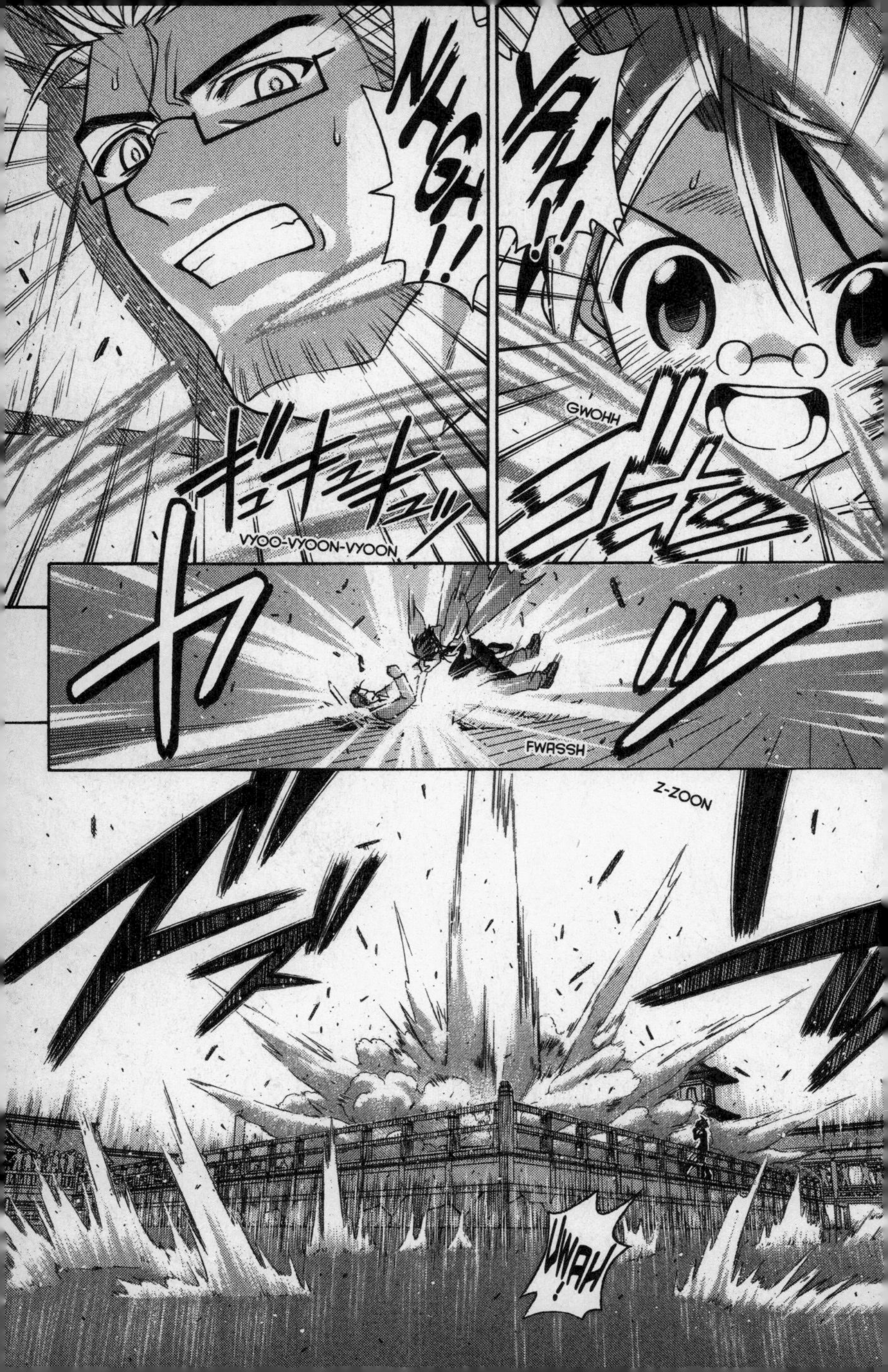
YAH!!
GWOHH
NHGH!!
VYOO-VYOON-VYOON
FWASSH
Z-ZOON
UWAH!

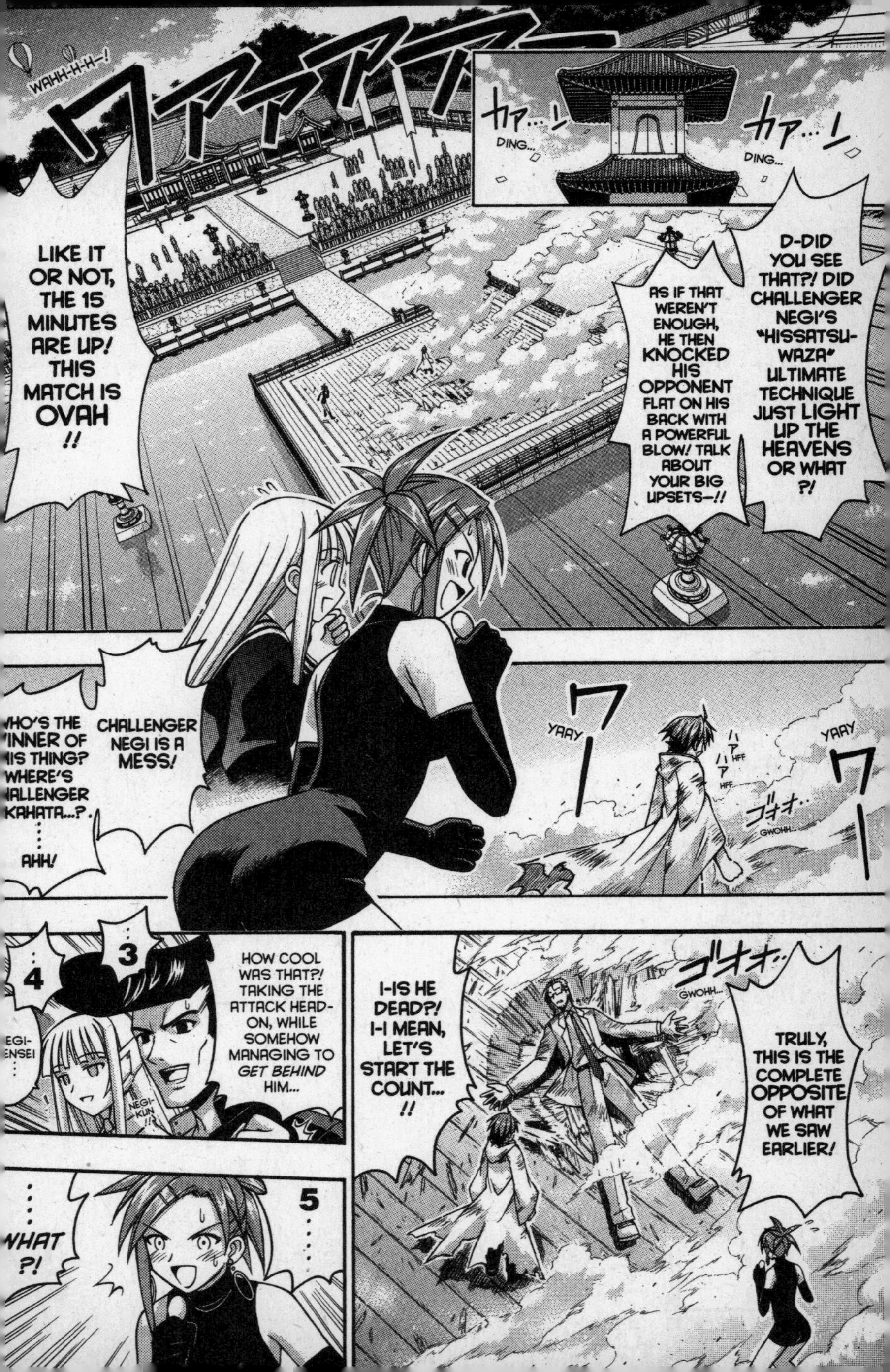

カァ…ン
DING...
カァ…ン
DING...
ワァァァアアー
WAHH-H-H-!
D-DID YOU SEE THAT?! DID CHALLENGER NEGI'S "HISSATSU-WAZA" ULTIMATE TECHNIQUE JUST LIGHT UP THE HEAVENS OR WHAT?!
AS IF THAT WEREN'T ENOUGH, HE THEN KNOCKED HIS OPPONENT FLAT ON HIS BACK WITH A POWERFUL BLOW! TALK ABOUT YOUR BIG UPSETS—!!
LIKE IT OR NOT, THE 15 MINUTES ARE UP! THIS MATCH IS OVAH!!
ワー
YAAY
ハァ
HFF
ハァ
HFF
ゴォォ…
GWOHH...
ワー
YAAY
CHALLENGER NEGI IS A MESS!
WHO'S THE WINNER OF THIS THING? WHERE'S CHALLENGER TAKAHATA...? ...AHH!
TRULY, THIS IS THE COMPLETE OPPOSITE OF WHAT WE SAW EARLIER!
ゴォォ
GWOHH...
I-IS HE DEAD?! I-I MEAN, LET'S START THE COUNT...!!
HOW COOL WAS THAT?! TAKING THE ATTACK HEAD-ON, WHILE SOMEHOW MANAGING TO *GET BEHIND* HIM...
...3
...4
NEGI-KUN!!
NEGI-SENSEI...
5...
...WHAT?!

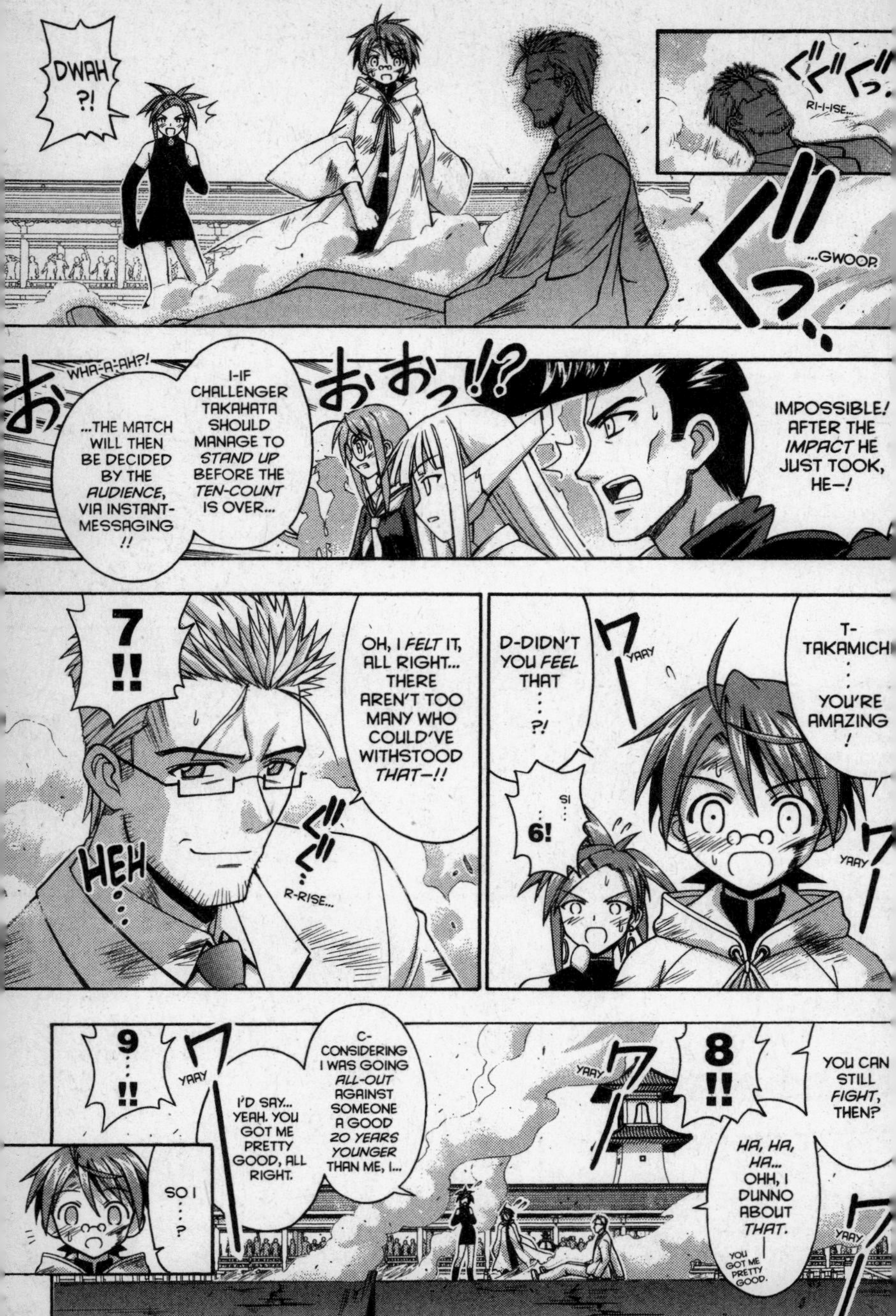
ぐぐぐっ
RI-I-ISE...
ぐぐっ
...GWOOP.
DWAH ?!
IMPOSSIBLE! AFTER THE *IMPACT* HE JUST TOOK, HE—!
おおっ!!?
WHA-A-AH?!
I-IF CHALLENGER TAKAHATA SHOULD MANAGE TO *STAND UP* BEFORE THE *TEN-COUNT* IS OVER...
...THE MATCH WILL THEN BE DECIDED BY THE *AUDIENCE*, VIA INSTANT-MESSAGING!!
T-TAKAMICHI... YOU'RE AMAZING!
YAAY
D-DIDN'T YOU *FEEL* THAT...?!
YAAY
SI... 6!
OH, I *FELT* IT, ALL RIGHT... THERE AREN'T TOO MANY WHO COULD'VE WITHSTOOD *THAT*—!!
7!!
R-RISE...
HEH...
YOU CAN STILL *FIGHT*, THEN?
8!!
YAAY
HA, HA, HA... OHH, I DUNNO ABOUT *THAT.*
YOU GOT ME PRETTY GOOD.
YAAY
C-CONSIDERING I WAS GOING *ALL-OUT* AGAINST SOMEONE A GOOD *20 YEARS YOUNGER* THAN ME, I...
I'D SAY... YEAH. YOU GOT ME PRETTY GOOD, ALL RIGHT.
9...!!
YAAY
SO I...?

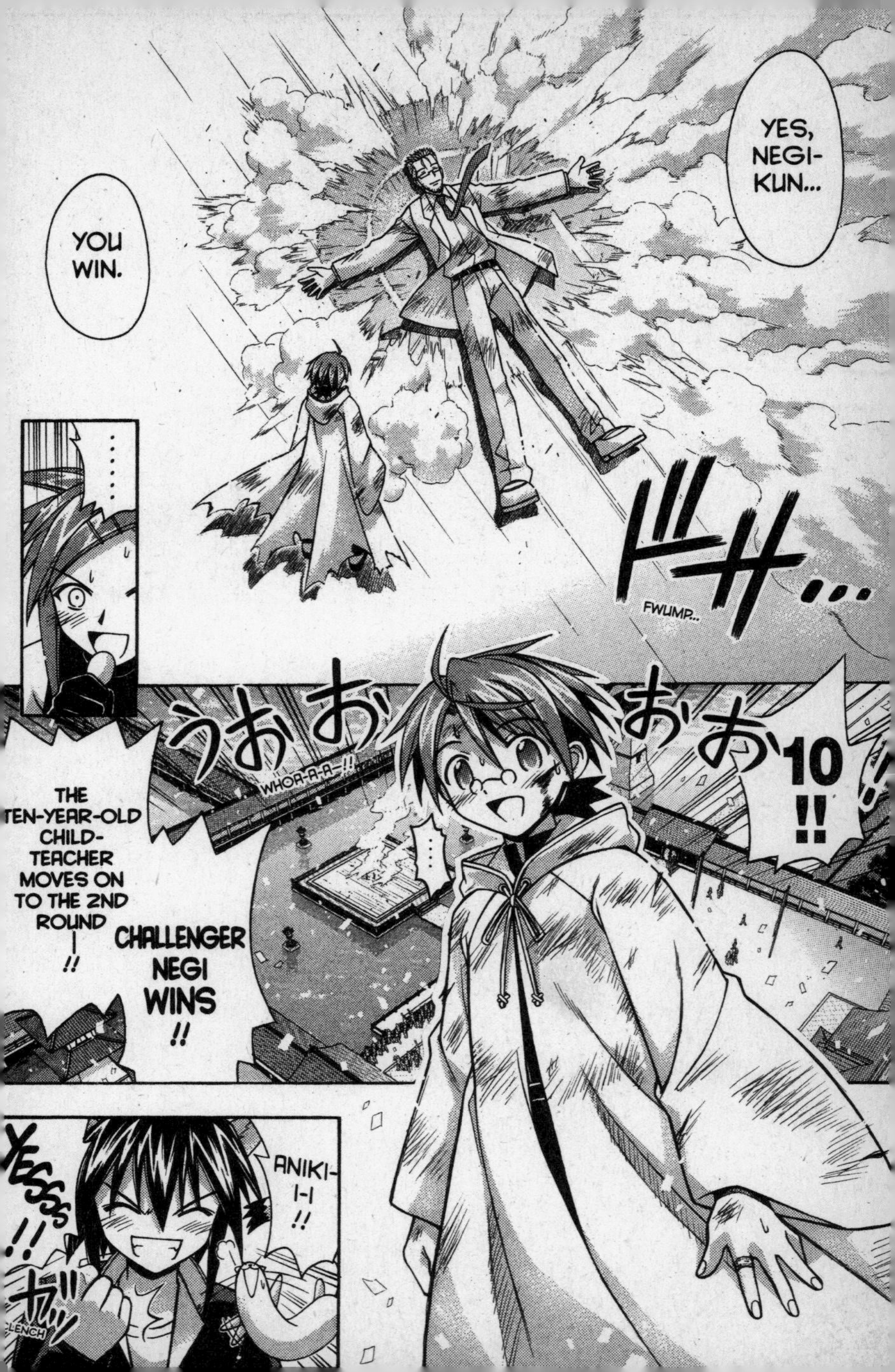
YES, NEGI-KUN...
YOU WIN.
ドサ…
FWUMP...
......
うおおおおお
WHOA-A-A-!!
10!!
THE TEN-YEAR-OLD CHILD-TEACHER MOVES ON TO THE 2ND ROUND -!!
CHALLENGER NEGI WINS!!
...
ANIKI-I-I!!
YESSSS!!
ガッ
CLENCH

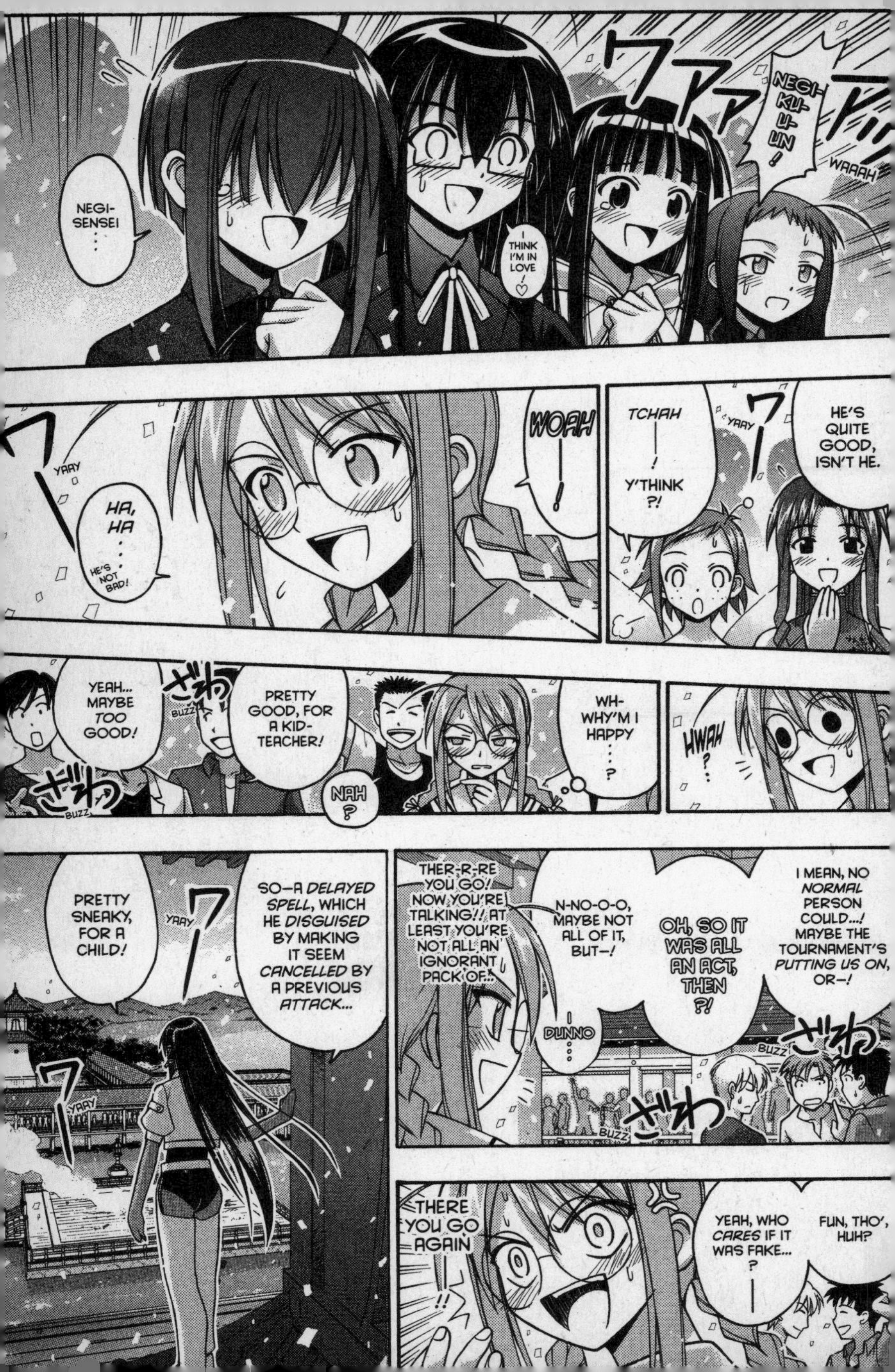
NEGI-KU-U-UN!
WAAAH
I THINK I'M IN LOVE ♡
NEGI-SENSEI...
HE'S QUITE GOOD, ISN'T HE.
YAAY
TCHAH—! Y'THINK?!
WOAH—!
YAAY
HA, HA... HE'S NOT BAD!
HWAH?
WH-WHY'M I HAPPY...?
NAH?
PRETTY GOOD, FOR A KID-TEACHER!
ざわ
BUZZ
YEAH... MAYBE TOO GOOD!
ざわ
BUZZ
I MEAN, NO NORMAL PERSON COULD...! MAYBE THE TOURNAMENT'S PUTTING US ON, OR—!
OH, SO IT WAS ALL AN ACT, THEN?!
N-NO-O-O, MAYBE NOT ALL OF IT, BUT—!
THER-R-RE YOU GO! NOW YOU'RE TALKING!! AT LEAST YOU'RE NOT ALL AN IGNORANT PACK OF...
I DUNNO...
ざわ
BUZZ
ざわ
BUZZ
FUN, THO', HUH?
YEAH, WHO CARES IF IT WAS FAKE...?
THERE YOU GO AGAIN—!!
SO—A DELAYED SPELL, WHICH HE DISGUISED BY MAKING IT SEEM CANCELLED BY A PREVIOUS ATTACK...
YAAY
PRETTY SNEAKY, FOR A CHILD!
YAAY

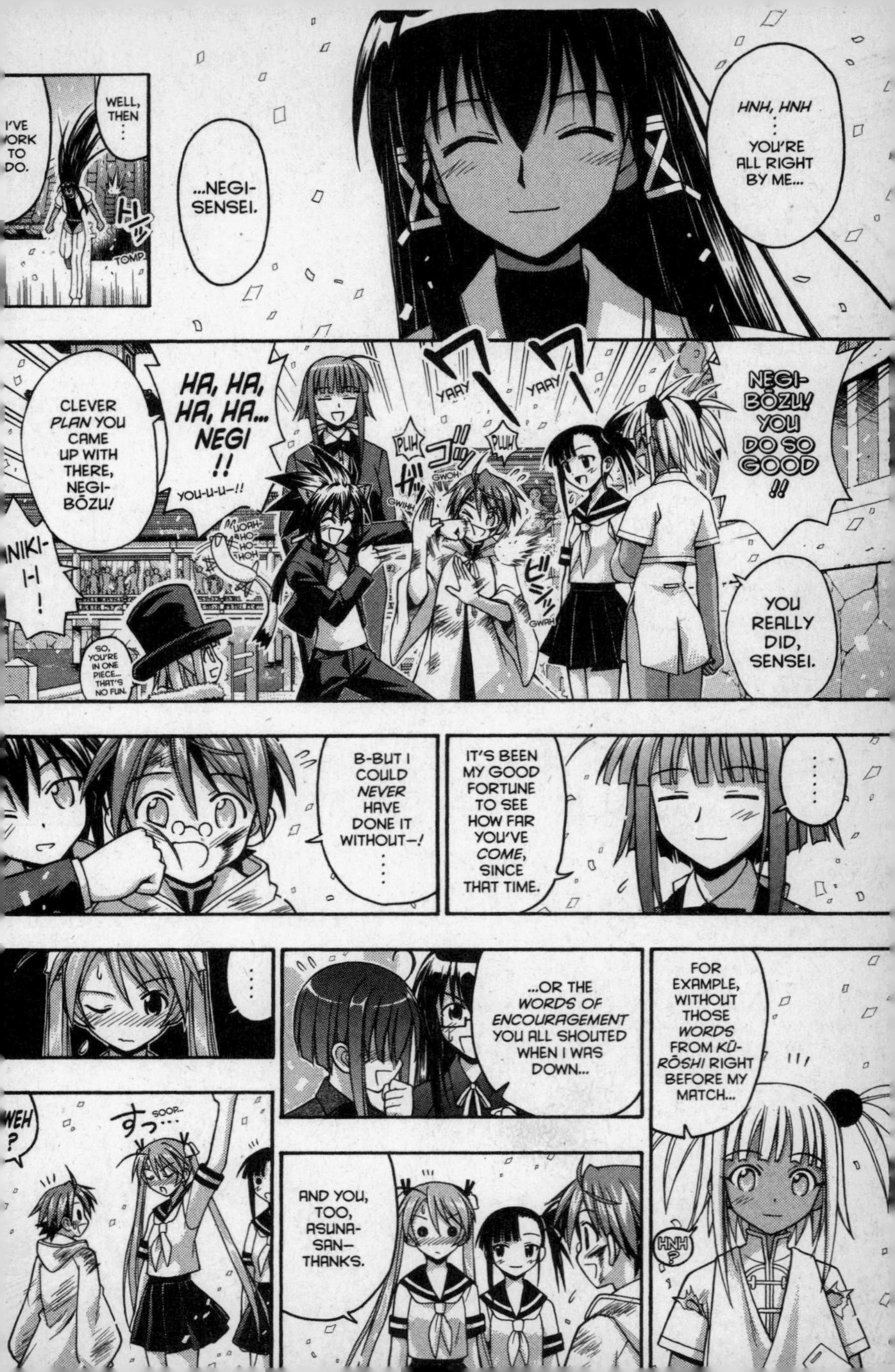
HNH, HNH ... YOU'RE ALL RIGHT BY ME...
...NEGI-SENSEI.
WELL, THEN ...
I'VE WORK TO DO.
TOMP
NEGI-BŌZU! YOU DO SO GOOD!!
YOU REALLY DID, SENSEI.
YAAY
YAAY
PLUH
GWOH
PLUH
GWIHH
GWAH
HA, HA, HA, HA... NEGI!!
YOU-U-U—!!
CLEVER PLAN YOU CAME UP WITH THERE, NEGI-BŌZU!
ANIKI-I-I!
UOAH-HO-HO-HOH
SO, YOU'RE IN ONE PIECE... THAT'S NO FUN.
......
IT'S BEEN MY GOOD FORTUNE TO SEE HOW FAR YOU'VE COME, SINCE THAT TIME.
B-BUT I COULD NEVER HAVE DONE IT WITHOUT—! ...
FOR EXAMPLE, WITHOUT THOSE WORDS FROM KŪ-RŌSHI RIGHT BEFORE MY MATCH...
HNH?
...OR THE WORDS OF ENCOURAGEMENT YOU ALL SHOUTED WHEN I WAS DOWN...
....
AND YOU, TOO, ASUNA-SAN—THANKS.
WEH?
すっ… SOOR..

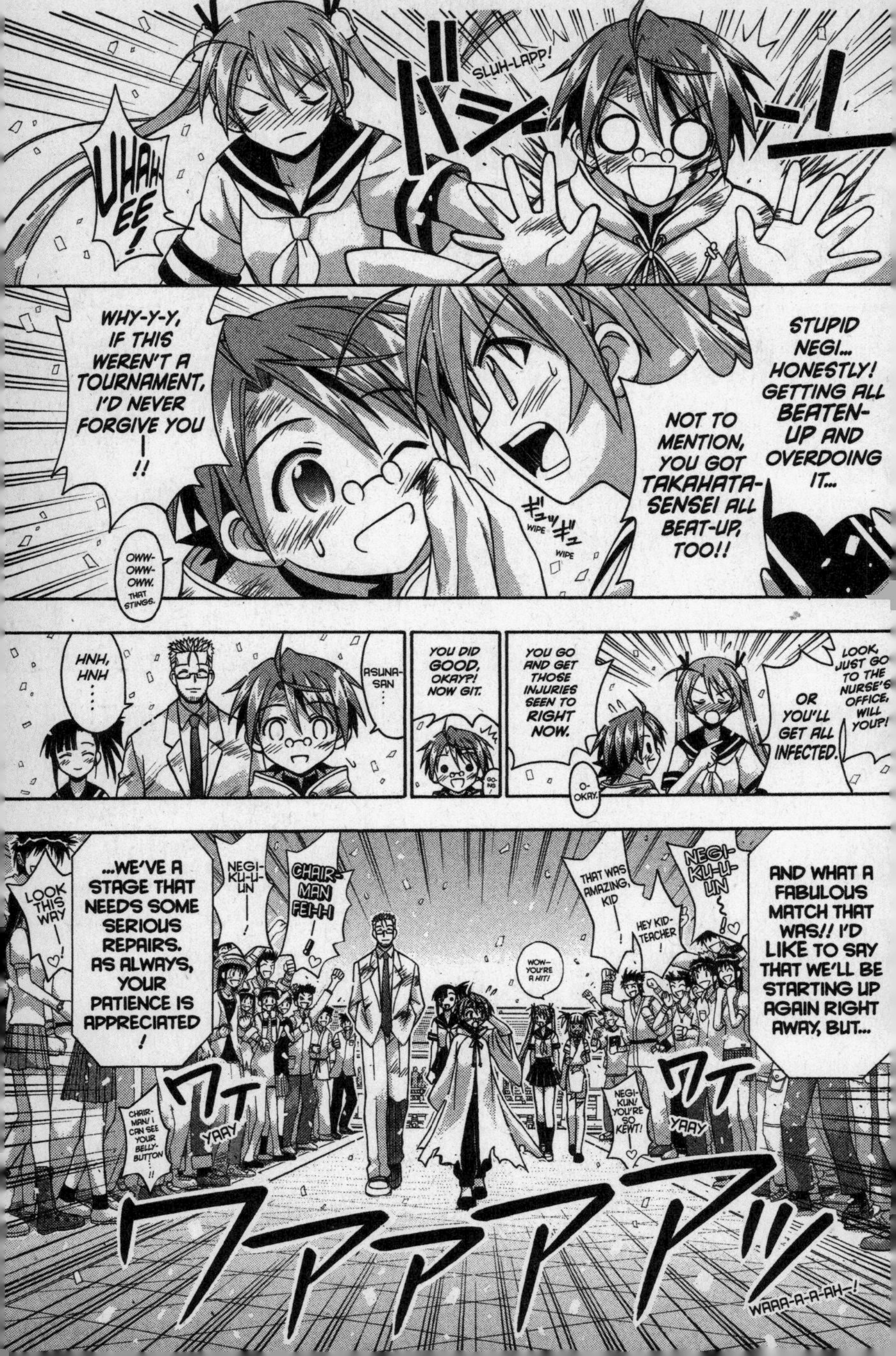
SLUH-LAPP!
UHAH-EE!
STUPID NEGI... HONESTLY! GETTING ALL BEATEN-UP AND OVERDOING IT...
NOT TO MENTION, YOU GOT TAKAHATA-SENSEI ALL BEAT-UP, TOO!!
WIPE
WIPE
WHY-Y-Y, IF THIS WEREN'T A TOURNAMENT, I'D NEVER FORGIVE YOU—!!
OWW-OWW-OWW. THAT STINGS.
LOOK, JUST GO TO THE NURSE'S OFFICE, WILL YOU?!
OR YOU'LL GET ALL INFECTED.
YOU GO AND GET THOSE INJURIES SEEN TO RIGHT NOW.
O-OKAY.
YOU DID GOOD, OKAY?! NOW GIT.
GO-ING!
ASUNA-SAN...
HNH, HNH...
AND WHAT A FABULOUS MATCH THAT WAS!! I'D LIKE TO SAY THAT WE'LL BE STARTING UP AGAIN RIGHT AWAY, BUT...
NEGI-KU-U-UN~!
THAT WAS AMAZING, KID!
HEY KID-TEACHER!
WOW—YOU'RE A HIT!
CHAIR-MAN FEI-I-I!
NEGI-KU-U-UN—!
...WE'VE A STAGE THAT NEEDS SOME SERIOUS REPAIRS. AS ALWAYS, YOUR PATIENCE IS APPRECIATED!
LOOK THIS WAY—!
YAAY
NEGI-KUN! YOU'RE SO KEWT!
YAAY
CHAIR-MAN! I CAN SEE YOUR BELLY-BUTTON...!!
WAAA-A-A-AH—!

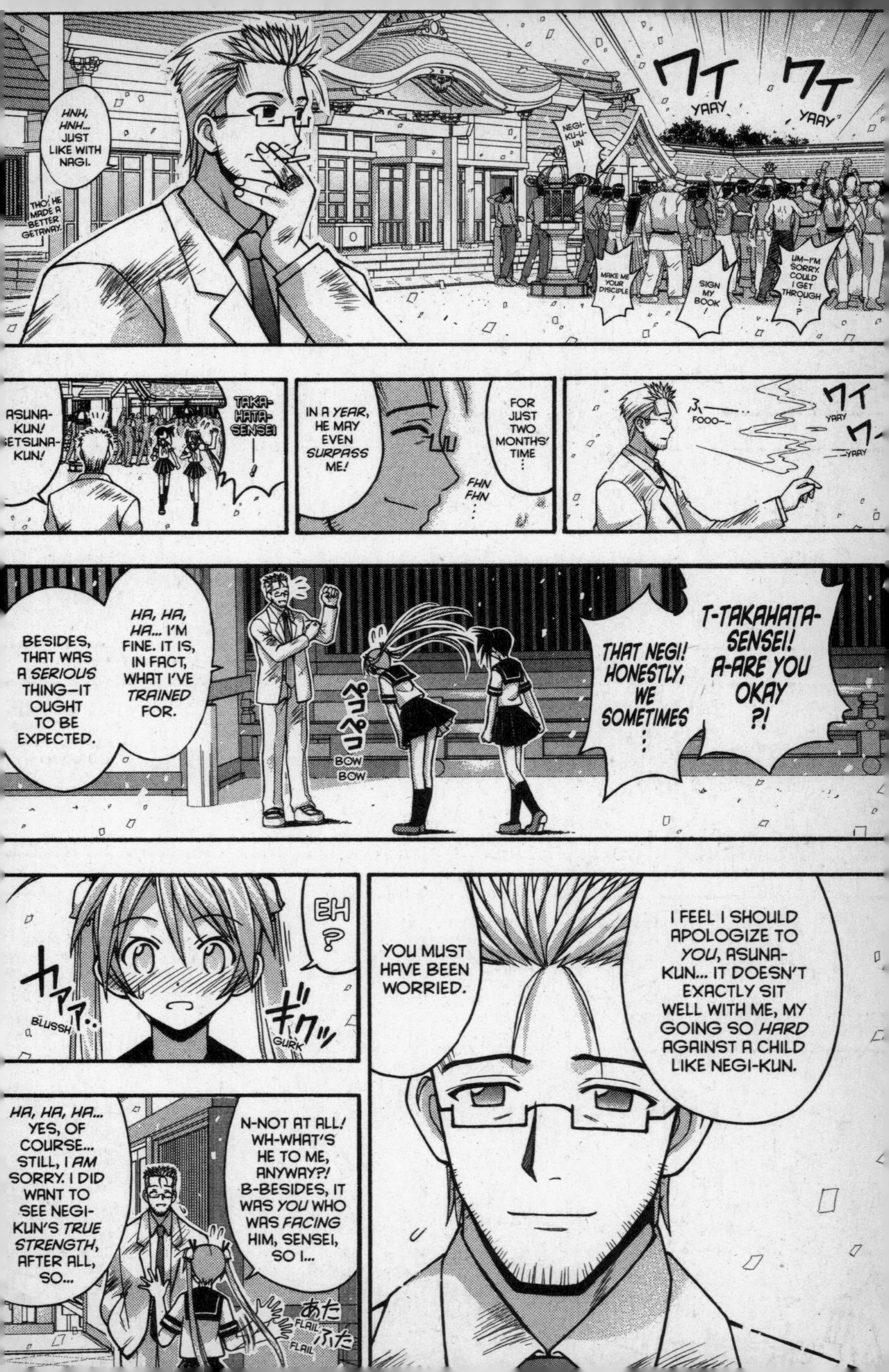
ワイ YAAY ワイ YAAY
NEGI-KU-U-UN!
UM—I'M SORRY. COULD I GET THROUGH...?
SIGN MY BOOK!
MAKE ME YOUR DISCIPLE!
HNH, HNH... JUST LIKE WITH NAGI.
THO' HE MADE A BETTER GETAWAY.
ワイ YAAY ワー YAAY
ふー FOOO-...
FOR JUST TWO MONTHS' TIME...
FHN FHN...
IN A YEAR, HE MAY EVEN SURPASS ME!
TAKA-HATA-SENSEI—!
ASUNA-KUN! SETSUNA-KUN!
T-TAKAHATA-SENSEI! A-ARE YOU OKAY?!
THAT NEGI! HONESTLY, WE SOMETIMES...
ペコペコ BOW BOW
HA, HA, HA... I'M FINE. IT IS, IN FACT, WHAT I'VE TRAINED FOR.
BESIDES, THAT WAS A SERIOUS THING—IT OUGHT TO BE EXPECTED.
I FEEL I SHOULD APOLOGIZE TO YOU, ASUNA-KUN... IT DOESN'T EXACTLY SIT WELL WITH ME, MY GOING SO HARD AGAINST A CHILD LIKE NEGI-KUN.
YOU MUST HAVE BEEN WORRIED.
EH?
ギクッ GURK
カアア.. BLUSSH
N-NOT AT ALL! WH-WHAT'S HE TO ME, ANYWAY?! B-BESIDES, IT WAS YOU WHO WAS FACING HIM, SENSEI, SO I...
HA, HA, HA... YES, OF COURSE... STILL, I AM SORRY. I DID WANT TO SEE NEGI-KUN'S TRUE STRENGTH, AFTER ALL, SO...
あたふた FLAIL FLAIL

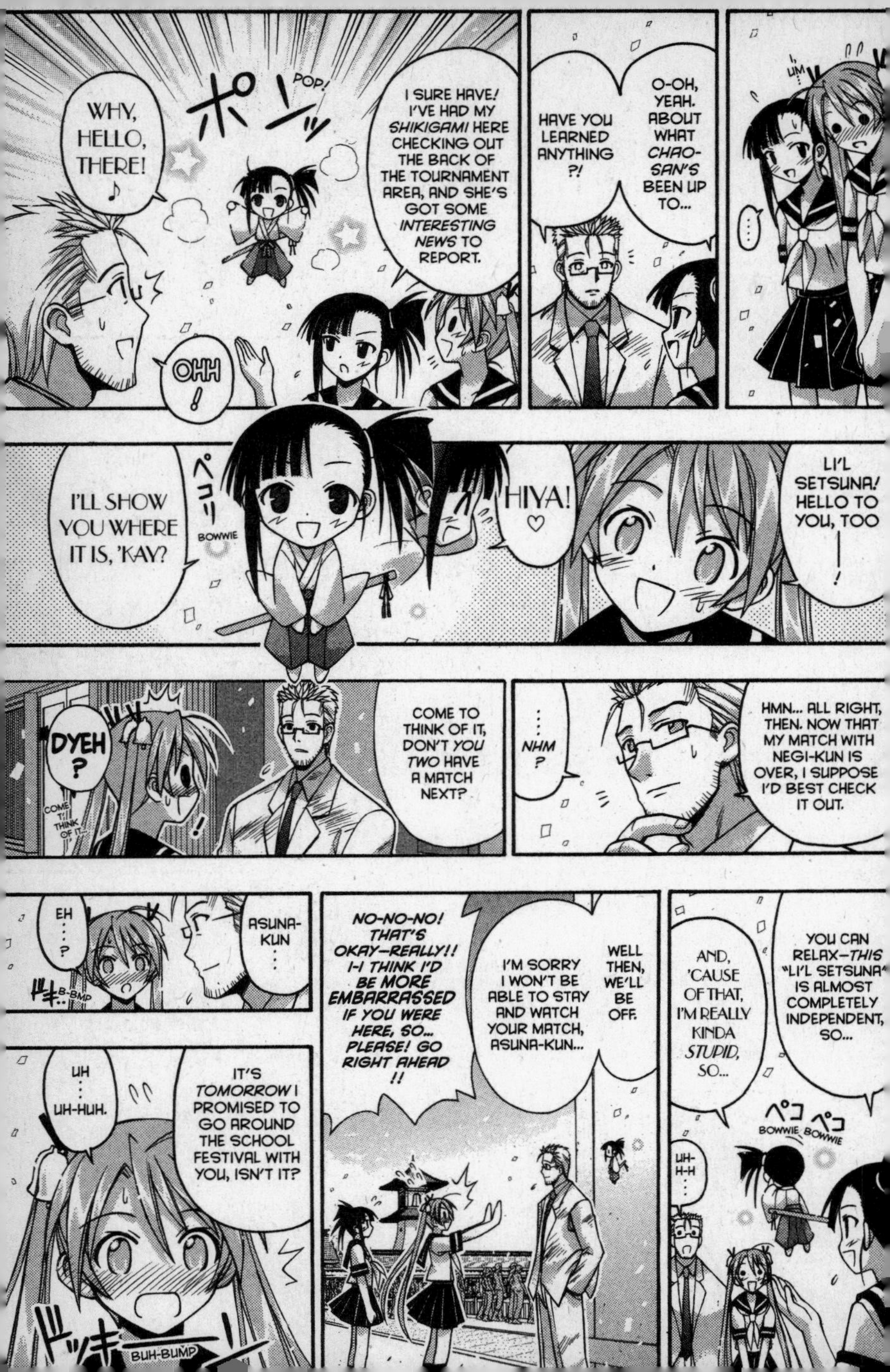
I, UM
...
O-OH, YEAH. ABOUT WHAT CHAO-SAN'S BEEN UP TO...
HAVE YOU LEARNED ANYTHING ?!
I SURE HAVE! I'VE HAD MY SHIKIGAMI HERE CHECKING OUT THE BACK OF THE TOURNAMENT AREA, AND SHE'S GOT SOME INTERESTING NEWS TO REPORT.
POP!
WHY, HELLO, THERE! ♪
OHH !
LI'L SETSUNA! HELLO TO YOU, TOO !
HIYA! ♡
BOWWIE
I'LL SHOW YOU WHERE IT IS, 'KAY?
HMN... ALL RIGHT, THEN. NOW THAT MY MATCH WITH NEGI-KUN IS OVER, I SUPPOSE I'D BEST CHECK IT OUT.
... NHM ?
COME TO THINK OF IT, DON'T YOU TWO HAVE A MATCH NEXT?
DYEH ?
COME T... THINK OF IT...
YOU CAN RELAX—THIS "LI'L SETSUNA" IS ALMOST COMPLETELY INDEPENDENT, SO...
AND, 'CAUSE OF THAT, I'M REALLY KINDA STUPID, SO...
BOWWIE BOWWIE
UH-H-H...
WELL THEN, WE'LL BE OFF.
I'M SORRY I WON'T BE ABLE TO STAY AND WATCH YOUR MATCH, ASUNA-KUN...
NO-NO-NO! THAT'S OKAY—REALLY!! I-I THINK I'D BE MORE EMBARRASSED IF YOU WERE HERE, SO... PLEASE! GO RIGHT AHEAD !!
ASUNA-KUN...
EH...?
B-BMP
IT'S TOMORROW I PROMISED TO GO AROUND THE SCHOOL FESTIVAL WITH YOU, ISN'T IT?
UH... UH-HUH.
BUH-BUMP

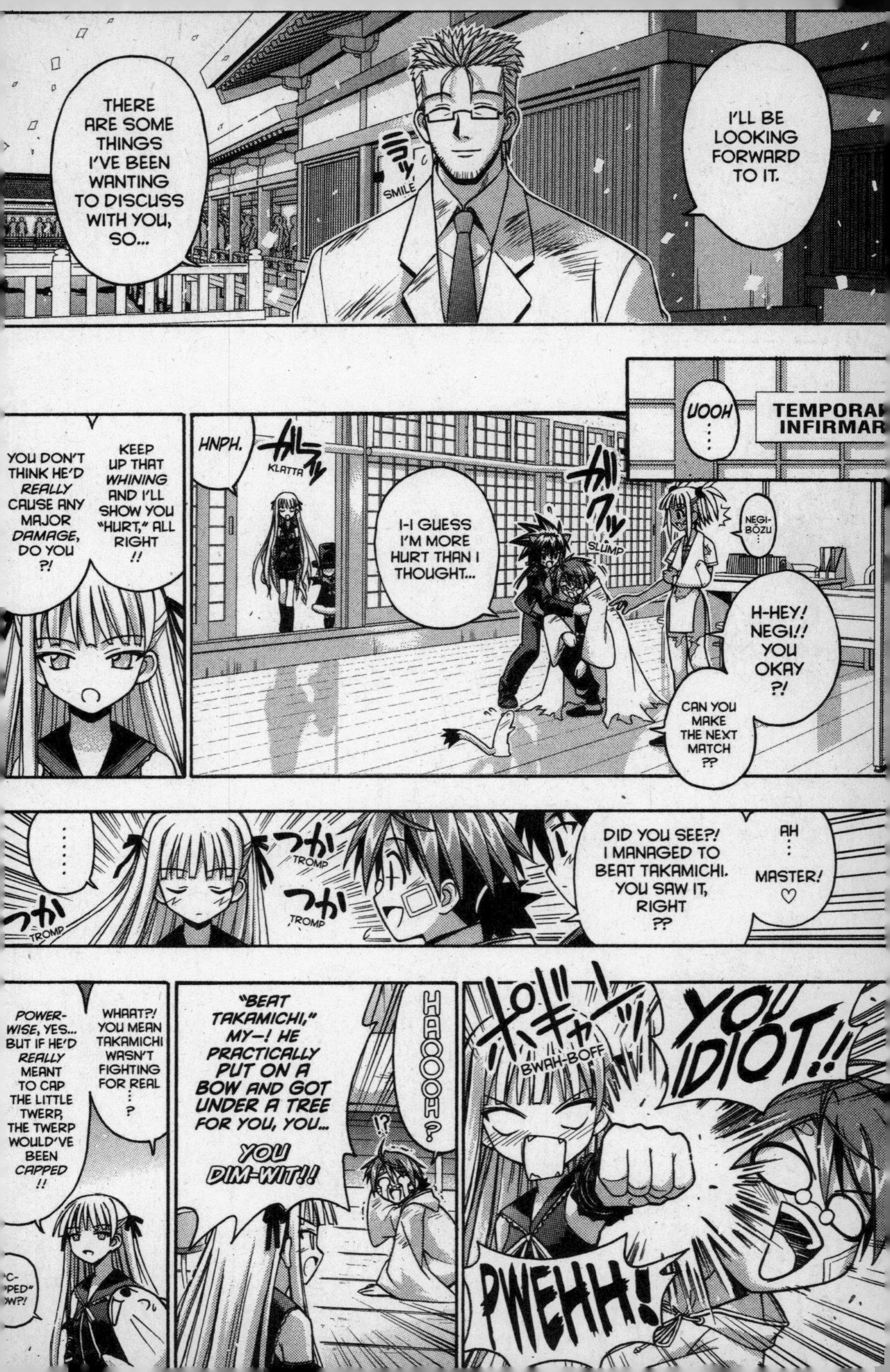

I'LL BE LOOKING FORWARD TO IT.
SMILE
THERE ARE SOME THINGS I'VE BEEN WANTING TO DISCUSS WITH YOU, SO...
TEMPORARY INFIRMARY
UOOH......
NEGI-BOZU...
H-HEY! NEGI!! YOU OKAY?!
CAN YOU MAKE THE NEXT MATCH??
SLUMP
I-I GUESS I'M MORE HURT THAN I THOUGHT...
KLATTA
HNPH.
KEEP UP THAT WHINING AND I'LL SHOW YOU "HURT," ALL RIGHT!!
YOU DON'T THINK HE'D REALLY CAUSE ANY MAJOR DAMAGE, DO YOU?!
AH... MASTER! ♡
DID YOU SEE?! I MANAGED TO BEAT TAKAMICHI. YOU SAW IT, RIGHT??
TROMP
TROMP
TROMP
......
YOU IDIOT!!
BWAH-BOFF
PWEHH!
HAOOOH?
!?
"BEAT TAKAMICHI," MY—! HE PRACTICALLY PUT ON A BOW AND GOT UNDER A TREE FOR YOU, YOU... YOU DIM-WIT!!
WHAAT?! YOU MEAN TAKAMICHI WASN'T FIGHTING FOR REAL...?
POWER-WISE, YES... BUT IF HE'D REALLY MEANT TO CAP THE LITTLE TWERP, THE TWERP WOULD'VE BEEN CAPPED!!

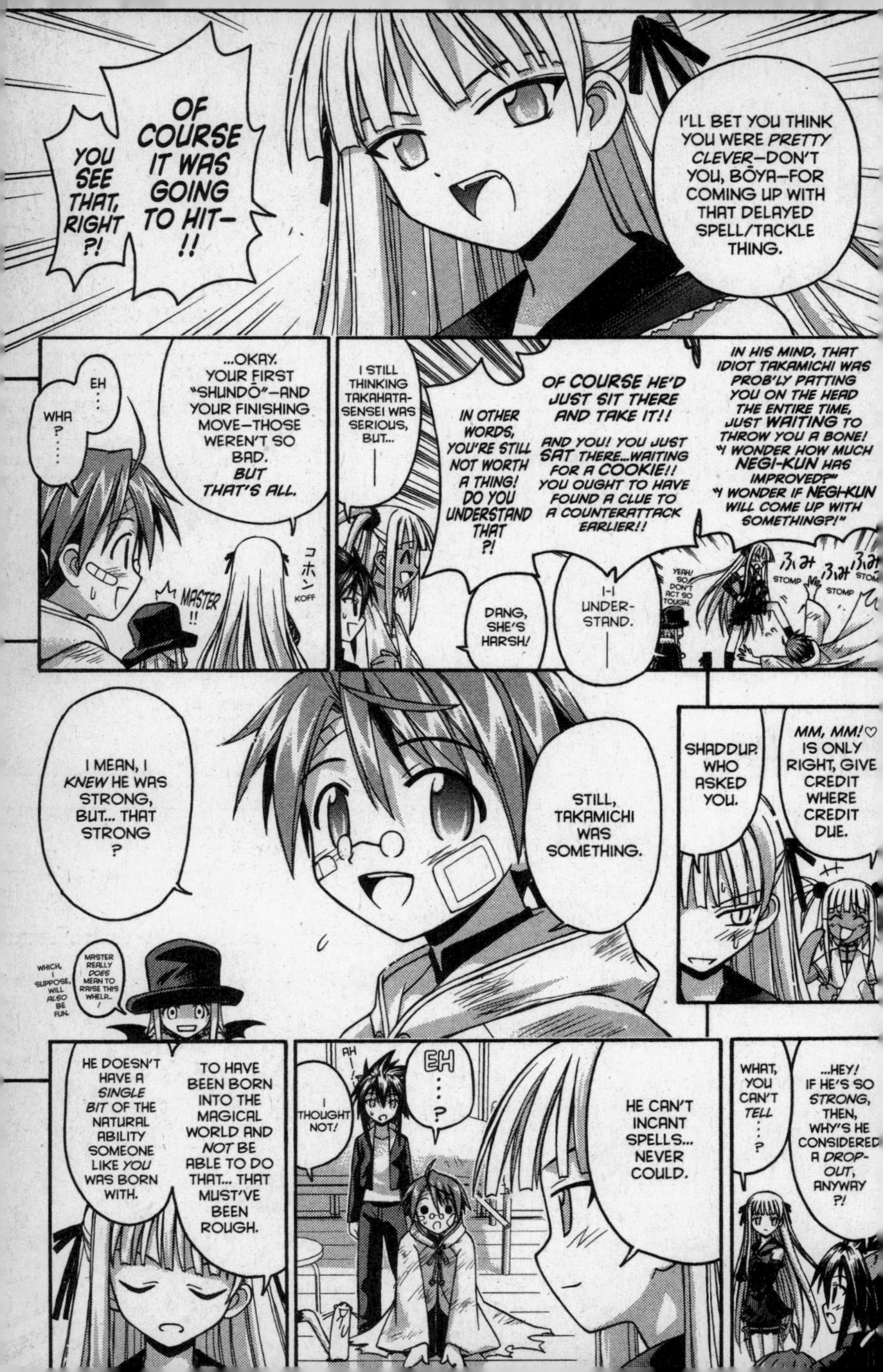
I'LL BET YOU THINK YOU WERE PRETTY CLEVER—DON'T YOU, BŌYA—FOR COMING UP WITH THAT DELAYED SPELL/TACKLE THING.
OF COURSE IT WAS GOING TO HIT—!!
YOU SEE THAT, RIGHT?!
IN HIS MIND, THAT IDIOT TAKAMICHI WAS PROB'LY PATTING YOU ON THE HEAD THE ENTIRE TIME, JUST WAITING TO THROW YOU A BONE! "I WONDER HOW MUCH NEGI-KUN HAS IMPROVED?" "I WONDER IF NEGI-KUN WILL COME UP WITH SOMETHING?!"
OF COURSE HE'D JUST SIT THERE AND TAKE IT!!
AND YOU! YOU JUST SAT THERE...WAITING FOR A COOKIE!! YOU OUGHT TO HAVE FOUND A CLUE TO A COUNTERATTACK EARLIER!!
IN OTHER WORDS, YOU'RE STILL NOT WORTH A THING! DO YOU UNDERSTAND THAT?!
I STILL THINKING TAKAHATA-SENSEI WAS SERIOUS, BUT... —
ふみ STOMP ふみ STOMP ふみ STOMP
YEAH! SO DON'T ACT SO TOUGH.
I-I UNDERSTAND. —
DANG, SHE'S HARSH!
...OKAY. YOUR FIRST "SHUNDŌ"—AND YOUR FINISHING MOVE—THOSE WEREN'T SO BAD. BUT THAT'S ALL.
EH...
WHA?.....
MASTER!!
コホン KOFF
MM, MM! ♡ IS ONLY RIGHT, GIVE CREDIT WHERE CREDIT DUE.
SHADDUP. WHO ASKED YOU.
STILL, TAKAMICHI WAS SOMETHING.
I MEAN, I KNEW HE WAS STRONG, BUT... THAT STRONG?
MASTER REALLY DOES MEAN TO RAISE THIS WHELP...!
WHICH, I SUPPOSE, WILL ALSO BE FUN.
...HEY! IF HE'S SO STRONG, THEN, WHY'S HE CONSIDERED A DROP-OUT, ANYWAY?!
WHAT, YOU CAN'T TELL...?
HE CAN'T INCANT SPELLS... NEVER COULD.
EH...?
AH...!
I THOUGHT NOT!
TO HAVE BEEN BORN INTO THE MAGICAL WORLD AND NOT BE ABLE TO DO THAT... THAT MUST'VE BEEN ROUGH.
HE DOESN'T HAVE A SINGLE BIT OF THE NATURAL ABILITY SOMEONE LIKE YOU WAS BORN WITH.

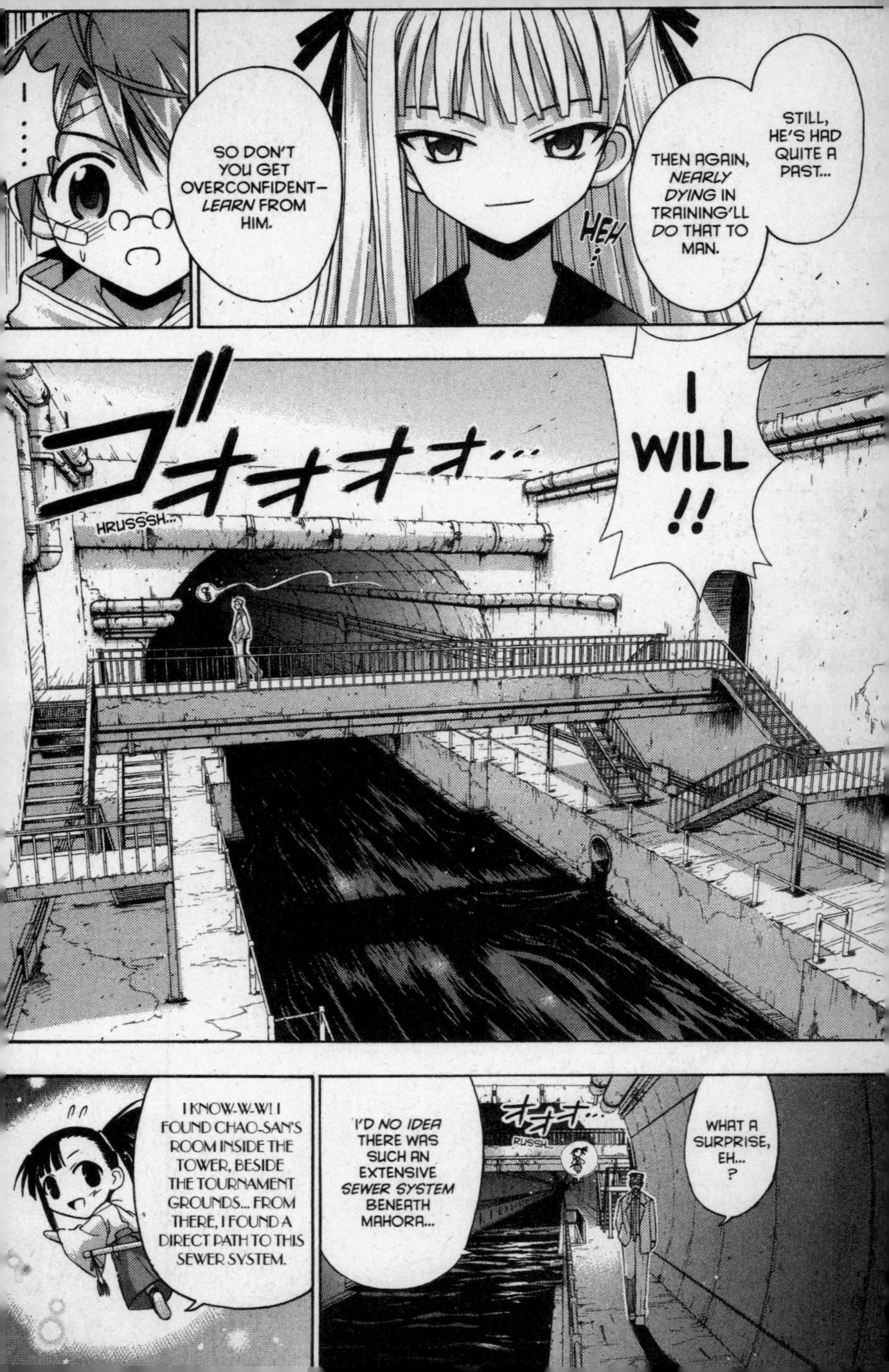
STILL, HE'S HAD QUITE A PAST...
THEN AGAIN, *NEARLY DYING* IN TRAINING'LL *DO* THAT TO MAN.
HEH
SO DON'T YOU GET OVERCONFIDENT— *LEARN* FROM HIM.
I ....
I WILL !!
ゴオオオオ…
HRUSSSH...
WHAT A SURPRISE, EH... ?
オオオ…
RUSSH...
I'D *NO IDEA* THERE WAS SUCH AN EXTENSIVE *SEWER SYSTEM* BENEATH MAHORA...
I KNOW-W-W! I FOUND CHAO-SAN'S ROOM INSIDE THE TOWER, BESIDE THE TOURNAMENT GROUNDS... FROM THERE, I FOUND A DIRECT PATH TO THIS SEWER SYSTEM.

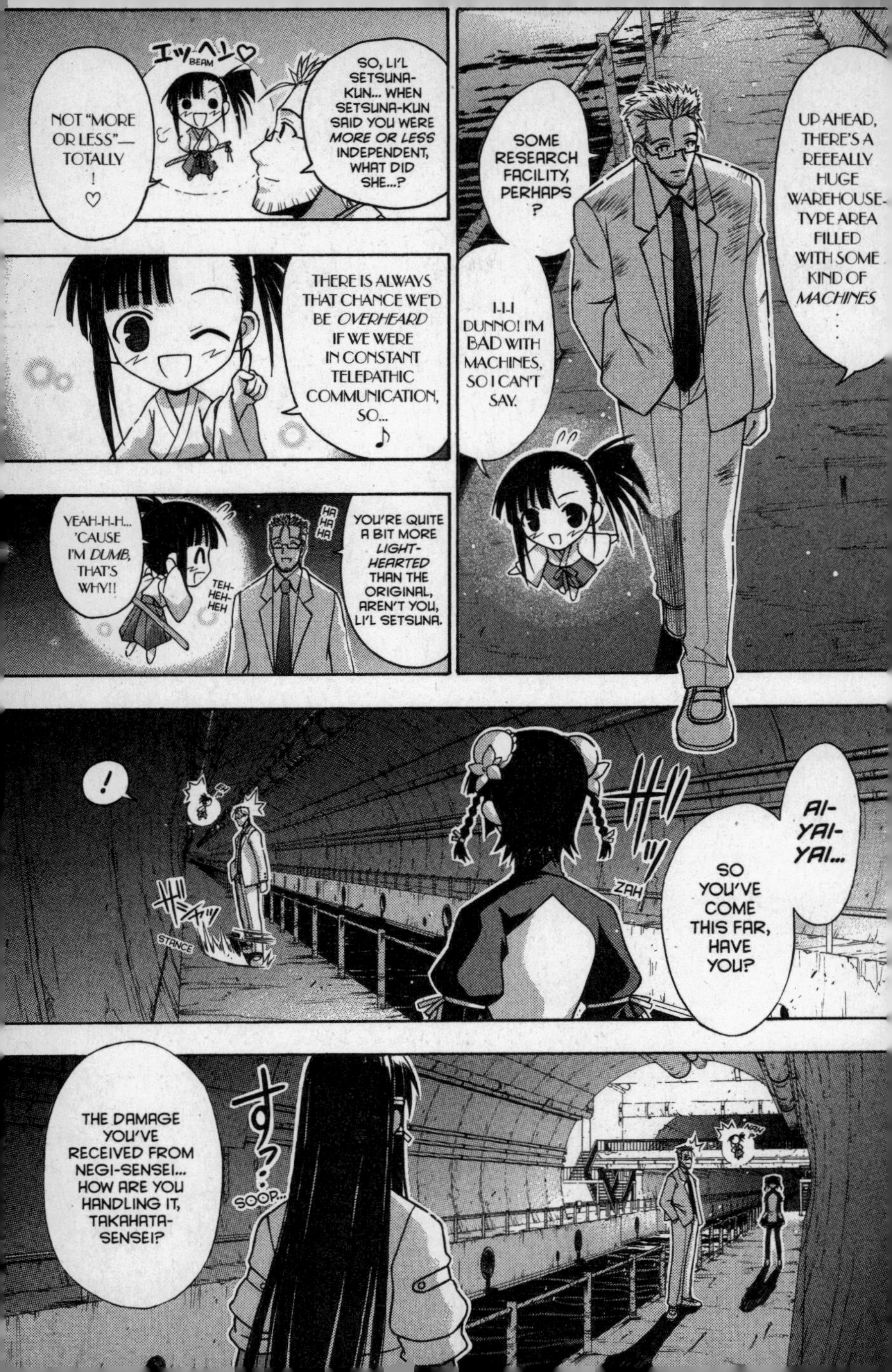
UP AHEAD, THERE'S A REEEALLY HUGE WAREHOUSE-TYPE AREA FILLED WITH SOME KIND OF *MACHINES* . . .
SOME RESEARCH FACILITY, PERHAPS?
I-I-I DUNNO! I'M BAD WITH MACHINES, SO I CAN'T SAY.
SO, LI'L SETSUNA-KUN... WHEN SETSUNA-KUN SAID YOU WERE *MORE OR LESS* INDEPENDENT, WHAT DID SHE...?
エッヘン♡
BEAM
NOT "MORE OR LESS"—TOTALLY! ♡
THERE IS ALWAYS THAT CHANCE WE'D BE *OVERHEARD* IF WE WERE IN CONSTANT TELEPATHIC COMMUNICATION, SO... ♪
YOU'RE QUITE A BIT MORE *LIGHT-HEARTED* THAN THE ORIGINAL, AREN'T YOU, LI'L SETSUNA.
HA HA HA
YEAH-H-H... 'CAUSE I'M *DUMB*, THAT'S WHY!!
TEH-HEH-HEH
AI-YAI-YAI...
SO YOU'VE COME THIS FAR, HAVE YOU?
ZAH
!
STANCE
THE DAMAGE YOU'VE RECEIVED FROM NEGI-SENSEI... HOW ARE YOU HANDLING IT, TAKAHATA-SENSEI?
SOOP...

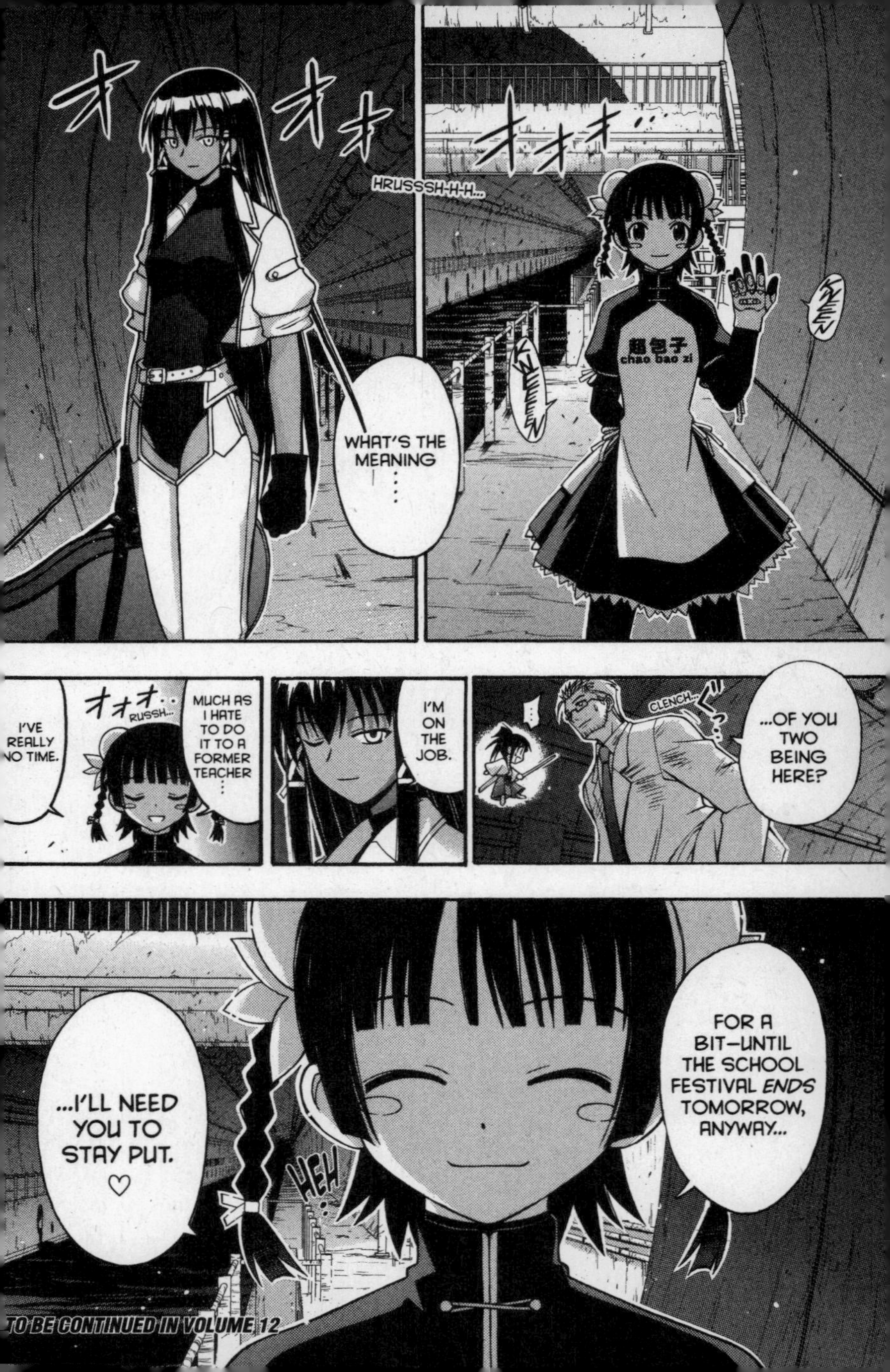
オオオ..
HRUSSSH-H-H...
KWEEN
超包子
chao bao zi
KWEEEN
WHAT'S THE MEANING ...
オ オオ
...OF YOU TWO BEING HERE?
CLENCH...
!
I'M ON THE JOB.
MUCH AS I HATE TO DO IT TO A FORMER TEACHER...
オオオ..
RUSSH...
I'VE REALLY NO TIME.
FOR A BIT—UNTIL THE SCHOOL FESTIVAL *ENDS* TOMORROW, ANYWAY...
HEH
...I'LL NEED YOU TO STAY PUT. ♡
TO BE CONTINUED IN VOLUME 12

—STAFF—

Ken Akamatsu
Takashi Takemoto
Kenichi Nakamura
Masaki Ohyama
Keiichi Yamashita
Tadashi Maki
Tohru Mitsuhashi

Thanks to
Ran Ayanaga

2003 MAHORA FESTIVAL • DAY ONE
TIME TABLE and SCHEDULE

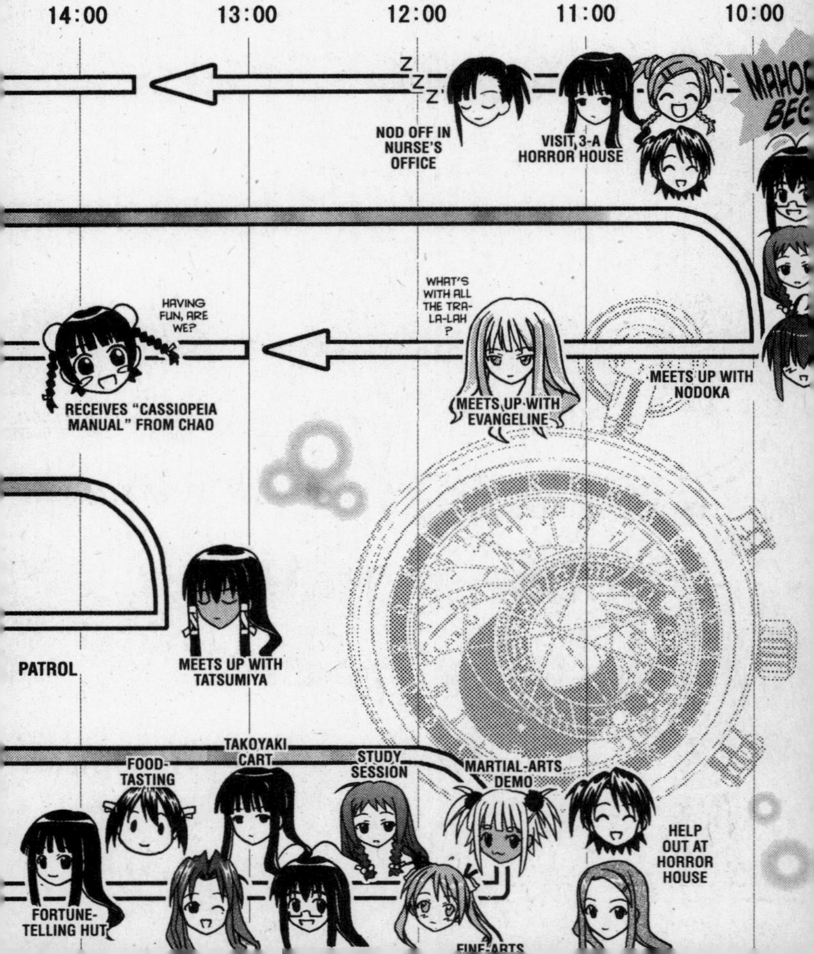
10:00
11:00
12:00
13:00
14:00
VISIT 3-A HORROR HOUSE
Z Z Z
NOD OFF IN NURSE'S OFFICE
MEETS UP WITH NODOKA
WHAT'S WITH ALL THE TRA-LA-LAH?
MEETS UP WITH EVANGELINE
HAVING FUN, ARE WE?
RECEIVES "CASSIOPEIA MANUAL" FROM CHAO
MEETS UP WITH TATSUMIYA
PATROL
HELP OUT AT HORROR HOUSE
MARTIAL-ARTS DEMO
STUDY SESSION
TAKOYAKI CART
FOOD-TASTING
FORTUNE-TELLING HUT

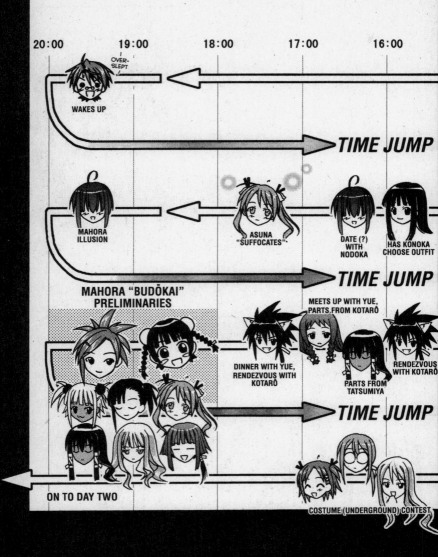

20:00　　19:00　　18:00　　17:00　　16:00

OVER-
SLEPT

WAKES UP

TIME JUMP

MAHORA
ILLUSION

ASUNA
"SUFFOCATES"

DATE (?)
WITH
NODOKA

HAS KONOKA
CHOOSE OUTFIT

TIME JUMP

MAHORA "BUDŌKAI"
PRELIMINARIES

MEETS UP WITH YUE,
PARTS FROM KOTARŌ

DINNER WITH YUE,
RENDEZVOUS WITH
KOTARŌ

PARTS FROM
TATSUMIYA

RENDEZVOUS
WITH KOTARŌ

TIME JUMP

ON TO DAY TWO

COSTUME (UNDERGROUND) CONTEST

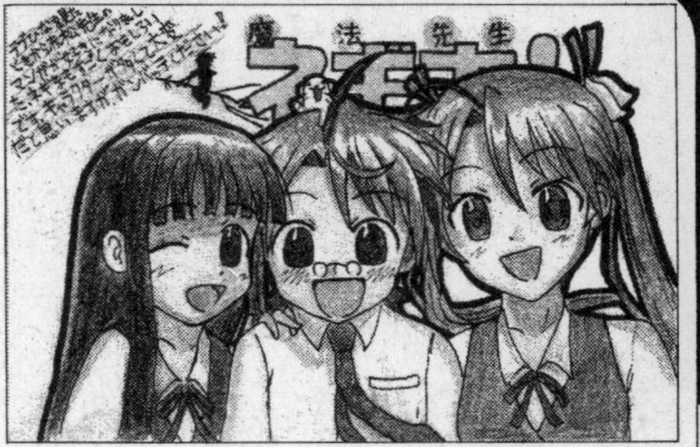
魔法先生ネギま!

DON'T THESE THREE SEEM TO BE HAVING FUN? (^^)

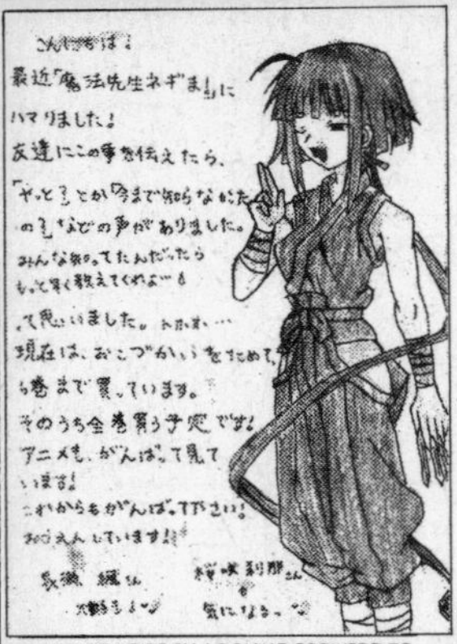
最近「魔法先生ネギま!」に
ハマりました!
アニメも、がんばって見ています!
これからもがんばって下さい!

KEEP THAT ENCOURAGEMENT COMING!

NEGIMA! FAN ART CORNER

THANKS AGAIN FOR ALL THE LETTERS! (^^) THE MAIN STORY IS JAM-PACKED WITH CHARACTERS FIGHTING IT OUT IN THE "BUDŌKAI" TOURNAMENT, SO LET'S USE THIS SPACE TO CHEER ON EVERYONE ELSE! IN THE FUTURE, PLEASE SEND ALL LETTERS AND ILLUSTRATIONS TO THE KODANSHA EDITORIAL OFFICE LISTED AT THE BACK OF (THE JAPANESE) EDITION. OKAY? (^^)

TEXT: ASSISTANT MAX

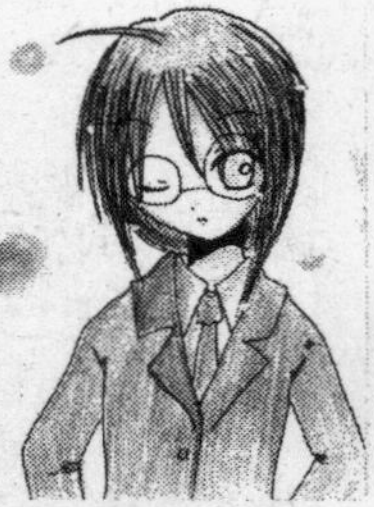

THERE ARE AT LEAST A FEW CHISAME FANS OUT THERE...AREN'T THERE? (HEH.)

I'M SURE WE'RE ALL LOOKING FORWARD TO SEEING THE MYSTERIOUS ZAZIE IN ACTION.

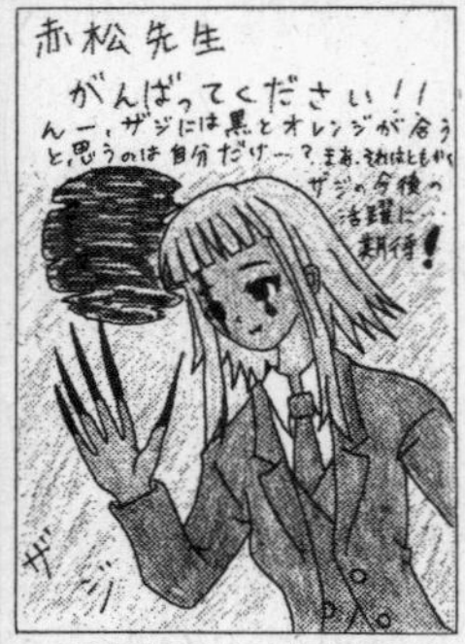
赤松先生
がんばってください!!
ザジの今後の活躍に期待!

THE "GOTHIC" FEEL HERE'S VERY GOOD.

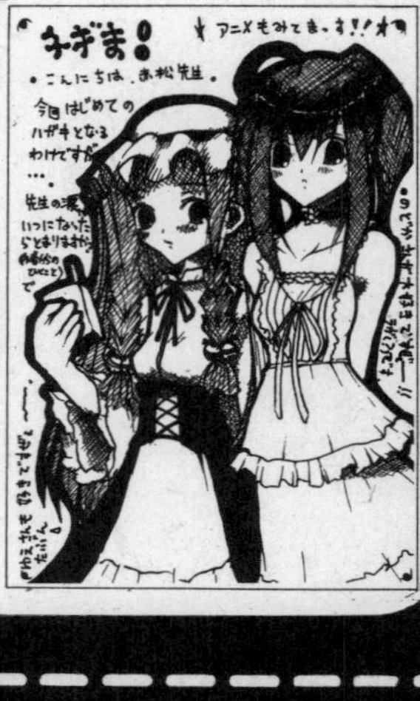
ネギま!
アニメもみてまーす!!
こんにちは、赤松先生。

THE "AKIRA LOVE" REALLY COMES THROUGH IN THIS.

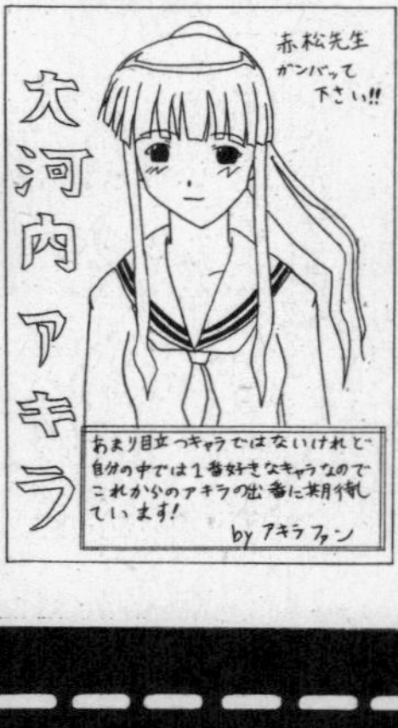
赤松先生
ガンバって下さい!!
大河内アキラ
あまり目立つキャラではないけれど
自分の中では1番好きなキャラなので
これからのアキラの出番に期待しています!
by アキラファン

THE FRIENDSHIP JUST KIND OF JUMPS OUT, DOESN'T IT.

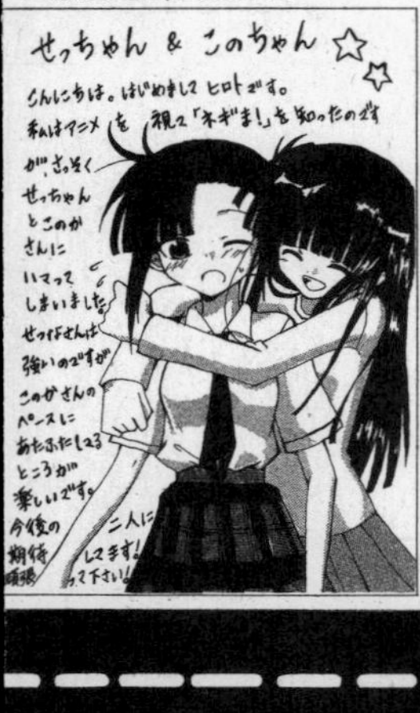
せっちゃん & このちゃん
こんにちは。はじめましてヒロトです。
私はアニメを視て「ネギま!」を知ったのです

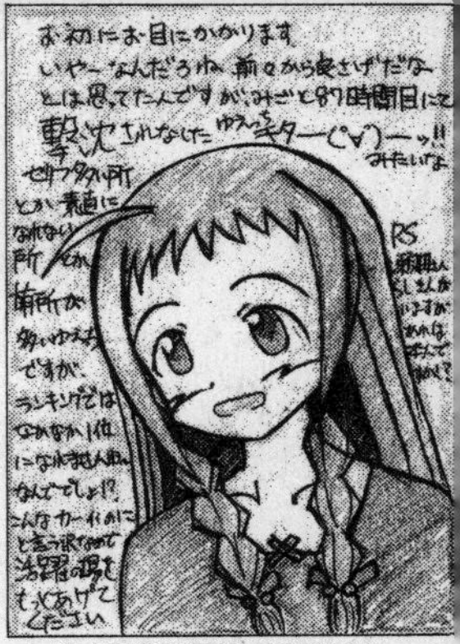
お初にお目にかかります

▲ AH, SO YUETCHI'S GOTTEN TO YOU, HASN'T SHE! (^^)

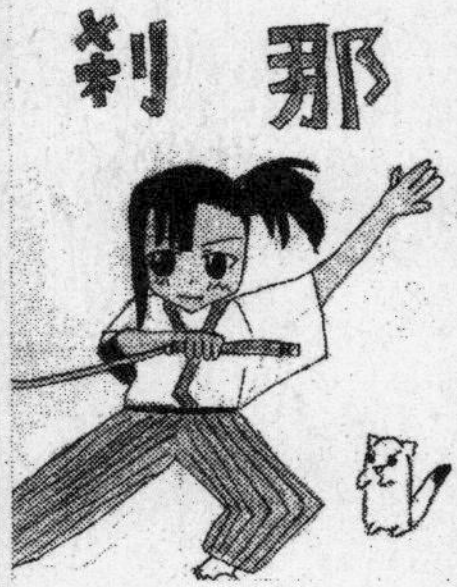
刹那

▲ IS CHAMO STRIKING A POSE HERE, TOO?! (HEH.)

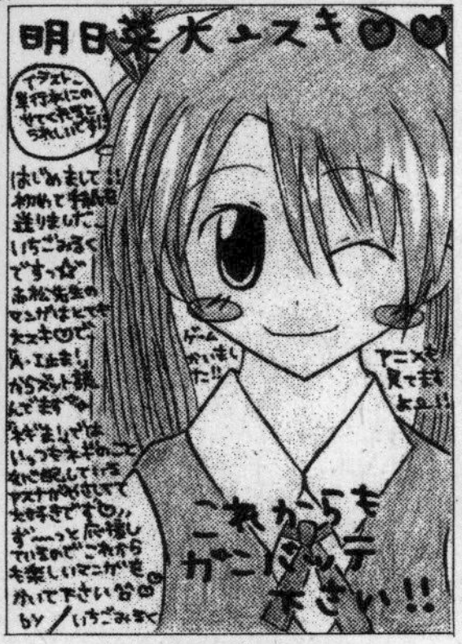
明日菜大ースキ♡♡
これからもガンバッテ下さい!!

LOVE THE BLUSHING OF HER CHEEKS. (^^) ▲

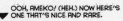

MAGISTER NEGI MAGI

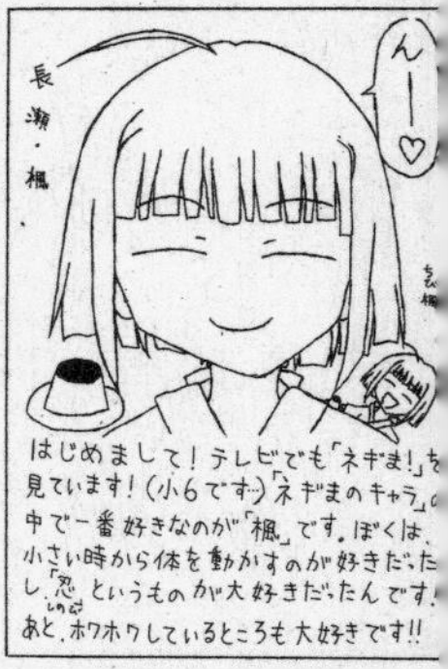
長瀬・楓
ん—!♡
はじめまして!テレビでも「ネギま!」を見ています!(小6です)「ネギまのキャラ」の中で一番好きなのが「楓」です。ぼくは、小さい時から体を動かすのが好きだったし、「忍」というものが大好きだったんです。あと、ホワホワしているところも大好きです!!

▼ A SOMEHOW REASSURING SMILE? (HEH.)

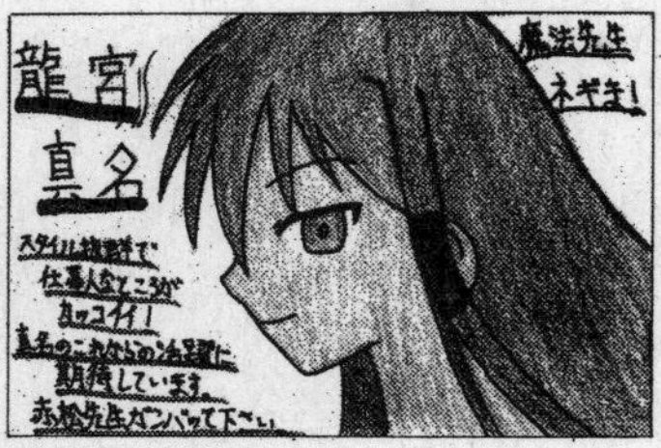
龍宮真名
魔法先生ネギま!
スタイル抜群で仕事人なとこがカッコイイ!
真名のこれからの活躍に期待しています。
赤松先生ガンバッて下さい

▲ TATSUMIYA ON THE JOB! (HEH.)

▼ IS NATSUMI ENTERING THE BUDŌKAI, TOO?! (HEH.)

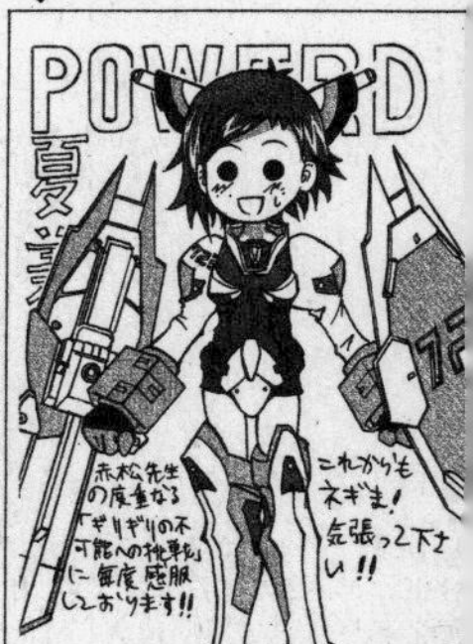
POWERD
夏美
赤松先生の度重なる「ぎりぎりの不可能への挑戦」に毎度感服しております!!
これからもネギま!頑張って下さい!!

▼ OOH, AMEKO! (HEH.) NOW HERE'S ONE THAT'S NICE AND RARE.

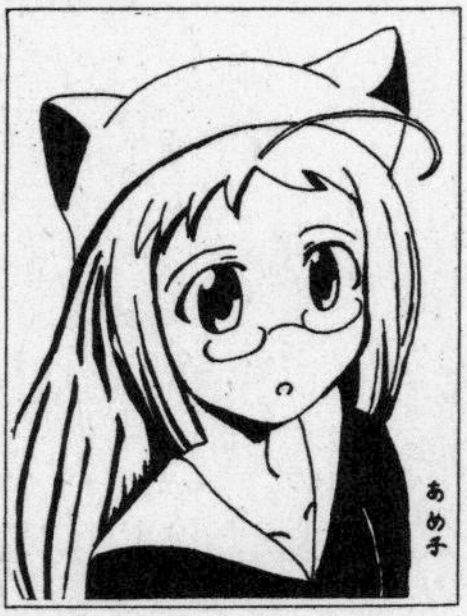
あめ子

▼ HOLDING AN ORIGAMI *SHURIKEN*... NOW *THAT* IS *CUTE*. (^^)

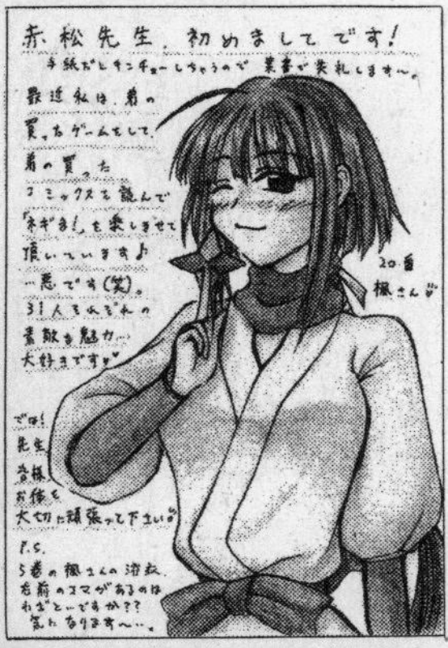
赤松先生、初めましてです!

3-D BACKGROUNDS EXPLANATION CORNER

• MAHORA BUDŌKAI EVENT PAVILION

SCENE NAME: MAIN STAGE   POLYGON COUNT: 900,966

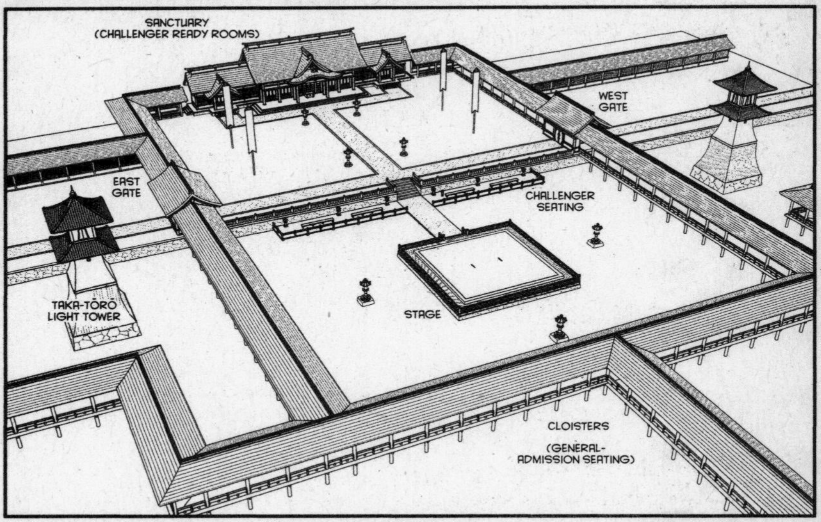

SANCTUARY
(CHALLENGER READY ROOMS)
WEST GATE
EAST GATE
CHALLENGER SEATING
TAKA-TŌRŌ LIGHT TOWER
STAGE
CLOISTERS
(GENERAL-ADMISSION SEATING)

SHOT OF THE TATSUMIYA SHRINE. LOCATED ALONG MAHORA LAKE, IT'S ALSO THE SITE OF THE MAHORA "BUDŌKAI" MARTIAL ARTS TOURNAMENT AND, WITH ITS LARGE STAGE, ITS POLYGON COUNT IS ONE OF THE HIGHEST EVER. LET'S TAKE A MORE DETAILED LOOK....

• SANCTUARY
SHRINE SANCTUARY, CURRENTLY IN USE AS DRESSING OR "READY" ROOMS FOR THE CHALLENGERS. IT'S BASED ON (REAL-WORLD) KIBI SHRINE.

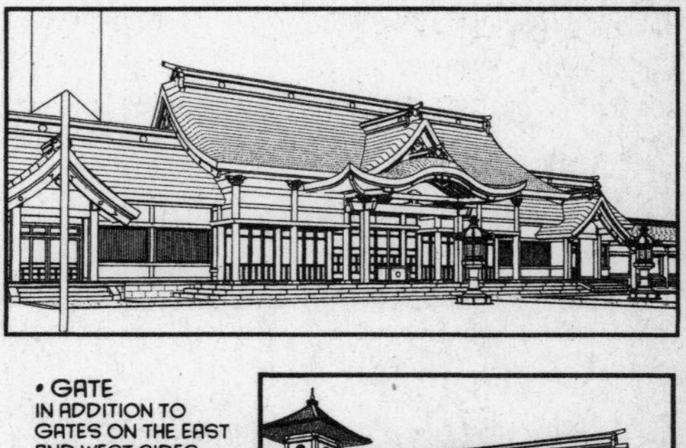

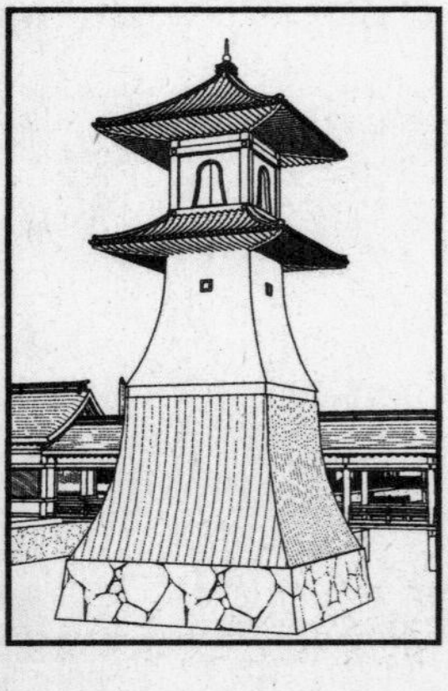

• GATE
IN ADDITION TO GATES ON THE EAST AND WEST SIDES, THERE IS ONE ON THE NORTH SIDE, AS WELL.

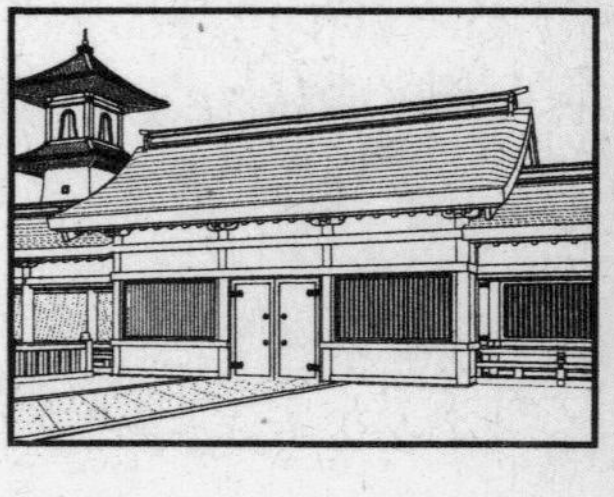

• *TAKA-TŌRŌ* LIGHT TOWER
ALTHOUGH ITS EXTERIOR IS TRADITIONAL, ITS INTERIOR IS HIGH-TECH.

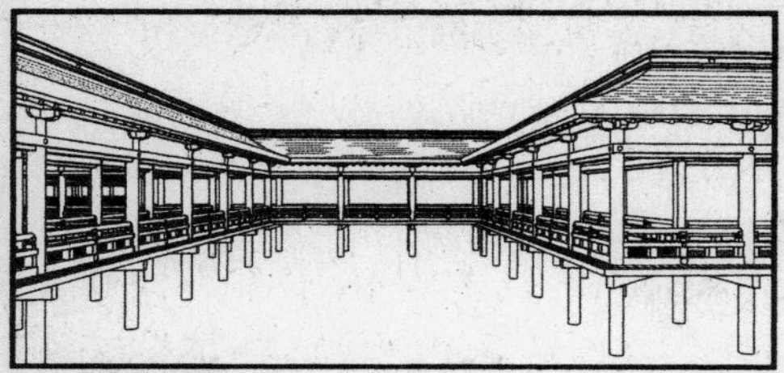

• CLOISTERS

DESIGN FOR LAKE-CIRCLING CLOISTERS TAKEN FROM (REAL-WORLD) ITSUKUSHIMA SHRINE.

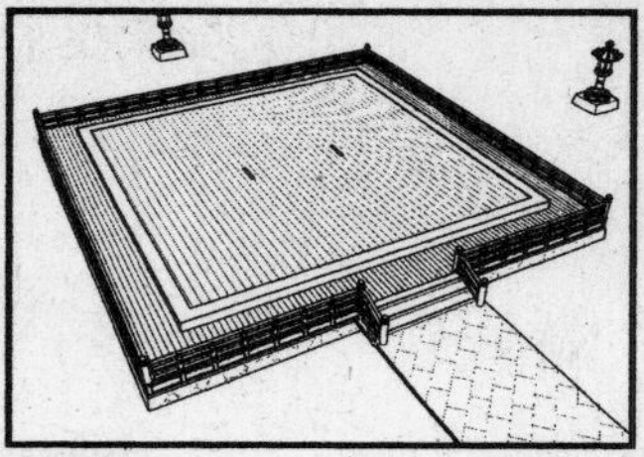

• STAGE

NORMALLY USED FOR "NOH" PLAYS, BUT CURRENTLY USED AS THE MAIN STAGE FOR THE MAHORA "BUDŌKAI" MARTIAL ARTS TOURNAMENT.

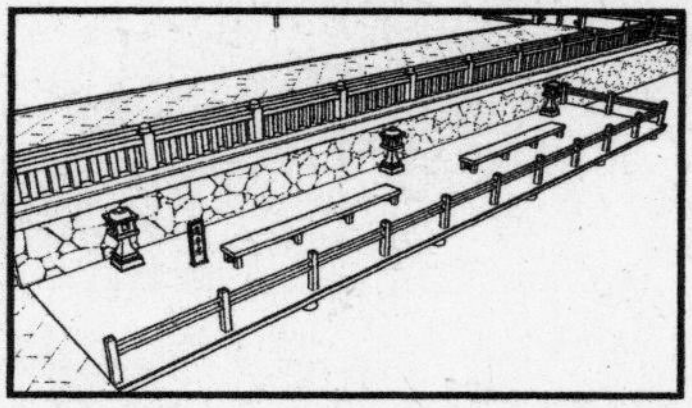

• CHALLENGER SEATING

WHERE ASUNA AND THE OTHERS ARE SEATED.

• POLY-MAN AND HIS FRIENDS

THOUGH IT'S NEGI AND KOTARŌ WHO GET ALL THE ATTENTION, THOSE WHO LABOR IN OBSCURITY—IN THE SHADOWS—ARE THE ONES WHO MAKE THEM REALLY EXCITING...POLY-MAN AND FRIENDS! (HEH.) THE TRUTH? EVERY LAST PERSON IN THE TOURNAMENT AUDIENCE IS MADE OF POLYGONS, IT BEING SUCH A PAIN TO DRAW EACH AND EVERY ONE OF THEM BY HAND! (^^)

INCIDENTALLY, WHILE THEIR POSES CAN BE ALTERED, MAKING EVERY SINGLE POSE UNIQUE WOULD BE TOO MUCH, SO WE TEND TO RELY ON SEVERAL REPEATED PATTERNS. LET'S TAKE A LOOK AT SOME OF THEM HERE.

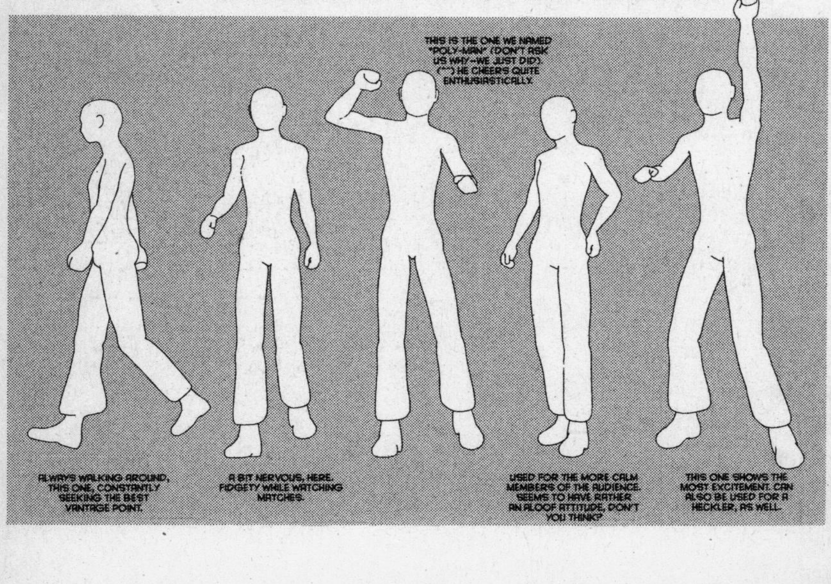
ALWAYS WALKING AROUND, THIS ONE, CONSTANTLY SEEKING THE BEST VANTAGE POINT.
A BIT NERVOUS, HERE. FIDGETY WHILE WATCHING MATCHES.
THIS IS THE ONE WE NAMED "POLY-MAN" (DON'T ASK US WHY—WE JUST DID). (^^) HE CHEERS QUITE ENTHUSIASTICALLY.
USED FOR THE MORE CALM MEMBERS OF THE AUDIENCE. SEEMS TO HAVE RATHER AN ALOOF ATTITUDE, DON'T YOU THINK?
THIS ONE SHOWS THE MOST EXCITEMENT. CAN ALSO BE USED FOR A HECKLER, AS WELL.

• STARBOOKS CAFÉ

SCENE NAME: STARBOOKS POLYGON COUNT: 120,110

STARBOOKS COFFEE

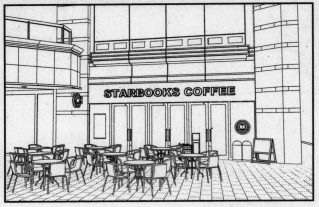

A FAVORITE HANGOUT OF MAHORA ACADEMY STUDENTS, THE "STARBOOKS CAFÉ" HAS APPEARED IN THE MANGA SINCE VOLUME 4, BUT HAS BEEN 3-D ONLY AS OF THIS MOST CURRENT VOLUME. AS FOR ITS INSPIRATION... YOU DON'T REALLY NEED ME TO SPELL IT OUT, DO YOU? (HEH.)

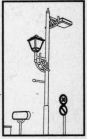

WE EVEN WENT SO FAR AS TO MAKE ROAD SIGNS AND LIGHT POSTS BUT, AS OFTEN HAPPENS, THEY'RE OUTSIDE THE FRAME MOST OF THE TIME. (^_^;)

• COSPLAY CONTEST HALL

SCENE NAME: CHAPEL POLYGON COUNT: 168,211

LOCATION FOR THE COSTUME CONTEST OR "COSPLAY" IN WHICH CHISAME AND THE OTHERS TOOK PART. WHAT WAS ONCE A CHAPEL HAS BEEN TURNED INTO A SECTION OF THE LIBRARY, AS IS APPARENT FROM THE TALL BOOKSHELVES LINING THE WALLS. THE BASIS FOR THIS LOCATION IS THE CHURCH OF SAN LORENZO IN FLORENCE, ITALY.

麻帆良祭㊙
コスプレコンテスト

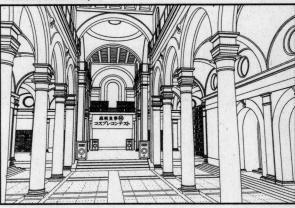

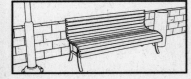

• BONUS

SEE, WE EVEN DID THE BENCH WHERE NEGI RESTS HIS HEAD ON THE LAP OF CLASS REP AYAKA IN 3-D. THIS ONE WOULD RE-E-EALLY HAVE BEEN A PAIN TO HAVE DONE BY HAND. (^_^;)

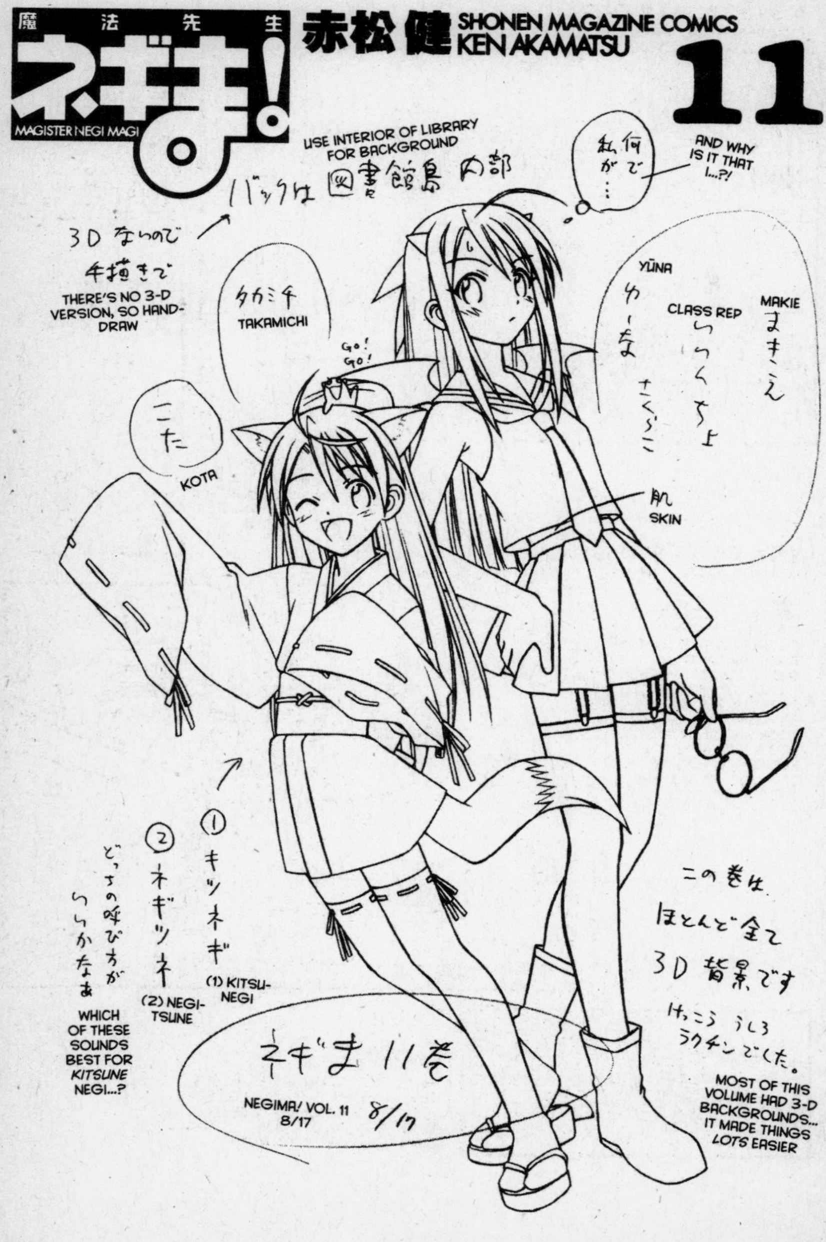

魔法先生
ネギま!
MAGISTER NEGI MAGI
赤松健
SHONEN MAGAZINE COMICS
KEN AKAMATSU
11
USE INTERIOR OF LIBRARY FOR BACKGROUND
バックは図書館島内部
何で私が…
AND WHY IS IT THAT I...?!
3Dないので手描きで
THERE'S NO 3-D VERSION, SO HAND-DRAW
タカミチ
TAKAMICHI
GO! GO!
こた
KOTA
ゆーな
YŪNA
いいんちょ
CLASS REP
まきえ
MAKIE
さくらこ
肌
SKIN
①キツネギ
②ネギツネ
(1) KITSU-NEGI
(2) NEGI-TSUNE
どっちの呼び方がいいかなぁ
WHICH OF THESE SOUNDS BEST FOR *KITSUNE* NEGI...?
ネギま11巻
8/17
NEGIMA! VOL. 11 8/17
この巻はほとんど全て3D背景です
けっこう うしろ ラクチンでした。
MOST OF THIS VOLUME HAD 3-D BACKGROUNDS... IT MADE THINGS *LOTS* EASIER

キャラ解説
CHARACTER PROFILE

⑫ 古菲
⑫ KŪ FEI

龍宮戦で一気に人気を
SINCE HER BATTLE AGAINST TATSUMIYA,
上げてきたクーフェイです!
KŪ FEI'S POPULARITY HAS SKYROCKETED!

けっこう登場回数の多いキャラ
FOR A CHARACTER THAT APPEARS PRETTY
なんですけど、それほど目立たないって
FREQUENTLY, SHE NEVER REALLY SEEMED TO STAND
言うか…し 今までは。
OUT MUCH...UNTIL NOW. SINCE 95TH PERIOD, THOUGH,
でも95時間目でホレたって
WE'VE BEEN DELUGED WITH MAIL FROM READERS
メールをたくさんもらいました。
SAYING THEY'VE FALLEN IN LOVE WITH HER.
よかったね、クー!
GOOD FOR YOU, KŪ!

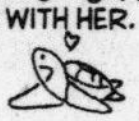

声優は田中葉月サン。
HER VOICE-ACTOR IN THE ANIME IS TANAKA HAZUKI...
口元がクーフェっぽくて好き。(笑)
WHOSE MOUTH IS SO "KŪ-LIKE," I LOVE IT! (HEH.)
新人さんだけど激ウマです。
FOR A NEWCOMER, SHE'S REALLY GOOD.
才能あるなぁ～。
TALK ABOUT TALENTED!

次の12巻も、大盛り上がりの
THE EXCITING MAHORA MARTIAL ARTS "BUDŌKAI"
まほら武道会が続きます。
TOURNAMENT CONTINUES IN THE NEXT VOLUME, AS WELL...
意外なアノ人もいよいよ登場!
AND THAT MYSTERIOUS PERSON WILL FINALLY BE REVEALED!
ご期待下さい。
PLEASE BE LOOKING FORWARD TO IT!

赤松
(AKAMATSU)

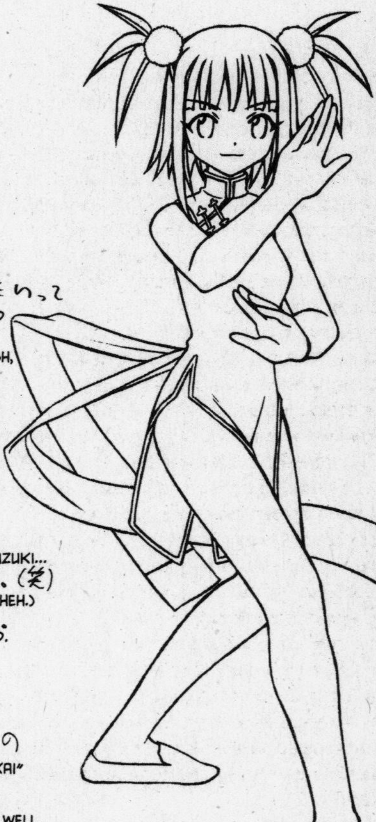

LEXICON MAGICUM NEGIMARIUM
—NEGIMA! VOLUME 11—

[92nd Period Through...]

■気

QI (AKA *KI*, OR *CHI*)

In combat theories of Chinese martial arts, *qi* has been seen and believed by many to be a mystical power. Such an explanation is said to have arisen from (A) many masters of their arts not wanting the secrets of their styles leaked to outsiders, and (B) for many martial artists, a lack of education and/or sophistication makes articulating the basis of *qi* too trying a task. The truth is that nothing really is known for certain. In the case of the Boxer Rebellion by the Righteous Harmony Society in China (1899–1901), for example, its members believed that mastery of the martial arts would render them impervious to swords, spears, and even the bullets of the Western world. From the end of the nineteenth century to the beginning of the twentieth, *qi* is documented again and again as a source for these mysterious powers.

An important concept often used to explain the uses of the *qi* technique is *qigong* (*kikō* in Japanese), which is further split into two subdivisions, medical treatment ("soft" *qigong*) and martial arts ("hard" *qigong*).

It is written in a book of the *I Ching* ancient art of divination that the "soft above and hard below, the two *qi* respond and meet." By the time the Spring and Autumn Periods (B.C. 770—B.C. 453) were nearing their ends, the concepts of the physical aspects of *qi* were nearly complete, although both Neo-Confucian scholar Zhu Xi (author of the famous book *Reflections on Things at Hand*) and philosopher and cosmologist Zhou Dunyi (1017-1073) believed that *qi* was not an aspect of martial arts but an essential element in the then-current theory of outer space. (Both men do allow that, as beings which exist on some level of the space-time continuum, *qi* may have its effect on mankind, as well.)

The concept of *qi* as a part of a person's physical being grew out of concepts within the Chinese medical sciences. The *Huangdi Neijing* (a medical text dating back to the Tang Dynasty [618 A.D.—907 A.D.]), for example, claims that *qi* may well be involved with the cause of many diseases—anger, sadness, fear, and other emotions being conditions capable of lowering one's quantity of *qi* in the body. In fact, "disease" in both the Chinese and Japanese languages is written with the characters for "ailment" and *qi*.

This same medical text goes on to explain that the heavens and the sun are the *yang* (light) aspects of *qi*, whereas the earth and the moon are of the *yin* (dark) aspects. Our understanding of the human body is enriched by these writings. According to the established medical practices of antiquity, the body's vital energy of *qi* circulates along specific, interconnected channels called "meridians." Disruptions of the body's energy flow—stagnations, blockages, redirections—are thought to be behind various emotional and physical illnesses.

In that the relation of *qi* to the human body has implications for the state of one's health, it also stands to reason that it may be connected to the body's ability to ecome honed as a weapon in martial arts. The connection between *qi* and the human body lends the study of martial arts a mystical resonance; it's no wonder, given the cultural context, that certain Chinese martial arts (Tai-chi, for example) are practiced not for bellicose ends, but for health benefits.

Within the story of *Negima!*, Chamo explains that the mystical energy coming from external sources such as Nature is known as "magical power," while the mystical power coming from within one's self is *qi*. It is true that, according to Chinese medical texts, the *qi* within a body has the aspect of *yang*, while the *qi* outside the body has the aspect of *yin*. It's stated that the five flavors of food are characterized by the aspect of *yin*, being that food comes from outside the body, and therefore cannot take on the aspect of *yang* until it is consumed. Looked at in that sense, what Chamo is saying is that magical power had a "dark" aspect, while *qi* has an aspect of "light."

Of the various illnesses that come with the four seasons, the *Huangdi Neijing* says, cures may be found within those above-mentioned five flavors of food. Today, this concept is reflected in the idea of *Ishoku Dōgen*, which holds that both medicines and one's daily diet are equally important in making a sick body well. It may well be that, along with martial arts and the sciences, one of the reasons Chao Lingshen maintains an active interest in cooking is a background in Chinese culture.

縮地

(*SUODI, AKA SHUKUCHI*)

In the fifth volume of Shenxianzhuan (*Shin-Senden* in Japanese), or "Hagiographies of the Gods and Immortals," a monk named Fei Chang-fang (Hichōbo in Japanese) learned the mystical *Suodi* or *Shukuchi* technique from a sage. According to that legend, the monk was taught the ability to shrink the land—to reach a point a thousand leagues away, as if it were right there, in front of one's eyes.

As a word, *Shukuchi*, quite reasonably, is composed of the characters "shrink" + "land." Although the inference may be taken that a mastery of it could give one the ability to move at supersonic speeds, in all likelihood this was not so in that, having been written during the Jin Dynasty (265 A.D.–420 A.D.), the thoroughly twentieth-century concept of somehow shrinking "space" and "time" could not possibly have existed.

As a side note, the concepts *Bunshin* (fission) and the above-mentioned *Shukuchi* are seen not only in the contemporary fields of martial arts, but in sports, as well—most notably, tennis.

■ VIRGA ANNULATA QUAE MOUET ARTEM MAGICAM

ウィルガ・アヌラータ・クヮエ・モウェット・アルテム・マギカム

VIRGA ANNULATA QUAE MOUET ARTEM MAGICAM

Inscription on the ring given to Negi by Evangeline (a rough Latin translation of which might be, "ring-shaped wand for activation of magic").

In the worlds of fantasy, myth, and legend, rings are not only magical tools, but also carry special symbolic meaning. In (the Wagner operatic tetralogy) *Der Ring des Nibelungen*, for example, Loki sings in "Das Rheingold" of how its wearer might wield supreme power over the entire world. That motif is a very powerful one, indeed.

Along with its image of great strength, then, the ring of myth and legend may have also the image of a great evil which infringes upon the just. In *The Republic*,

Plato's famous dialogue, there is the well-known story of the "Ring of Gyges," about a shepherd who finds a gold ring on a dead body:

> Now the shepherds met together, according to custom, that they might send their monthly report about the flocks to the king; into their assembly he came having the ring on his finger, and as he was sitting among them he chanced to turn the collet of the ring inside his hand, when instantly he became invisible to the rest of the company and they began to speak of him as if he were no longer present. He was astonished at this, and again touching the ring he turned the collet outwards and reappeared; he made several trials of the ring, and always with the same result—when he turned the collet inwards he became invisible, when outwards he reappeared. Whereupon he contrived to be chosen one of the messengers who were sent to the court; where as soon as he arrived he seduced the queen, and with her help conspired against the king and slew him, and took the kingdom [....] If you could imagine any one obtaining this power of becoming invisible, and never doing any wrong or touching what was another's, he would be thought by the lookers-on to be a most wretched idiot, although they would praise him to one another's faces, and keep up appearances with one another from a fear that they too might suffer injustice. (*Republic*, 359e–360d)

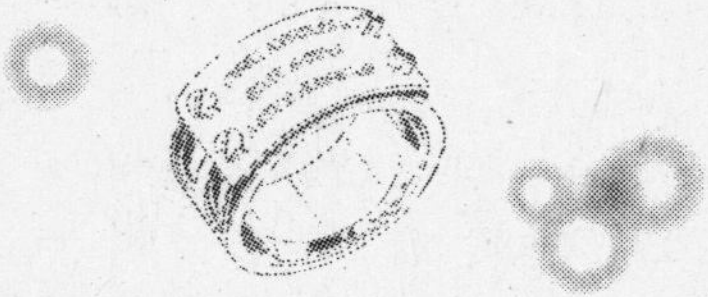

[97th Period]

■「『魔法の射手　集束・雷の三矢』」

サギタ・マギカ・コンウェルゲンティア・フルグラーリス

SAGITTA MAGICA CONVERGENTIA FULGURALIS

Spell incanted to concentrate the trajectory of multiple magical arrows upon a single target location (in the story, it was cast as an unincanted spell). Normally, when multiple magic arrows are cast, the caster chants "SERIES"; however, when the arrows must strike a single point (and not multiple locations), the incantation is changed to "CONVERTIA." Since all magic arrows strike a single point, the effectiveness and penetration and damage levels become much greater... although, since the attack is no longer coming from various directions, it also becomes that much easier to avoid.

[98th Period]

■「特殊術式、夜に咲く花、リミット30　無詠唱用発動鍵設定　キーワード　風精の主〔…〕『術式封印』」

アルティス・スペキアーリス・フロース・ノクティクルス・リミタートゥス・ペル・トリーギンタ・セクンダース・シネ・カントゥ・クラウィス・モウェンス・シット・ウェルバ・ドミヌス・アエリアーリス〔…〕ディラティオー・エフェクトゥス

ARTIS SPECIALIS FLOS NOCTICULUS LIMITATUS PER TRIGENTA SECUNDAS, SINE CANTU CLAVIS MOVENS SIT VERBA, "DOMINUS AERIALIS" (...) DILATIO EFFECTUS

A spell that delays the effect of another spell (again, story-wise, this was cast as an unincanted spell). This is normally called a "Delayed Spell," but is in this particular instance a special case, in which specific keyword(s) may be set as a condition to activate the spell.

In the story, Negi sets the delay for thirty seconds and makes the keywords "Dominus Aerialis" (King of the Wind-Spirits). If the keywords had not been invoked within the time-limit of the delayed spell, the effect would have been lost. In order to make the period of delay longer, then, a greater amount of training and magical power was therefore required.

About the Creator

Negima! is only Ken Akamatsu's third manga, although he started working in the field in 1994 with *AI Ga Tomaranai* (released in the United States with the title *A. I. Love You*). Like all of Akamatsu's work to date, it was published in Kodansha's *Shonen Magazine*. *AI Ga Tomaranai* ran for five years before concluding in 1999. In 1998, however, Akamatsu began the work that would make him one of the most popular manga artists in Japan: *Love Hina*. *Love Hina* ran for four years, and before its conclusion in 2002, it would cause Akamatsu to be granted the prestigious Manga of the Year award from Kodansha, as well as going on to become one of the best-selling manga in the United States.

Translation Notes

Japanese is a tricky language for most Westerners, and translation is often more art than science. For your edification and reading pleasure, here are notes on some of the places where we could have gone in a different direction in our translation of the work, or where a Japanese cultural reference is used.

Mahora Academy signs, page 8

Ken Akamatsu's panels are always deeply detailed, and panel 2 on page 8 is an especially good example. Here's a closer look at the signs decorating Mahora Academy's façade:

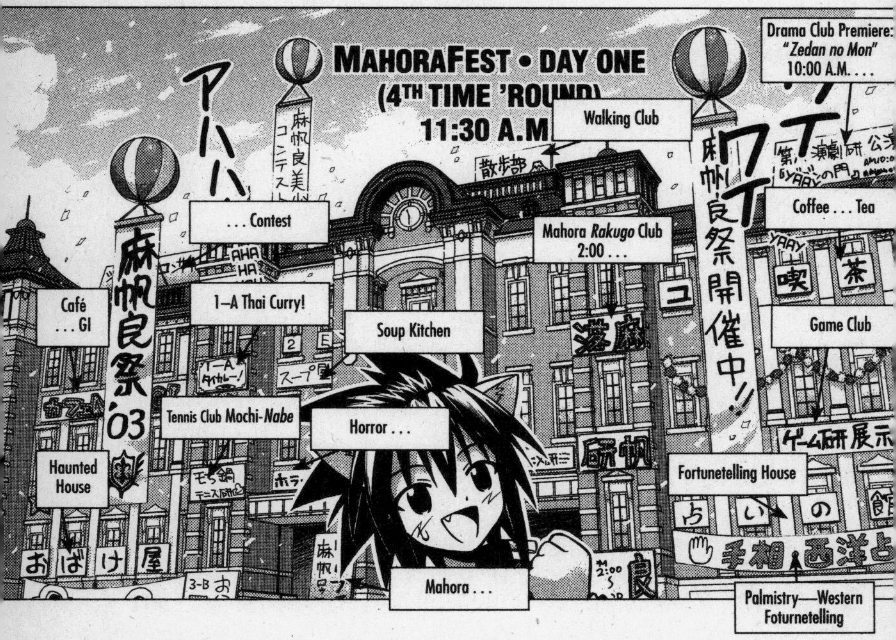
Drama Club Premiere:
"Zedan no Mon"
10:00 A.M. . . .
MAHORAFEST • DAY ONE
(4TH TIME 'ROUND)
11:30 A.M
Walking Club
散歩部
Coffee . . . Tea
喫 茶
Mahora *Rakugo* Club
2:00 . . .
Game Club
ゲーム研展示
麻帆良祭開催中!!
Fortunetelling House
占 い の 館
Palmistry—Western Foturnetelling
手相 西洋占
. . . Contest
アハハ
AHA HA
1–A Thai Curry!
1−A タイカレー!
Soup Kitchen
スープ
Café . . . GI
麻帆良祭 '03
Tennis Club Mochi-*Nabe*
Horror . . .
ホラ
Haunted House
おばけ屋
Mahora . . .
3-B

In addition to being the name of the play staged by one of Mahora Academy's drama clubs, the "Gate of Zedan" is also a completely unrepentant throwaway gag by the artist. The name of a well-known-by-fans space fortress in the Japanese animation series *Mobile*

Suit Zeta Gundam, in the expansive history of the ever-expanding Gundam universe, "Gate of Zedan" was once also known as "A Bao A Qu" (which, according to Wikipedia, is itself a Malayan legend described in Jorge Luis Borges' *Book of Imaginary Beings* [1967]). A Bao A Qu or "Gate of Zedan," then, is also the site of the final battle in the anime series that pioneered the Gundam franchise, *Mobile Suit Gundam*.

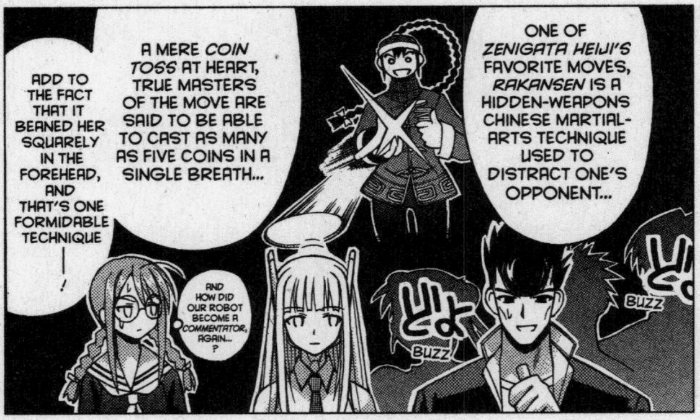
ONE OF ZENIGATA HEIJI'S FAVORITE MOVES, RAKANSEN IS A HIDDEN-WEAPONS CHINESE MARTIAL-ARTS TECHNIQUE USED TO DISTRACT ONE'S OPPONENT...
A MERE COIN TOSS AT HEART, TRUE MASTERS OF THE MOVE ARE SAID TO BE ABLE TO CAST AS MANY AS FIVE COINS IN A SINGLE BREATH...
ADD TO THE FACT THAT IT BEANED HER SQUARELY IN THE FOREHEAD, AND THAT'S ONE FORMIDABLE TECHNIQUE—!
BUZZ
BUZZ
AND HOW DID OUR ROBOT BECOME A COMMENTATOR, AGAIN...?

"Zenigata Heiji," page 82

Character from a story set during the Edo period of Japan about a constable who upholds the law with his secret weapon—tossing down a fistful of yen to distract and disable criminals (the kanji for "zeni" is the character for "coin"). Starting out as a series of novels by Nomura Kodo, *Zenigata Heiji* starred the same actor (Ogawa Hashizo) for 888 episodes, from 1966 until his death in 1984 and, since then, by two subsequent actors (in the '90s, by Kitaoji Kinya and, as of 2005, Murakami Hiroaki). In the popular manga/anime *Lupin the Third*, the ancestors of many of the series' characters were themselves famous. Inspector Zenigata of Interpol, Lupin's nemesis, was one of Zenigata Heiji's descendants...only, instead of coins, this more modern version threw handcuffs.

Preview of Volume Twelve

Because we're running about one year behind the release of the Japanese *Negima!* manga, we have the opportunity to present to you a preview from volume 12. This volume will be available in English on November 28, 2006.

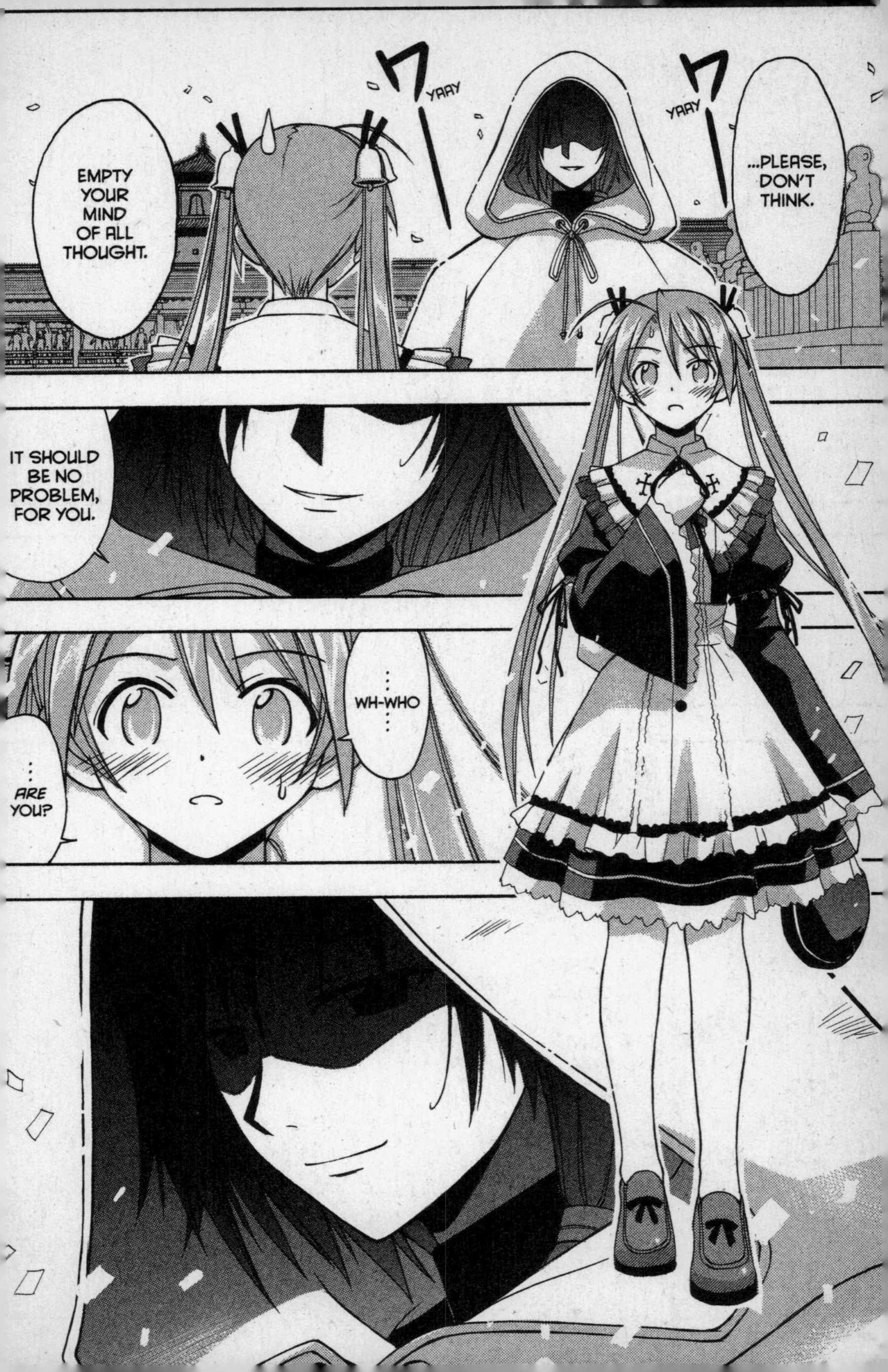
YAAY
...PLEASE, DON'T THINK.
YAAY
EMPTY YOUR MIND OF ALL THOUGHT.
IT SHOULD BE NO PROBLEM, FOR YOU.
...WH-WHO...
...ARE YOU?

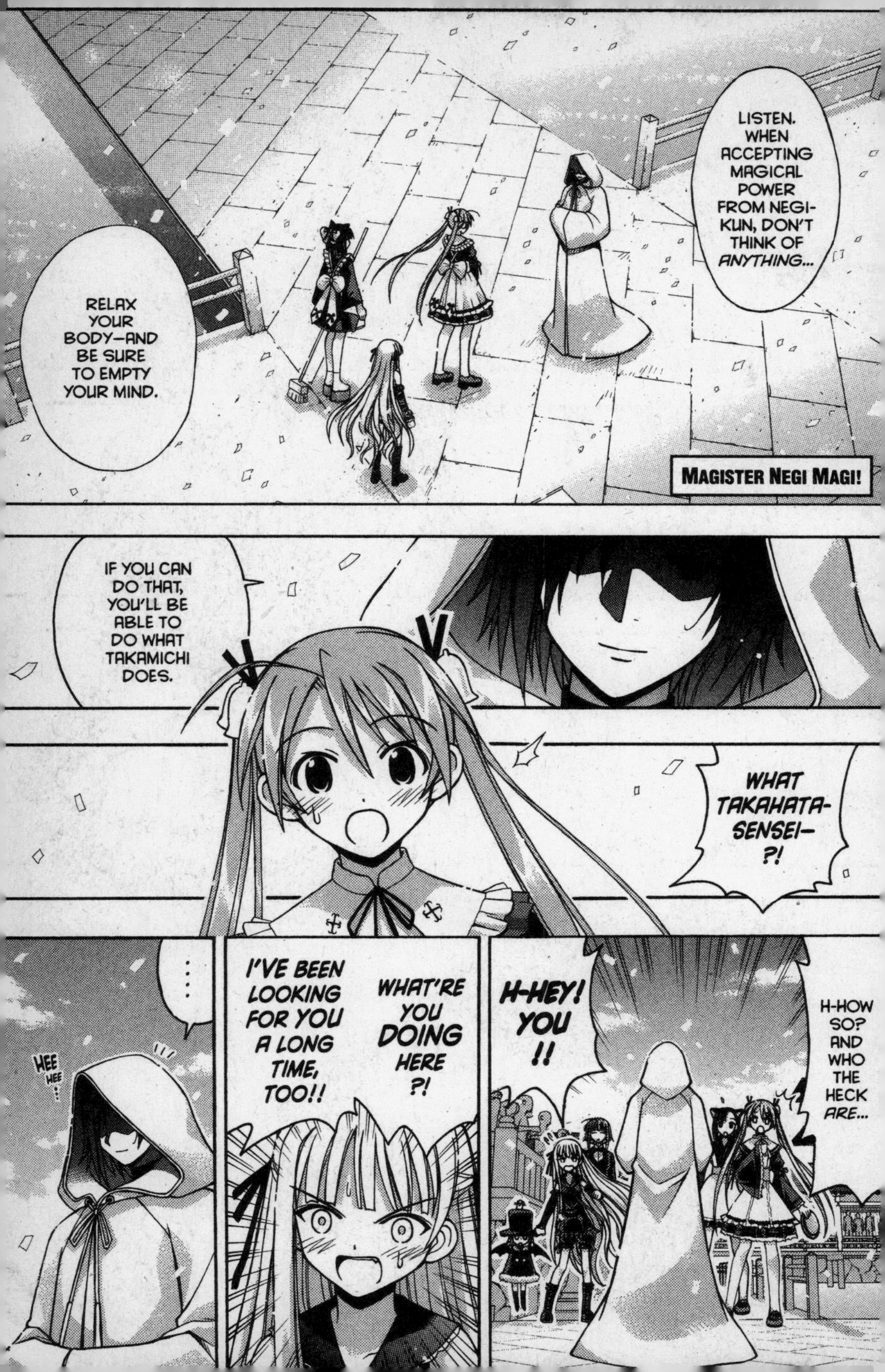
LISTEN. WHEN ACCEPTING MAGICAL POWER FROM NEGI-KUN, DON'T THINK OF *ANYTHING...*
RELAX YOUR BODY—AND BE SURE TO EMPTY YOUR MIND.
MAGISTER NEGI MAGI!
IF YOU CAN DO THAT, YOU'LL BE ABLE TO DO WHAT TAKAMICHI DOES.
WHAT TAKAHATA-SENSEI—?!
H-HOW SO? AND WHO THE HECK ARE...
H-HEY! YOU!!
WHAT'RE YOU DOING HERE?!
I'VE BEEN LOOKING FOR YOU A LONG TIME, TOO!!
....
HEE HEE...

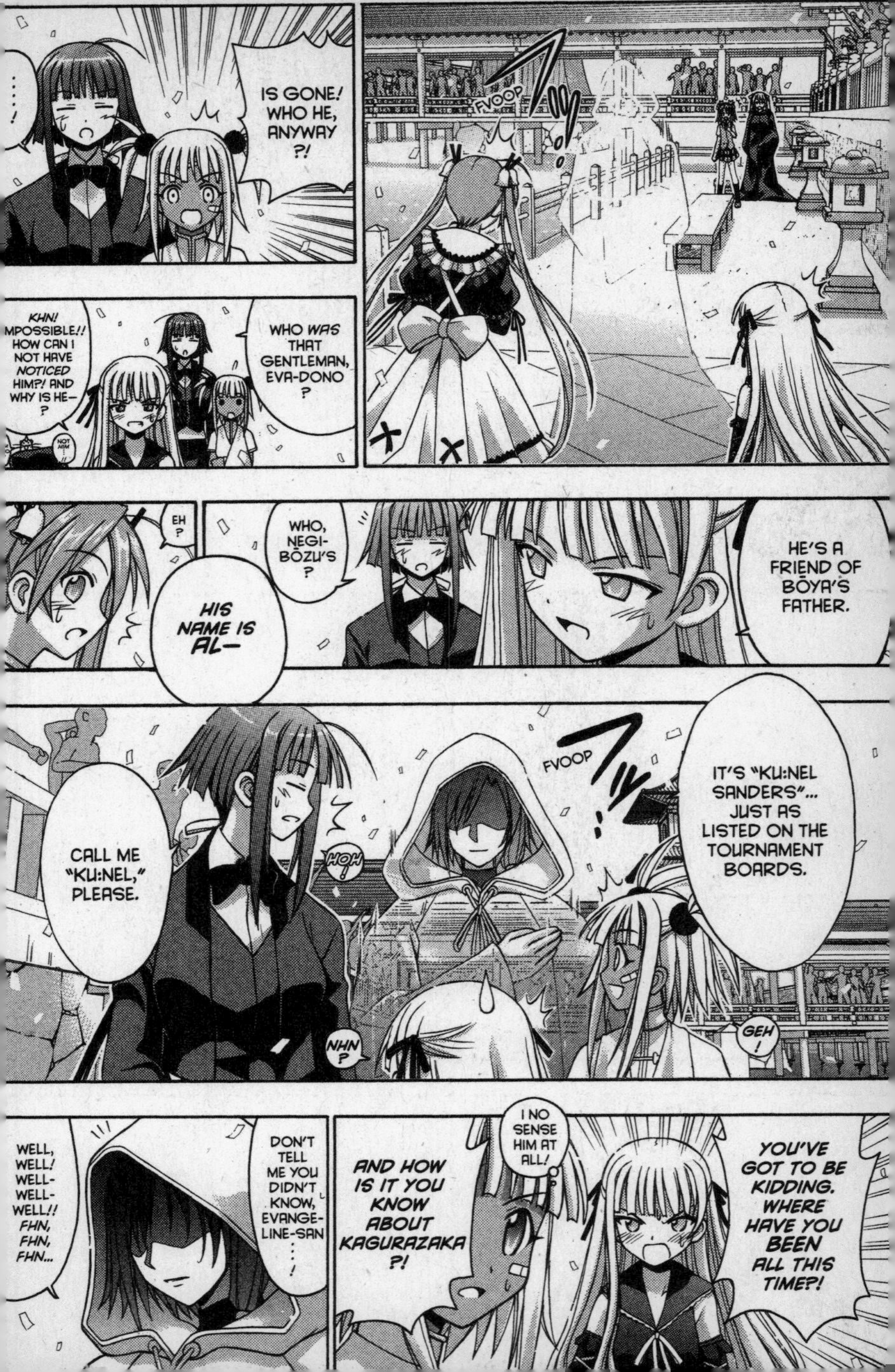
FVOOP
IS GONE! WHO HE, ANYWAY?!
...!
WHO WAS THAT GENTLEMAN, EVA-DONO?
KHN! IMPOSSIBLE!! HOW CAN I NOT HAVE NOTICED HIM?! AND WHY IS HE—?
NOT HIM...!!
HE'S A FRIEND OF BŌYA'S FATHER.
WHO, NEGI-BŌZU'S?
HIS NAME IS AL—
EH?
IT'S "KU:NEL SANDERS"... JUST AS LISTED ON THE TOURNAMENT BOARDS.
FVOOP
GEH!
HOH!
CALL ME "KU:NEL," PLEASE.
NHN?
YOU'VE GOT TO BE KIDDING. WHERE HAVE YOU BEEN ALL THIS TIME?!
I NO SENSE HIM AT ALL!
AND HOW IS IT YOU KNOW ABOUT KAGURAZAKA?!
DON'T TELL ME YOU DIDN'T KNOW, EVANGELINE-SAN...!
WELL, WELL! WELL-WELL-WELL!! FHN, FHN, FHN...

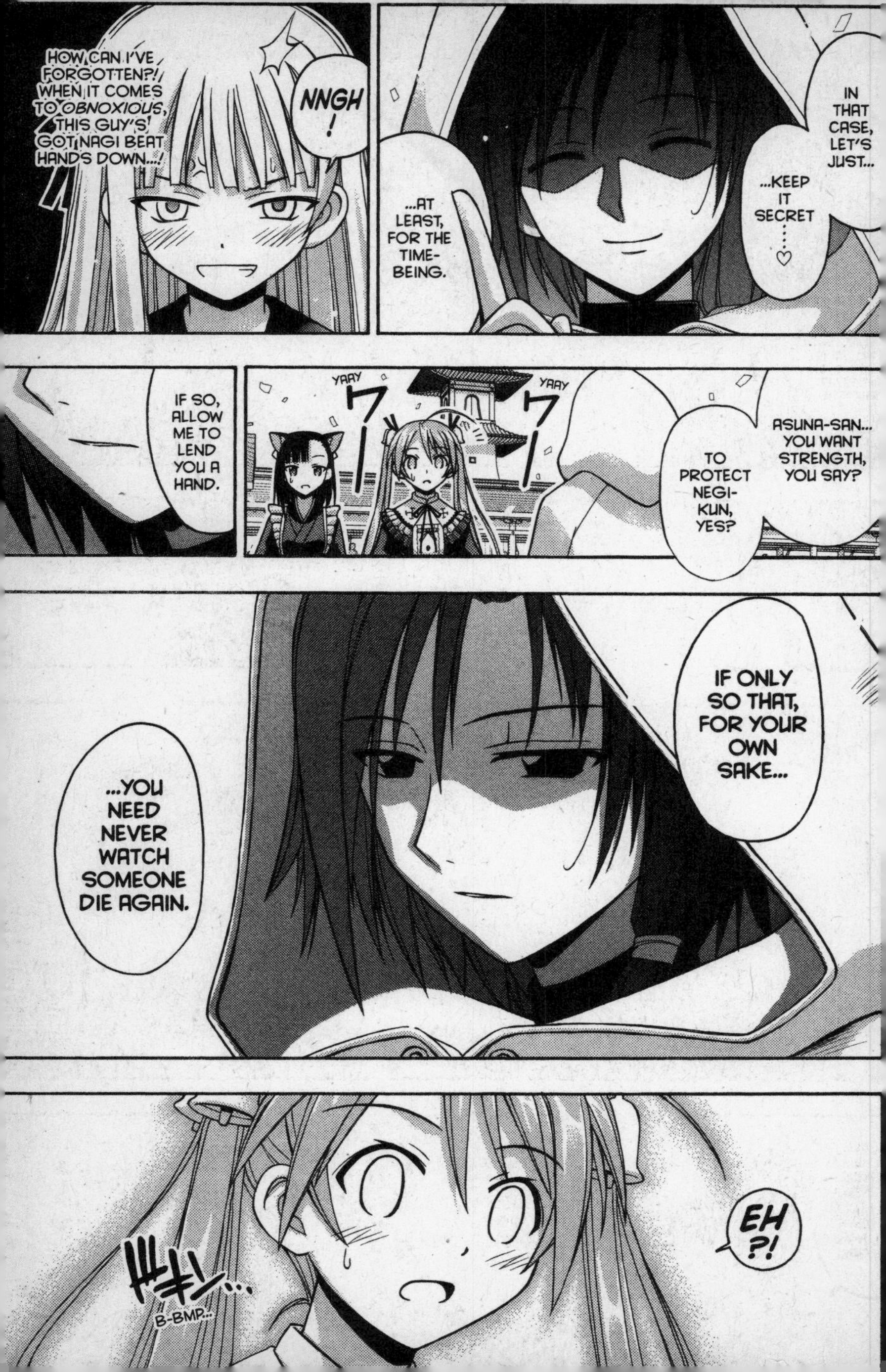
IN THAT CASE, LET'S JUST...
...KEEP IT SECRET ...♡
...AT LEAST, FOR THE TIME-BEING.
NNGH!
HOW CAN I'VE FORGOTTEN?! WHEN IT COMES TO *OBNOXIOUS*, THIS GUY'S GOT NAGI BEAT HANDS DOWN...!
ASUNA-SAN... YOU WANT STRENGTH, YOU SAY?
TO PROTECT NEGI-KUN, YES?
YAAY
YAAY
IF SO, ALLOW ME TO LEND YOU A HAND.
IF ONLY SO THAT, FOR YOUR OWN SAKE...
...YOU NEED NEVER WATCH SOMEONE DIE AGAIN.
EH?!
B-BMP...

TOMARE!

[STOP!]

You're going the wrong way!

Manga is a completely different type of reading experience.

To start at the *beginning*,
go to the *end*!

That's right! Authentic manga is read the traditional Japanese way—from right to left. Exactly the *opposite* of how American books are read. It's easy to follow: Just go to the other end of the book, and read each page—and each panel—from right side to left side, starting at the top right. Now you're experiencing manga as it was meant to be.